Hairdressing: Level 2

The Interactive Textbook

An Interactive Multimedia Blended eLearning System

ATT Training
World leader in multimedia blended eLearning

Alison Read and Charlotte Church, ATT TRAINING

Routledge
Taylor & Francis Group
LONDON AND NEW YORK

First published 2012
by Routledge
2 Park Square, Milton Park, Abingdon, Oxon OX14 4RN

Simultaneously published in the USA and Canada
by Routledge
711 Third Avenue, New York, NY 10017

Routledge is an imprint of the Taylor & Francis Group, an informa business

British Library Cataloguing in Publication Data
A catalogue record for this book is available from the British Library

Library of Congress Cataloging in Publication Data
Read, Alison, 1974-
Hairdressing : level 2 : the interactive textbook / by Alison Read and Charlotte Church. — 1 [edition].
p. cm
Includes index.
ISBN 978-0-203-10992-2 — ISBN 978-0-415-52867-2 (alk. paper) 1. Hairdressing—Textbooks. I. Church, Charlotte, 1981- II. Title.
TT972.R42 2012
646.7'24—dc23

2012000180

ISBN: 978-0-415-52867-2 (pbk)
ISBN: 978-0-203-10992-2 (ebk)

Typeset in Helvetica
by RefineCatch Limited, Bungay, Suffolk

Contents

Preface

All of us at ATT Training are proud to be producing the best multimedia blended eLearning materials available for hairdressing training. We have achieved this by working with the best hairdressers, product manufacturers and salons, as well as great colleges and training centres. We started this about fifteen years ago and our materials have got better every year since!

To keep improving, as well as continuing to develop our computer-based and online learning materials, we are very pleased to have teamed up with a leading publisher to produce this full-colour and interactive textbook. It can be used on its own or in conjunction with our multimedia materials online. All the essential materials are free for students and even more is available to teachers for a very low annual fee. Please contact us for details: info@atthairdressing.com

This book is the second in the "Hairdressing: Multimedia Blended eLearning" series:

- Hairdressing — Level 1
- Hairdressing — Level 2
- Hairdressing — Level 3

We hope you find the content useful and informative. Comments, suggestions and feedback are always welcome at our website: **www.atthairdressing.com.** You will also find links to lots of free online resources to help with your studies.

WWW **Website**

www.atthairdressing.com

We also have interesting and useful materials and ideas on these sites; come and join in:

Facebook: www.facebook.com/atthairdressing

Twitter: www.twitter.com/atthairdressing

YouTube: www.youtube.com/atthairdressing

Flickr: www.flickr.com/atthairdressing

Acknowledgements

ATT Training is grateful to the following companies and individuals for supplying assistance and/or materials and working to help with the production of our books and computer based materials:

- Kennadys, Ingatestone, Essex (Salon of the Year winner) www.kennadys.co.uk
- Splinters, London www.splintersacademy.com
- Inter Training Service (ITS)
- Bexley College
- The Manchester College
- Wella
- L'Oréal
- Sandra Brock (consultant)
- John Cornell (photographer)
- Beth Denton
- Shutterstock for supplying chapter opener images for chapters 1, 4, 5, 6, 8, 9, 10, 13 and 14.

Pronunciation of useful words

There are quite a few unusual words and phrases that we come across as hairdressers. In this short section we have listed as many as we can think of – please let us know via the website if you find any more.

To keep it simple we have not used complicated and unusual characters so our method is not perfect, but it is very close. The word is shown followed by the same word spelt phonetically (fon-et-ik-a-lee). A quick tip is that a single vowel like -o- is sounded as in 'lock' or if it is shown as -**oh**- then it is said as in 'broke' and if shown as -oo- then it is sounded as in 'food'.

If you have access to all our online multimedia screens than you can listen to how our narrator says the words – he gets most of them right!

Abrasion	(a-bray-shon)
Acetic acid	(a-see-tick asid)
Adhesion	(a-dee-shon)
Alcohol	(al-coh-hol)
Alkaline	(al-ca-line)
Alopecia areata	(al-oh-pee-sha a-ree-ah-ta)
Alpha keratin	(al-fa keh-ra-tin)
Amino acid	(a-me-no asid)
Ammonia	(am-oh-nee-a)
Androgenic alopecia	(an-droh-jen-ik al-oh-pee-sha)
Asymmetric	(ay-sim-et-rik)
Barbicide	(bar-be-side)
Canities	(can-it-eez)
Capillary	(cap-ill-ah-ree)
Catagen	(cat-a-jen)
Ceramic	(sir-am-ic)
Cetrimide	(set-rim-ide)
Cicatrical alopecia	(sik-at-rik-al al-oh-pee-sha
Collodion	(coll-odd-ee-on)
Contraindication	(con-tra-in-dik-ay-shon)
Cysteine	(siss-teen)
Cystine	(siss-tyn)
Defamatory	(de-fam-a-tor-ee)
Dermal papilla	(der-mal pa-pil-a)
Dermatitis	(der-ma-ty-tiss)
Diffuse alopecia	(dy-fuze al-oh-pee-sha)
Di-sulphide	(dy-sull-fide)
Effleurage	(eff-lu-rage)
Epidermis	(ep-ee-der-miss)
Eumelanin	(you-mel-a-nin)
Follicle	(fol-ik-al)
Folliculitis	(fol-ik-you-ly-tiss)
Fragilitas crinium	(fraj-ill-i-tus krin-e-um)
Hexachlorophene	(hex-a-klor-oh-feen)
Hydrogen	(hy-dro-jen)

Hydrophilic	(hy-dro-fill-ik)
Hydrophobic	(hy-droh-foe-bik)
Hygroscopic	(hy-grow-skop-ik)
Keloid	(key-loyd)
Keratin	(ke-ra-tin)
Lanolin	(lan-o-lin)
Lanugo	(lan-oo-go)
Libellous	(ly-bell-uss)
Magnesium	(mag-nee-zee-um)
Medulla	(me-dull-a)
Melanin	(mel-a-nin)
Melanocytes	(mel-a-no-sites)
Monilethrix	(mon-i-lee-thriks)
Oxymelanin	(ox-ee-mel-a-nin)
Pediculosis capitis	(ped-ik-u-loh-sis cap-it-iss)
Petrissage	(pet-re-sarge)
Pheomelanin	(fee-oh-mel-a-nin)
Pityriasis capitis	(pit-ih-ry-ah-sis cap-it-iss)
Polythene	(pol-ih-theen)
Porosity	(por-ross-it-ee)
Psoriasis	(sor-rye-a-sis)
Scabies	(scay-bees)
Sebaceous cyst	(seb-ay-shus sist)
Seborrhoea	(seb-or-ee-ah)
Sodium hydroxide	(soh-dee-um hy-drok-side)
Sulphur	(sul-fur)
Telogen	(tel-oh-jen)
Tinea capitis	(tin-ee-a cap-it-iss)
Trichologist	(try-kol-oh-jist)
Trichorrhexis nodosa	(tri-kor-rex-iss noh-doh-sa)
Vellus	(vel-uss)
Zinc pyrithione	(zink py-rith-ee-on)

CHAPTER 1

Introduction

This chapter explains how to use this book. It is also a general introduction to the hairdressing industry and covers part of the VRQ unit 201, Working in the hairdressing industry (the remainder of which can be found within Chapter 7).

In this chapter you will learn about:

- how to use this book to help you learn more and have fun in the process
- development routes and career prospects
- how to gain information that will help you in the industry.

Why do you want to be a hairdresser?

Well, I am sure we all have different answers to this question but I bet most are similar. My answer would have been something like: "Because it is an amazing industry to work in. It is wide-ranging as well as being creative and you get to meet lots of really nice people."

Hairdressing is so much more than cutting hair with scissors! Each chapter of this book therefore covers an important area such as colouring, perming, styling and more.

In this first chapter we look at the information you will need to know if you wish to work as a hairdresser or barber, including career prospects, opportunities for development and gaining helpful information.

1.1 How to use this book

Introduction

Most of all, relax, take your time, and enjoy it!

This book is fine if used just on its own. However, if used in conjunction with the associated online learning material, it is even better. Most of the text and images are the same on screen and in this book – the resources on screen may be larger and animations and videos are often used. Lots of learning activities are included, either in boxes to the side, or at the end of each chapter. These are a great way to learn so complete them as you work through the book.

You may be accessing the computer based materials through a college or training centre. However, the learning screens, questions, activities (and more!) are also available if you are at home from: **www.atthairdressing.com**

You will also find a forum where you can talk to other students and teachers as well as links to other useful sites and resources.

Structure

This textbook is set out in chapters that cover the mandatory and optional units needed for a qualification. Each chapter is split into sections and has activity sheets at the end. Remember, the structure of the computer based material is exactly the same. At the start of each chapter you will find a page showing the contents with the free online multimedia materials colour coded as follows:

CHAPTER 2 HEALTH AND SAFETY: CONTENTS, SCREENS AND ACTIVITIES

Key:
Sections from the book are set in this colour
Screens available online are set in this colour
Online activity screens are set in this colour

Website
www.atthairdressing.com

Hazards and risks at work

Introduction
Likely hazards
Risks associated with the hazards and avoiding of risks
Identify the risks
Displaying rules and regulations
Five in a row

Reduce risks to health and safety at work

Introduction
Health and Safety at Work Act 1974 1
Health and Safety at Work Act 1974 2
Select correct bars
COSHH 1
COSHH 2
Fire
Fire safety
General rules
Emergency fire procedure
Fire extinguishers
Correct selection

Photographs and diagrams

Some of the photographs and diagrams in this book may need information to be added (labels, sketches, notes, etc.). Use the online or computer based material to find out what should be added to the book. In some cases there may be a blank space where a diagram or information from the computer screen should be drawn or written.

Use this book as a workbook, make notes, underline things, make sketches and highlight important points. However, you should only do this if you own it; if it is a library or college book, use a separate piece of paper!

Margin boxes

Throughout the book you will find lots of boxes in the margins similar to the ones shown here:

Safety first
Important health and safety points will be highlighted here.

Definition
Unusual words and phrases are put into this type of box.

Key information
Special and important facts that you should remember will be added in boxes like this.

Website
www.atthairdressing.com

Glossary

There is a comprehensive glossary at the back of this book. It is also available online at www.atthairdressing.com where you can search for important words and phrases and even translate them into other languages.

We have also added a guide to the pronunciation of unusual words in this format: (proh-nun-see-ay-shun), at the front of the book. This method is called phonetic spelling, and is not perfect but it will help!

Activities

Online activities are a very important part of the book and you should use them as you work through the text. When you see the following symbol, carry out the activity stated by going to the website and completing the interactive multimedia screen.

WWW **Online activity (the activity number and name are also shown here)**

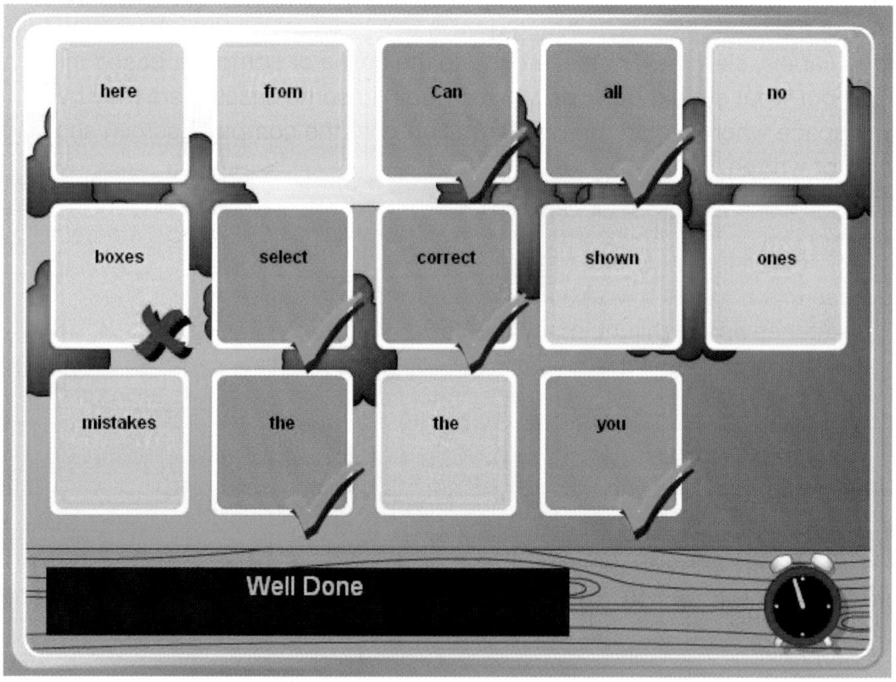

Choosing the correct options activity

Worksheets

As well as the 'Activity' boxes there are some worksheets available online, an example of which is presented at the end of each main chapter. You can carry out these tasks during your study of a chapter or unit, or at the end. If your college or company is registered with ATT Training, lots more of these activity sheets are available. Please visit **www.atthairdressing.com** for more details.

Assessment

There are multiple-choice quizzes available online and you should do these after you have studied a complete unit. You will see the following icon at the end of each chapter:

Online multiple-choice quiz

. . . and good luck in the final exam, which will be arranged by your tutor/assessor.

You can also print a certificate of achievement – but only if you answer all the questions correctly of course!

Website

www.atthairdressing.com

1.2 Development routes and career prospects

You can train to become a hairdresser or barber in the following ways:

- colleges and training providers offer full- or part-time NVQ (National Vocational Qualification), SVQ (Scottish Vocational Qualification) and VRQ (Vocationally Related Qualification) courses in awards, certificates or diplomas
- trainees are taken on at salons which allow you to learn from colleagues, take part in training in-house and attend a day-release programme at college (these are often known as apprenticeships)
- if still at school then there are courses that you can become involved in which will lead you on to the above steps.

There are four different levels of work in hairdressing and therefore the training courses and qualifications are set to match these levels. This book covers the knowledge required for Level 2.

Table 1.1 Levels of work

Level 1	Level 2	Level 3	Level 4
This is often the place school leavers start and can include work such as shampooing, conditioning and helping with work such as perming and colouring as well as supporting the rest of the team and helping clients.	This can be thought of as the junior stylist or barber and will include cutting, colouring and more complex tasks.	A stylist or senior stylist will be at this level and above. It will include more complex work such as consultations as well as supervision of others.	At this level you will usually be employed in management of a large salon or arranging shows and exhibitions.

Once you are trained as a stylist you can take short courses in specialist areas such as colouring, hair extensions, etc. through manufacturers, hair shows and seminars. Some colleges and universities offer higher level qualifications once you are experienced in hairdressing. For more information you can visit the government website www.direct.gov.uk.

The salons in which we may work are many and varied, but there are also lots of other places where a good hairdresser can work. Here are some examples but I am sure there are more:

- leisure clubs and gyms
- health and fitness clubs
- spa industry
- fashion/photographic industry
- film/television/theatre
- clients' homes
- cruise liners
- clinics and hospitals
- residential homes
- holiday resorts and hotels
- department stores
- product manufacturers and suppliers.

Key information

Vidal Sassoon, Nicky Clarke and Lee Stafford and many other top hairdressers all started at the bottom and worked their way up.

The type of career path we take can also be varied. Vidal Sassoon, Nicky Clarke and Lee Stafford all started at the bottom and worked their way to the top. We won't all do that but just being a good stylist in a salon is a great job, or you may end up running your own salon or working in television or films.

Here are some examples of more varied roles in our industry that may interest you:

- Trichologist:
  Clients with scalp or hair disorders may need to be referred to a doctor but in many cases a trichologist, who is a specialist in hair and scalp disorders, may be the best choice. It takes a few years to qualify but can be a fascinating career.
- Management:
  Many hairdressers go on to run their own salon, which means you will need management skills. You could also take on a managerial role in a large salon or even manage training courses for new students.
- TV, film and theatre:
  The creative industries are difficult to get into as there are not many openings. However, never let that put you off; if you are determined you will get there in the end with enthusiasm and hard work.
- Manufacturers:
  The large manufacturers need sales representatives, technical representatives and demonstrators for their products.
- Teaching:
  A career in teaching a skill such as hairdressing usually follows significant experience in the industry and will also require additional qualifications.
- Writing books and learning materials:
  And of course you may have ambitions to write a book – I did and here it is!

Whatever career path you follow in hairdressing, it will be interesting, challenging and exciting, so go on out there and have fun!

1.3 Helpful information

This section explains the services that are offered, job roles available and how you can become a hairdresser/barber. If more information is needed then some organisations that can help are highlighted throughout this section.

Gaining information about the hairdressing industry

If you are interested in training to become a hairdresser, you can find information from:

- the Internet
- magazines/trade journals
- course leaflets/prospectuses
- education and training providers
- awarding bodies such as City & Guilds, VTCT, Edexcel
- job centres
- organisations specialising in professional career guidance
- shows/seminars
- advertisements/word of mouth
- work experience
- Habia (sector skills council).

Figure 1.1 The Internet can be a useful source of information

Hairdressing salons do not only offer haircutting services. They offer a great range of services. The different types of salon will offer their own types of services. They do not often offer all of the services as it is based on their clients' wishes.

Key information

Hairdressing services may include:

shampooing and conditioning
cutting and blow-drying
styling and dressing
colouring
perming
relaxing
shaving
facial haircutting
face massage
scalp massage
Indian head massage.

Occupational roles within the hair industry

You should understand all the job titles and roles in the salon. These include:

- shampooist
- junior/trainee
- receptionist
- junior stylist/stylist
- colour technician
- artistic director
- manager
- salon owner
- barber.

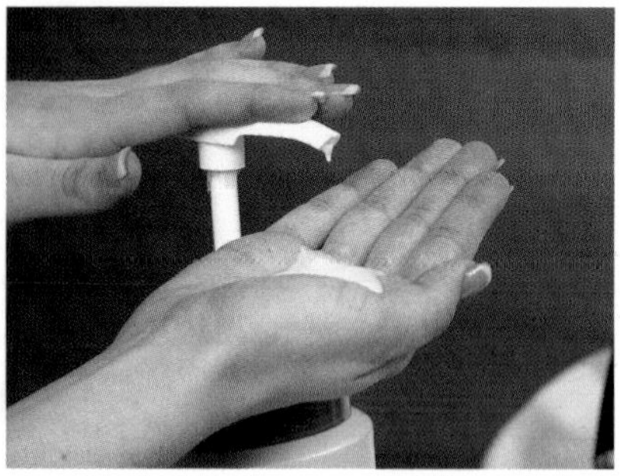

Figure 1.2 Dispensing shampoo

Shampooist

The shampooist, as the name suggests, shampoos the clients' hair and prepares them for the stylist. They may also look after the washbasin area.

Figure 1.3 A junior/trainee will assist clients by offering refreshments, for example

Junior/trainee

The junior or trainee works under the direction of a higher ranking member of staff. They help with many different tasks including assisting with clients (getting refreshments, taking coats, etc.), shampooing, perming, colouring, styling, blow-drying and reception duties.

Figure 1.4 The receptionist will take payment

Receptionist

The receptionist attends to visitors and enquiries, answers the telephone, takes bookings for appointments, takes and records payments for services and retail items. He/she will also maintain the reception area.

Figure 1.5 The stylist provides hair care services to enhance appearance

Junior stylist/stylist

The junior stylist will carry out only basic hairdressing services on the client, guided by a stylist. The stylist provides hair care services to enhance the client's appearance. They deliver a wide range of services including giving advice, styling, cutting and colouring.

Colour (chemical) technician

The colour technician specialises in the application of tint to clients' hair. Therefore they have an in-depth knowledge of the use of chemicals in salons. Many will also offer other chemical services, for example perming and relaxing.

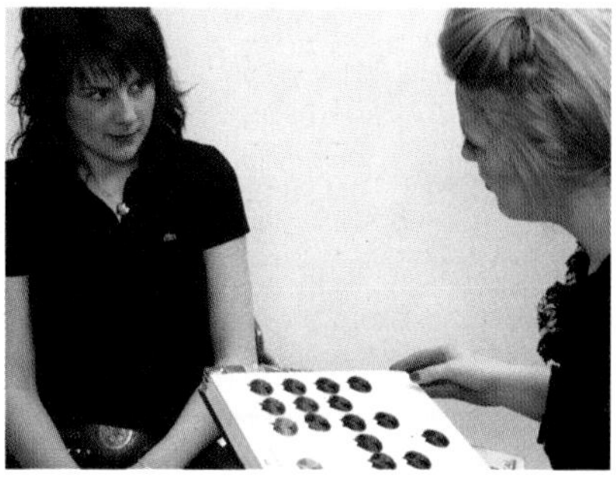

Figure 1.6 The colour technician specialises in the application of colour

Artistic director

Artistic directors are responsible for all hairdressing design work. This will include any publicity and promotional work for the salon. They also help with management of the salon and training of staff.

Figure 1.7 Artistic directors are responsible for design work

Manager

The manager participates in the smooth running of the salon on a day to day basis. He/she is normally responsible for:

- overseeing the team in the salon
- employing staff
- organising training and promotions
- ordering supplies
- paying bills.

It is up to the salon manager to ensure the salon is a profitable business whilst adhering to health and safety legislation with the rest of the team.

Figure 1.8 The manager ensures that the salon runs smoothly

Salon owner

The salon owner may also be the manager of the salon and he/she usually carries out a wide range of business tasks. Many salon owners will also style clients' hair.

Tasks that the owner may carry out include:

- hiring employees
- dealing with customer queries/complaints
- overseeing health and safety policy and legal requirements
- ordering stock and supplies
- pricing retail products
- creating new business
- managing finances.

Figure 1.9 The salon owner will hire employees

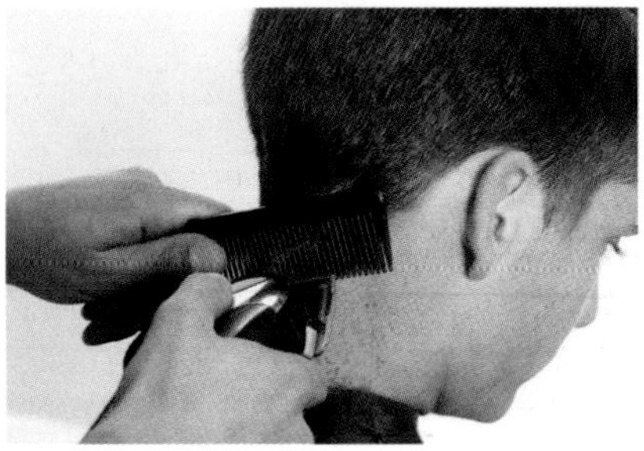

Figure 1.10 Barbers specialise in men's hair

Barber

Barbers specialise in the styling of men's hair. This includes cutting hair and maintaining facial hair, or shaving.

Employment characteristics

There are many different options when working in the hair industry. Your employment characteristics could be as follows:

- full- or part-time
- self-employed
- employed seasonally.

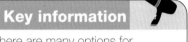

Key information

There are many options for employment within the hairdressing industry.

Some staff are employed on certain days of the week only, for example on a Saturday. This may be the case early on in your career. Your hours of work can vary from day to day. Many salons have 'late night openings' on certain days and you may be required to work until closing. Renting a chair is another choice that you may be given at some point through your hairdressing career. This allows you to be self-employed and you would pay the salon to use their space and facilities.

Figure 1.11 You may rent a chair within a salon

Career patterns

Your first role when you start working in the hairdressing industry will usually be as a trainee. From here you can progress to becoming a stylist, then a senior stylist. Once you have reached this stage you can move into management if you wish. The speed of your progression will not only depend on the training and qualifications you achieve but also how well you work within the salon. Most salons have their own career progression paths that you will follow once you start working.

Figure 1.12 You will usually start work as a trainee

Key information

The speed of your progression will not only depend on the training and qualifications you achieve but also how well you work within the salon.

Organisation types

As a hairdresser you may need to access the following organisations:

- salons
- professional membership organisations
- industry lead bodies
- manufacturers and suppliers.

Salons

Salons offer hairdressing services and products to meet clients' requirements. A great deal of experience can be gained working in a salon whilst training to become a hairdresser or barber.

Figure 1.13 A salon (Kennadys in Ingatestone, Essex)

Key information

Professional membership organisations will also provide information about ethical issues and legislation within the industry.

Professional membership organisations

One of the roles of this type of organisation is to allow hairdressers or barbers to be state registered. Becoming a SRH (state registered hairdresser) gives you official recognition under the Hairdressers Registration Act. The Hairdressing Council is an example of this type of organisation. Professional membership organisations will also provide information about ethical issues and legislation within the industry.

Industry lead bodies

The lead body organisations' (or sector skills councils') main role is to set the standards for a particular industry, e.g. hair and beauty. Qualifications are formed from these standards. These bodies are appointed by the government.

Figure 1.14 Lead bodies set standards which form qualifications

Figure 1.15 Manufacturers make the products used in the salon

Manufacturers and suppliers

These organisations make and supply products and other equipment, e.g. brushes, hair dryers, rollers, etc. that salons both use and sell on to the client. You may come into contact with manufacturers and suppliers if you have to return items, check their pricing or find out the ingredients of products.

1.4 Preparing for assessments

1.4.1 Simple steps

Assessment can be stressful time for a student. However, there are some simple steps you can take to increase your confidence and performance:

1 Study the course materials as you are going along – don't leave it all to the last minute!

2 Nearer to the exam/assessment, set aside a certain time each day to practise and study.
3 Take advantage of all pre-test material in this book, online and of course any that your teacher provides.
4 Attend all revision sessions even if you feel you don't really need it.
5 Ask your teacher to clear up any uncertainties.
6 Take time off work a few days before your assessment to allow extra time to study.
7 Sleep well the night before the assessment/exam.
8 Eat a healthy breakfast the morning of your assessment to help you wake up and get your brain working.
9 Don't put too much pressure on yourself to perform.
10 Don't 'cram' too much at the last minute (for you will almost certainly forget things if you do).
11 Remember, if you worked hard to get this far you can only do your best.

1.4.2 Multiple-choice tests

Multiple-choice exams are easy for some and hard for others. The best thing about a multiple-choice quiz is that all the information you will need is given to you. The downside is that the additional information given to you is designed to make sure you really know the correct answer – and don't just guess. Here are some tips on how to prepare for a multiple-choice test:

- Practise, practise, practise.
- Do the online quizzes and other examples of the tests several times to get used to the format.
- Read all the answer options; it is often possible to rule out one or two easily so that then, even if you need to guess, you have a 50:50 chance of getting it right!
- Answer ALL the questions – don't miss any out.

Figure 1.16 On reflection, you will do fine in your exams . . .

1.4.3 Practical exams

Practical work is clearly the most important part of being a hairdresser. For this reason you will have to do a number of practical examinations or tests either in your college or at your salon. These are often described as observed assessments.

If you only read one part of this section make sure it is this bit:

For your practical assessments you should:

- show a professional attitude
- look the part – be smart, clean and looking good
- not have doubts about your abilities; it will show – so be confident
- not allow other students to influence you; concentrate on your work not on that of others
- pause, relax and take a moment if you forget a procedure or process – it will come back to you
- relax and don't panic!

Remember, the job of your assessor or examiner is to make a professional judgement that you have met the necessary standards and are therefore competent to do your job. They do not want to fail you but of course they will ensure you have reached the necessary standard before saying you have passed. It is easy to feel intimidated because the assessor will not talk much and will be making notes. This is not designed to put you off; it is to make sure they are fair to everyone and that they judge you against set criteria.

They may ask you some oral questions during or after the assessment procedure. Don't panic, take your time and answer clearly and confidently.

- If you have practised and studied hard during your training, the assessments will be easy – I promise!

Personal appearance

Figure 1.17 Look good, feel good

Now, there is an old saying that I am sure you agree with: '*If you look good you feel good.*' In addition, your appearance should show the 'client' (model and an assessor in this case) that you are capable of caring for your own appearance, and therefore are capable of caring for others.

Here are some important tips; you may like to add notes after each one such as how you will prepare yourself and what you will wear:

Shoes – your footwear should be comfortable, clean, polished if appropriate and in good repair (so no trainers and flip-flops then!)

Clothes – these should be professional in appearance, clean, ironed and comfortable (so no jeans and jogging suits then!)

Hair – it is very important that your own hair looks good and it should be clean and styled. Showing your assessor/examiner/client that you look after your own appearance is important (so no bed-heads then!)

Facial hair – men should ensure that they are either clean shaven or that their beard or moustache is neatly shaped and trimmed (so no one-day stubble then!)

Make-up – don't overdo it, make sure it is practical and appropriate for a day's work. Maybe just a soft shade of lipstick and some light mascara would be ideal. (Guys using make-up is fine, but don't overdo it either!)

Fresh breath – In necessary use breath mints, but don't chew gum – it is very unprofessional (so, you may need get that appointment at the dentist too!)

Perfume or cologne or aftershave – in a salon, either at your work or at college, there will be many other people and odours from different products. Some clients may be allergic or sensitive to strong scents (so, the floral perfume from gran is probably not the best choice then!)

Nails – you should avoid extreme nails as they can be distracting. They should be practical so that you can carry out the procedures required for your assessments. Nails should be clean and cared for (so don't bite them during the exams!)

Personal hygiene – No client, model or examiner wants to be close to a hairdresser with bad body odour. Bath or shower daily, use deodorant and change clothes regularly (so don't jog 5 miles on your way to the exam then!)

Jewellery – keep this to a minimum; too many rings and bracelets will prevent you working properly. Excessive body jewellery such as facial piercings can be distracting (but, don't refuse that diamond engagement ring!)

Mobile phones – these should always be turned off when working and in fact for an exam they may be prohibited (so, not on vibrate, turn it off!)

CHAPTER 2

Health and safety

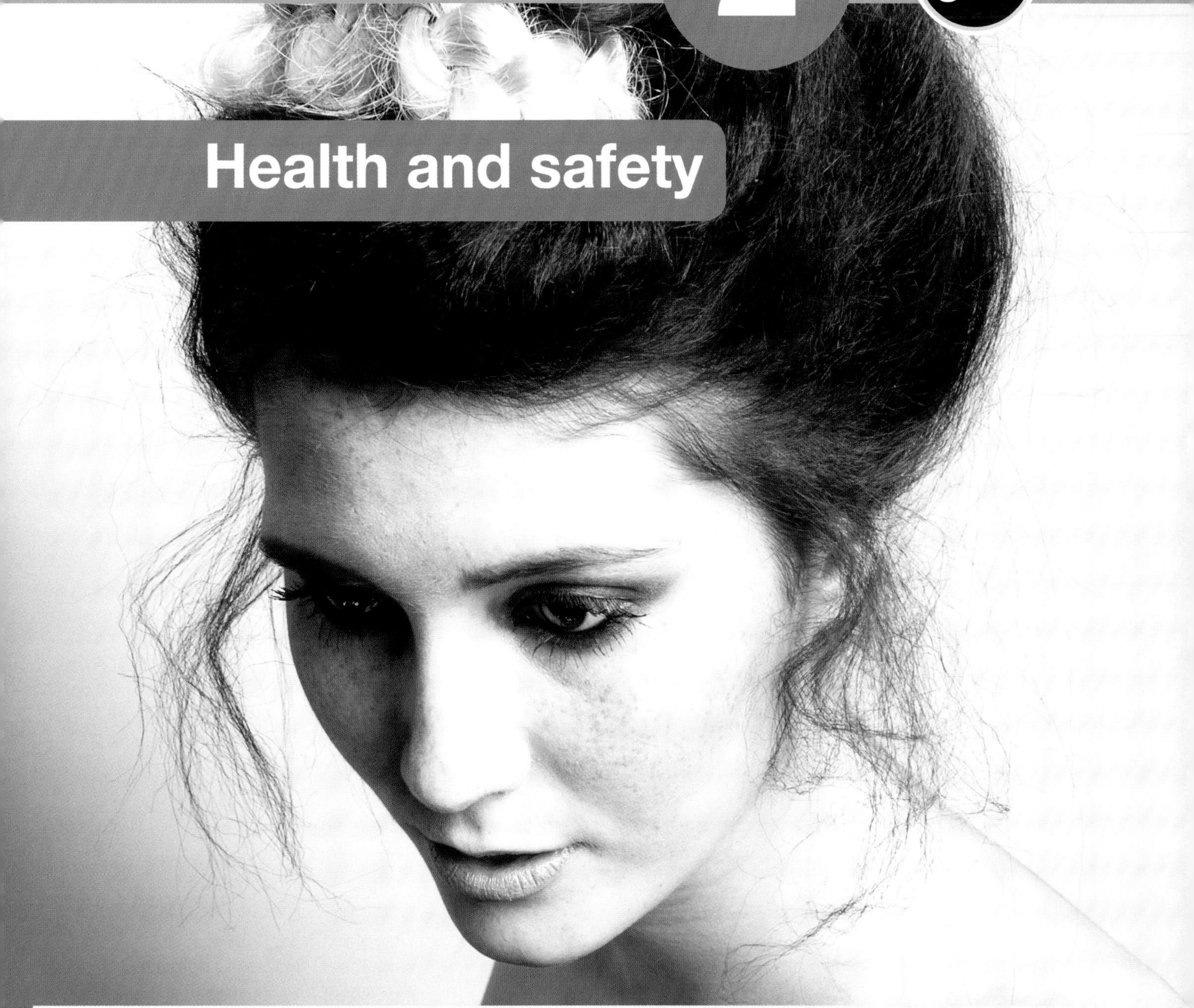

This chapter covers the NVQ/SVQ unit G20, Make sure your own actions reduce the risk to health and safety and VRQ unit 202, Follow health and safety in the salon.

In this chapter you will learn about supporting health and safety in the workplace. Health and safety is the responsibility of all persons at work. Employers and supervisors in particular have a greater responsibility for health and safety than trainees. Staff should be aware of their own competence levels in the workplace. All staff should not only adhere to legal responsibilities but also manufacturers' and workplace instructions whilst keeping in mind environmental issues at all times.

In this chapter you will learn about:

- identifying the hazards and evaluating the risks in your workplace
- reducing the risks to health and safety in your workplace.

Website
www.atthairdressing.com

CHAPTER 2 HEALTH AND SAFETY: CONTENTS, SCREENS AND ACTIVITIES

Key:
Sections from the book are set in this colour
Screens available online are set in this colour
Online activity screens are set in this colour

Hazards and risks at work

Introduction
Likely hazards
Risks associated with the hazards and avoiding of risks
Identify the risks
Displaying rules and regulations
Five in a row

Reduce risks to health and safety at work

Introduction
Health and Safety at Work Act 1974 1
Health and Safety at Work Act 1974 2
Select correct bars
COSHH 1
COSHH 2
Precautions
Manual Handling Operations Regulations 1992
Lifting 1
Lifting 2
Electricity at Work Regulations 1989
RIDDOR 1996
Dermatitis
The Provision and Use of Work Equipment Regulations 1998
Personal Protective Equipment at Work Regulations 1992
Workplace Regulations 1992
Operate safely in the salon 1
Select correct boxes
Operate safely in the salon 2
Equipment
Methods of sterilisation
Disposal of waste
First aid
Round the board
First aid problems
Fire
Fire safety
General rules
Emergency fire procedure
Fire extinguishers
Correct selection
Calling emergency services
Periodic checks
Other emergencies
Security
Recording accidents
Select correct group
Client care
Client records
Data protection
Personal presentation and hygiene 1
Personal presentation and hygiene 2
Five in a row
Jewellery
Posture and deportment
Exercise and rest
Worksheet – First aid
Worksheet – PPE at Work Regulations
Worksheet – Dermatitis
Worksheet – Hazards and risks
Worksheet – Legislation
Worksheet – Sterilisation
Online multiple choice quiz

2.1 Hazards and risks at work

Likely hazards

Many things around the salon can be a hazard. A hazard is a source of danger. Examples of hazards include:

- electrical equipment
- storage boxes
- products
- trailing leads.

Hazards should be identified, acted upon and reported depending on the individual salon policy. This is to minimise the risk of accidents. You should know the right person to approach if there is a health and safety problem or a risk of one.

Definition

Hazard: A source of danger.

Risks associated with the hazards and avoiding these risks

The risk is the likelihood of an accident occurring from a hazard.

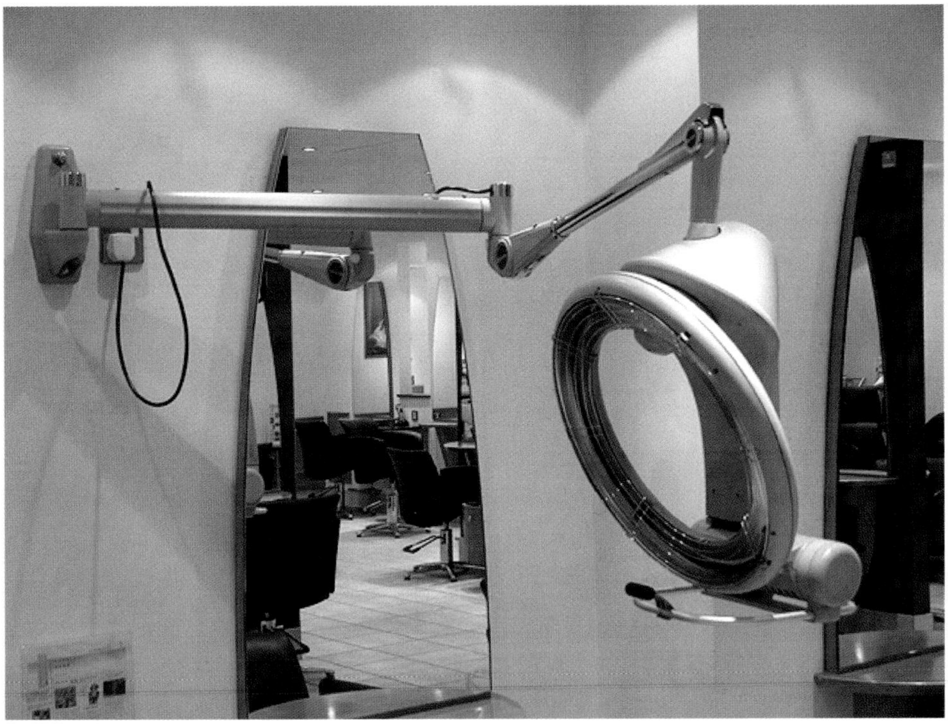

Figure 2.1 Electrical equipment

A risk from electrical equipment is that it will cause somebody an injury when using or repairing it. To avoid this happening it is important that staff are trained in its use and it is tested for correct working order.

Storage boxes may be a risk if they are stored in front of a fire exit for example. There is a strong likelihood that they will cause an accident. The boxes must be moved to an area that does not cause a risk to injury.

Products may cause a risk due to them containing chemicals that are flammable and toxic. They must be stored securely and only be available to hairdressers who have been trained in their use.

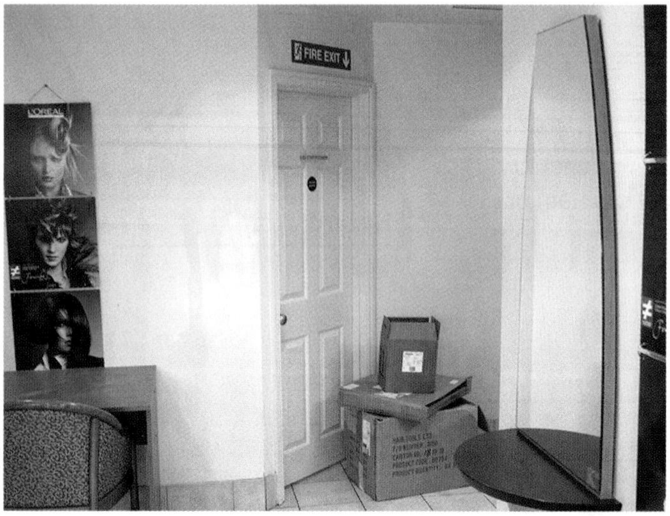

Figure 2.2 Storage boxes

Figure 2.3 Products

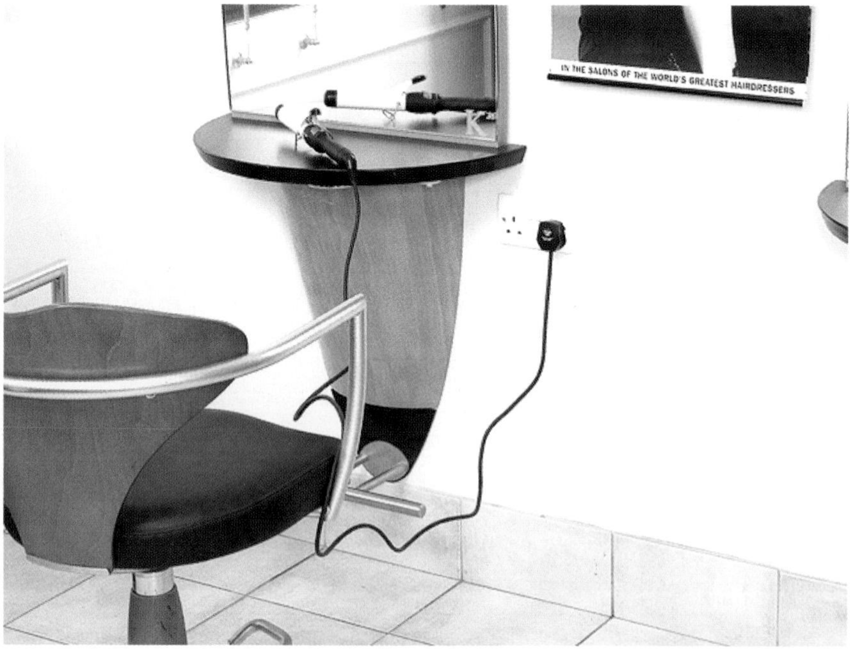

Figure 2.4 Trailing leads present a risk

Key information

A risk is the likelihood of an accident occurring from a hazard.

Trailing leads are a risk if it is likely that somebody may trip over them. Make sure they are not in the passageway of a client or another member of staff.

Identify the risks

You must be able to identify risks and understand the actions that should be taken to avoid an accident occurring (risk assessment).

Online activity 2.1 WWW

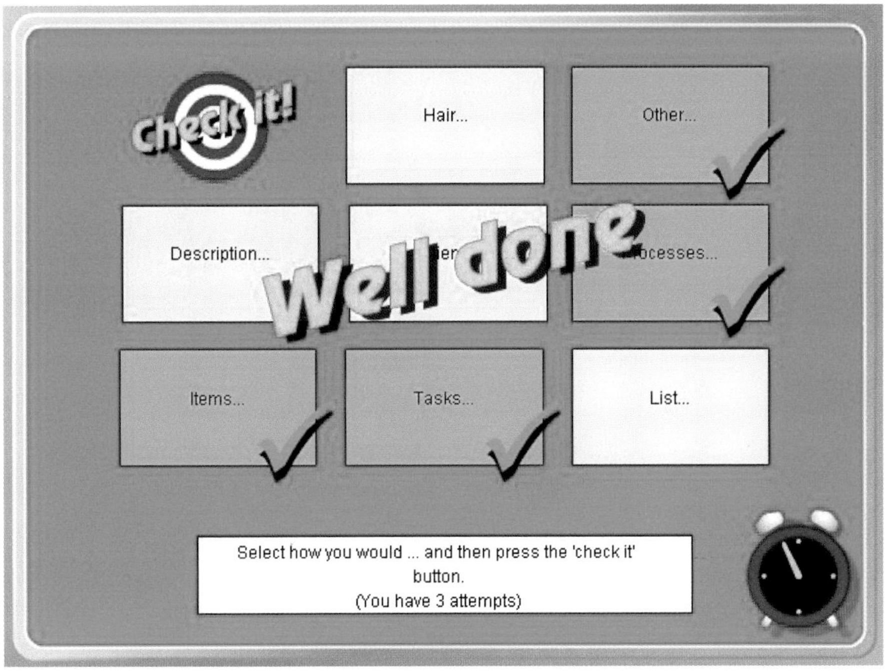

Identify the risks

Displaying rules and regulations

Every salon must by law display the rules and regulations for health and safety on the wall in a position that can be seen by everyone.

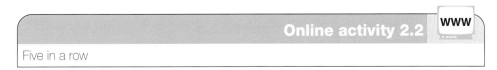

Figure 2.5 Rules and regulations poster

Online activity 2.2 WWW

Five in a row

2.2 Reducing risks to health and safety at work

In order to reduce the risks to health and safety in your workplace, there is certain legislation that must be followed. It is also important to act according to the health and safety policies that the salon operates, manufacturers'/suppliers' instructions and also your own competence levels. Doing this at all times will significantly reduce the risks, thus allowing you to control them.

Figure 2.6 Act accordingly with health and safety policies in the salon

The Health and Safety at Work Act 1974

This Act places a strict duty on employers to ensure, so far as is reasonably practicable, safe working conditions and the absence of risks to health in connection with the use, handling, storage and transport of articles and substances.

Key information

Under the Health and Safety at Work Act an employer must provide:

- safe equipment and safe systems of work
- safe handling, storage and transport of substances
- a safe place of work with safe access and exit
- a safe working environment with adequate welfare facilities
- all necessary information, instruction, training and supervision
- all necessary personal protective equipment free of charge.

WWW Online activity 2.3

Correct selection

Control of Substances Hazardous to Health Regulations 2002

These are commonly called the COSHH regulations and they lay down the essential requirements for controlling exposure to hazardous substances and for protecting people who may be affected by them.

A substance is considered to be hazardous if it can cause harm to the body. It only poses a risk if it is:

- inhaled (breathed in)
- ingested (swallowed)
- in contact with the skin
- absorbed through the skin
- injected into the body
- introduced into the body via cuts etc.

Figure 2.7 Hazardous substance symbols showing that materials are flammable, corrosive, harmful/irritant or (very) toxic

Precautions

- Follow manufacturers' instructions.
- Always wear personal protective equipment (PPE).
- Avoid contact of the chemical with skin, eyes and face.
- Do not use on sensitive or damaged skin.
- Always use a non-metallic bowl to avoid rapid decomposition of the product.
- Store the product in a cool, dry place away from sunlight or other sources of heat. Make sure containers are properly sealed when not in use.
- Store the product in the container and replace the cap immediately after use.
- Never mix products unless recommended by the manufacturer.
- Rotate stock.
- Keep products, especially aerosols, away from naked flames or heat.

Figure 2.9 Always follow instructions

Figure 2.10 Store products in a cool, dry place away from sunlight

Key information

Under the COSHH regulations employers must:

- identify substances in the workplace which are potentially hazardous
- assess the risk to health from exposure to the hazardous substances and record the results
- make an assessment as to which members of staff are at risk
- look for alternative less hazardous substances and substitute if possible
- decide what precautions are required
- introduce effective measures to prevent or control the exposure
- inform, instruct and train all members of staff
- review the assessment on a regular basis.

Activity

The associated learning screen for this part is interactive

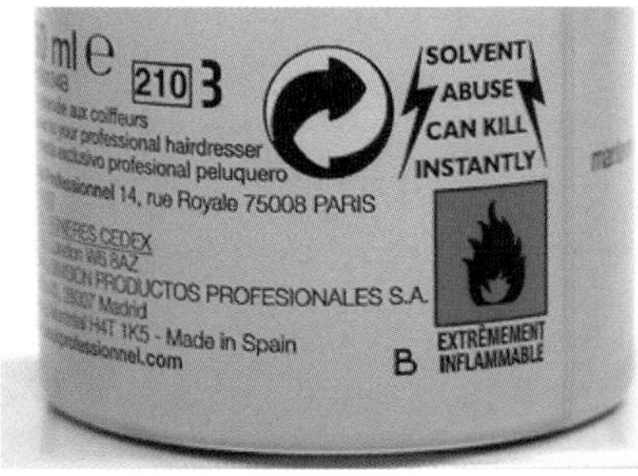

Figure 2.8 Hazard symbol shown on a product

Manual Handling Operations Regulations 1992

These regulations cover the lifting of loads as well as lowering, pushing, pulling, carrying and moving them, whether by hand or other bodily force. You should carry out an assessment of the risks involved by looking at the following:

- the weight of the load
- the shape of the load (e.g. some loads may not be particularly heavy but can be awkward to lift)

- the working environment (e.g. if the area is damp the employee's hands could be wet and the load might slip)
- where the task is to be carried out (e.g. are there cramped conditions which make it difficult to lift?)
- the individual's capability.

If packages are too heavy, politely ask another member of staff to help you.

Safety first

When lifting heavy packages keep your back straight, feet slightly apart, and bend your knees.

Figure 2.11 Incorrect lifting

Figure 2.12 Correct lifting

Lifting

If you send a member of staff to collect stock or equipment, for example, from a wholesaler or another salon, make sure that:

- the member of staff has suitable car insurance
- the member of staff is capable of lifting the stock or equipment without difficulty.

Figure 2.13 Incorrect method of lifting from a shelf

Figure 2.14 Correct method of lifting from a shelf

Electricity at Work Regulations 1989

These regulations state that you must:

- Always check electrical equipment before using it. Look for loose wires and that the plug is not cracked or damaged in any way. Check that the cord is not frayed or cracked.
- Never use electrical equipment when your hands are wet.
- Electrical equipment should be maintained regularly and checked by a suitably qualified person. Once checked the equipment should have a certificate or label acknowledging it.
- Faulty electrical equipment in the workplace must be removed, labelled as faulty and reported to the relevant person.

Figure 2.15 Checking electrical equipment for damage

Figure 2.16 Correct labelling of faulty equipment

Reporting of Injuries, Diseases and Dangerous Occurrences Regulations Act 1996 (RIDDOR)

The Act states that work related accidents, diseases and dangerous occurrences must be reported. You must keep these records for three years and they can be in written form and kept in a file or a computer file.

Key information

RIDDOR records must include:

- date and method of reporting
- date, time and place of event
- personal details of those involved
- brief description.

Dermatitis

This is a very common skin disease in hairdressers and is caused by hands being exposed to certain products and carrying out wet work regularly. Dermatitis can be prevented by:

- ensuring shampoo and conditioner are rinsed from your hands
- drying hands thoroughly
- moisturising regularly
- wearing disposable gloves.

Safety first

Dermatitis is a reportable disease.

Definition

Dermatitis: Inflammation of the skin resulting from irritation from an external agent.

The Provision and Use of Work Equipment Regulations 1998

The following requirements apply to all equipment:

- Work equipment must be suitable for the purpose for which it is used.
- Equipment must be properly maintained and a maintenance log kept, for example for portable electrical hand tools.
- Users and supervisors of equipment must be given adequate health and safety training and written instructions where required.

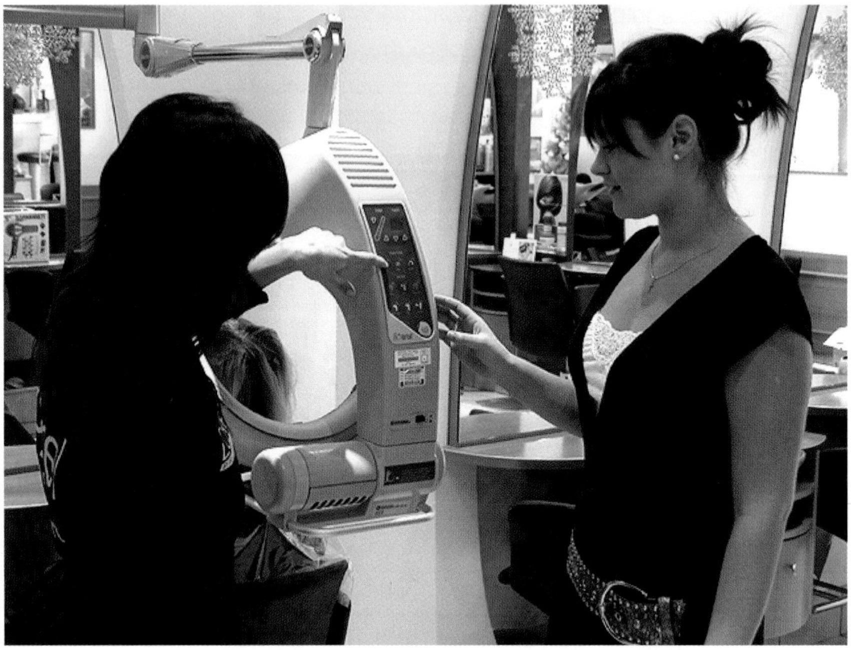

Figure 2.17 Users of equipment must be given adequate health and safety training

Personal Protective Equipment at Work Regulations 1992 (PPE)

The requirements under this Act are met when you comply with the COSHH regulations. These regulations require every employer to provide suitable personal protective equipment (PPE) to each of his or her employees who may be exposed to any risk while at work.

The PPE supplied must be properly maintained and the users must be trained and monitored to ensure that the PPE is properly used. Employees are required to report to the employer any loss of or damage to PPE.

In the average salon, PPE will involve the use of gloves and wearing tinting aprons when handling perm lotion, relaxers, tints and bleach; possibly eye protection when handling and mixing strong bleach solutions. It is the duty of the workforce to use PPE when required.

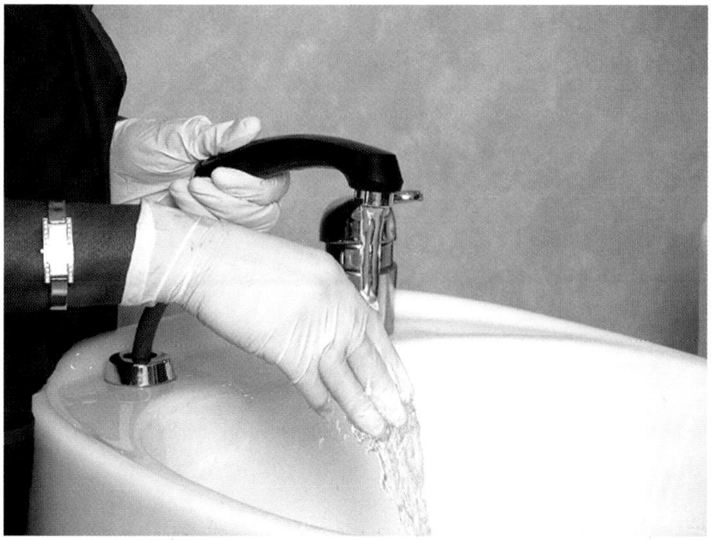

Figure 2.18 PPE equipment

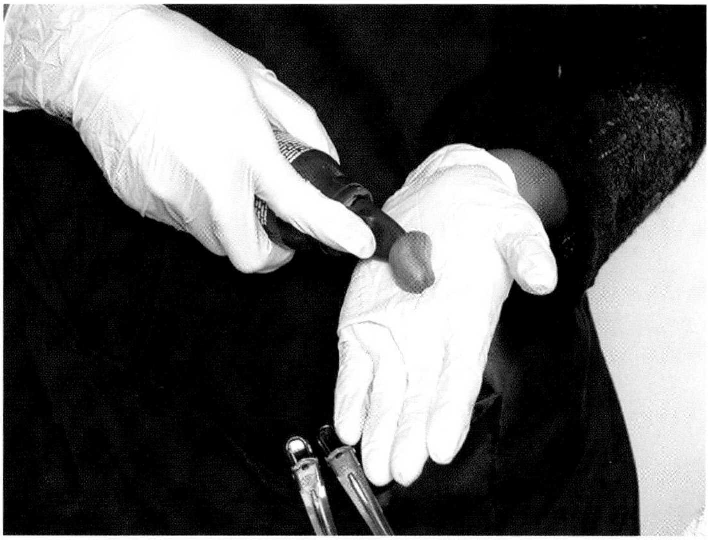

Figure 2.19 Gloves and aprons should be worn when handling chemicals

Figure 2.20 Gloves must be worn when colouring hair

Key information

In the average salon, PPE will involve the use of gloves and wearing tinting aprons when handling perm lotion, relaxers, tints and bleach.

Key information

It is the responsibility of the employee to work safely to ensure the safety of clients and colleagues.

Definition

Micro-organisms: Tiny forms of life, only seen through a microscope.

Safety first

Micro-organisms need warmth, moisture and food for multiplication, all of which are present in salons; therefore it is of great importance to keep the working environment clean.

Definitions

Ringworm: A highly contagious fungal skin infection.

Lice: Tiny insects that are spread by head-to-head contact.

Impetigo: Contagious bacterial skin disease.

The Workplace (Health Safety and Welfare) Regulations 1992

This Act states that the employer is to provide a safe working environment for employees and members of the public. The employer must legally:

- maintain equipment
- regulate temperature
- ensure adequate lighting.

Operate safely in the salon

Micro-organisms cannot be seen but are found in air, clothing, dirt, on the surface of the skin and under the nails. Some of them can cause disease and are said to be infectious. Micro-organisms need warmth, moisture and food for multiplication, all of which are present in salons; therefore it is of great importance to keep the working environment clean.

They are divided into three groups:

- fungi
- bacteria
- viruses.

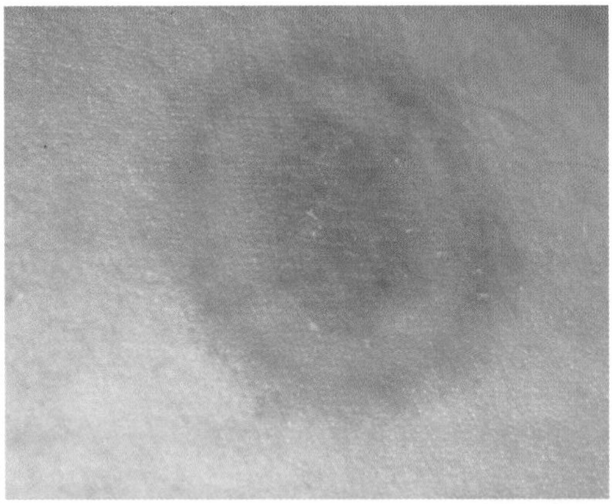

Figure 2.21 Ringworm is from the fungi group

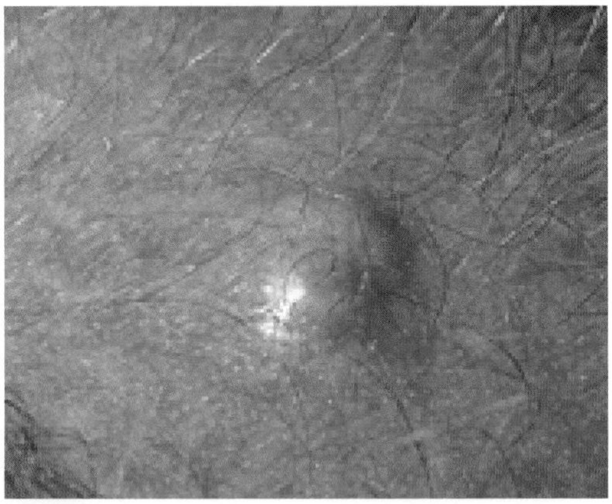

Figure 2.22 Boils are from the bacteria group

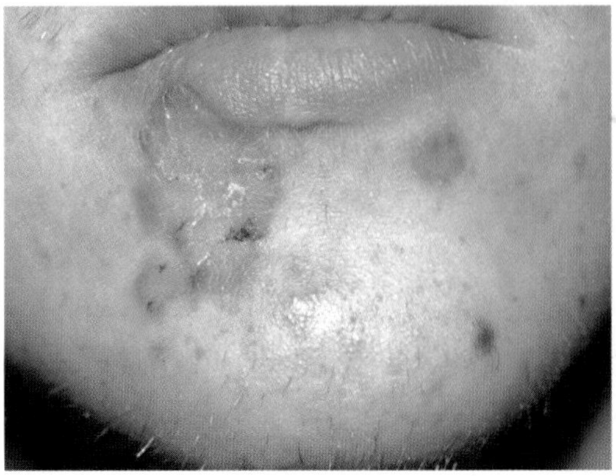

Figure 2.23 Impetigo is from the bacteria group

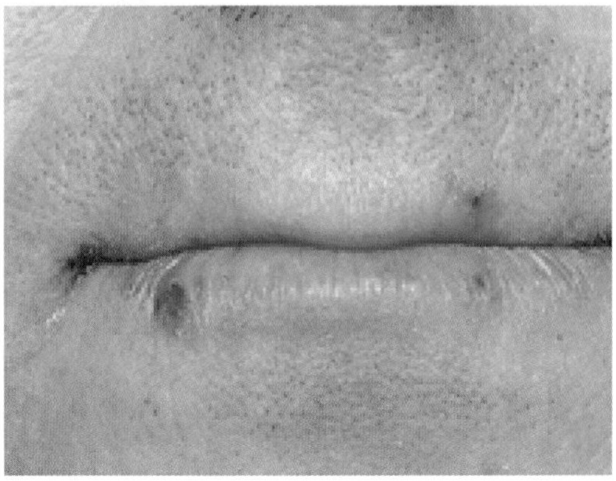

Figure 2.24 Cold sores are from the virus group

Online activity 2.4

WWW

Select correct boxes

Make sure the working environment is clean and dry at all times; this includes clothing, work areas and all equipment. Floors should be kept clean; hair clippings should be swept up to prevent diseases and accidents. If floors are wet, notices should be left to warn clients and other staff. Surfaces should be washed down once a day. Mirrors should be cleaned before the clients arrive.

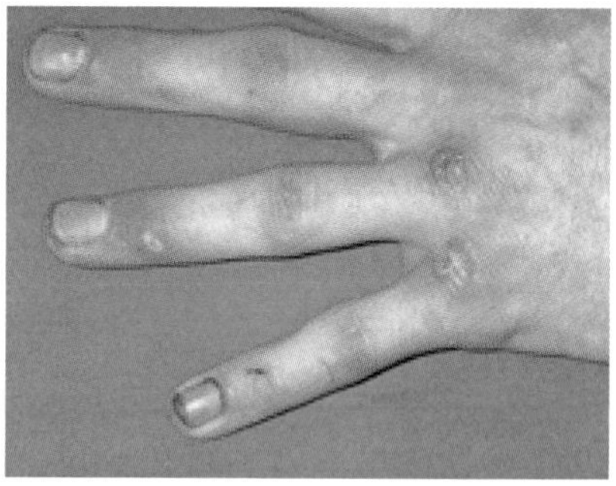

Figure 2.25 Warts are from the virus group

Figure 2.26 Clean work surfaces and mirrors

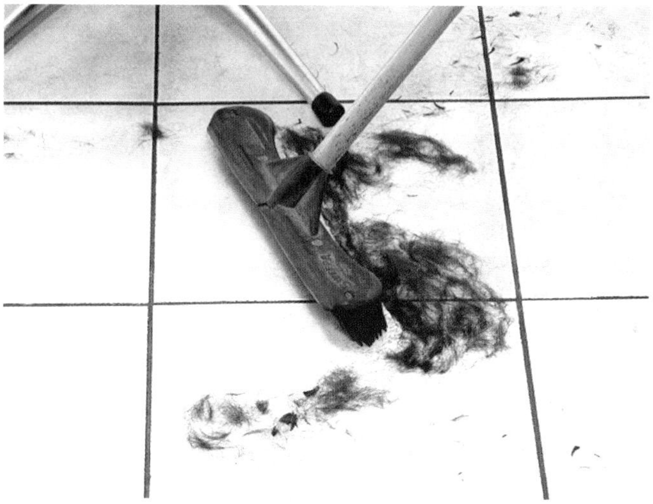

Figure 2.27 Sweep up hair clippings

Figure 2.28 Inform clients and other staff if floors are wet

Safety first

Keep the used towels in a closed container to reduce the risk of the spread of infection.

Equipment

Always use fresh, clean and sterile towels and gowns for each client. All towels should be washed after each client. Keep the used towels in a closed container to reduce the risk of the spread of infection. This prevents cross infection of fungal diseases such as ringworm of the head (tinea capitis) or infestations of lice (pediculosis capitis). Bacterial diseases are also spread from dirty towels, especially impetigo.

Brushes and combs should be washed after use. All other equipment should have hair clippings removed and be cleaned carefully.

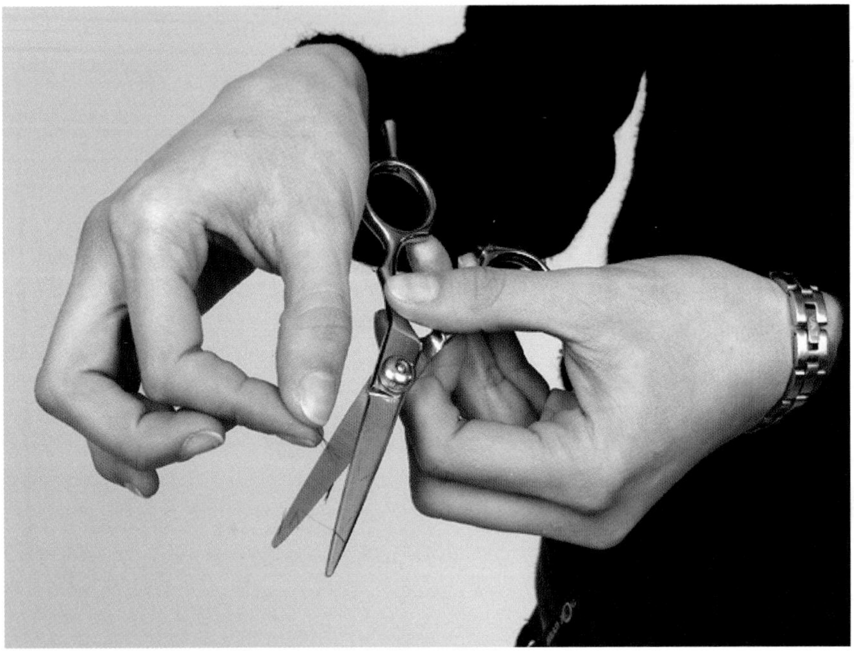

Figure 2.29 Remove hairs from scissors after use

Key information

Remember to always wash brushes and combs before sterilising.

Methods of sterilisation

Salons may use a variety of ways to sterilise equipment (make free of micro-organisms). Remember to always wash brushes and combs before sterilising.

Autoclave (heat)

This is the recommended method of sterilisation for small metal items. The high temperature steam produced destroys all micro-organisms. Note that it is important always to follow the manufacturer's instructions when using an autoclave.

UV cabinet (ultraviolet radiation)

Clean tools can be stored in a UV cabinet once they have been sterilised.

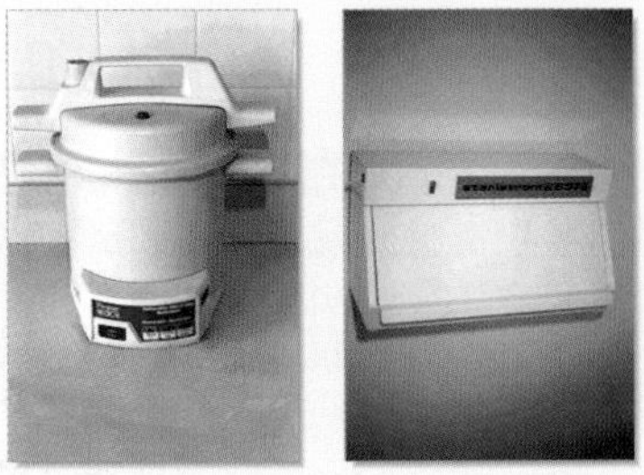

Figure 2.30 Autoclave and UV cabinet

Chemical sterilisation

Proprietary sterilising solutions and sprays are available for sterilising equipment. To be effective the chemical solutions should be used for the correct length of time and mixed following the manufacturer's instructions. Sterilising sprays are used for wiping scissors and clippers.

Figure 2.31 Chemical sterilising solution

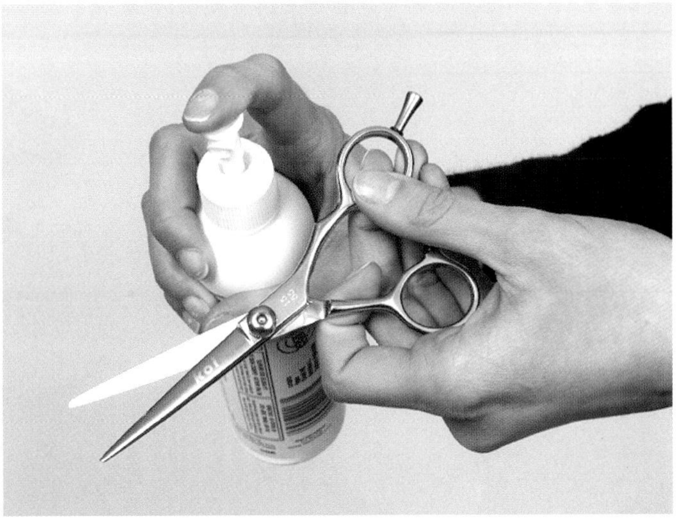

Figure 2.32 Sterilising spray

Disposal of waste

Salons produce waste as do other businesses. This waste will have a negative effect on the environment and it can cause pollution. In order to reduce this, it should be managed correctly.

Covered waste bins which contain a polythene bin liner should be used for everyday items of salon waste. These should be emptied daily or when full.

Razor blades and any other sharp items should be kept away from general salon waste and placed in a safe closed container before disposal.

Key information

Waste will have a negative effect on the environment and it can cause pollution.

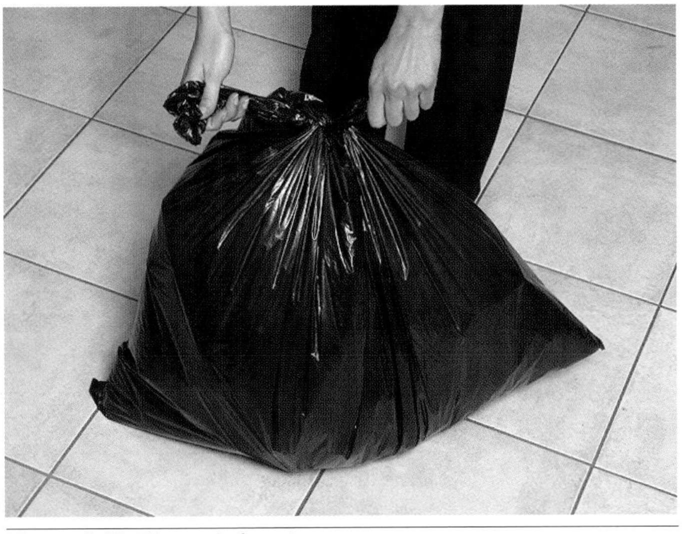

Figure 2.33 Disposal of waste

Figure 2.34 Sharps boxes are used to dispose of razors

Safety first

Chemical waste should be kept away from general waste.

Any contaminated waste should be put in a bag separately and disposed of immediately.

Waste that can be recycled should be dealt with according to your local by-laws.

Safety first

Ensure you know who the registered first-aider in your salon is and locate where the first aid box is kept.

Definition

RIDDOR stands for the Reporting of Injuries, Diseases and Dangerous Occurrences Regulations.

Key information

Ensure that you are wearing gloves when performing basic first aid and you ONLY carry out basic first aid.

First aid - Regulations for First Aid 1981

All establishments should have a registered first-aider. Ensure you know who the registered first-aider in your salon is and locate where the first aid box is kept. The health and safety regulations RIDDOR require the salon to have a first aid kit available. The box is green with a white cross on it.

Figure 2.35 First aid box

WWW Online activity 2.5

Round the board

First aid problems

If an accident occurs in the salon, you should have a basic knowledge of what to do. The table below shows some common first aid problems and the action to take if they occur.

Table 2.1 Problems and actions

Problem	Action taken
Chemicals on the skin	Flush with cool water
Chemical enters eye	Wash out the eye with cool water until first aider arrives Make sure the water is clean
Burns from heat	Flush with cool water Call for first aid assistance if needed
Burns from chemicals	Remove any clothing that is contaminated as long as it is not stuck to the skin Flush with cool water Call for first aid assistance if needed
Unconscious state	Put into recovery position Call for first aid assistance
Cut to the skin	Put pressure on the area using pad from first aid box If a deep cut or bleeding does not stop, call for first aid assistance

Fire

Accidents involving fire are very serious. If a fire should break out the priority is to remove clients to safety. If it is a small fire it can be extinguished with a glass fibre 'fire blanket' or an extinguisher. If the fire is too big or clearly out of control . . .

GET OUT – STAY OUT – CALL OUT THE FIRE BRIGADE!

Safety first

If a fire should break out the priority is to remove clients to safety.

Figure 2.36 Fire blanket and fire extinguisher

Definition

Flammable: Can catch fire.

Fire safety

Fire precautions that should be carried out include checking that:

- exits are not obstructed
- doors to escape routes are not closed
- fire doors are kept closed but not locked
- fire fighting equipment is available and in working order
- the correct type of fire extinguisher is readily available.

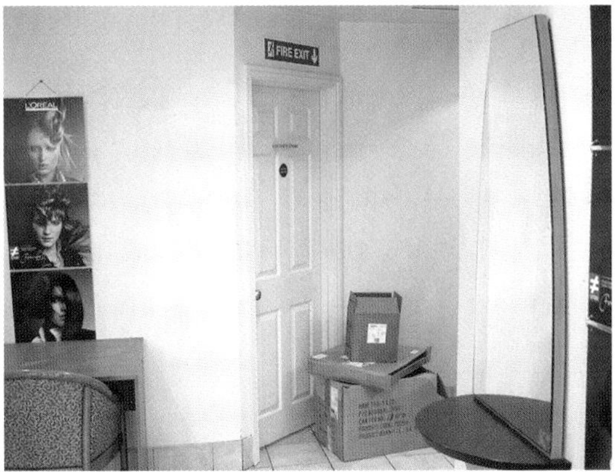

Figure 2.37 This obstruction is unsafe

General rules

To prevent fires occurring the following rules can help:

- A 'No Smoking' policy inside salons should be supported.
- Towels should not be placed over heaters.
- Electrical sockets should not be overloaded.
- Check that electrical wires are not bare or frayed.
- Switch off electrical appliances when not in use.
- Store flammable liquids away from heat.
- Do not obstruct electric or gas heaters.

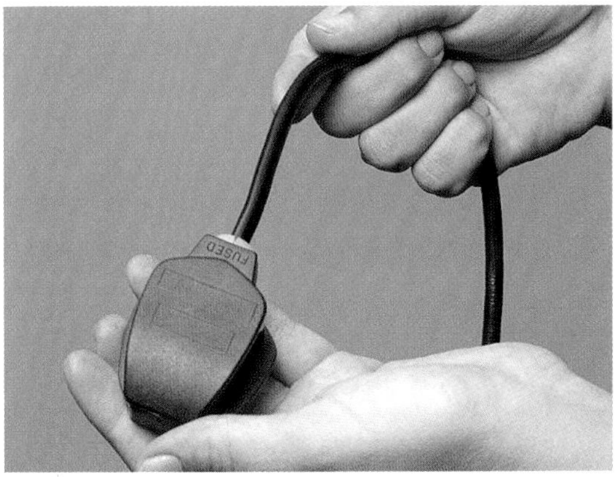

Figure 2.38 Check electrical wires

Safety first

Ensure that you know the emergency fire procedures in your workplace.

Emergency fire procedure

If a fire does happen your workplace should have a set procedure; so, for example, you will know:

1 how the alarm is raised
2 what the alarm sounds like
3 what to do when you hear the alarm
4 your escape route from the building
5 where to go to assemble
6 who is responsible for calling the fire brigade.

Safety first

All extinguishers have instructions written on them. Read them now before it is too late.

Fire extinguishers

These can be dangerous if used incorrectly or on the wrong type of fire. They are colour coded to allow easy recognition. The table below shows the substances each type contains and its uses.

Black and blue extinguishers are recommended for the salon because they are suitable for use with electrical equipment and flammable liquids.

Table 2.2 Fire extinguisher colours and use

Colour label	Substance	Use
Red	Water	Wood, paper, textiles, not electrical
Black	CO_2	Flammable liquids, safe for all voltages
Green	Vaporising liquids	Flammable liquids, safe for all voltages
Blue	Dry powder	Flammable liquids, safe for all voltages
Cream	Foam	Flammable liquids, not electrical

WWW Online activity 2.6

Correct selection

Calling emergency services

If it is necessary to call out the emergency services then follow these rules:

- do not panic
- dial 999
- speak slowly and clearly
- tell the operator which service or services you require
- give your name, address and telephone number
- give relevant details of the fire, accident etc.
- listen and answer questions carefully
- if the fire brigade has been requested, wait in a safe place for its arrival.

Figure 2.39 Speak slowly and clearly when calling for help!

Figure 2.40 Your salon should have periodic checks by the fire prevention officer

The salon owner or employer should authorise periodic checks by the fire prevention officer. The fire brigade will offer help and advice on fire safety, evacuation procedures and choice of fire fighting equipment.

Definition

Periodic: Occurring at intervals.

Other emergencies

Study this table to see what action you should take in certain situations.

Table 2.3 Emergencies and actions

Emergency	Action
Flood	• Turn off water • Alert the fire brigade Make sure you know where the mains stopcock is
Bomb alert	• Phone emergency services • Evacuate
Gas leak	• Open windows • Phone emergency services • Evacuate
Suspicious person and/ or package	• Report to the manager

Definition

Stopcock: A valve that opens and closes a gas or water supply pipe.

Security

Employees should pay attention to:

- locking doors at night
- closing and securing windows at night
- keeping the back door closed during salon hours
- never leaving money or valuables unattended or in the salon overnight
- unauthorised or suspicious people in the salon
- not leaving the till open and unattended
- making sure clients' handbags, jewellery etc. remain with them at all times
- marking their own equipment.

Key information

Salon security is essential.

If in any doubt always report to your manager.

Figure 2.41 Don't leave tills open like this

Key information

Details which should be recorded are:

- full name and address of casualty
- date and time of the accident
- accident details
- signature of the person making the entry.

Recording accidents

All accidents should be recorded in the accident book, which all salons should possess.

WWW Online activity 2.7

Drag into correct group

Client care

The client should be cared for throughout their time at the salon. Remember to:

- gown the client properly to protect their clothing
- remove all obstacles when clients are moving around the salon to prevent accidents
- if the client needs to be evacuated whilst in the middle of a treatment always cover their hair with a towel
- make sure the client's handbag, jewellery etc. are kept with the client at all times
- when using products which are hazardous, always read the manufacturer's instructions and ask for assistance if unsure.

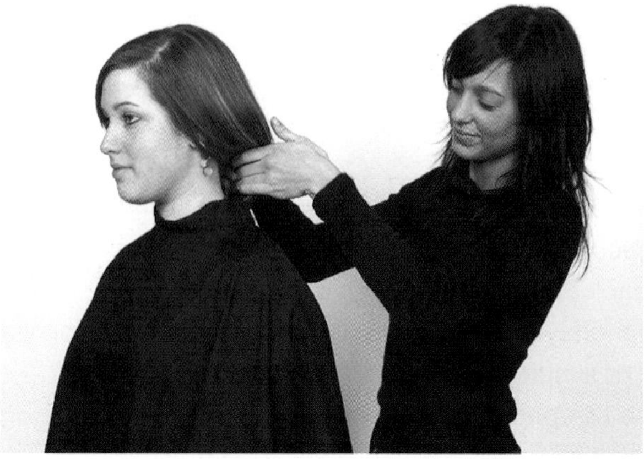

Figure 2.42 Gowning the client

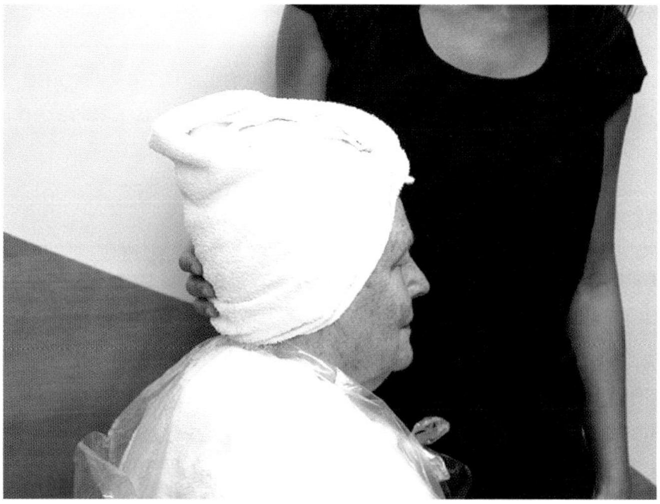

Figure 2.43 Covering client's head with a towel

Figure 2.44 Make sure clients carry their possessions at all times

Client records

Client records should be updated regularly with all relevant details, for example if a client has an allergic reaction to a chemical used in the salon. This can prevent an accident occurring at a later date. Record home care products sold to the client with date of purchase.

> **Safety first**
>
> Client records should be updated regularly with all relevant details, for example if a client has an allergic reaction to a chemical used in the salon.

Figure 2.45 Take care with hazardous products

Figure 2.46 Make sure you record it if a client has bought any products

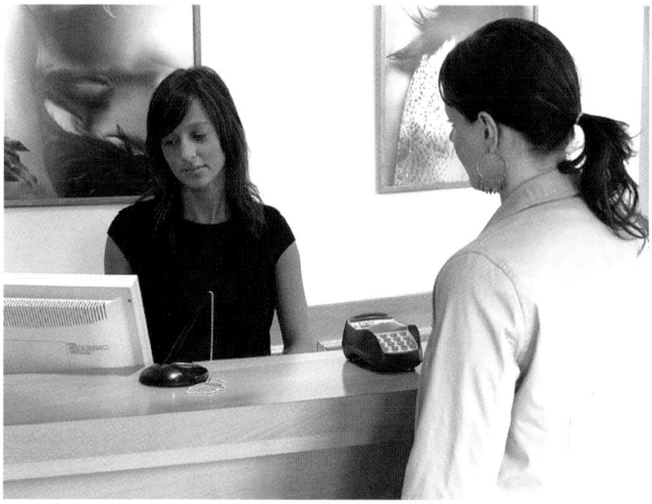

Figure 2.47 Update client records

Key information

Clients must have access to their details if they request it.

Definition

Data Protection Act: An Act that provides rights for individuals regarding the obtaining, use, holding and disclosure of information about themselves.

Data protection

If you keep client information on the computer, the company must be registered with the Data Protection Register. The information must be accurate and treated as confidential. Clients must have access to their details if they request it.

Personal presentation and hygiene

The stylist must always ensure his or her own personal hygiene and presentation are of a high standard. This includes:

- Hair – Your hair and make-up should reflect the standards of the salon. It should be clean, fashionable and smart.
- Clothing – Salon dress should reflect the style of the salon; however, it should also protect the hairdresser, be comfortable and clean. Clothing that is too loose is a risk to the client and the stylist. There is a risk of clothing coming into contact with the client or being caught in equipment. Some salons wear overalls as they lend an air of efficiency to the salon. They should protect the clothing, match the colour scheme of the salon and be neat, clean and attractive. Clothes should not be stained or creased. When colouring, perming, neutralising and relaxing you should wear an apron for extra protection. Always wash your salon clothes/overalls when they are dirty or smelly; do not wait until the end of the week.
- Mouth and teeth – Bad breath is unpleasant to clients. Regular visits to the dentist will guard against bad breath. Certain foods will make your breath smell; don't eat pickled onions at lunchtime. Brush your teeth regularly. If you smoke, try to give it up.
- Hands and nails – Both should be clean as the risk of spreading infection is then minimised. They should not be stained with hair colourant. Nails should not be bitten and should not be too long (dirt can get trapped underneath). Wear disposable gloves where necessary.
- Shoes – Should be comfortable and allow feet to breathe. Leather shoes would be ideal. Cut down on foot odour by washing tights or socks frequently.

Figure 2.48 Ensure your personal hygiene and presentation are of a high standard

Hair in the salon can harm the skin. It may break the surface of the skin leaving the hairdresser open to risk of infection. The wearing of open toed shoes will increase the risk of infection.

- The skin – A bath or shower every day is essential because of the hot, humid atmosphere of the salon and the close contact the hairdresser has with the client. Always use deodorant or an antiperspirant (reduces underarm sweating). A little perfume is pleasant but too much can be overpowering.

Online activity 2.8 WWW

Five in a row

Jewellery

This should at no time interfere with the client's comfort; only the minimum of jewellery should be worn. Jewellery may scratch a client's skin. It may also react with the chemicals, possibly contributing to the development of contact dermatitis.

Safety first

Jewellery may react with chemicals, possibly contributing to the development of contact dermatitis.

Figure 2.49 This is too much jewellery to wear in the salon

Posture and deportment

The back should be kept straight; bend from the knees, feet apart with weight evenly distributed. If the spine is bent the back will have excess strain and the body will tire. The lungs will also be constricted; this lowers the intake of oxygen, which induces tiredness. Poor posture looks sloppy and will not give a good impression of the hairdresser.

Safety first

Your back should be kept straight. Bend from the knees, feet apart with weight evenly distributed.

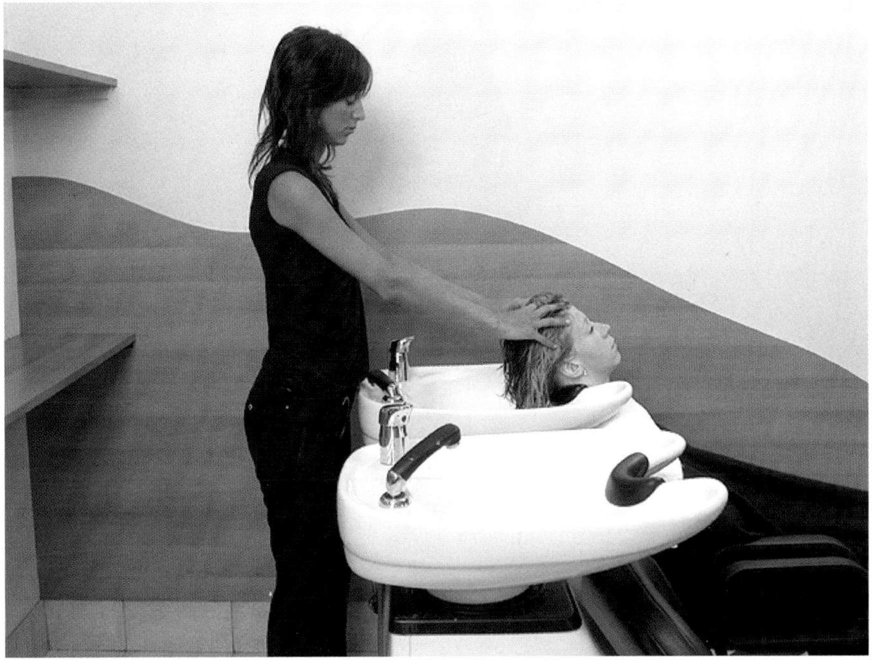

Figure 2.50 Correct posture

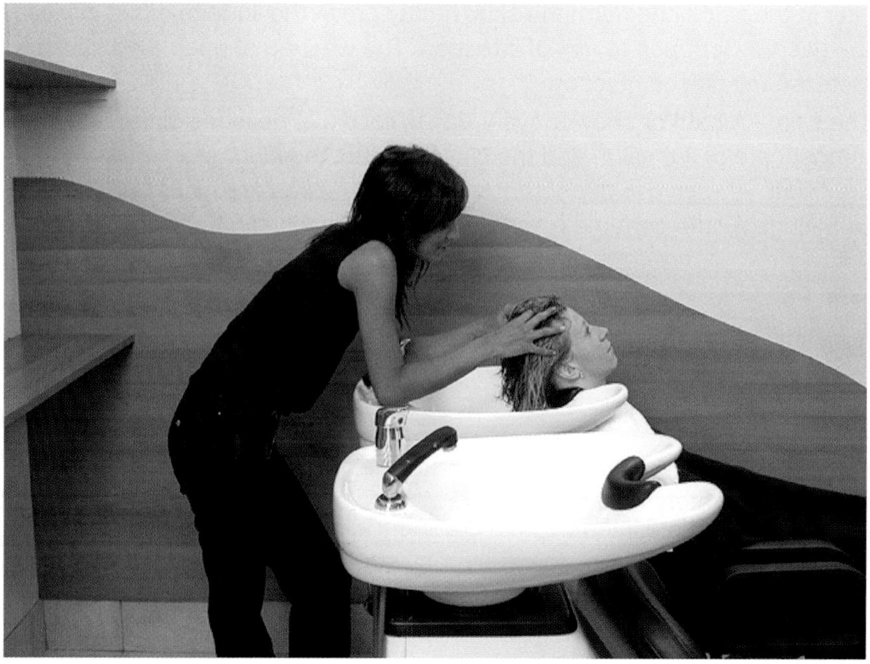

Figure 2.51 Incorrect posture

Definition

Regenerate: To renew or replace.

Key information

Exercise is vital to health; it firms muscles and moves joints, keeping the body supple.

Exercise and rest

Hairdressing means standing for long hours so it is necessary to be fit and healthy. Exercise is vital to health; it firms muscles and moves joints, keeping the body supple. During sleep, the body regenerates its energies, refreshing the brain and the body. Lack of sleep reduces the quality of life when you are awake.

Figure 2.52 Exercise and rest will help you to be good at your job

2.3 Worksheets

WORKSHEETS

You can carry out the worksheets during your study of a chapter or unit, or at the end. An example is presented here and there are more online. If your college or company is registered with ATT Training, lots more are available. Write your answers directly in the book, but only if you own it of course – if it is a library or college book, use a separate piece of paper!

2.3.1 First aid

Regulations for First Aid 1981

All establishments should have a registered first-aider. Ensure you know who the registered first-aider in your salon is, and locate where the first aid box is kept. The health and safety regulations RIDDOR require the salon to have a first aid kit available. The box is green with a white cross on it.

Who is the first-aider in your salon?

____

Where is the first aid kit kept in your salon?

____

First aid problems

If an accident occurs in the salon, you should have a basic knowledge of what to do. Ensure that you are wearing gloves when performing basic first aid and that you ONLY carry out basic first aid.

Complete the following table by referring back to Chapter 2, or with the help of the online learning screens. Add any other information that you can think of.

Problem	Action taken

2.4 Assessment

Well done! If you have studied all the content of this unit you may be ready to test your knowledge.

Check out the 'Preparing for assessments' section in Chapter 1 if you have not already done so, and always remember:

- You can only do your best if you have. . .
  - studied hard
  - completed the activities
  - completed the worksheets
  - practised, practised, practised
  - and then revised!

? Now carry out the online multiple-choice quiz

. . . and good luck in the final exam, which will be arranged by your tutor/assessor.

CHAPTER 3

Create a positive impression

This chapter covers the NVQ/SVQ unit G17, Give clients a positive impression of yourself and your organisation.

Giving clients a positive image of yourself and your salon is about giving the best service you can. Your reputation is earned in this way.

In this chapter you will learn about:

- establishing effective rapport with clients
- responding appropriately to clients
- communicating information to clients.

Website www

www.atthairdressing.com

CHAPTER 3 CREATE A POSITIVE IMPRESSION: CONTENTS, SCREENS AND ACTIVITIES

Key:

Sections from the book are set in this colour

Screens available online are set in this colour

Online activity screens are set in this colour

Establish effective rapport

Introduction	Handling clients' behaviour
Effective rapport with clients	Correct selection
Welcoming clients	If a client is confused
Client comfort	Being part of a team

Respond to clients

Introduction	Good knowledge
Suggestions	Five in a row

Communicating with clients

Introduction	Unexpected or unwanted news
Verbal communication	Dealing with unexpected or unwanted news
Non-verbal communication	Wordsearch
Check It	Worksheet – handling clients' behaviour
Written communication	Worksheet – being part of a team
Electronic communication	Worksheet – communicate information to clients
Body language	Online multiple choice quiz

3.1 Establish effective rapport

Developing a professional attitude with clients is very important. You must treat clients in a friendly and helpful manner at all times.

Key information

You must treat clients in a friendly and helpful manner at all times.

Figure 3.1 Making the right impression

Welcoming clients

Follow your salon's procedure for welcoming clients, making sure that you make the correct impression from the moment you greet the client. Ensure a high standard of personal appearance, as this will affect how the client views you and the salon as a whole. Make sure that if appointments are running late, you explain to the client why they may have to wait. Give an estimated waiting time and offer the client a magazine and a drink, possibly another stylist.

Definition

Impression: The first and immediate effect of an experience.

Figure 3.2 Offer the client a magazine if they have to wait

Key information

If the client is comfortable and pleased with the finished result they will book again.

Client comfort

Ensure the client's comfort is maintained throughout the client's stay in the salon. Ask if they are comfortable, confirm they are satisfied with the treatment. For example, ask questions such as: Do you like the colour? Tell me how you feel about your haircut. If the client is comfortable and pleased with the finished result they will book again. Communicating with the client will be covered in more detail in section 3.

Handling clients' behaviour

If a client is angry you should:

- maintain a friendly approach
- stay calm
- not argue with the client
- listen
- try to establish why they are angry
- ensure communication is clear
- always inform a senior member of staff if you cannot deal with the situation.

WWW Online activity 3.1

Correct selection

Figure 3.3 Maintain good customer care, especially if a client is confused

If a client is confused:

- ask questions to find out what is it the client is confused about
- be precise with your response
- take time to make sure you understand and confirm their expectations.

Maintain good customer care and inform a more senior member of staff.

Figure 3.4 Be courteous to other members of your team

Being part of a team

A happy team working together promotes good working practices and leads to satisfied clients. Always be co-operative and courteous. Consider yourself part of a team, rather than an individual merely responsible for your own specific duties. Offer help and assistance to others; remember that the 'favour' may be returned when you are busy, e.g. if you have completed your duties see if you can help others.

Key information

Consider yourself part of a team, rather than an individual merely responsible for your own specific duties.

Definitions

Co-operative: To join in and help others in your team.

Courteous: To be polite.

3.2 Responding to clients

You must always respond to clients if they wish for assistance. Do this in a friendly and helpful manner, clarifying that you have understood their expectations. It is important to respond quickly to clients. As you can see in the photograph below, if the stylist did not respond quickly to this situation it could have resulted in a potential accident.

Safety first

It is important to respond quickly to clients.

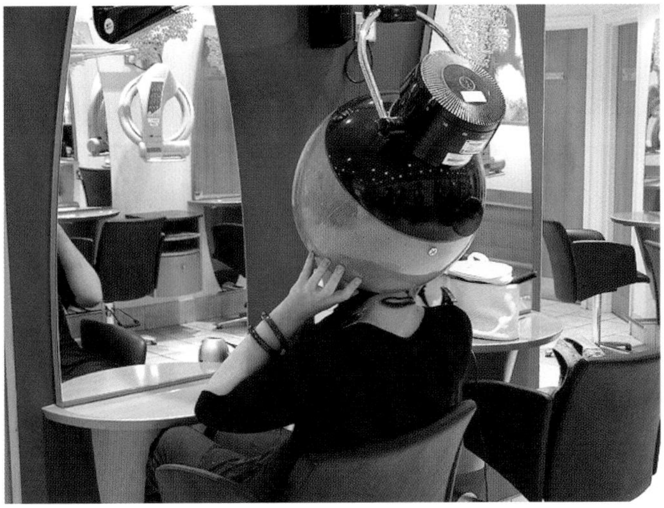

Figure 3.5 A potentially dangerous situation . . .

Figure 3.6 . . . avoided as the stylist responded quickly

Clients welcome suggestions, maybe a new look, a change of hairstyle, highlights, colour to hide grey hair and conditioning treatment to improve the quality and appearance of their hair. Suggesting services is helpful to the client. Give the client time to think, but be positive. You should try to convince the client that the service or treatment is a must and that you particularly want to provide it. Give the client time to consider all the facts.

Figure 3.7 Offering suggestions to the client can be helpful

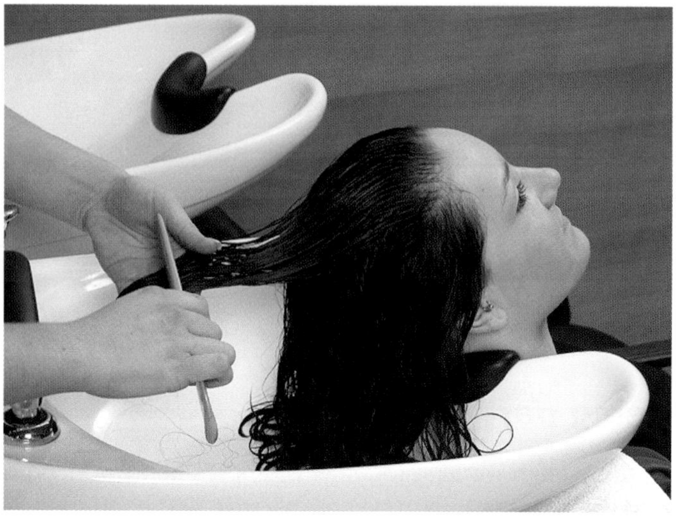

Figure 3.8 Good knowledge about treatments is essential

Key information

Find out the answers to any questions you do not know the answer to. Do not make up the answers.

Have a good knowledge about the treatments that you give to clients as you should be able to answer any questions that they have about them. Find out the answers to any questions you do not know the answer to. Do not make up the answers.

WWW Online activity 3.2

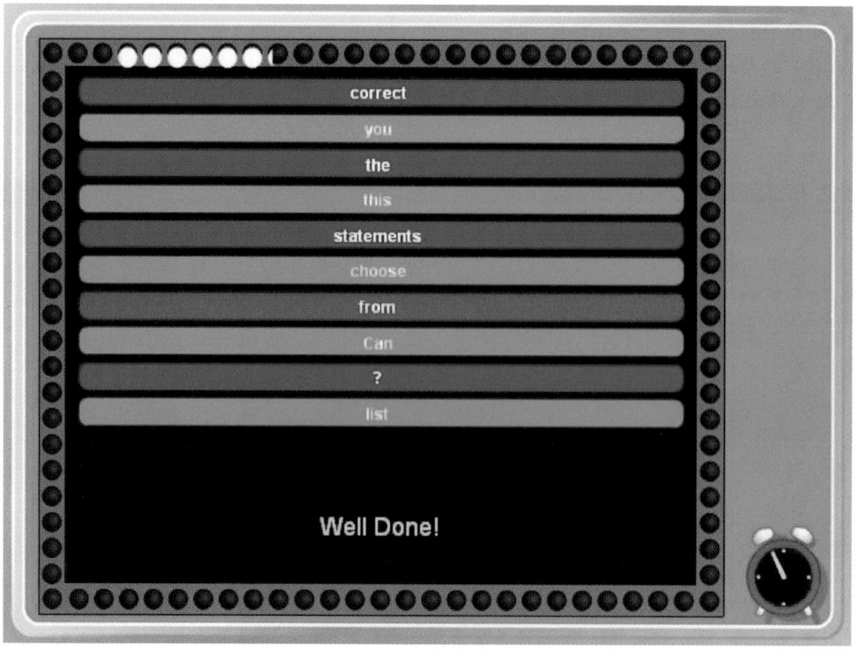

Five in a row

3.3 Communicating with clients

Good communication in the salon is always important, especially if a business is to succeed. Communication can be in many different forms including verbal, non-verbal, written and electronic. You should be aware of your own communication and your clients in order to judge how they are feeling.

Key information

You should be aware of your own communication and your clients in order to judge how they are feeling.

Verbal communication

This is spoken information. In the salon this includes:

- talking to the client
- talking to other staff members
- answering or making telephone calls.

Always speak clearly, be polite, check the information received is correct and pass it on to the appropriate person.

Figure 3.9 Talking to a client

Figure 3.10 Talking to other staff members

Figure 3.11 Answering or making telephone calls

Non-verbal communication

This is the way we convey information without speaking. This includes:

- gestures
- body posture
- facial expressions.

Online activity 3.3

Check it

Figure 3.12 Always check the details in written communication

Definitions

Concise: Expressing a lot but in few words.

Accurate: Exact and correct in all details.

Written communication

Written messages and information should always be clear, concise and accurate. It may be necessary to ask questions to ensure you have all the relevant details. Always check the details; ensure it gets to the person intended.

Electronic communication

This form of communication includes:

- using the salon's website to give out information regarding prices, special offers etc.
- sending text messages to clients to confirm their appointments
- emailing clients with information
- using the intranet in your salon to make sure information is up to date at all times.

Figure 3.13 Using the computer to communicate

Body language

Body language is a very important form of communication. Our stance, gestures or facial expressions say a lot about how we feeling, for example smiling implies friendliness, frowning implies hostility. Maintain eye contact with the client when talking and listening to show you are paying attention and to convey friendliness and trust. Always listen carefully to the client, making sure you take in everything the client is telling you.

Key information

Our stance, gestures or facial expressions say a lot about how we are feeling, for example smiling implies friendliness, frowning implies hostility.

Figure 3.14 Positive body language

Figure 3.15 Negative body language

Giving client unexpected or unwanted news

Definitions

Diagnosis: To identify the problem, need or want.

Sympathetically: To be sympathetic. To understand how someone may feel.

For some, dealing with the public and providing a service can be the most enjoyable aspect of a hairdresser's job. For others, creating or delivering a treatment or style may be the most enjoyable aspect. What is certain is that an effective hairdresser needs to be good at both, because sometimes the client has to receive news that was not expected or wanted. As a result of a test and diagnosis the hairdresser may realise that the treatment or service requested by the client is not possible. This news should be delivered as sympathetically but as positively as possible.

Here are two suggestions on how to deal with this situation.

1 Suggest an alternative to the original requested service that you think will be just as suitable for the client. It will of course not be the same, but it could be just as acceptable, maybe more so once the client has had time to consider.

2 Suggest a course of action that will enable the original treatment or service that was requested to take place. There is no doubt that if you explain this carefully you will gain the full confidence of the client.

Figure 3.16 Use colour charts to suggest an alternative

Figure 3.17 Ensure that you explain the alternative fully to gain confidence

WWW Online activity 3.4

Wordsearch

3.4 Worksheets

WORKSHEETS

You can carry out the worksheets during your study of a chapter or unit, or at the end. An example is presented here and there are more online. If your college or company is registered with ATT Training, lots more are available. Write your answers directly in the book, but only if you own it of course – if it is a library or college book, use a separate piece of paper!

3.4.1 Handling clients' behaviour

If a client is angry you should:

- maintain a friendly approach
- stay calm
- not argue with the client
- listen
- try to establish why they are angry
- ensure communication is clear
- always inform a senior member of staff if you cannot deal with the situation.

If a client is confused:

- ask questions to find out what is it the client is confused about
- be precise with your response
- take time to make sure you understand and confirm their expectations.

Maintain good customer care and inform a more senior member of staff.

Work in pairs or a small group. One person should act as a client and another as a staff member. Read the following scenarios and use role play to establish a satisfactory method of dealing with the problems.

1. The client is unhappy about being kept waiting in reception for their appointment. They have been waiting for 20 minutes due to the stylist running over with their previous client.
2. The client shouts at the stylist for pulling their hair whilst combing it.
3. A client seems happy with their treatment whilst in the chair, but when they get to reception they start complaining that it took too long.
4. A client arrives at reception and complains that their hair is breaking off after having a treatment at your salon a week previously.

3.5 Assessment

Well done! If you have studied all the content of this unit you may be ready to test your knowledge.

Check out the 'Preparing for assessments' section in Chapter 1 if you have not already done so, and always remember:

- You can only do your best if you have. . .
    - studied hard
    - completed the activities
    - completed the worksheets
    - practised, practised, practised
    - and then revised!

? Now carry out the online multiple-choice quiz

. . . and good luck in the final exam, which will be arranged by your tutor/assessor.

CHAPTER 4

Advise and consult

This chapter covers the NVQ/SVQ unit G7, Advise and consult with clients and VRQ unit 203, Client consultation for hair services.

The consultation with a client is very important because it is the time when you find out what they want. You will also check their hair, skin and scalp condition to ensure services and products are safe and meet their needs.

In this chapter you will learn about:

- identifying what clients want
- analysing the hair, skin and scalp
- advising your client and agreeing on services and products.

Website
www.atthairdressing.com

CHAPTER 4 ADVISE AND CONSULT: CONTENTS, SCREENS AND ACTIVITIES

Key:
Sections from the book are set in this colour
Screens available online are set in this colour
Online activity screens are set in this colour

Identify clients' requirements

Introduction
Identify what clients want
Effective communication 1
Drag Into correct group
Effective communication 2
Confidentiality

Analyse the hair, skin and scalp

Introduction
Hair structure and growth
Layers of a strand of hair
Hair growth cycle
Wordsearch
Checking the client visually - hair growth patterns
Lifestyle and head/face shapes
Head/face shapes 1
Head/face shapes 2
Head/face shapes 3
Five in a row
Tests - porosity
Elasticity test
Incompatibility test
Skin test
Pre-perm test curl
Test cutting
Development test curl
Shoot the target
Strand test
Contraindications
Infections
Preventing infection
Correct selection
The salon
Equipment
Hair and scalp conditions
Round the board
Non-contagious - damaged cuticle
Pityriasis capitis (dandruff)
Seborrhoea
Fragilitas crinium (split ends)
Trichorrhexis nodosa
Monilethrix
Psoriasis
Check It
Alopecia
Androgenic alopecia
Diffuse alopecia
Alopecia areata
Cicatrical alopecia
Check it
Sebaceous cyst
Warts
Canities (grey hair)
Contagious - folliculitis
Tinea capitis (ringworm of the scalp)
Impetigo
Pediculosis capitis (head lice)
Scabies
Drag into correct group

Advise clients

Agreeing treatment
Advise clients on aftercare procedures and future salon services
Advise on equipment
Supplying client with information
Record keeping 1
Record keeping 2
Five in a row
Worksheet – identify what the client wants
Worksheet – hair structure and growth
Worksheet – hair and scalp conditions
Online multiple choice quiz

4.1 Identify clients' requirements

Before starting any treatment all clients, new and existing, should have a meeting with the stylist to discuss what the client wants or needs. This is known as the consultation. It will require obtaining information from the client in order to carry out their wishes.

The consultation starts with the stylist communicating with the client by asking the client several questions. The way this is carried out is very important in order to establish a good relationship between client and hairdresser.

Key information

Before starting any treatment all clients, new and existing, should have a meeting with the stylist to discuss what the client wants or needs.

Definition

Consultation: Discuss individual needs with the client.

Figure 4.1 A consultation between client and stylist

Effective communication

Develop different questioning skills using both open and closed questions. Asking questions that require a yes or no reply are known as closed questions. Using words such as when, who, what, if etc. will enable the client to discuss their needs. This method is known as open questioning and is used to expand on what the client's wishes are and help you to ensure a good service is provided.

Key information

Closed questions usually have a 'yes' or 'no' answer.

Open questions use words such as 'when', 'who' and 'what' and encourage discussion.

Online activity 4.1 WWW

Drag into correct group

Always listen carefully to the client, making sure you take in everything the client is telling you. Maintain eye contact whilst the client is speaking. Clarify the information you have obtained and update the client's record card throughout the consultation.

Key information

Maintain eye contact whilst the client is speaking.

Figure 4.2 This kind of gossiping can result in you losing your job!

Confidentiality

Key information

All clients' personal details are confidential.

Definitions

Confidential: Keep secret.

Disclose: To make something known.

Contraindication: Condition preventing a treatment.

All clients' personal details are confidential. This means you must never give out client addresses or telephone numbers. The client is the most important person in the salon and you must gain their trust. You must not gossip about clients or disclose anything a client has told you in confidence. A broken confidence could result in you losing your job.

4.2 Analyse the hair, skin and scalp

Safety first

If any contraindications are found, under no circumstances must you perform the service on the client.

Key information

To establish the condition of the hair, skin and scalp, there are visual checks and tests you must perform, the results of which must always be recorded.

The condition of the hair will determine whether it is advisable to perform certain services or use particular products. To establish the condition of the hair, skin and scalp, there are visual checks and tests you must perform, the results of which must always be recorded. If any contraindications are found, under no circumstances must you perform the service on the client.

Hair structure and growth

In order to diagnose, the hairdresser should understand the structure and growth of hair.

Figure 4.3 shows the structure of a hair follicle (with the sebaceous gland attached to the papilla). This is the capillary network through which the hair obtains its food and oxygen supply from the blood.

There are three layers to a strand of hair: cuticle, cortex and medulla (shown in Figures 4.3 and 4.4).

The cuticle is translucent (the hair colour shows through it) and has a protective function; it is made up of layers of scales. There are more layers around the base of the hair due to wear and tear at the tip.

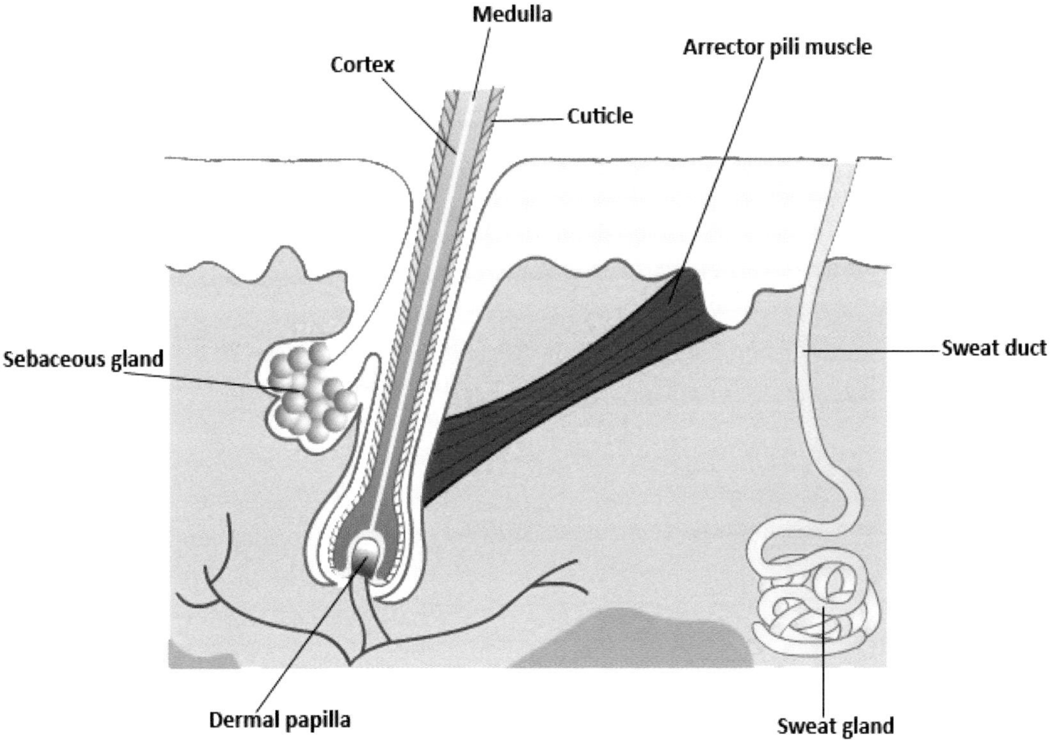

Figure 4.3 Structure of the hair follicle

The cortex forms the bulk of the hair. In this part of the hair the chemical changes of bleaching, tinting, perming and straightening take place. Melanin and pheomelanin are found in the cortex, which gives the hair its colour.

The medulla is the centre of the hair shaft and is mainly found in medium or coarse hair.

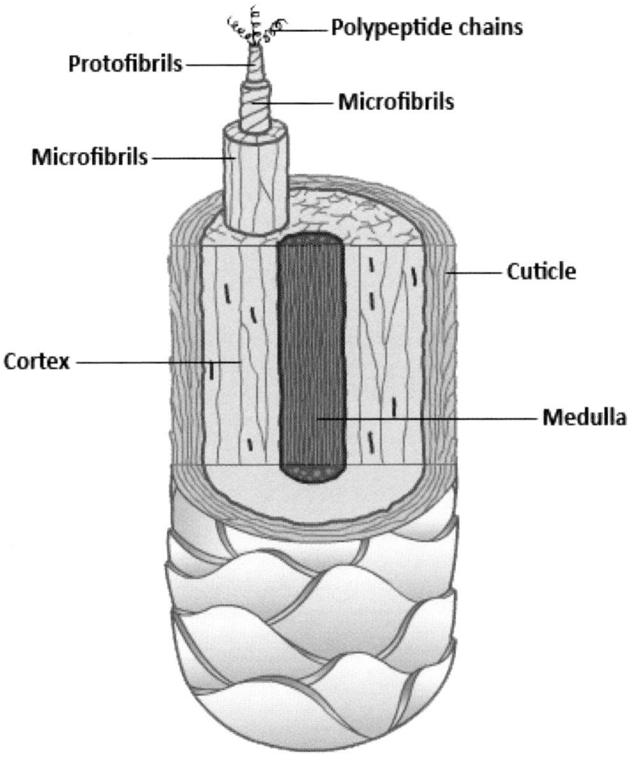

Figure 4.4 Hair structure

Definitions

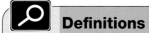

Follicle: Sac containing the hair shaft in the epidermis.

Sebaceous gland: Produces sebum.

Definitions

Melanin: Colouring pigment of the hair.

Pheomelanin: Natural pigment of hair causing a red/yellow hair colour.

Hair growth cycle

Hair grows from the follicle. Hair above the skin is dead, below the skin in the follicle it is actively growing. A new hair grows for a number of years (this varies from person to person; the period is longer in young people) and then dies at the base of the follicle. The follicle rests for a few months before a new hair starts to grow. Hair grows at an average of 1.25 centimetres (half an inch) per month.

The terms used in this growth cycle are:

- anagen (when the hair grows actively)
- catagen (when the old hair falls out and the follicle shrinks)
- telogen (when the follicle and papilla are in a stage of rest).

Website WWW
www.atthairdressing.com

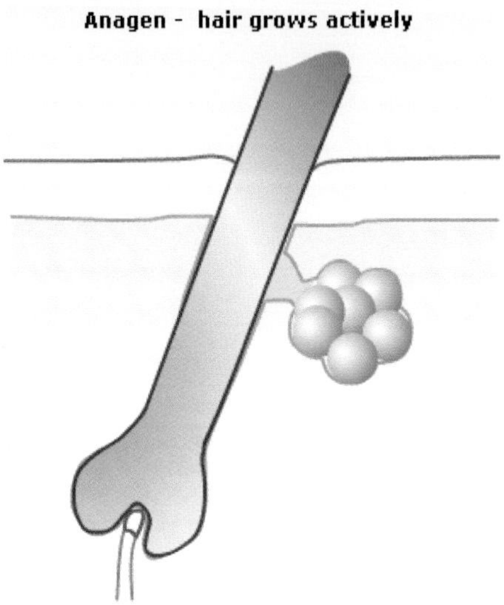

Figure 4.5 Anagen

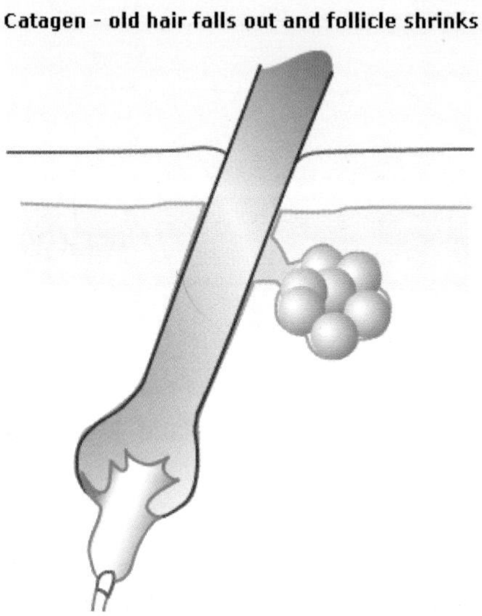

Figure 4.6 Catagen

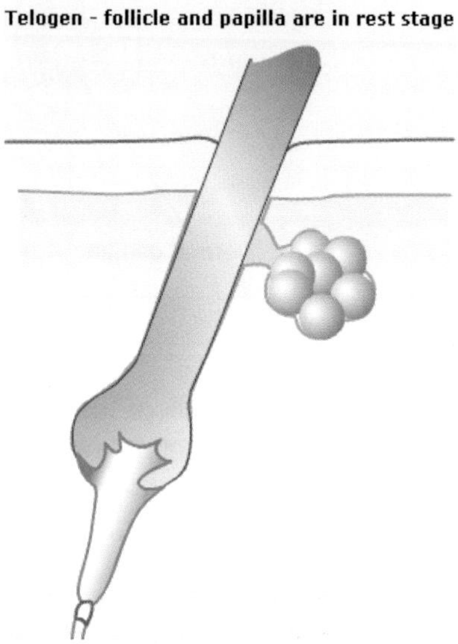

Figure 4.7 Telogen

WWW **Online activity 4.2**
Wordsearch

Checking the client visually – hair growth patterns

The hairdresser should always try to work with the natural hair growth patterns. Do not try to force the hair into an unnatural direction. The hair growth patterns are classified as follows:

Figure 4.8 Cowlick

Cowlick – A cowlick is usually found on the front hairline across the forehead. The roots of the hair grow backwards and the mid-lengths and ends of the hair are forwards, causing the hair to spring up.

Figure 4.9 Crowns

Crowns – A crown is a circular movement of the hair (whorl) positioned towards the back, on top of the head. It is important to identify the crown area because it can be a very strong movement, or in some cases a double crown or two crowns are present, moving in different directions. This may restrict styling.

Figure 4.10 Inward and upward nape

Inward and upward nape – This describes the movement of the hair in the nape area which is below the occipital bone. Some hair grows from the outside of the hairline into the middle and in some cases the hair grows from the middle of the nape area towards the hairline. In extreme cases the hair grows and lies in one direction only.

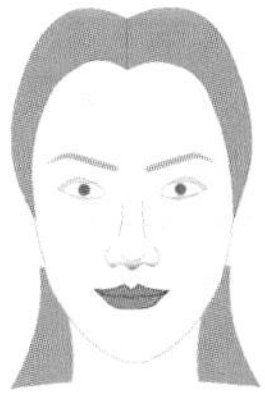

Figure 4.11 Natural partings

Natural partings – A natural parting is where the hair falls in a dividing line. It can be in the centre of the front sections, to the left or to the right. It is advisable to work with a natural parting and adapt any style. It is difficult to maintain a style that goes against a natural parting.

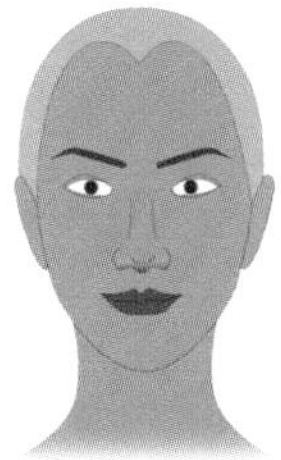

Figure 4.12 Widow's peak

Widow's peak – A widow's peak is a very strong centre forward growth on the front hairline.

Lifestyle and head/face shapes

It is important to create a style that is appropriate to the client's lifestyle and the way the client manages his or her hair at home or work. The style should be determined by the shape of the client's face, but other factors could be the shape of the client's body and the shape of the client's head.

The client may have the following head or face shape:

- oval
- round
- long
- square
- heart
- pear.

The oval shaped face is considered to be the perfect shape that suits any style. However, many people have differing features and it is therefore important to choose the hairstyle to suit both features and face shape.

Key information

It is important to create a style that is appropriate to the client's lifestyle and the way the client manages his or her hair at home or work.

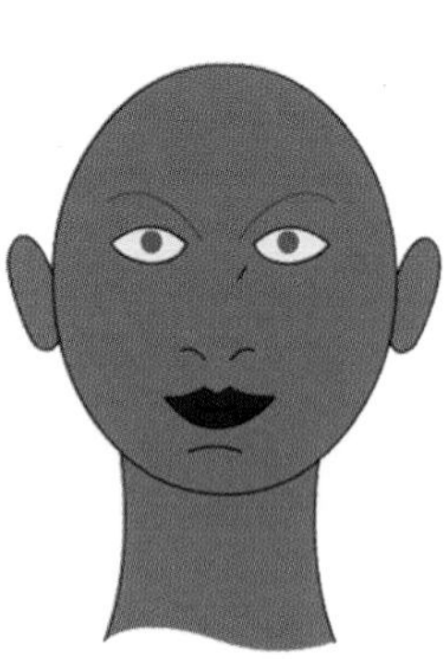

Figure 4.13 An example of a round face

If your client has a round face, a hairstyle will be needed that is flat at the sides and high on the top. This will enhance the client's features.

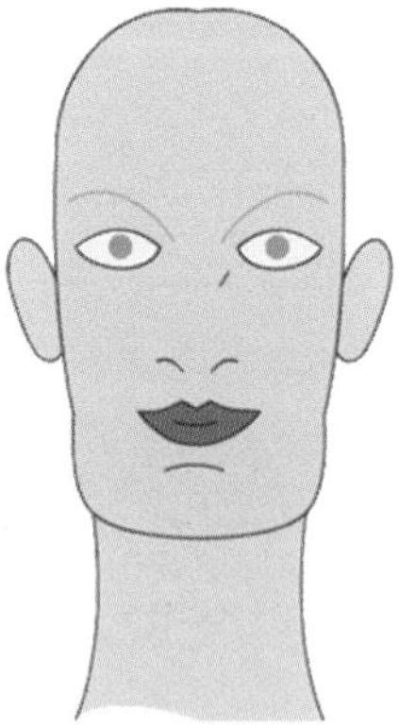

Figure 4.14 An example of a narrow or long face

If the client has a narrow or long face, the hairstyle needs to be fuller at the sides and flatter on top.

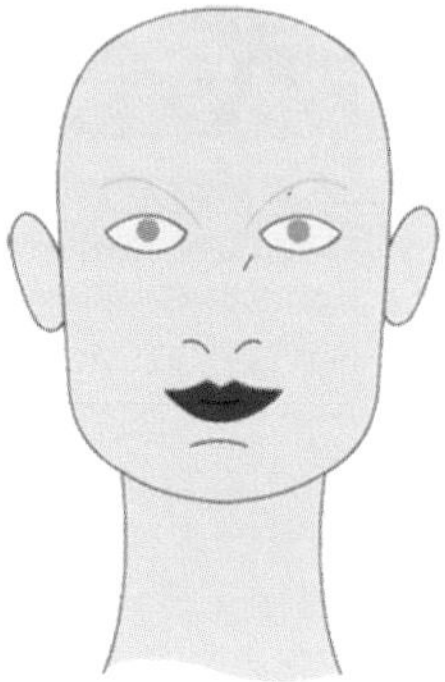

Figure 4.15 An example of a square shaped face

If a client has a square or angular jawline, the hairstyle will need to be softer in style and covering part of that area. This will flatten the face.

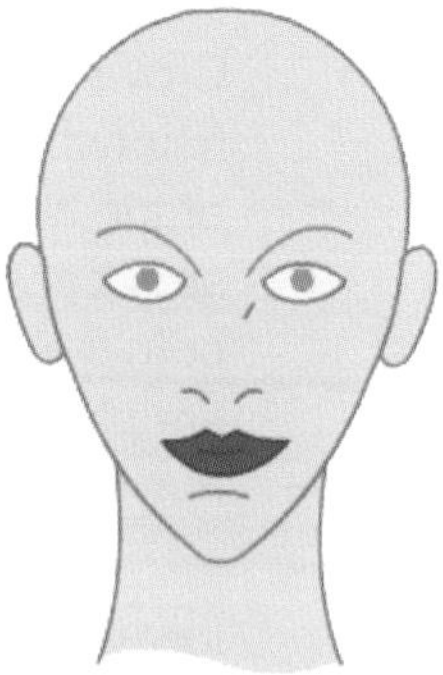

Figure 4.16 An example of a heart shaped face

A client with a heart shaped face will usually be very wide around the eyes and cheek-bones. They may also have a very wide forehead. A fringe would help to narrow the forehead and hair will need to be brought onto the face to create more fullness between the jaw and the bottom of the ear.

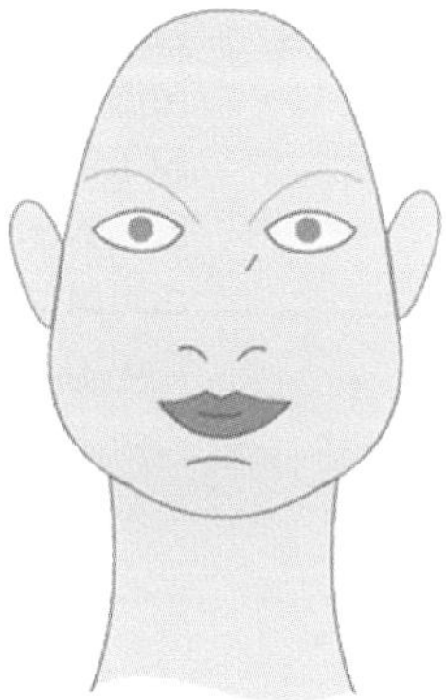

Figure 4.17 An example of a pear shaped face

If a client has a pear shaped face, the hairstyle will have to be flat around the jawline but have lots of volume and fullness around the temples. This will narrow the appearance of the face.

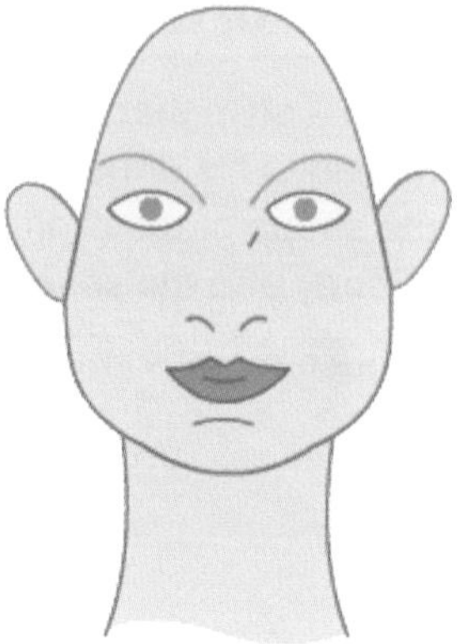

Figure 4.18 Large ears

Large ears that protrude need to be covered for a flattering effect.

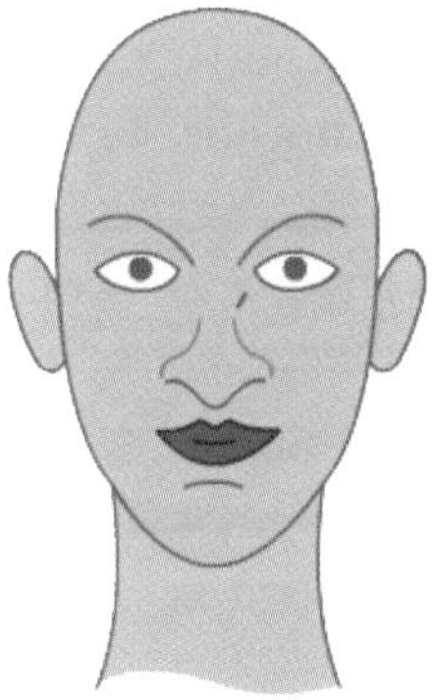

Figure 4.19 Large nose

If the client has a big nose or broken nose a centre parting will exaggerate this. Choose an asymmetric style. This will be more flattering.

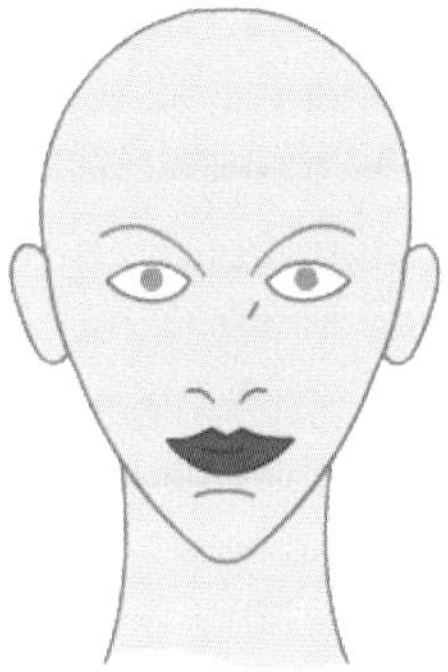

Figure 4.20 High forehead

A fringe will achieve the best effect for a client with a high forehead or receding hairline.

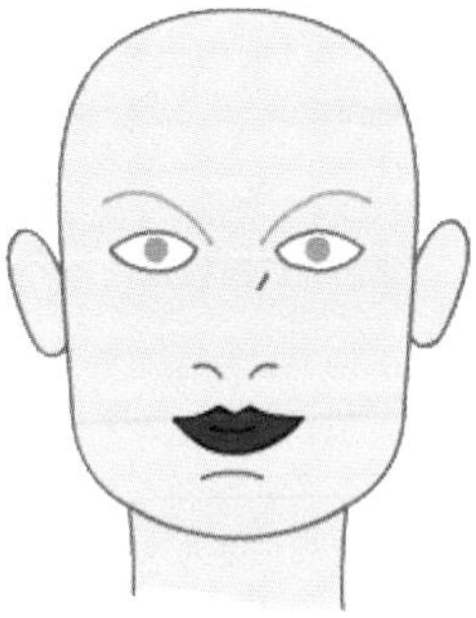

Figure 4.21 Short neck

A short stocky neck requires a softer hairstyle which is more flattering to the client.

Online activity 4.3 WWW

Five in a row

Tests – porosity test

The porosity test assesses the degree of damage to the cuticle. A damaged cuticle absorbs more moisture, which makes the hair feel rougher.

Hold a few strands of hair at the end and slide your fingers towards the root. If it feels rough the cuticles are raised and this indicates the condition of the hair is poor. If it feels smooth then the cuticles are flat and the condition of the hair is good.

Definition

Porosity: Ability to absorb moisture.

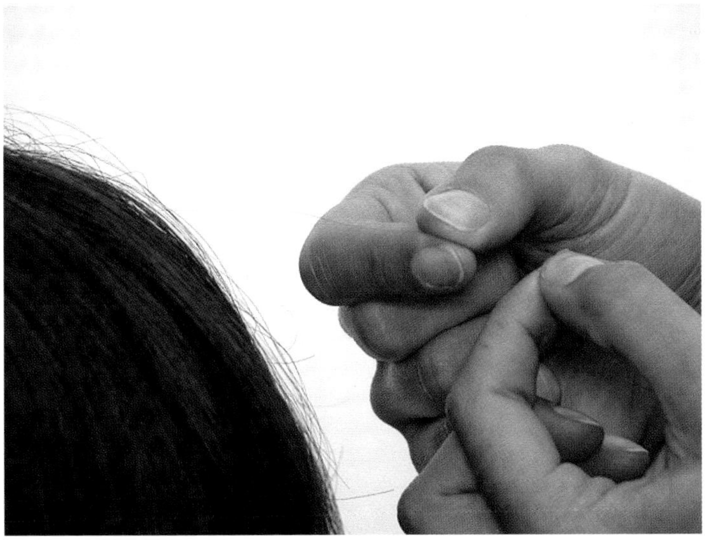

Figure 4.22 Carrying out the porosity test

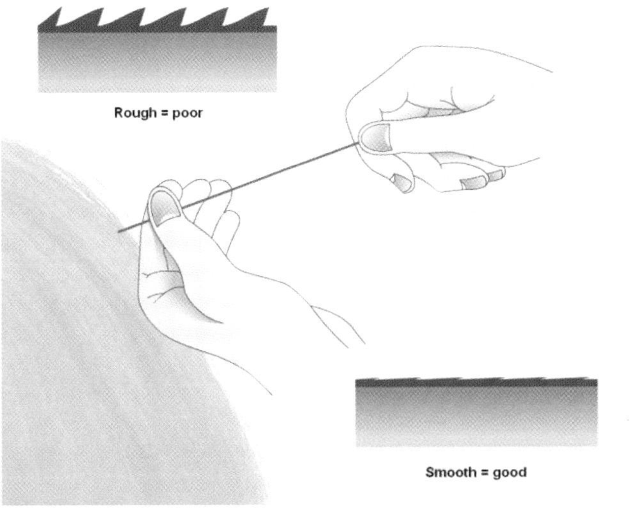

Figure 4.23 Raised and flat cuticles

Elasticity test

This test assesses the extent of damage to the cortex of the hair. It measures the ability of the hair to be stretched.

Hold a single strand of dry hair firmly at each end with finger and thumb. Pull back gently and see how much the hair stretches and springs back.

A hair in good condition can stretch up to a third of its length and return to its original length. If the hair snaps it indicates that the hair has a weak cortex.

Definition

Cortex: Middle layer of the hair shaft.

Figure 4.24 Conducting the elasticity test

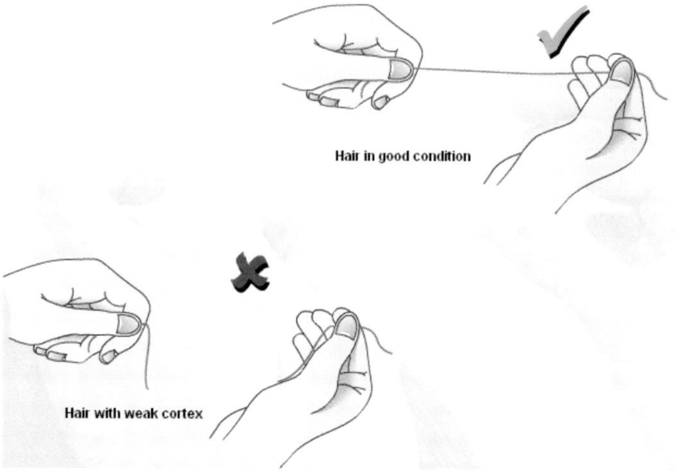

Figure 4.25 Elasticity test results

Safety first

The hairdresser should make sure that any products that have been used previously on the hair do not react unfavourably with products that the hairdresser intends to use.

Incompatibility test

The hairdresser should make sure that any products that have been used previously on the hair do not react unfavourably with products that the hairdresser intends to use. This incompatibility test detects metallic salts used in colour preparations, so-called 'hair colour restorers'.

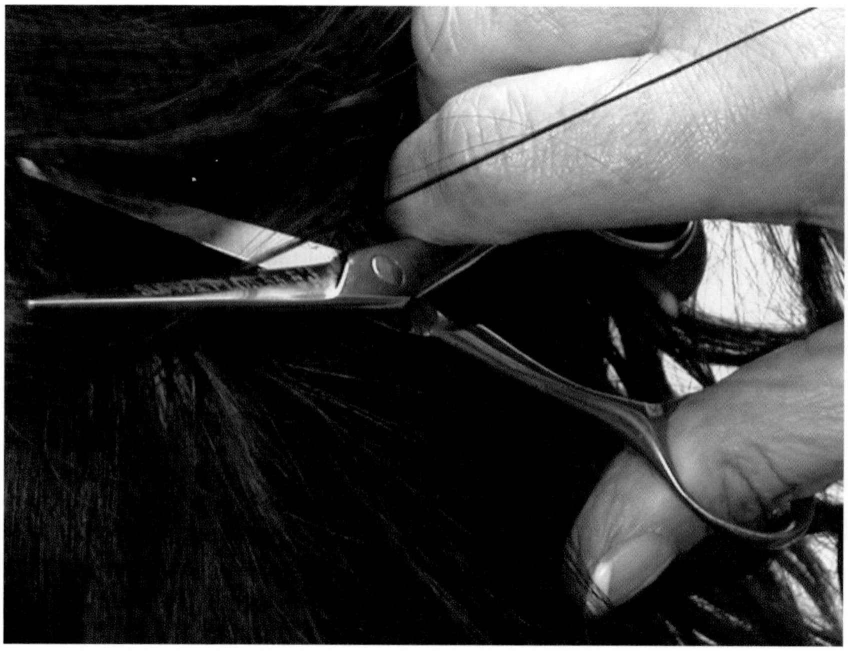

Figure 4.26 Cut a piece of hair from the root

Prepare a solution of twenty parts hydrogen peroxide and one part ammonia. Sellotape together a small group of hairs taken from the client's head, at the root end. Immerse the hairs in the solution for 30 minutes. A positive reaction will show the presence of bubbles, give off heat (the beaker gets warmer), or the hair will change colour.

Definitions

Hydrogen peroxide: An agent used for oxidising when colouring and perming.

Ammonia: Colourless fluid used as a solvent.

Figure 4.27 Incompatibility test in progress

Skin test

This is conducted to see if a client will develop an allergic reaction to the chemicals contained in colouring products. They are usually carried out before tinting and semi-permanent services. About one in twenty-five clients develops a positive reaction to the test; under no circumstance should the service be completed.

Gown the client, prepare a solution of the chemical to be used in the salon service. Cleanse behind the ear with cotton wool and alcohol. Place a penny sized smear of the chemical on the cleansed area. To protect the area from water it may be covered with collodion. Ask the client to return after 48 hours. Redness, swelling or irritation would indicate a positive reaction and the treatment should not be supplied. Colouring companies recommend this method to comply with legal requirements.

Safety first

About one in twenty-five clients develops a positive reaction to the test; under no circumstance should the service be completed.

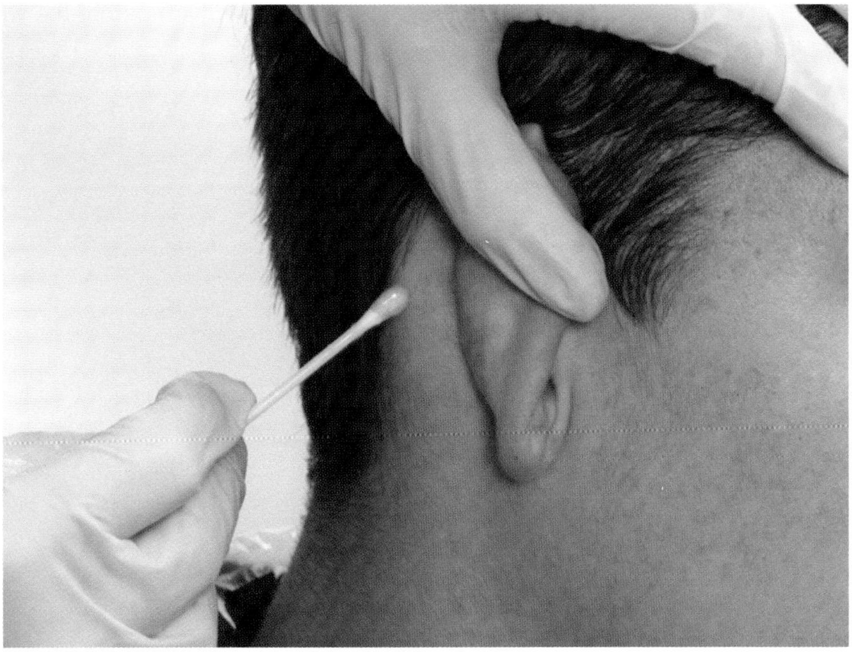

Figure 4.28 Carrying out a skin test

Definition

Collodion: A syrupy, clean solution of pyroxylin, alcohol and ether.

Pre-perm test curl

If the hair has been damaged through perming or colouring, a sample of hair should be tested to find out if the full head can be permed.

Take a cutting of the hair, apply perm lotion and wind around a perm rod. Leave the hair to develop and neutralise. Dry the hair and test the elasticity strength. If the results are satisfactory, the hairdresser can continue with the perm. If the result is unsatisfactory, do not perm.

Safety first

If the result of this test is unsatisfactory, do not perm.

Figure 4.29 Pre-perm test curl

Test cutting

This method can be used to assess the effects of an application before the whole head is treated.

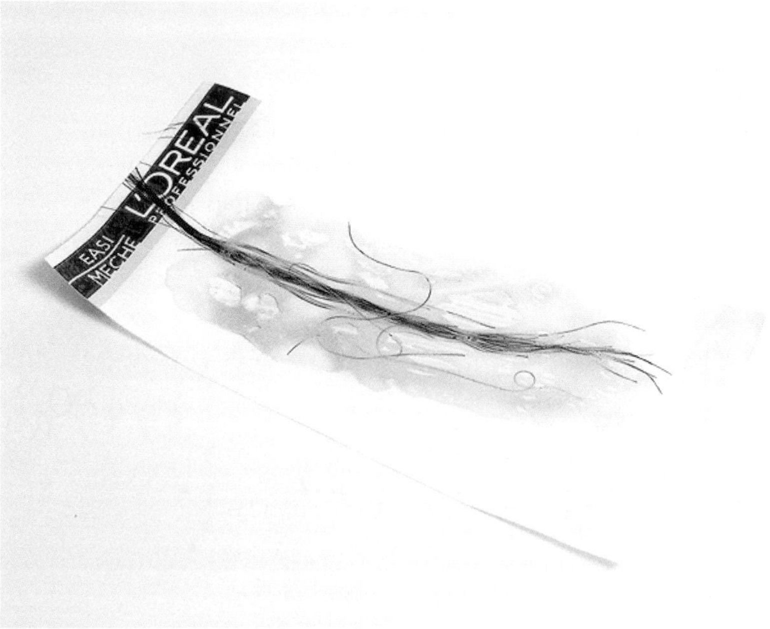

Figure 4.30 Test cutting

Key information

Uneven colouring will indicate damaged hair and whether it can take further chemical treatment.

Cut a few strands of hair and Sellotape them at the roots. Immerse the strands of hair in the intended products and process according to the manufacturer's instructions. Examine the results for colour effects. Uneven colouring will indicate damaged hair and whether it can take further chemical treatment.

Development test curl

After a perm lotion has been on the hair for a certain length of time, this test can be carried out to see if the hair has reached the correct development.

Unwind four rods in different sections to check development. The curl should show an 'S' shaped bend and separation of the strands, and the hair should look shiny. The curl should be checked after five minutes. Gloves must always be worn when you are carrying out this test.

Safety first

Gloves must always be worn when you are carrying out this test.

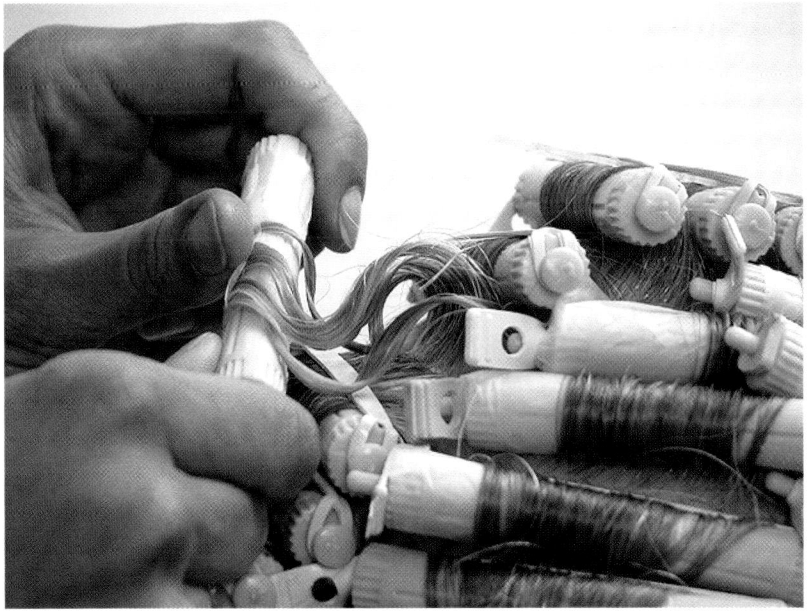

Figure 4.31 The 'S' shaped bend

Colour/strand test

This test monitors the colour development along a strand of hair during processing. This should be done before the colourant is rinsed from the hair.

Remove the colourant from a small mesh of hair. Check to see if the target shade has been reached. If not, leave the colour to develop further. If it has, then remove colour.

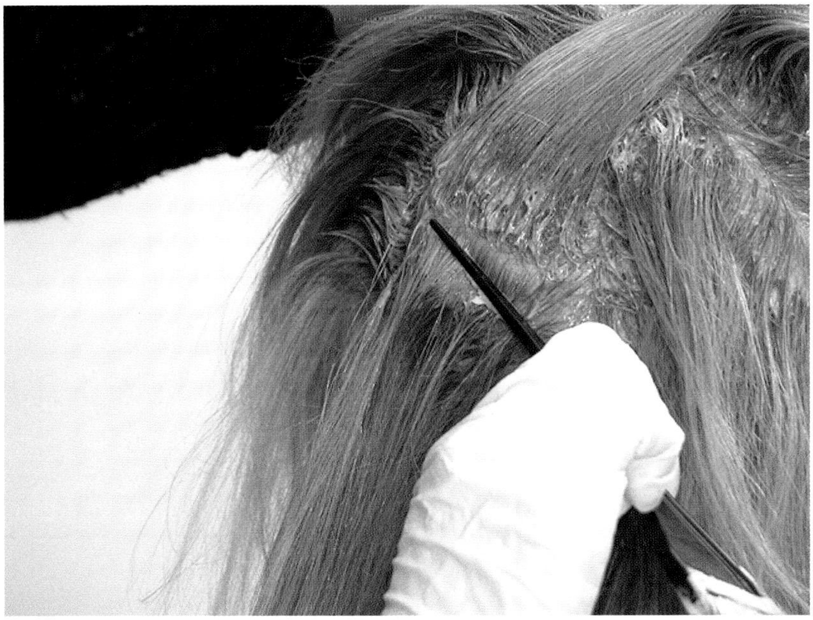

Figure 4.32 Carrying out a colour/strand test

Online activity 4.4

Shoot the target

Contraindications

Definition

Contraindications: A condition preventing a treatment.

There are many contraindications which may prevent the hairdresser performing a treatment. Problems that may stop the client receiving the service requested need to be identified and dealt with sympathetically. There will be times when the stylist needs to seek advice or report a situation that is proving difficult to handle. The stylist will seek advice promptly from the salon owner or manager/manageress.

Figure 4.33 Seek advice from the salon owner or manager if necessary

Infections

Micro-organisms cannot be seen but are found in the air, clothing, dirt, on the surface of the skin and under the nails. Some of them can cause disease and are said to be infectious.

They are divided into three groups:

- fungi e.g. ringworm
- bacteria e.g. boils, impetigo
- viruses e.g. cold sores, warts, influenza and the common cold.

They need warmth, moisture and food for multiplication, all of which are present in salons.

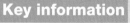

Key information

Micro-organisms cannot be seen but are found in the air, clothing, dirt, on the surface of the skin and under the nails.

Preventing infection

Major sources of infection are:

- unclean hands and nails
- unclean equipment

- open cuts
- pus
- mouth and nose discharge
- sharing crockery
- coughing and sneezing.

In carrying out the examination of the client's hair and scalp the hairdresser must follow good hygiene practice. The importance of hygiene in the salon is essential to not only prevent the spread of infectious diseases but also because clients prefer to patronise a salon which has high hygiene standards. Infectious diseases should always be treated by a doctor.

Safety first

Infectious diseases should always be treated by a doctor.

Online activity 4.5 www

Correct selection

Figure 4.34 Sweep up hair to keep floors clean

The salon

It is important to keep the salon clean and dry at all times; this includes clothing, work areas and all equipment. Floors should be kept clean, hair clippings should be swept up to prevent diseases and accidents. If floors are wet, notices should be left to warn clients and other staff. Surfaces should be washed down once a day. Mirrors should be cleaned before the clients arrive.

Safety first

If floors are wet, notices should be left to warn clients and other staff.

Equipment

Always use fresh, clean and sterile towels and gowns for each client. All towels should be washed after each client. Keep the used towels in a closed container to reduce the risk of the spread of infection. This prevents cross infection of fungal diseases such as ringworm of the head (tinea capitis) or infestations of lice (pediculosis capitis). Bacterial diseases are also spread from dirty towels, especially impetigo.

Key information

Always use fresh, clean and sterile towels and gowns for each client.

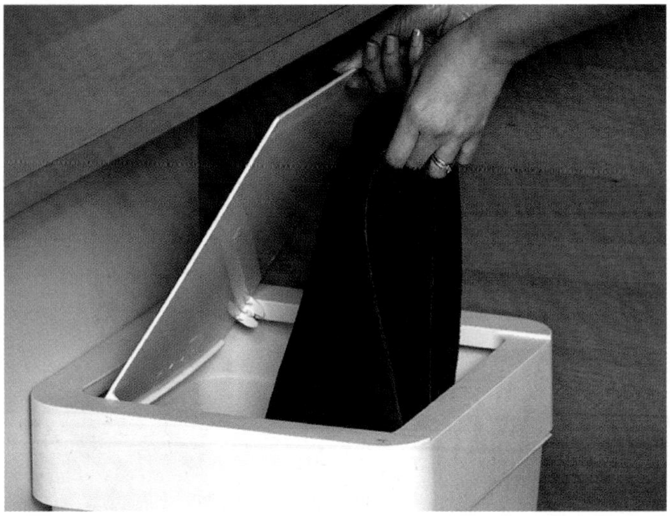

Figure 4.35 Place towels into a closed container

Figure 4.36 Wash brushes and combs

Hair and scalp conditions

A hairdresser should be able to recognise abnormal hair and scalp (skin) conditions. There are two categories of abnormal conditions:

- contagious (can be caught by contact)
- non-contagious (cannot be caught by contact).

Online activity 4.6

Round the board

Non-contagious – damaged cuticle

Definition

Cuticle: A series of overlapping scales that form the outer layer of the hair shaft.

The cuticles are a series of overlapping scales that form the outside layer of the hair shaft. When the cuticles are in a good condition they lie flat and feel smooth to the touch. When they are damaged they become raised and feel rough. In extreme conditions of neglect or severe chemical damage some of the cuticles break off. Physical and chemical abuse to the hair are often the causes. The application of a protein conditioner will smooth down the scales and make the hair more manageable.

Figure 4.37 Cuticle in good condition

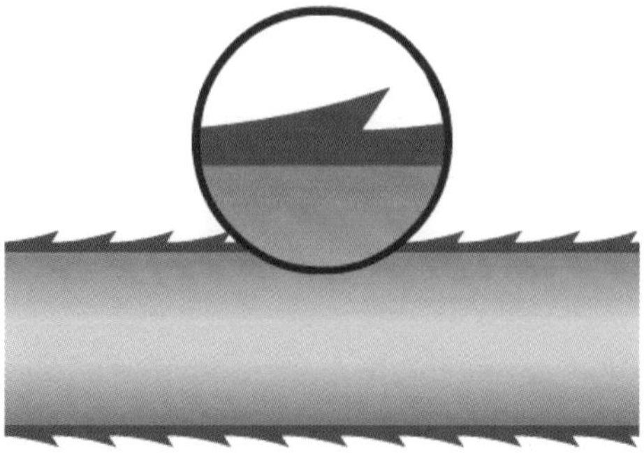

Figure 4.38 Cuticle in poor condition

Pityriasis capitis (dandruff)

Pityriasis capitis (dandruff) can be recognised by dry flaky scales that are shed from the scalp. Some irritation can be experienced by the client. The disorder is caused by the overproduction of skin cells. In severe cases white, grey or yellowish scales are continually falling from the scalp. This produces a breeding ground for bacteria or induces infections. Conditioners that contain antiseptic properties such as cetrimide or hexachlorophene are useful for this disorder.

Key information

Conditioners that contain antiseptic properties such as cetrimide or hexachlorophene are useful for treating dandruff.

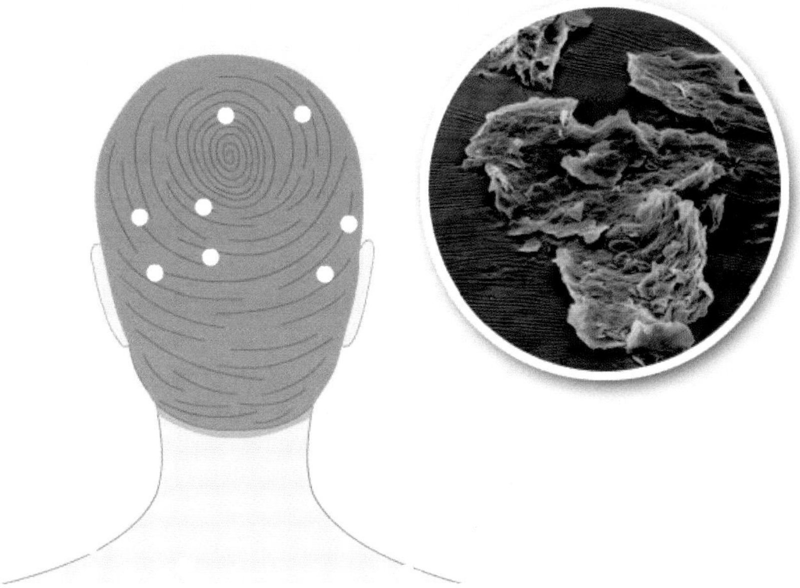

Figure 4.39 Dandruff is caused by the overproduction of skin cells

Safety first

If the condition is severe refer the client for medical treatment.

Seborrhoea

Seborrhoea is caused by the excess production of sebum from the sebaceous gland. The hair and scalp appear to be in a very oily state. Special conditioning treatments are available for this problem. Take care not to massage the scalp. If the condition is severe refer the client for medical treatment.

Definitions

Sebum: An oily discharge from the sebaceous gland.

Sebaceous gland: A small skin gland which secretes sebum into the hair follicle.

Fragilitas crinium (split ends)

Fragilitas crinium is a condition where the hair becomes very dry and brittle. Splits occur on the points of the hair shaft. It is caused by chemical and physical damage. Some conditioners enable the split ends to stick together but this is a temporary arrangement. The only real treatment is to have the hair cut.

Trichorrhexis nodosa

Trichorrhexis nodosa is a condition in which areas towards the point of the hair shaft swell. The hair fractures at this point and leaves a very broken and exposed cortex. Chemical and physical damage can cause this condition but in some cases it is due to genetic or metabolic disorders. Conditioners will improve the quality of the hair.

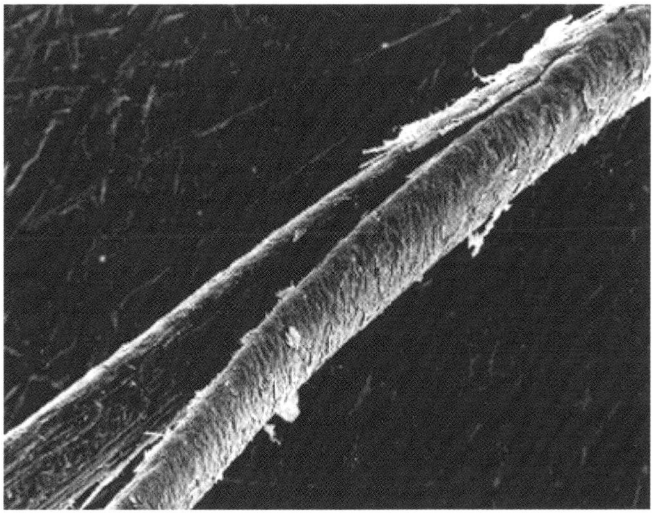

Figure 4.40 Split end

Key information

Chemical and physical damage can cause this condition but in some cases it is due to genetic or metabolic disorders.

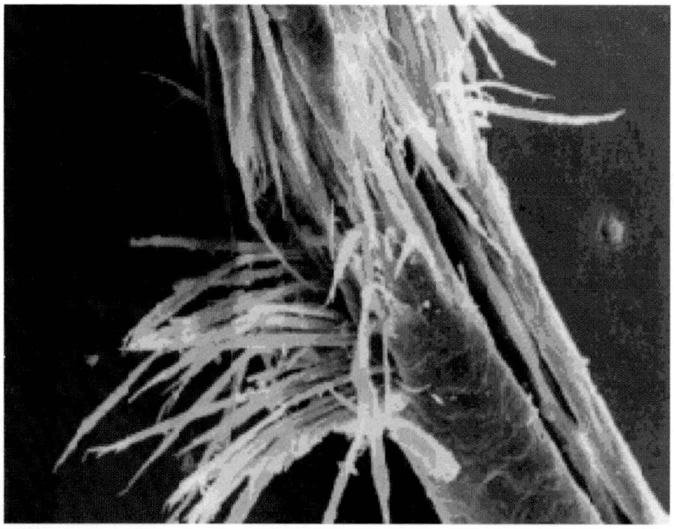

Figure 4.41 Trichorrhexis nodosa

Monilethrix

Definition

Hereditary: Passed on from parents (genetic).

This condition is caused by the uneven production of cells in the dermal papilla of the hair. The hair breaks easily, keeping the hair short or showing evidence of baldness. The cause is hereditary. No treatment is available.

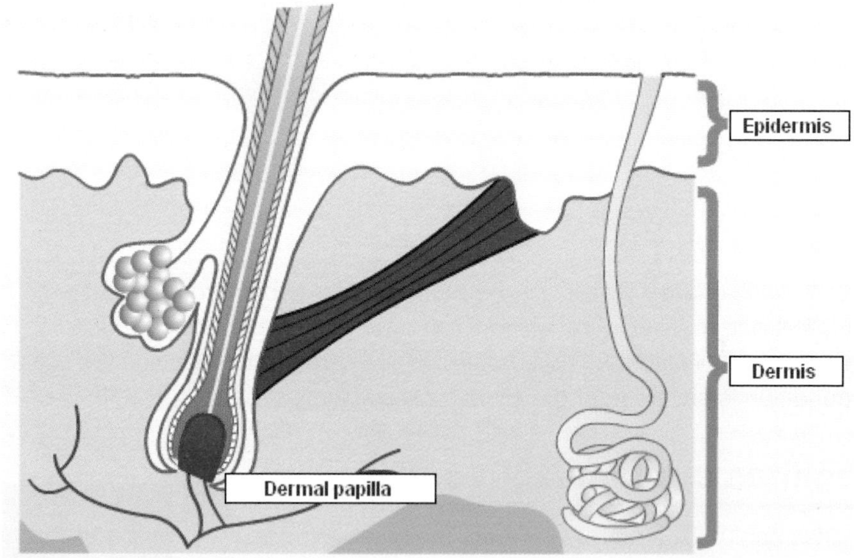

Figure 4.42 Monilethrix is caused by uneven production of cells in the dermal papilla

Psoriasis

This condition is caused by the overproduction of cells in the epidermis. On the scalp there are red patches which are covered by silvery-white scales. This condition is hereditary but can be brought on by emotional stress. Normal salon services can be given but extra care is needed. Special coal tar shampoos and ointments can be used for this condition.

Definition

Epidermis: Outer layer of the skin.

Online activity 4.7

Check it

Alopecia (baldness)

Symptoms include a receding hairline, balding on the top and the crown of a male head. There are several types of baldness.

Androgenic alopecia (male pattern baldness)

Androgenic alopecia starts with a receding hairline followed by thinning and may result in complete baldness. It is often hereditary. Normal salon services can be given.

Diffuse alopecia

Diffuse alopecia is a gradual thinning of the hair. Normal salon services can be given but medical advice should be sought.

Alopecia areata

Alopecia areata starts as small circular patches of baldness, irregularly spread over the head. Causes are hereditary but may be brought on by the client being stressed. This condition requires medical treatment.

Key information

Alopecia areata is hereditary but may be brought on by the client being stressed.

Cicatrical alopecia

Cicatrical alopecia is baldness caused by physical or chemical damage to the skin preventing hair from growing. Normal salon services can be given.

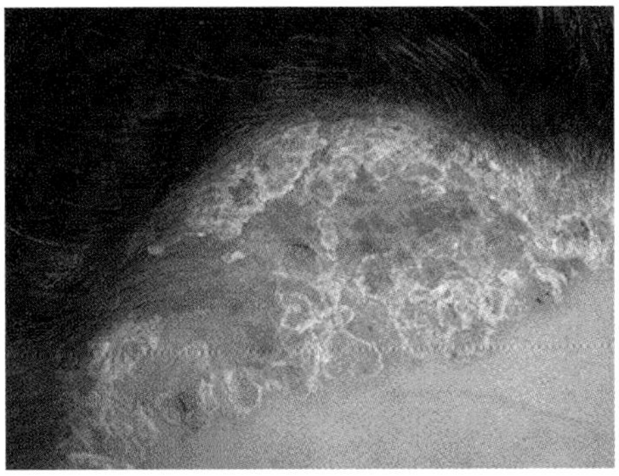

Figure 4.43 Psoriasis

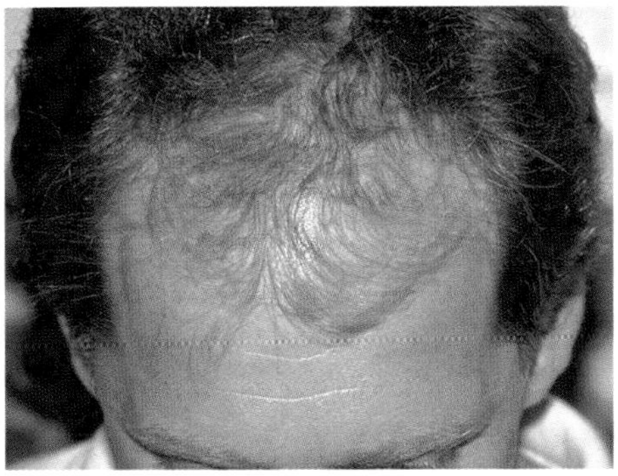

Figure 4.44 Receding hairline

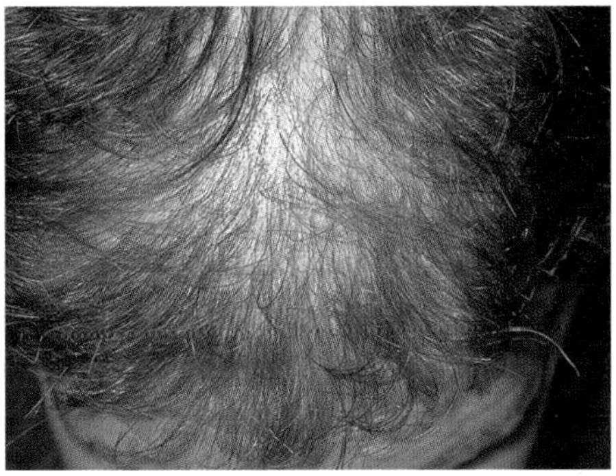

Figure 4.45 Thinning hair

Figure 4.46 Gradual thinning of the hair

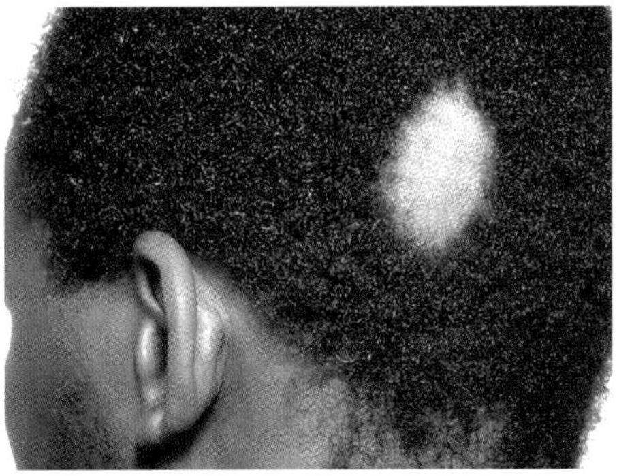

Figure 4.47 Circular patch of baldness

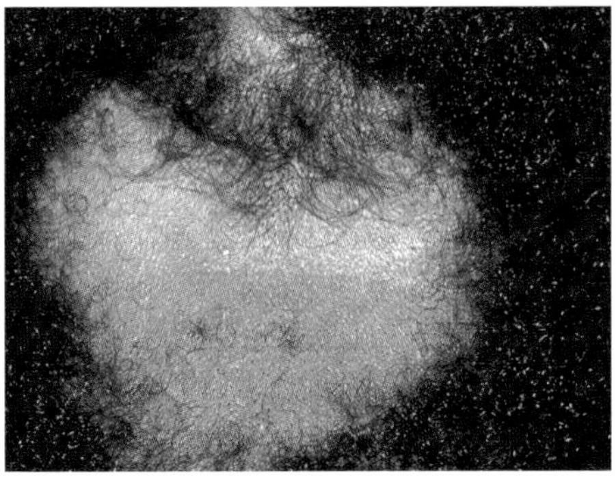

Figure 4.48 Cicatrical alopecia

Online activity 4.8

Check it

Sebaceous cyst

This is a small lump on the scalp or skin caused by a blockage of the sebaceous gland. Normal services can be given but this condition requires medical treatment.

Warts

These can be smooth or rough and are caused by a viral infection of the epidermis. The warts are non-contagious provided they are not damaged. Normal services can be given provided great care is taken.

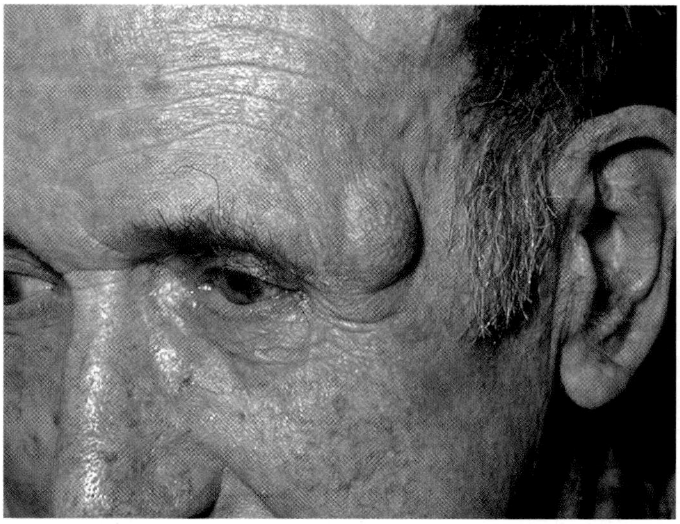

Figure 4.49 Sebaceous cyst on the face

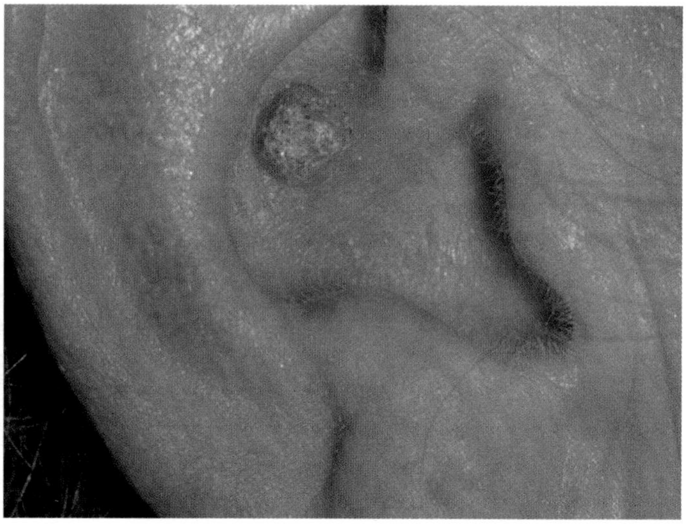

Figure 4.50 Wart in the ear

Key information

Hairs go white when the pigmentation cells (melanocytes) do not function properly.

Safety first

Folliculitis and tinea capitis will need medical treatment. No service should be given to the client.

Definition

Fungi: Parasitic organisms that do not contain chlorophyll. Includes mushrooms and yeast.

Canities (grey hair)

Hairs go white when the pigmentation cells (melanocytes) do not function properly. The greyness is a mixture of white and coloured hairs. Shock can cause coloured hairs to fall out. The hair of the client can be tinted.

Contagious – Folliculitis

With this disease the hair follicles become inflamed due to an infection. It may appear anywhere on the skin, not just on the scalp. The condition will need medical treatment. No service should be given to the client.

Tinea capitis (ringworm of the scalp)

Symptoms include a red ring which causes irritation to the client. It is a red circular rash with a white centre and brittle short hair in the patches. It is caused by a fungal infection and is contagious. This condition requires medical treatment. No service should be given.

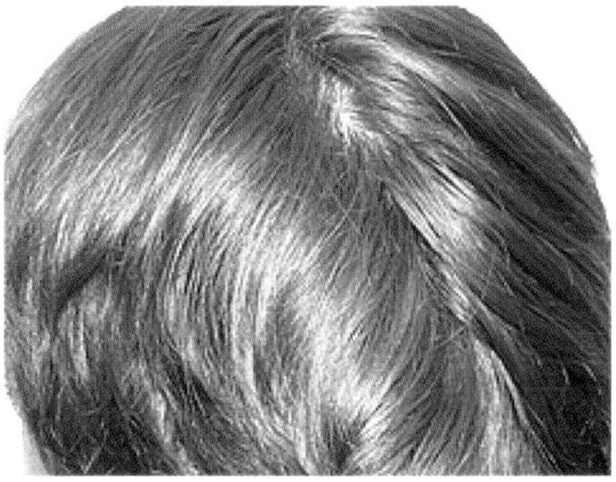

Figure 4.51 Grey hair

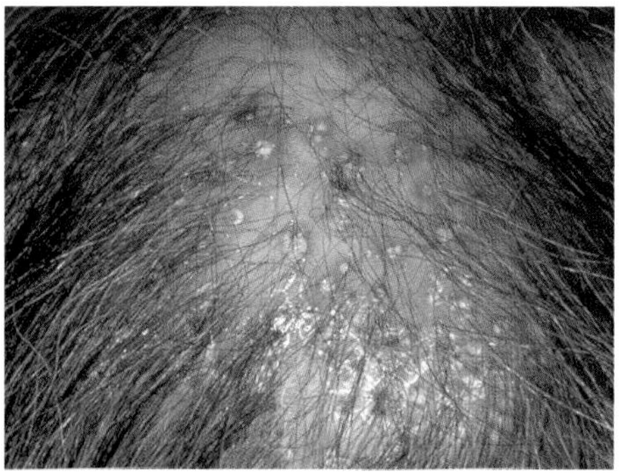

Figure 4.52 Folliculitis

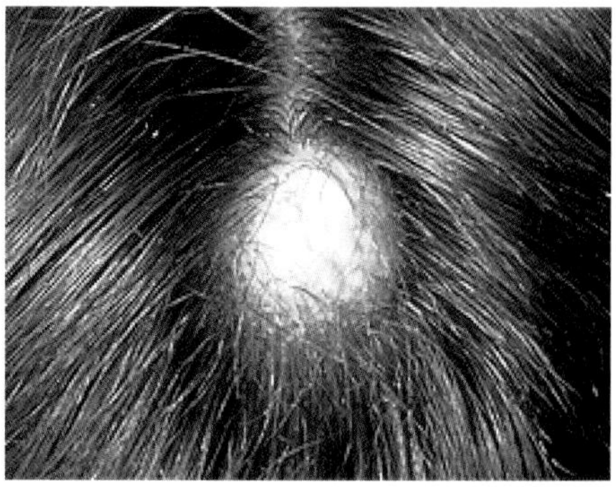

Figure 4.53 Ringworm of the scalp

Impetigo

This condition starts as a red sore and then forms a yellow crust. It is caused by a bacterial infection and can be transferred by using dirty towels. This condition is highly contagious. It requires medical treatment. No salon service should be given.

Safety first

Impetigo is caused by a bacterial infection and can be transferred by using dirty towels.

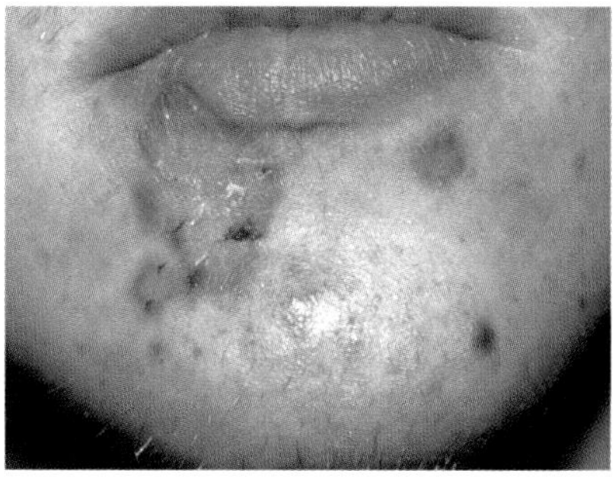

Figure 4.54 Impetigo around the mouth

Pediculosis capitis (head lice)

Infestations of head lice are fairly common. How does the stylist know the difference between dandruff and lice? The dandruff or skin flake will drop from the hair shaft but the head lice will slide up and down the hair shaft. Marks where the client has scratched may indicate the presence of head lice. Look for eggs attached to the hair shaft or insects that can be match-head size. The lice cling to a hair and feed on blood by biting into the scalp. Eggs are laid and cemented to the hair shaft. The condition is highly contagious by contact. Head lice are found in warm places on the head, at the nape and behind the ears. The condition requires medical treatment.

Key information

How does the stylist know the difference between dandruff and lice? Dandruff will drop from the hair shaft but the head lice will slide up and down the hair shaft.

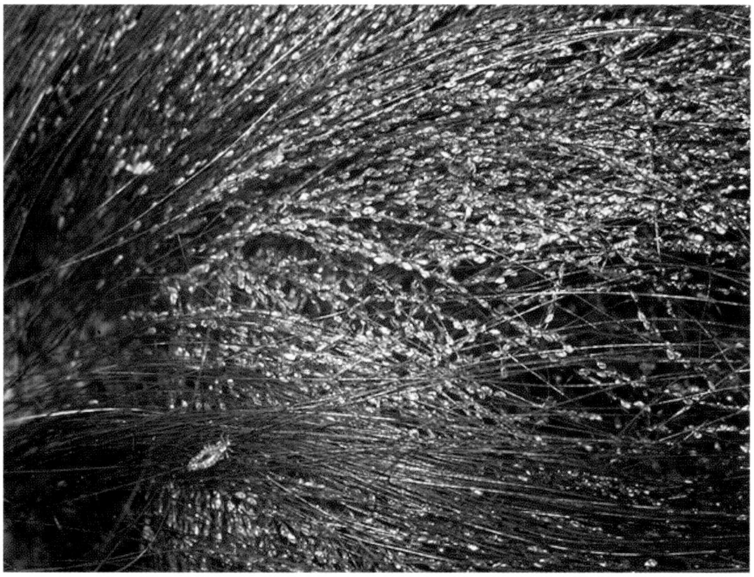

Figure 4.55 Head lice

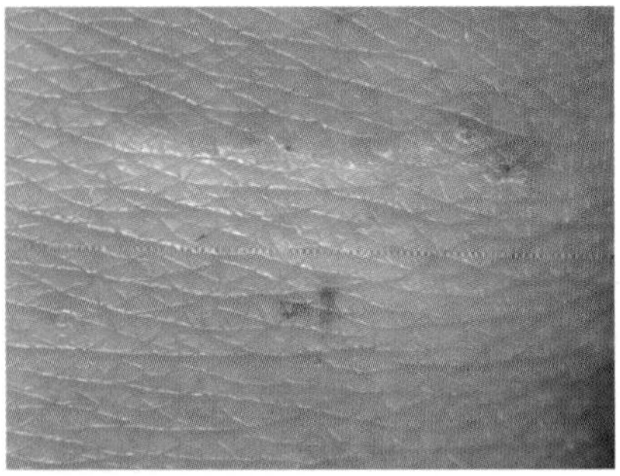
Figure 4.56 Scabies

Scabies

Scabies can be recognised as tiny raised and red lines on the skin. It is caused by an itch mite which burrows into the skin. It is highly infectious. No salon services should be given and the client should be referred for medical advice.

WWW Online activity 4.9

Drag into correct group

4.3 Advise clients

As a result of the consultation, observations and tests, a decision will finally need to be agreed about which treatment is required. At this point the hairdresser can confirm the arrangements by agreeing with the client the following details:

- when the treatment or service will take place
- how you or your salon will provide the treatment or service.

Figure 4.57 Decide how the treatment will be provided

Advise clients on aftercare procedures and future salon services

It is vital that all staff know the most suitable products for every hair and scalp condition. Product training is available to all salons but always read the manufacturer's instructions yourself. Aftercare procedures are varied. Product advice will include shampoos, conditioners, styling products and finishing products. Spend time advising and listening to clients' questions. Clients with families may be encouraged to buy other products to suit their husbands or children.

Key information

It is vital that all staff know the most suitable products for every hair and scalp condition.

Figure 4.58 Spend time advising clients on what products to use

The client will appreciate advice on how to use hairdressing equipment, for example how to use curling tongs or straightening irons. A little extra time communicating with the client on how they can style their hair at home, builds trust and ensures client loyalty resulting in the client returning to the salon.

Figure 4.59 Give advice on how to use electrical equipment

Key information

Remember to supply all clients with:

- the salon telephone number
- the salon contact name
- the salon opening and closing times
- the dates, times and duration of agreed repeat appointments
- prices of services and products.

Record keeping

Efficient record keeping cannot be over-emphasised during the consultation and throughout the hairdressing service as it serves to ensure the safety of your clients, yourself and your colleagues at all times. Information should be full, accurate and clear.

Figure 4.60 Use the client's records during the consultation

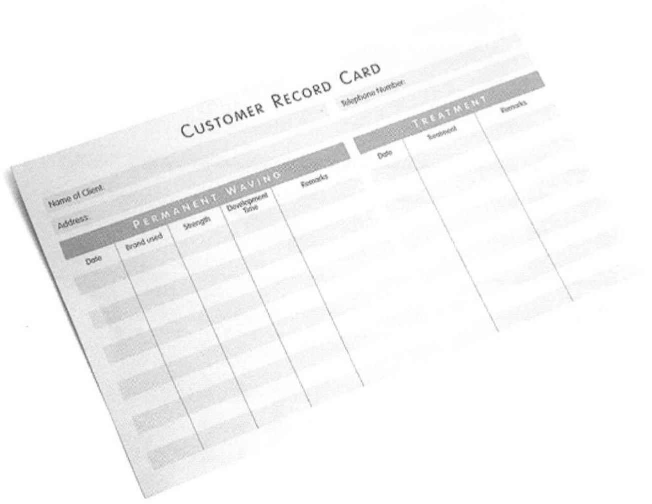

Figure 4.61 An example of a client record card

Key information

Remember your duties and responsibilities under the Data Protection Act to keep the information confidential.

The record card should contain the following information about the client:

- name, address, telephone number and occupation
- record number
- contraindications
- previous treatments
- previous products used
- length of treatment and cost
- who performed the treatment
- result of treatment
- any aftercare given
- any recommendations given
- products bought from salon.

Figure 4.62 Computerised record keeping

Online activity 4.10 www

Five in a row

WORKSHEETS

4.4 Worksheets

You can carry out the worksheets during your study of a chapter or unit, or at the end. An example is presented here and there are more online. If your college or company is registered with ATT Training, lots more are available. Write your answers directly in the book, but only if you own it of course – if it is a library or college book, use a separate piece of paper!

4.4.1 Identify what the client wants

1 Write down information about your salon's policy for consultations.
Does every client have one? If not, why not?

____

____

How long should a consultation last?

____

____

What is the purpose of a consultation?

____

____

2 Both open and closed questions are used during a consultation. Give (a) two examples of open questions and (b) two examples of closed questions that you have used in a consultation before. (If you haven't ever done a consultation before then note down questions that you think would be useful to ask.)

(a) ______________________________

____

(b) ______________________________

____

3 State what is good and bad in these two photos:

Figure 4.63 Consultation 1

Figure 4.64 Consultation 2

____

____

4.5 Assessment

Well done! If you have studied all the content of this unit you may be ready to test your knowledge.

Check out the 'Preparing for assessments' section in Chapter 1 if you have not already done so, and always remember:

- You can only do your best if you have. . .
  - studied hard
  - completed the activities
  - completed the worksheets
  - practised, practised, practised
  - and then revised!

Now carry out the online multiple-choice quiz

. . . and good luck in the final exam, which will be arranged by your tutor/assessor.

CHAPTER 5

Reception duties

This chapter covers the NVQ/SVQ unit G4, Fulfil salon reception duties and VRQ unit 216, Salon reception duties.

The salon reception is the first point of contact for a client. The duties of a receptionist are therefore very important and will ensure a good first impression.

In this chapter you will learn about:

- maintaining the reception area
- attending to clients and enquiries
- scheduling appointments for salon services
- handling payments from clients for the purchase of services and retail products.

Website WWW
www.atthairdressing.com

CHAPTER 5 RECEPTION DUTIES: CONTENTS, SCREENS AND ACTIVITIES

Key:
Sections from the book are set in this colour
Screens available online are set in this colour
Online activity screens are set in this colour

Reception area

Introduction
Receptionist's tasks
Correct selection
Sale of Goods Act
Trades Description Act
Product checks

Attending to clients

Client and visitor enquiries
Checklist
Stationery items
Select correct boxes
Receiving clients and visitors
Enquiries
Dealing with enquiries
Round the board
Taking telephone messages
Dealing with telephone calls
Making calls
Incoming calls
Complaints
Complete the sentences
Busy reception area
Correct selection

Making appointments

Appointment system
Service times and cost
Scrambled words
Records
Next appointment

Handling payments

Till payments
Round the board
Calculating and settling the bill
Method of payment
Payment by cash
Bank notes and coins 1
Bank notes and coins 2
Correct selection
Receipt
Cheques 1
Cheques 2
Cheques 3
Cheques 4
Credit or debit card 1
Wordsearch
Credit or debit card 2
Credit or debit card 3
Credit or debit card 4
Credit or debit card 5
Payment disputes
Reception security
Five in a row
Worksheet – records and next appointments
Worksheet – complaints
Worksheet – attend to visitors and enquiries
Online multiple choice quiz

5.1 Reception area

There are a number of tasks in the reception area that the receptionist may be required to carry out:

- cleaning, dusting, polishing and vacuuming the reception area to keep it clean
- keeping magazines up to date and tidy
- re-stocking retail displays.

Figure 5.1 Cleaning the reception desk

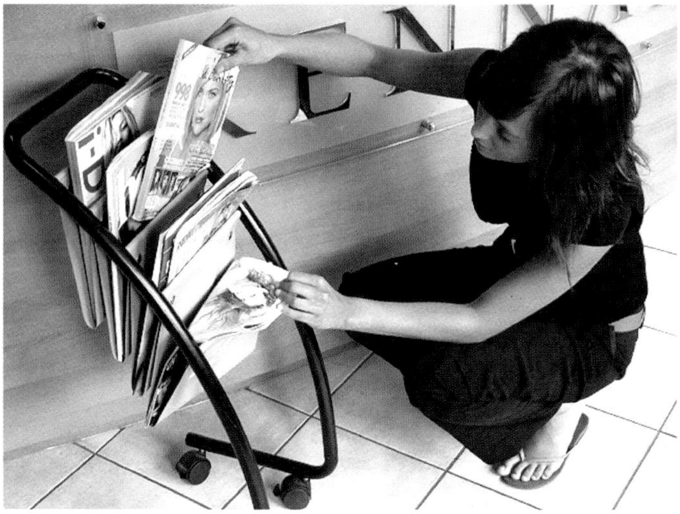

Figure 5.2 Keeping magazines up to date

Figure 5.3 Re-stocking retail displays

Online activity 5.1 WWW

Correct selection

Sale of Goods Act

This states:

- products sold must be fit for the purpose you have stated and are able to do what you claim
- products sold must be of good quality.

Consumers can reject the products if they do not meet these requirements and have a refund as long as it's done within a set time.

Key information

Consumers can reject the products if they do not meet these requirements and have a refund as long as it's done within a set time.

Trades Description Act

This states products must:

- be labelled correctly
- be labelled so as not to mislead the buyer
- state what the product is used for
- show the ingredients
- state where they were made
- be clearly priced.

All product information in writing and verbal recommendations must be accurate.

When checking the retail merchandise, look for product damage. It may be the product is leaking, or the package may be damaged. Always check the sell-by date. Checking the price of the sale goods is essential. The till must balance at the end of the day. If the clients are undercharged there will be a loss of profit and it is embarrassing to ask to pay more after the transaction.

Definitions

Merchandise: Goods that are to be sold.

Transaction: The agreement between a seller and buyer for a good or service.

Figure 5.4 Product information must be correct

Figure 5.5 Check product for signs of damage

Figure 5.6 Ensure you know the correct price of products

5.2 Attending to clients

Creating a good first impression with the client and visitors is essential. The receptionist is the first and last contact clients and visitors have in the salon. The receptionist is the focal point of the salon. The smooth running of the salon depends on the efficiency of the receptionist.

Key information

Creating a good first impression with the client and visitors is essential.

Figure 5.7 The receptionist can ensure a smooth-running salon

Checklist

Here is a checklist for the receptionist to follow:

- Be friendly, have a pleasing smile.
- Be cheerful and enthusiastic, show interest and be alert.
- Be courteous when dealing with clients, using 'please' and 'thank you' as much as possible.

- Be efficient and well organised.
- Be quick, do not keep clients waiting.
- Be accurate, speak clearly, listen and try not to make mistakes.
- Develop different questioning skills using both open and closed questions. Asking questions that require a yes or no reply are known as closed questions. Using words such as when, who, what, if, etc., will enable the client to discuss their needs. This method is known as open questioning and is used to expand on what the client's wishes are and help you to ensure a good service is provided.
- Be well groomed, wear clean and well-presented clothes, neatly styled hair and have a fresh look made-up face.

Definitions

Enthusiastic: Showing interest and being eager.

Accurate: Correct in all details.

Stationery items

Stationery items to keep at the reception are:

- service price lists
- product information leaflets
- appointment cards
- message pad
- appointment book
- promotional information or vouchers.

Online activity 5.2

Select correct boxes

Receiving clients and visitors

Welcome the client on arrival, take their coat and confirm their appointment. Seat the client and offer magazines and a cup of tea or coffee. Next, make sure the client is gowned appropriately, depending on the treatment, to protect his or her clothes. Visitors should be asked to state their names, whether they have an appointment, who they represent and the nature of their business. The appropriate member of staff should then be contacted.

Figure 5.8 Take your client's coat

Figure 5.9 And seat them with a magazine

Figure 5.10 Ask visitors their name and purpose of their business

Enquiries

Enquiries may be made by a variety of visitors, regular clients, new clients and casual clients. Some may have been recommended by other people and have knowledge about the salon, others may not. Enquiries may be internal from within the salon or external. They may be made directly, face to face, in person or indirectly, by telephone, letter, another person or existing client.

Key information

Enquiries may be made by a variety of visitors, regular clients, new clients and casual clients.

Figure 5.11 A telephone enquiry

Dealing with enquiries

When dealing with an enquiry it is essential to establish the purpose of the enquiry and the information required. All messages should be recorded accurately and completely. They should then be passed on promptly to the correct person. The receptionist must have knowledge of the product and services sold in the salon, e.g. cost of products and treatments as well as the time required.

Figure 5.12 Pass messages on promptly

Online activity 5.3

Round the board

Taking telephone messages

The receptionist will be required to take messages. The details should be recorded clearly and the following points should be observed when taking a message:

- identify the name of the salon to the caller
- state your own name
- enquire who is calling
- write down the telephone number of the caller
- note the company that the caller represents
- note the date and time of the call
- check whether or not the message is urgent
- note the name of the person to whom the message should be given
- note who recorded the message.

Definitions

Observe: To look at and be aware of.

Identify: To recognise and establish the identity of something.

Dealing with telephone calls

To deal with telephone calls efficiently, find out:

1. the telephone number of the salon (and remember it!)
2. the telephone engineer's number in case a fault or problem needs reporting
3. the operator's number
4. the business services available
5. how to use a telephone directory
6. the international operator's number
7. the number of the emergency services
8. the type of emergency services available
9. the number for directory enquiries
10. if there is an extension to the salon phone, e.g. the staff room
11. how to transfer calls to extension numbers.

Website

www.atthairdressing.com

Making calls

The receptionist often makes calls from the salon, for instance in the case of:

- telephoning for a taxi for a client
- obtaining credit card authorisation
- contacting clients
- contacting suppliers.

Incoming calls

The receptionist receives incoming calls for:

- clients booking, cancelling, altering or checking appointments
- clients speaking to members of staff
- clients enquiring about salon prices
- clients asking for directions
- dealing with client complaints.

Figure 5.13 A receptionist may need to obtain credit card authorisation on the phone

Figure 5.14 Clients may wish to speak with other members of staff

Complaints

If a client has a complaint, always be polite, stay calm and remain courteous at all times. Never be argumentative, rude or contradictory. Remember, the client is the most important person in the salon. Inform the supervisor, i.e. stylist or manageress. They have sufficient experience and authority to decide on an appropriate course of action.

Definitions

Argumentative: To argue.

Contradictory: To give conflicting information.

Busy reception area

If the reception area is crowded you will need to:

- ask for assistance if possible
- offer clients a seat and refreshments
- apologise for keeping them waiting
- tell the clients you will deal with them as soon as possible
- keep calm and smile.

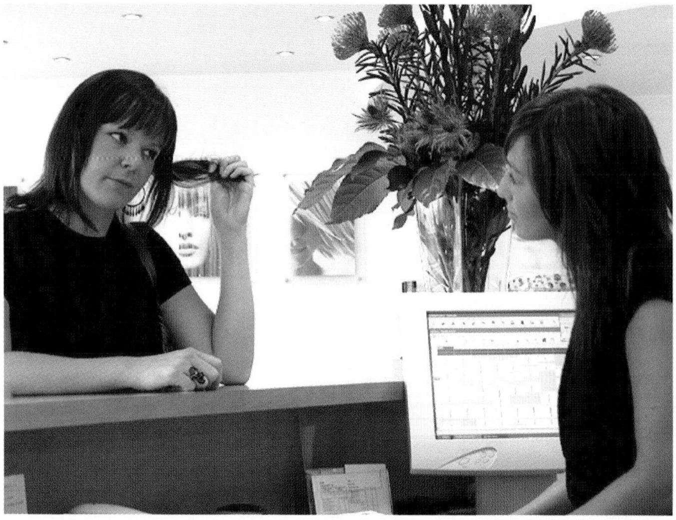

Figure 5.15 If a client complains, stay calm and remain courteous

Figure 5.16 Keep calm and smile!

WWW Online activity 5.4

Correct selection

5.3 Making appointments

Figure 5.17 Computerised appointment system

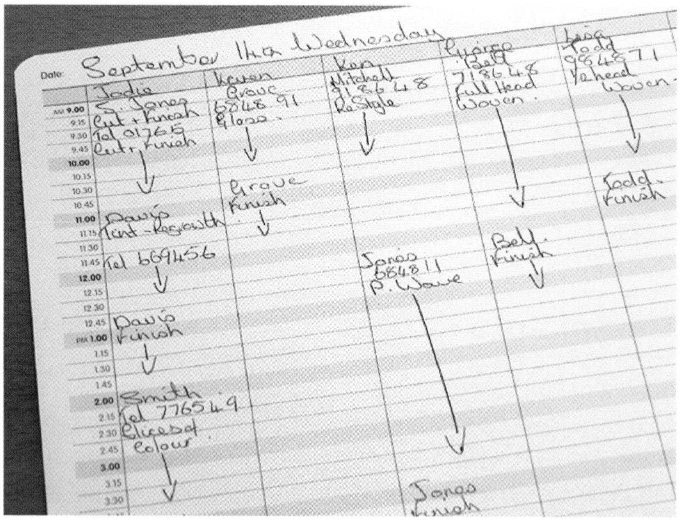

Figure 5.18 An appointment book

Appointment system

To ensure the efficient running of the salon the appointment system must be well organised. Each salon will have its own system for making appointments, with many using a computerised system. Some salons use an appointment book and divide it into columns with the stylists' names at the top and the times down the side.

Whichever system is used, it is recommended that the following points be recorded: date, client's name, telephone number, service required and the member of staff responsible for the scheduled service. The details entered should be pencilled in so that any alterations are easily made. The receptionist needs to know the time of the last appointment to ensure that there will be no overlap or double booking.

Key information

The following points should be recorded:

- date
- client's name
- telephone number
- service required
- member of staff responsible for the scheduled service.

Service times and costs

The receptionist needs to be able to explain the length of time of the services and the cost. This is essential so as not to disappoint clients or lose appointments by over- or under-booking. Some typical timings are shown in Table 5.1, although they will vary from salon to salon.

Table 5.1 Service times

Cutting	30-45 minutes
Shampoo & set	1–1½ hour
Blow-dry	30-45 minutes
Permanent waving	2½ hours
Semi-permanent colour	1 hour
Tinting	2 hours
Bleaching	2½ hours
Highlighting	2½ hours
Lowlighting	2½ hours
Conditioning treatments	1½ hours
Hair extensions from	1 hour

Online activity 5.5 WWW

Scrambled words

Figure 5.19 Look up the client's records before they arrive

Key information

Remember to observe the rule of confidentiality because records contain personal details. Observe the Data Protection Act – all clients' personal details are confidential.

Records

Before the client arrives, look up the client's records. If using a manual system have the client's record card ready for the stylist who will return it after the treatment. Take care to file it back correctly. Remember to observe the rule of confidentiality because records contain personal details. Observe the Data Protection Act – all clients' personal details are confidential.

Next appointment

When the client has made his or her next appointment, the details (time, service, date and stylist) should be entered onto an appointment card. This should then be handed to the client. The receptionist should thank the client for their custom and verbally confirm the next appointment. If appointments are made over the phone repeat the details back to the client so that these can be confirmed.

Figure 5.20 Note the details onto an appointment card

Figure 5.21 And hand it to the client

Figure 5.22 Open the till with a float

5.4 Handling payments

Till payments

An important task for the receptionist is to be able to handle payments from clients for the purchase of services and retail products. It is customary to open the till each day with a float. The float consists of small change and is usually £20.00/ £30.00. It is removed each night ready for the next day; this is not part of the daily takings.

Online activity 5.6

Round the board

Calculating and settling the bill

The bill must include the cost of the service and value added tax (VAT). The bill can be written on a bill pad or receipt slip which can usually be torn off, given to the client for checking before payment is made or electronically produced from the cash register.

Definition

VAT: Value Added Tax is a tax that is charged on most goods and services in the UK.

Method of payment

This can be carried out by:

- cash
- cheque
- credit or debit card.

Figure 5.23 Cash

Payment by cash

When handling a cash transaction you should:

- carefully ring the amount of each product or service into the till
- inform the client of how much has to be paid.

Adding up payments can be done using a calculator, pen and paper, pricing scanner or electronic point-of-sale.

Bank notes and coins

Check that the bank notes have a watermark. This is apparent when the note is held up to the light or it can be checked electronically. The metallic strip which is woven into the paper should also be checked. Check for correct colour and paper type. The banknote number should also be checked against a list of known forgeries if appropriate. Coins should be checked for accepted currency, i.e. the correct currency for that country. Place the money on or beside the till, NOT in the till, so you can see what the client gave you.

Definitions

Currency: A unit of exchange used as a form of money.

Forgery: A copy that is illegal.

Watermark: A design that is visible when held up to the light.

Figure 5.24 Check the bank note to see if there is a watermark

Figure 5.25 Ensure the metallic strip is visible

Figure 5.26 Place money beside the till

Change

Count out the change into the client's hand. NEVER place all the change at once into a client's hand. Counting the change out serves as a double check that the client has not been under- or over-charged. Ensure that the client agrees that the change given is correct. If there is doubt, count the change out again. If incorrect change has been given, this error will show up at the end of the day's trading and the till will not balance when it is being cashed up. Next, place the money in the till and close the drawer.

Figure 5.27 Count change into client's hand

Figure 5.28 Place money in the till once the transaction is complete

Online activity 5.7

Correct selection

Receipt

Finally, give the client a receipt, smile and say 'thank you'. If insufficient cash is available to enable change to be given, report to the manager or designated person who will act as necessary to rectify the problem.

Figure 5.29 Smile and say thank you

Clients paying by cheque

In some salons it may be necessary to have the manager authorise payment by cheque. The receptionist should ensure that cheques are completed correctly. The details on the cheque must include:

- the correct date
- the salon name (or business name) and correct spelling
- the amount written (in figures and words)
- changes made to the cheque in the form of alterations must be initialled by the client
- signature of the client which must match the one on the cheque guarantee card.

Figure 5.30 This cheque has been written correctly

Cheque cards

Cheques must be backed by a cheque guarantee card. Check that:

- the cheque and guarantee card have the same bank name and bank account number
- the sort code matches on the cheque and the card
- the amount to be paid does not exceed the card limit
- the cheque guarantee card is in date.

Figure 5.31 A cheque guarantee card

Figure 5.32 Write the relevant details on the back of the cheque

The receptionist must write the cheque card number on the back of the cheque, check the expiry date and initial it. If any corrections to the cheque have been made they should be initialled by the client. The cheque can then be passed (if necessary) to the supervisor for authorisation.

The amount of the cheque should be keyed into the till, the cheque placed into the till and the receipt and cheque guarantee card returned to the customer.

Figure 5.33 Place the cheque into the till

Payment by credit or debit card

Some of the most commonly used cards are:

- Visa
- MasterCard
- American Express
- Switch
- Delta
- Connect.

Figure 5.34 The most commonly used cards

Online activity 5.8 WWW

Wordsearch

Figure 5.35 Check card details

Checks to make on credit or debit cards

Check that:

- it is a card that the salon accepts
- the card date is valid
- hologram is clear and sharp
- Mr, Mrs, Miss or Ms match the sex of the client
- the signature strip is sound
- the cardholder's signature matches the name on the front of the card
- card account number is not on the warning list.

Electronic method – EFTPOS

This method reduces the paperwork and risk of transposing (copying) errors. In order to use this method the salon will need a special payment terminal through which the card is 'swiped'. The amount is keyed into the terminal and the details of the client's card are relayed quickly and automatically via a central computer.

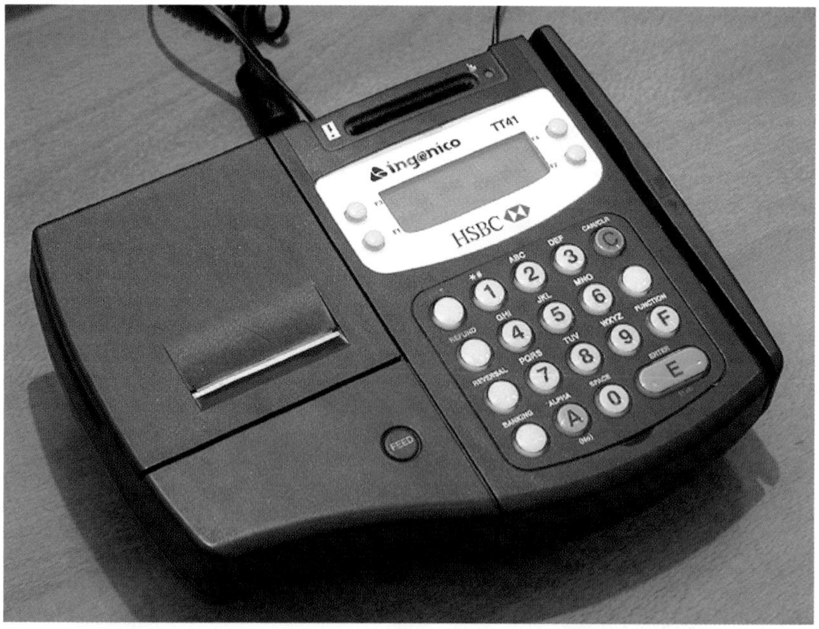

Figure 5.36 EFTPOS terminal

The receptionist should key the correct amount into the computer and wait for the credit card slip to appear. Next, ask the client to check that all the information is correct and then sign it. Check that the signature matches the signature on the card and double check the expiry date on the card. Also, if the amount exceeds the 'floor limit' (this is the limit set by the credit company) special authorisation will be necessary to accept the card. The client should be provided with a copy of this with a receipt and thanked for his or her custom.

Definition

Authorisation: To officially permit something.

Figure 5.37 The client should check the details and sign

Figure 5.38 Check that the signature matches

Chip and PIN

Most salons have switched over to the Chip and PIN system, which helps safeguard cards against fraud. The receptionist must ask the client to enter a 4-digit PIN code instead of signing a receipt.

Figure 5.39 Place the card in the machine

Figure 5.40 Ask the client to enter their PIN code

Payment disputes

If any problems arise, for example, complaints about the bill, make sure you use excellent interpersonal skills by staying calm, polite and courteous. Never be argumentative, rude or contradictory. In most cases refer to the manager or supervisor. These employees have sufficient experience and authority to decide on an appropriate course of action.

Key information

If any problems arise, for example, complaints about the bill, make sure you use excellent interpersonal skills by staying calm, polite and courteous.

Figure 5.41 Keep calm when dealing with complaints

Reception security

- Always keep the till closed.
- Only authorised staff to handle the money and access the stock.
- Never leave the reception desk unattended.
- Keep display areas locked and always in full view of the staff.
- Stock open displays with 'dummy' products.
- Lock draws and remove the key.
- Maintain confidentiality of credit and payment card slips.
- File away client record cards.
- Remind clients to keep their belongings with them at all times.
- Stock checks done randomly will help track any loss of products.

Figure 5.42 Always keep the till closed

Figure 5.43 Stock open displays with 'dummy' products

WWW Online activity 5.9

Five in a row

5.5 Worksheets

WORKSHEETS

You can carry out the worksheets during your study of a chapter or unit, or at the end. An example is presented here and there are more online. If your college or company is registered with ATT Training, lots more are available. Write your answers directly in the book, but only if you own it of course – if it is a library or college book, use a separate piece of paper!

5.5.1 Records

Before the client arrives, look up the client's records. If using a manual system, have the client's record card ready for the stylist who will return it after the treatment. Take care to file it back correctly. Remember to observe the rule of confidentiality because records contain personal details. Observe the Data Protection Act – all clients' personal details are confidential.

Answer these questions:

1 Why is it important to keep client records?

2 Why should you check client records before a treatment?

3 Why is it important to file records correctly?

4 What does confidentiality mean?

5.6 Assessment

Well done! If you have studied all the content of this unit you may be ready to test your knowledge.

Check out the 'Preparing for assessments' section in Chapter 1 if you have not already done so, and always remember:

- You can only do your best if you have. . .
  - studied hard
  - completed the activities
  - completed the worksheets
  - practised, practised, practised
  - and then revised!

? Now carry out the online multiple-choice quiz

. . . and good luck in the final exam, which will be arranged by your tutor/assessor.

CHAPTER 6

Promote additional services or products

This chapter covers the NVQ/SVQ unit G18, Promote additional services or products to clients and VRQ unit 205, Promote products and services to clients in the salon.

Sales of additional products and services make up a significant part of the income to the salon, and that of course is what pays our wages! Working with clients so that they are willing to commit to using additional services and products is therefore a key task and will also ensure that the client's hair is kept in best possible condition after services have been carried out.

In this chapter you will learn about:

- identifying additional products or services that are available
- informing clients about additional products or services
- gaining client commitment to using additional products or services.

Website www

www.atthairdressing.com

CHAPTER 6 PROMOTE ADDITIONAL SERVICES OR PRODUCTS: CONTENTS, SCREENS AND ACTIVITIES

Key:

Sections from the book are set in this colour

Screens available online are set in this colour

Online activity screens are set in this colour

Promoting products or services

Introduction
Identify additional products or services
Listening to clients
Round the board
Opportunities to identify needs
Knowledge of products and services
Complaints
Five in a row
Legislation
The Consumer Protection Act
Sale of Goods Act
Supply of Goods and Services Act
Correct selection
Trades Description Act

Inform clients about products and services

Introduction
Times to inform clients
Opportunities to inform clients of products and services
Other methods of promoting products and services
Check it
Giving information to clients 1
Giving information to clients 2

Gain client commitment

Introduction
Buying signs
Client showing no interest
Correct selection
Delivery of products
Booking additional services and record keeping
Worksheet – opportunity to identify needs
Worksheet – booking additional services and record keeping
Online multiple choice quiz

6.1 Identify products or services

Promoting products and services not only makes for a greater revenue for your salon but it also helps to keep the client's hair in the best possible condition after services have been carried out, for example colouring. Before recommending a product or service to a client, make sure that it is suitable. If you give an incorrect recommendation, and the client has a reaction or feels it is unsuitable, it can have a very negative effect on your reputation or that of your salon. Therefore be quick to pick up on each individual client's needs and be aware of the legislation regarding products and services that your salon offers.

Key information

If you give an incorrect recommendation, and the client has a reaction or feels it is unsuitable, it can have a very negative effect on your reputation or that of your salon.

Figure 6.1 Use your communication skills to find out what the client needs or wants

Listening to clients

This is the perfect way of establishing your client's needs in order to identify whether they may need additional products or services. During the consultation, use your communication skills to find out from your client how they currently style their hair and whether they use certain products.

Online activity 6.1 WWW

Round the board

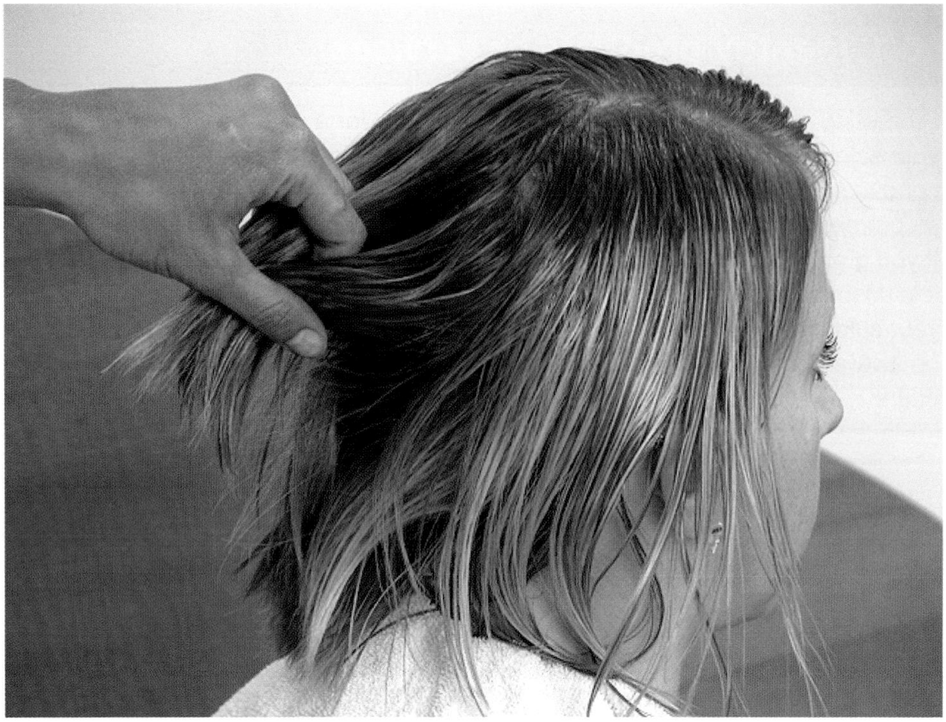

Figure 6.2 Oily hair calls for a suitable shampoo which you can recommend

There are many more opportunities other than during the consultation where you can identify a client's needs regarding products or services. For example you may be shampooing a client's hair and you notice that the hair is particularly oily. You could then recommend a suitable shampoo and/or conditioner that would help this and also styling products that would be suitable. It is important to gauge your client's reaction when suggesting products or services. The client may show interest through facial expressions or they may ask you about a particular product from which you could then give advice.

Key information

The client may show interest through facial expressions or they may ask you about a particular product from which you could then give advice.

Knowledge of products and services

Make sure you know what your salon can offer your clients. It is important to have a thorough knowledge of all the services, products and costs. This includes the features and benefits. If you do not know much about a particular product or service that your salon offers, make sure you ask another member of staff.

Safety first

If you do not know much about a particular product or service that your salon offers, make sure you ask another member of staff.

Make sure that any information regarding the products and services is kept updated. Many salons have times when a product representative comes to the salon to give information about new products that will be used/sold in the salon. Make sure that you attend these but if you miss them for any reason, ask other members of staff about the products.

Figure 6.3 Have good knowledge of all products

Complaints

If a client has a complaint, always be polite, stay calm and remain courteous at all times. Never be argumentative, rude or contradictory. Remember, the client is the most important person in the salon. Inform the supervisor, e.g. stylist or manageress. They have sufficient experience and authority to decide on an appropriate course of action.

Key information

Remember, the client is the most important person in the salon.

Figure 6.4 Stay calm when dealing with complaints

Online activity 6.2

Five in a row

Legislation

You must be aware of the following legislation when promoting products or services to clients:

- The Consumer Protection Act (1987)
- Sale of Goods Act (1979)
- Supply of Goods and Services Act (1982)
- Trades Description Act (2010).

Definition

Legislation: A law.

The Consumer Protection Act

This Act protects the buyer's safety from products by following European directives. This means that there must be clear information on the use of the product. Your salon must only sell products from a reputable supplier. Make sure that they remain in good condition whilst in your salon.

Figure 6.5 Ensure that the client has clear information about the product

Sale of Goods Act

This states:

- products sold must be fit for the purpose stated and able to do what they claim
- products sold must be of good quality
- consumers can reject the products if they do not meet these requirements and have a refund as long as it is done within a set time.

Figure 6.6 Products must be fit for the purpose stated

Supply of Goods and Services Act

This states that services must be:

- at a price that is reasonable
- provided within a timescale that is reasonable
- given with reasonable skill and care.

Goods provided within this service must be:

- of satisfactory quality
- fit for their purpose
- as described.

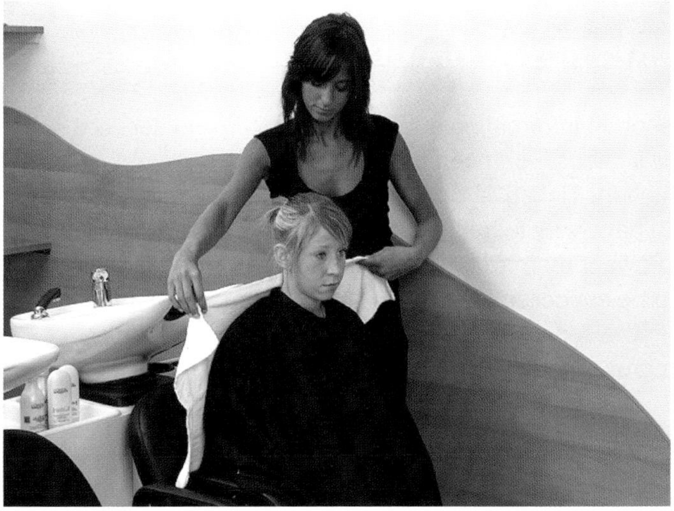

Figure 6.7 Services must comply with the Sale of Goods Act

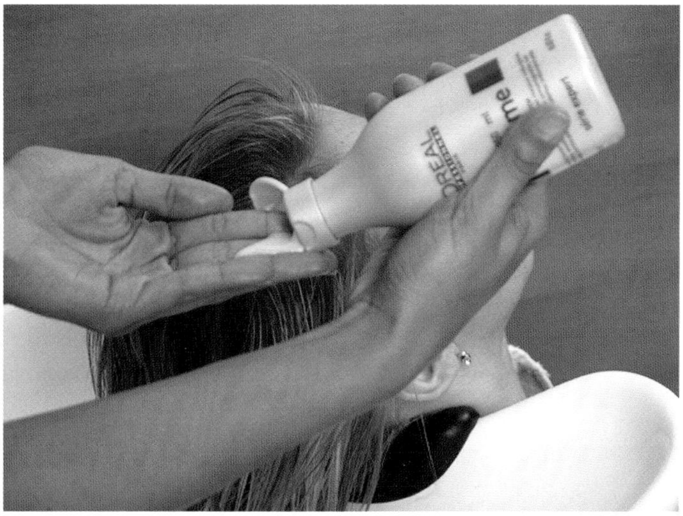

Figure 6.8 Goods must comply with the Sale of Goods Act

Online activity 6.3

Correct selection

Trades Description Act

This states products must:

- be labelled correctly
- be labelled so as not to mislead the buyer
- state what the product is used for
- show the ingredients
- state where they were made
- be clearly priced.

All product information in writing and verbal recommendations must be accurate.

Figure 6.9 Product information must be accurate

6.2 Inform clients about products or services

Key information

Timing is most important because if you choose an unsuitable time, it can have very negative consequences.

Once you have gained enough information about the products and services and found out your client's needs, you need to judge the correct time to communicate this information. Timing is most important because if you choose an unsuitable time, it can have very negative consequences. You do not want to annoy the client as you want them to visit your salon again. Repeat business is essential for a salon to be successful as it shows customer loyalty. If the customer is satisfied with the services you are providing they will tell others, allowing the business to grow and increase its profits.

Times to inform clients

Timing of communicating information about products or services is important. Judging your client's body language will help you to decide when this should be. For example if a client looks annoyed, then it is not a good time. A time that would be appropriate is when they look calm and they have enough time to think about what you have just advised.

Figure 6.10 Choose a suitable time to communicate

Figure 6.11 This client looks annoyed so now is not a good time!

Opportunities to inform clients of products and services

These include, when the client is:

- waiting for a treatment
- having their consultation
- having their hair shampooed
- having their treatment
- paying for their treatment.

But remember to do this only if the client's body language and mood are positive.

Key information

But remember to do this only if the client's body language and mood are positive.

Figure 6.12 Brochures are a good way of promoting products and services

Other methods of promoting products and services

These include the following:

- visual aids
- posters
- newsletters
- promotional flyers
- vouchers
- mailing out information
- word of mouth
- testers/samples
- winning competitions
- loyalty promotions.

It is important to show lots of enthusiasm about products and services that you are promoting as this will hold the client's interest.

Definition

Promotional: To advertise or publicise.

Online activity 6.4 WWW

Check it

Giving information to clients

Key information

Be honest and explain how the product or service will benefit the client.

Definition

Misconception: To have an impression that is incorrect.

Information must be given to clients accurately and must not be confusing. Be honest and explain how the product or service will benefit the client. Let the client take a look at the product that they may wish to buy. Then show the client how to use it through a demonstration, explaining how it will benefit them.

Give timings of treatments correctly so the client is not under any misconception as to how long it will take. If you do give inaccurate information here, clients will not believe you in the future. Price lists should be shown clearly and the prices of treatments should have no hidden extras. Make sure the client is aware of vouchers that they could buy for friends and family. If there are any offers at a particular time, you should always have knowledge of these in order for you to promote them.

Figure 6.13 Allow the client to look, feel, touch and smell the product

Figure 6.14 Timings of treatments should be given accurately

6.3 Gain client commitment

Once you have given all the information to the client, you should give them time to decide whether they wish to buy. You can usually pick up on signs to show if they seem interested.

Buying signs

A client is likely to buy if they:

- show positive body language, e.g. are nodding or smiling
- want to know more about the product
- smell or touch the product
- want to try the product
- want to know the price of the product
- want to know how the product works.

Figure 6.15 This client is touching the product so it's likely she is interested in buying it

Client showing no interest

If a client is not interested in additional products or services they will:

- tell you that they are not interested
- start a conversation about another matter
- be interested in other activities in the salon.

If this is the case then check that you are giving the client the correct information and that you are explaining yourself correctly. It may be that you are giving too much information or that you are giving it at the wrong time. Try another way of giving information but don't carry on if your client still does not show any interest. Change the conversation to a subject that you know your client will be interested in.

Key information

Try another way of giving information but don't carry on if your client still does not show any interest.

Figure 6.16 This client does not look interested

Figure 6.17 Change the conversation to something you know the client is interested in

www Online activity 6.5

Correct selection

Delivery of products

Safety first

If anything is unclear, run through the details carefully, repeating any information that you feel the client is confused about.

The delivery details must be explained carefully to the client. If anything is unclear, run through the details carefully, repeating any information that you feel the client is confused about. If the client has to wait for their product then you should tell them for how long. Ring up the supplier or wholesaler directly if there are any problems with the client's delivery. Give clients information about this as soon as possible. Always ask your manager or supervisor if you do not feel you have adequate knowledge about a product or service.

Booking additional services and record keeping

If the client wishes to book additional services, do this straight away at a time that is convenient to them. Always record details of products or additional services that the client buys or books on that client's record card and keep on file.

Figure 6.19 Book additional services straight away

Figure 6.18 Speak to your supervisor if you are unsure about anything

6.4 Worksheets

WORKSHEETS

You can carry out the worksheets during your study of a chapter or unit, or at the end. An example is presented here and there are more online. If your college or company is registered with ATT Training, lots more are available. Write your answers directly in the book, but only if you own it of course – if it is a library or college book, use a separate piece of paper!

6.4.1 Opportunities to identify needs

There are many more opportunities other than during the consultation where you can identify a client's needs regarding products or services. For example you may be shampooing a client's hair and you notice that the hair is particularly oily. You could then recommend a suitable shampoo and/or conditioner that would help this and also styling products that would be suitable. It is important to gauge your client's reaction when suggesting products or services. The client may show interest through facial expressions or they may ask you about a particular product from which you could then give advice.

Answer these questions:

1 In the example above, which shampoo and/or conditioner would you recommend to a client who has oily hair?

2 Why would you recommend this/those particular products?

3 How does the shampoo and/or product work and why does that make it suitable for this client?

6.5 Assessment

Well done! If you have studied all the content of this unit you may be ready to test your knowledge.

Check out the 'Preparing for assessments' section in chapter 1 if you have not already done so, and always remember:

- You can only do your best if you have. . .
  - studied hard
  - completed the activities
  - completed the worksheets
  - practised, practised, practised
  - and then revised!

Now carry out the online multiple-choice quiz

. . . and good luck in the final exam, which will be arranged by your tutor/assessor.

CHAPTER 7

Effectiveness at work

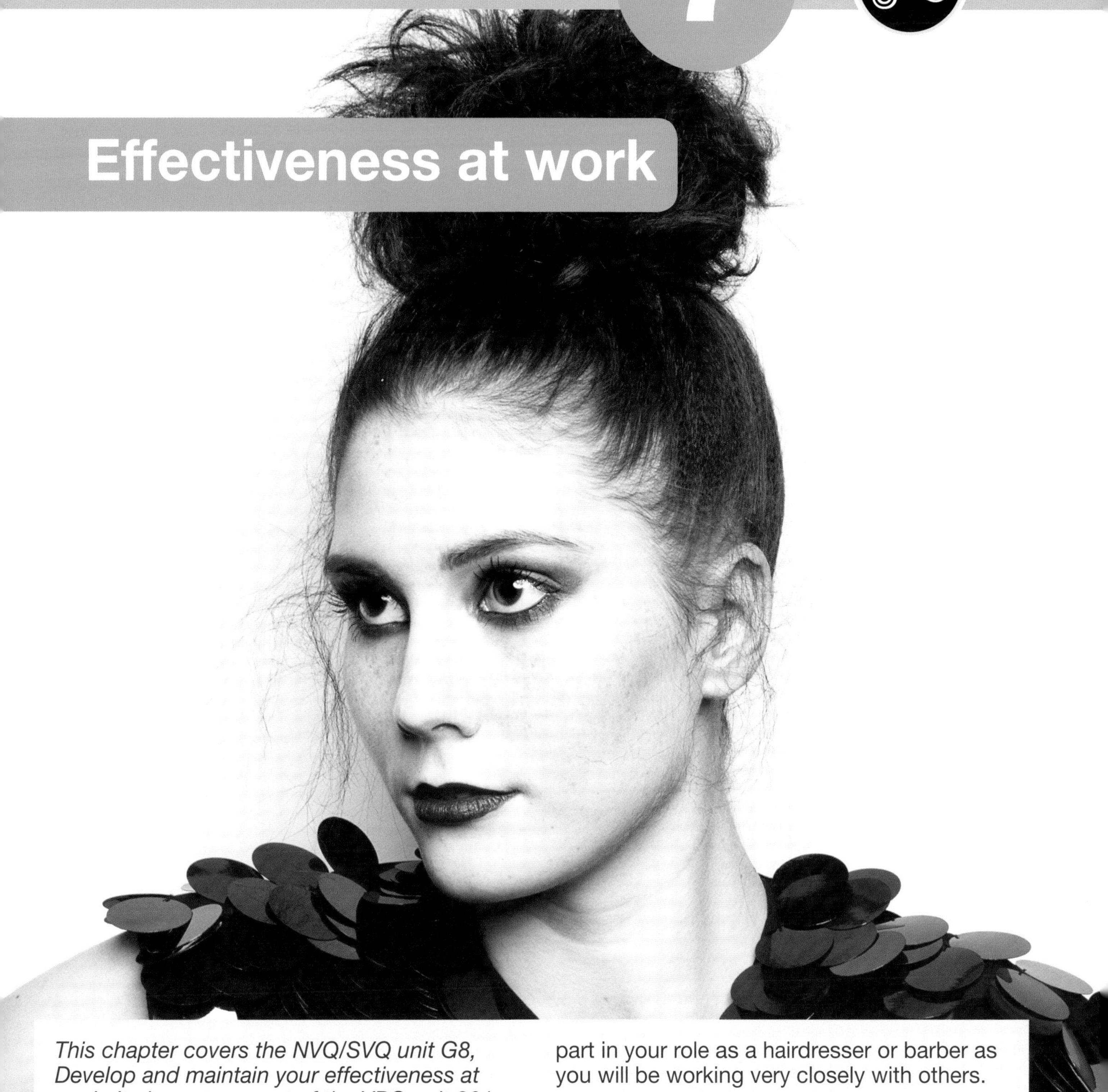

This chapter covers the NVQ/SVQ unit G8, Develop and maintain your effectiveness at work. It also covers part of the VRQ unit 201, Working in the hair industry.

This chapter will enable you to develop personally and professionally so that you become successful in the workplace by using your own initiative and adapting to changing circumstances. Teamwork also plays a big part in your role as a hairdresser or barber as you will be working very closely with others.

In this chapter you will learn about:

- improving your personal effectiveness at work
- working effectively as part of a team.

Website

www.atthairdressing.com

CHAPTER 7 EFFECTIVENESS AT WORK: CONTENTS, SCREENS AND ACTIVITIES

Key:

Sections from the book are set in this colour

Screens available online are set in this colour

Online activity screens are set in this colour

Improve your personal effectiveness at work

Introduction	Short and long-term goals
Round the board	Five in a row
Improve your personal effectiveness at work	Training and Keeping skills up to date
Meeting standards	Shadowing
Job description	Asking others for help
Select correct boxes	Setting yourself a personal training plan
Appraisals	Review your training plan
Self-appraisal	Problems and how to address them
Strengths, weaknesses and targets	Correct selection

Working effectively as part of a team

Work effectively as part of a team	Organising your own work
Round the board	Correct selection
Your role in the team 1	Worksheet – self appraisal
Your role in the team 2	Worksheet – structure of the salon
Structure of the salon	Worksheet – problems and how to address them
Resolving conflicts	Online multiple choice quiz

7.1 Improve your personal effectiveness at work

This chapter will enable you to develop personally and professionally. It will help you adapt to changing circumstances which may occur during your working day. If problems do arise, ask yourself if you can solve them. If you can't, then you should know who to ask advice from in the team, thus communicating with the team and members of the public.

Figure 7.1 Know who to ask if you have a problem

Online activity 7.1 WWW

Round the board

When we refer to the term personal effectiveness, we mean working to meet standards that are expected of you. So here you will learn how to evaluate your current performance and ways in which you can improve this.

Key information

When we refer to the term personal effectiveness, we mean working to meet standards that are expected of you.

Meeting standards

When you first start working in a salon as a trainee, your main job will be to help other members in the salon. This is a great way of learning about all the treatments and services that your salon offers. You must remember to carry out your work to the relevant standards at all times (NVQ or VRQ). These standards make up your qualifications. If you do not do this, it will greatly hinder your reputation and that of your salon.

If a task has been given to you by another member of staff, make sure that you ask them to clarify if you are unclear about it. This is another method of ensuring that the highest possible standard of service is given.

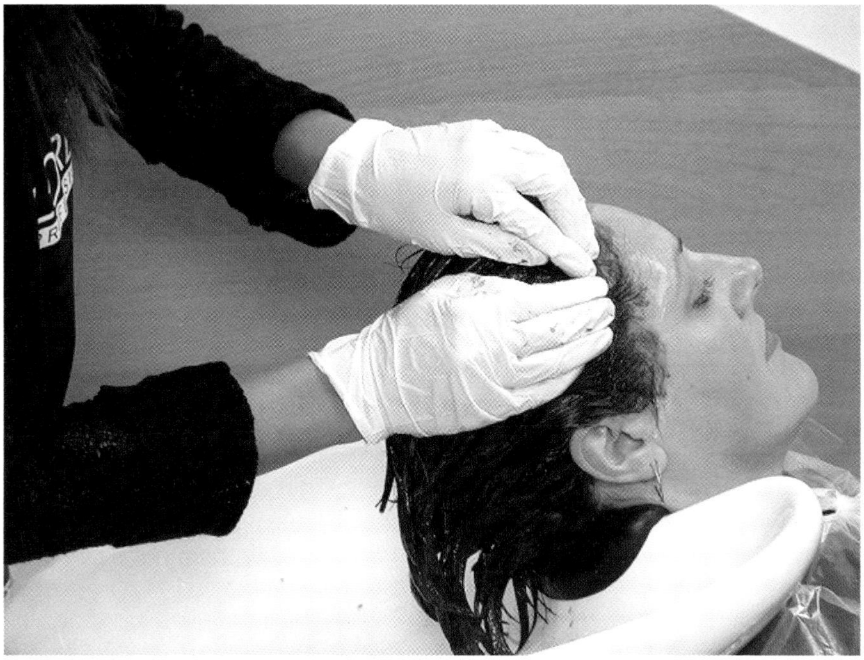

Figure 7.2 Carry out all work to the relevant standards

Job description

Having a clear understanding of your job role is essential for you to work effectively. You must make sure that you and your manager have the same defined role for your position. If you are confused in any way about part of your job role, then speak to your manager in order to clarify any misunderstandings. When you start working in a salon, you will be given a job description.

Key information

A job description outlines your:

- title
- person you are responsible to
- location
- purpose
- duties
- standards needed.

Job Description

Job title:	Stylist
Responsible to:	Salon Manager
Based at:	The Hair Salon, Surrey
Purpose:	To provide services and treatments in the salon, whilst maintaining a high standard of customer care working in-line with company standards.
Duties:	Consult with clients, giving advice on services and treatments Provide high quality services and treatments to clients Give advice on products including aftercare Attend regular training sessions Assist salon manager Achieve performance targets set
Standards needed:	Ensure company policy is adhered to at all times

Figure 7.3 A basic job description

WWW Online activity 7.2

Select correct boxes

Appraisals

An appraisal is a system where you and your manager discuss your progress and personal contribution in the salon. Each salon will have its own staff appraisal system but they should be regular. Many salons will carry them out every three months.

The appraisal process will identify:

- what you have achieved
- what you want to achieve
- how to achieve it.

Key information

An appraisal is a system where you and your manager discuss your progress and personal contribution in the salon.

Therefore it is not just about how you are doing in your job role, but how you are developing as an individual. It should be thought of as a conversation between the two of you and not just your manager telling you how he or she feels about your work.

Figure 7.4 Appraisals should be a two-way conversation

Self-appraisal

Some companies will give a self-appraisal form for their staff to fill in themselves and then a performance appraisal form that the employer will complete. This gives you a chance to discuss any points that you or your manager have made on your performance. It's not always easy to take a look at yourself and so your manager should help by giving his or her opinion. Always listen to this opinion calmly even if you do not agree. Self-appraisal forms will contain whatever information your manager or salon manager feels is required for your position.

Figure 7.5 Self-appraisal forms are filled in by you

Strengths, weaknesses and targets

Part of the self-appraisal process will be to assess your own strengths and weaknesses. This will enable you to tackle any problem areas you may have. Be as honest as you can when establishing your strengths and weaknesses.

You can see the strengths and weaknesses on the following sample job appraisal. Simon regards his strengths to be styling, cutting, reception duties and client care whereas his weaknesses he regards as colouring and asking for help.

Self Appraisal

Name: *Simon Turner*	**Salon:** *Cuts 4U*
Position: *Trainee stylist*	**Age:** *25*
Period covered: *Oct 2005 Oct 2006*	**Time in current position:** *2 years*
Appraiser: *Marie Turner*	**Date:** *24th November 2006*

1. What do you consider to be your main responsibilities?
Train in all aspects of styling, cutting and colouring hair.
Carry out client care at all times.
Shampoo/condition hair.

2. Areas where you perform well.
I feel I am good at styling and cutting. I also feel I do well when I am on the reception desk. I am very good at client care as I have had very positive comments from clients about this.

3. Areas that you could improve.
I struggle sometimes deciding on the right colour to use on clients. Also I do not ask for help as much as I should.

4. What do you feel have been your best achievements in your job role?
I won an in-house competition for Best Style in May 2005.

5. Likes and dislikes about the company.
Likes: friendly atmosphere, everyone gets on very well.
Dislikes: sometimes it can be too busy to take breaks.

6. Areas in your position that you are most interested in/least interested in.
Most interested in cutting.
Least interested in shampoo/conditioning.

7. Reasons you feel you find certain tasks difficult.
I feel I find colouring difficult because I do not completely understand the principles of colouring.

8. How can you improve your performance?
If I learn more about colouring I feel this will greatly increase my performance as I will need less time when colouring and will not need to ask another member of staff to help.

9. What are your short-term goals?
To fully understand the colouring principles.
Help others out more often.

10. What are your long-term goals?
In about two years' time I wish to become a stylist in the salon.

11. What training do you feel would help you to achieve your goals?
A colour course.

Figure 7.6 Sample self-appraisal form

Short- and long-term goals

From your strengths and weaknesses you can set targets, i.e. short- and long-term goals that you wish to achieve. This helps to overcome any weaknesses you may have and shows that you are keen to learn. Your manager will then discuss these with you and can tell you whether he or she feels your short- and long-term goals are feasible.

In Figure 7.6 you can see that Simon's short-term goals are to fully understand the colouring principles and to help others whereas his long-term goals are to look ahead in two years' time when he is aiming to become a stylist.

WWW Online activity 7.3

Five in a row

Training and keeping skills up to date

You will notice on the self-appraisal form (Figure 7.6) that Simon feels to gain a full understanding of the colouring principles he should take part in a training course. This is important throughout your career as a hairdresser as you must make sure your skills are kept up to date. You can do this not just through regular training but also by attending hair shows, seminars and trade events.

Key information

You can do this not just through regular training but also by attending hair shows, seminars and trade events.

Shadowing

Shadowing another member of staff is a great way to learn. If you get the opportunity to do this it will enable you to learn from somebody in the business who has a greater amount of experience.

Definition

Shadowing: Following a more experienced member of staff for training purposes.

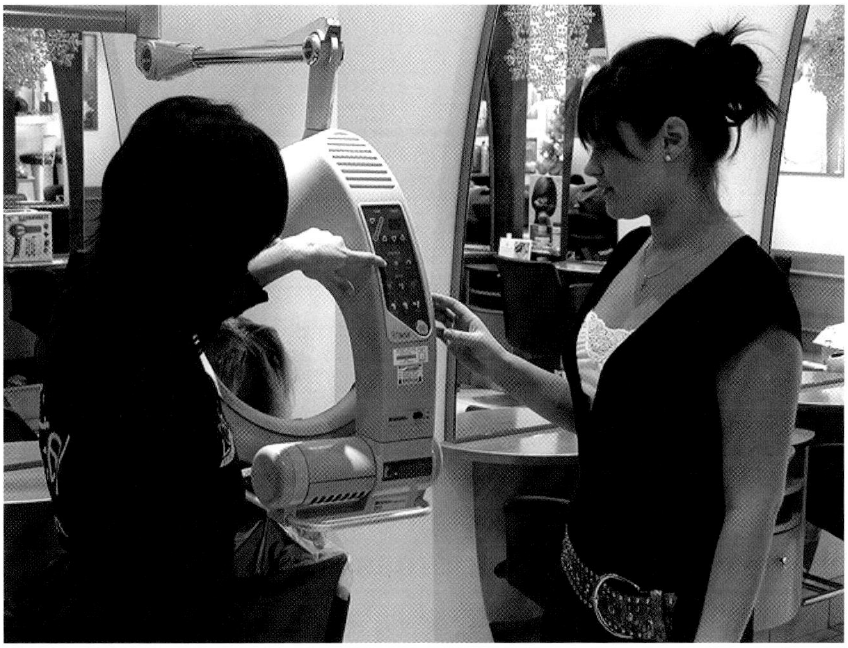

Figure 7.7 Shadowing is a great way to learn

Asking others for help

In Simon's self-appraisal (Figure 7.6) he wrote that he did not ask others for help as much as he should. This is something he will need to tackle as when you are training you will need to ask others for help on many different occasions. His colleagues will understand that it is necessary to be asked for help in order for Simon to be an effective member of staff.

Definition

Effective: To work well.

Setting yourself a personal training plan

You can set up your own personal training plan by creating an action plan. Your long-term goal could be for example that in a year's time you wish to complete your NVQ Level 2 in Hairdressing. You must break down the units that you wish to complete including the correct number of optional units. Let's say you wish to complete the shampooing/conditioning unit in one month's time.

You should write down how you wish to achieve this and so your training plan may look something like that shown in Figure 7.8.

Definition

Action plan: A method of outlining steps and actions in order achieve a particular goal.

Review your training plan

The training plan is a guide enabling you to assess your progress. It should be reviewed and updated at regular periods in order to check that the objective or goal is being achieved. Figure 7.9 shows an example schedule that is a good way to help you keep track of your progress.

Training Plan

Watch junior shampooist - observe client care.

Listen to instructions - health and safety, salon security (client's belongings), how much shampoo to use (resources).

Learn about the products used in the salon.

Practise on models - until competent.

Shampoo clients - until competent.

Answer oral questions correctly.

Complete assignments.

Pass written question papers.

Figure 7.8 Sample training plan

Areas	With help	Some help	Own work	Date
Shampoo			Yes	28/11
Condition			Yes	16/11
Blow-dry		Yes		17/11
Setting				
Permanent wave	Yes			04/01
Winding				
Neutralise		Yes		04/01
Semi-perm colour	Yes			15/02
Temp colour		Yes		17/11
Cuts	Yes			06/01
Reception				
Stock control		Yes		13/01

Figure 7.9 Example schedule

Problem	Resolve
Overbooking	Apologise to the client Say how long the wait will be Offer a drink and magazines Offer another stylist if need be
Client changes her requirement	Notify stylist Carry out another client consultation
Staff absent	Book appointments with other stylist if possible Otherwise phone, apologise and rearrange if possible
Complaint from a client	Inform your superiors

Figure 7.10 Problems that you may encounter

Key information

A happy team working together promotes good working practices and leads to satisfied clients.

Problems and how to address them

Problems do occur from time to time and it is essential you know the correct way to deal with them. Figure 7.10 shows you certain problems that may occur in the salon and what you must to do to resolve them.

WWW Online activity 7.4

Correct selection

7.2 Work effectively as part of a team

A happy team working together promotes good working practices and leads to satisfied clients. In this section you will learn about forming relationships and keeping them the best they can be.

WWW Online activity 7.5

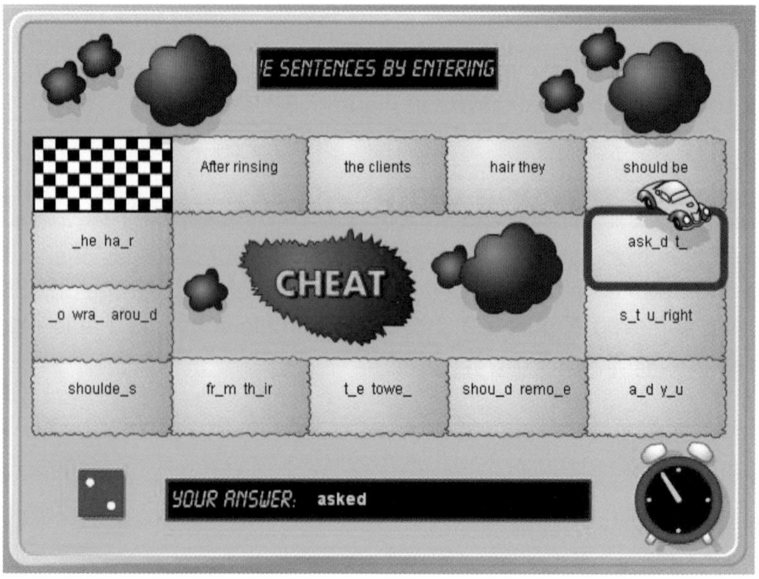

Round the board

Your role in the team

During your training as a hairdresser you will start each day assisting the stylists by sweeping the floor, making tea and coffee, washing towels and general cleaning. You will progress to shampooing clients where your knowledge of shampoo and conditioning products is vital as you will recommend and select the appropriate product needed. Your technical skills improve through your own dedication as your role in the team changes. You neutralise perms, answer the telephone, book appointments, generally help in the salon and at the reception desk. Your role in the team is gradually developing.

Always be co-operative and courteous. Consider yourself part of a team, rather than an individual merely responsible for your own specific duties. Offer help and assistance to others, remember that the 'favour' may be returned when you are busy; e.g. if you have completed your duties see if you can help others.

Key information

Your technical skills improve through your own dedication as your role in the team changes.

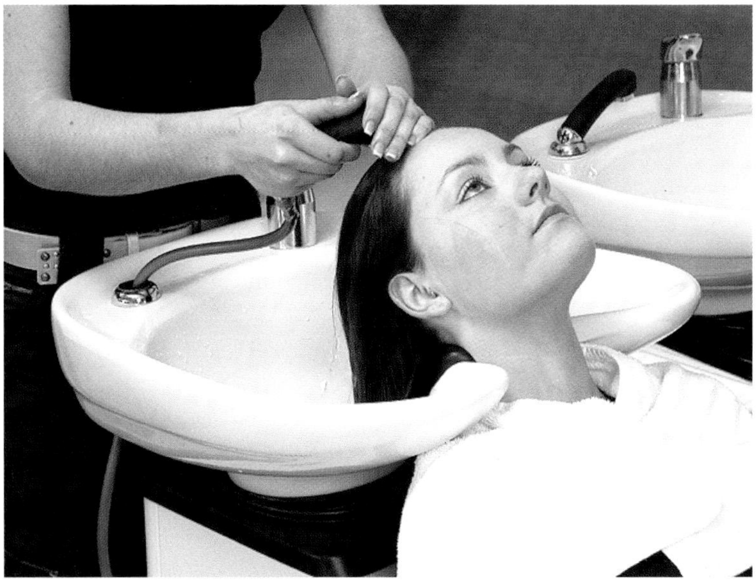

Figure 7.11 You will be shampooing as you progress through your training

Figure 7.12 Work as a team

Structure of the salon

You will need to find out how your salon operates and the hierarchy within it. It may be that the structure in your salon looks similar to this one.

Definition

Hierarchy: A group of people ranked in order of job position.

Salon Owner

Salon Manager/Manageress

Salon Trainer

Senior Stylist

Stylist

Senior Technician

Junior Stylist/Technician

Trainee

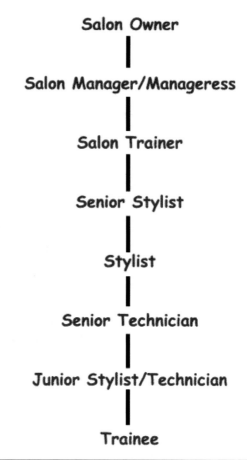

Figure 7.13 Example of the hierarchy in a salon

Website

www.atthairdressing.com

Know the team members, their names, job titles and responsibilities. This will enable you to know who to go to with any particular issues you may have.

Make sure you also know the following:

1 What to do if you are unable to go to work, who do you contact?
2 How many days' holiday are you entitled to?
3 Who do you ask when you book your holiday time?
4 Who do you speak to if you have personal problems?

Resolving conflicts

Key information

Awkward situations can occur at work and it is important to know the correct procedure to follow if they become problems.

Awkward situations can occur at work. It is important to know the correct procedure to follow if they become problems. You should first of all approach the person you find the problem with. Make sure that no-one else can listen in and be calm. Knowing what you are going to say beforehand will help. Don't forget it is most important also to listen to what your colleague has to say. If you still do not resolve the conflict you should then go to your manager and discuss the issue with them.

Figure 7.14 Try to speak directly to your colleague

Figure 7.15 But talk to your manager if you cannot resolve the conflict on your own

Organising your own work

Work out what has to be done each day. When you first start as a trainee, you will get instructions from your trainer or senior trainee. As you become more experienced your own role will change and you will progress to senior trainee. Write out a list of your tasks for the day. Tick off your tasks as you do them.

An example of such a list is:

- Assist stylist during all procedures of the day.
- Prepare trolley before each service begins.
- Get record cards ready for the stylist.
- Prepare PPE and towels.
- Check stock.
- Launder towels when bin is full.

Online activity 7.6 WWW

Correct selection

WORKSHEETS

7.3 Worksheets

You can carry out the worksheets during your study of a chapter or unit, or at the end. An example is presented here and there are more online. If your college or company is registered with ATT Training, lots more are available. Write your answers directly in the book, but only if you own it of course – if it is a library or college book, use a separate piece of paper!

7.3.1 Self-appraisal

Some companies give a self-appraisal form for their staff to fill in themselves. It's not always easy to take a look at yourself and so your manager should help by giving his or her opinion. Always listen calmly to this opinion, even if you do not agree.

Here is a sample self-appraisal form. Fill it in as best as you can on your own and then ask your tutor to help you complete it.

Self Appraisal

Name:	**Salon:**
Position:	**Age:**
Period covered:	**Time in current position:**
Appraiser:	**Date:**

1. What do you consider to be your main responsibilities?

2. Areas where you perform well

3. Areas that you could improve

Figure 7.16 Self-appraisal form part 1 (Continued)

4. What do you feel have been your best achievements in your job role?

5. Likes and dislikes about the company

6. Areas in your position that you are most interested in/least interested in

7. Reasons you feel you find certain tasks difficult

8. How can you improve your performance?

10. What are your long-term goals?

11. What training do you feel would help you to achieve your goals?

Figure 7.16 Self-appraisal form part 1

7.4 Assessment

Well done! If you have studied all the content of this unit you may be ready to test your knowledge.

Check out the 'Preparing for assessments' section in Chapter 1 if you have not already done so, and always remember:

- You can only do your best if you have. . .
  - studied hard
  - completed the activities
  - completed the worksheets
  - practised, practised, practised
  - and then revised!

Now carry out the online multiple-choice quiz

. . . and good luck in the final exam, which will be arranged by your tutor/assessor.

CHAPTER 8

Shampoo, condition and treat the hair and scalp

This chapter covers the NVQ/SVQ unit GH8, Shampoo, condition and treat the hair and scalp and the VRQ unit 204, Shampoo and condition the hair and scalp.

The techniques of shampooing, conditioning and treating the hair and scalp are an essential part of the hairdressing service. Care must be taken to choose the correct products suitable for the client's hair and scalp.

In this chapter you will learn about:

- maintaining effective and safe methods of working when shampooing, conditioning and treating the hair and scalp
- shampooing hair and scalp
- conditioning and treating the hair and scalp
- providing aftercare advice.

Website www
www.atthairdressing.com

CHAPTER 8 SHAMPOO, CONDITION AND TREAT THE HAIR AND SCALP: CONTENTS, SCREENS AND ACTIVITIES

Key:
Sections from the book are set in this colour
Screens available online are set in this colour
Online activity screens are set in this colour

8.1 Working safely

This section covers the health and safety issues concerned with shampooing, conditioning and treating the hair and scalp. Chapter 2 covers health and safety working methods in more detail. Refer to this chapter if needed.

Figure 8.1 Ask the client about the condition of their hair

Check the condition of the hair and scalp

Before starting the service, it is essential that the condition of the hair and scalp is checked. This will establish which products will be suitable for the client.

To find out the condition, you should:

- ask the client directly
- visually check
- check the client's records.

Report any skin or scalp conditions that are not recognised to your manager. All responses to questioning should be recorded so that information is kept up to date.

Online activity 8.1

Check it

Key information

Before starting the service, it is essential that the condition of the hair and scalp is checked.

Safety first

Report any skin or scalp conditions that are not recognised to your manager.

Condition of hair

The following table shows types of hair condition and causes.

Table 8.1 Condition types and causes

Hair condition	Main causes
Chemically damaged	Colouring Bleaching Perming
Heat damaged	Use of heated equipment
Environmentally damaged	Sun Wind
Product build up	Gel Mousse Dressing cream

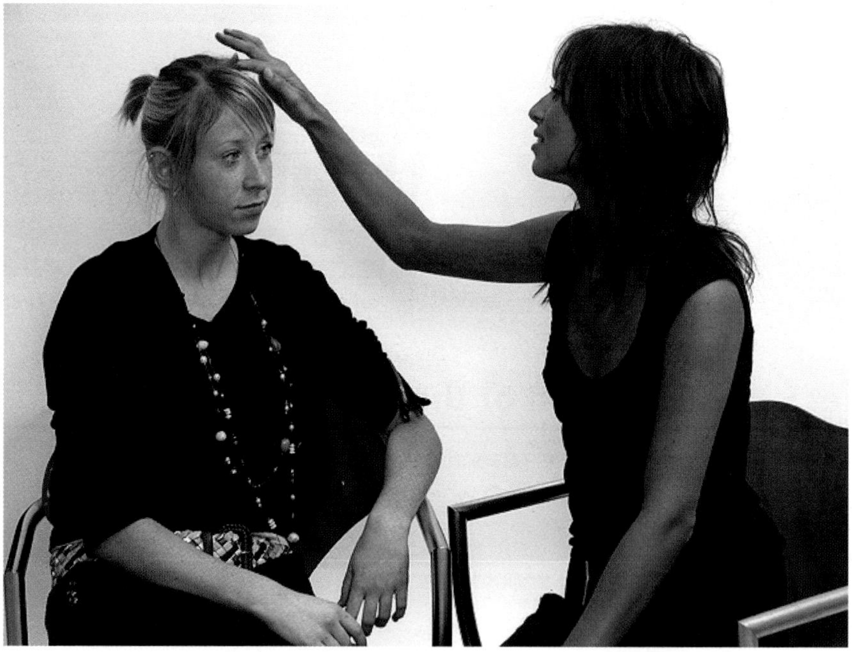

Figure 8.2 Checking for contraindications

Contraindications

These include:

- allergies to any products
- abrasions to the skin
- skin and scalp disorders
- skin and scalp disease
- damage to area where treatment will be
- fresh scar tissue.

If you do find any of these, you must NOT treat the hair and scalp. Record these results.

Safety first

If you do find any of these, you must NOT treat the hair and scalp.

Prepare client for service

Assist the client to put on a gown to protect his or her clothing while in the salon. Always use fresh, clean and sterile towels and gown for each client. Ask the client to remove any jewellery that may interfere with the service, for example large loop earrings or heavy chains around the neck. After the consultation direct the client from the workstation to the basin at which the treatment will be provided. Offer physical support if necessary to an incapacitated or infirm client. Ensure that there are no obstacles or hazards in the way.

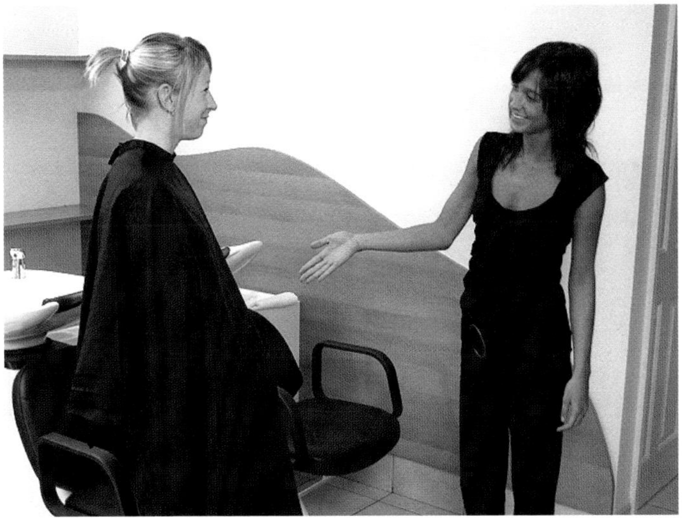

Figure 8.3 Assist the client to the washbasin

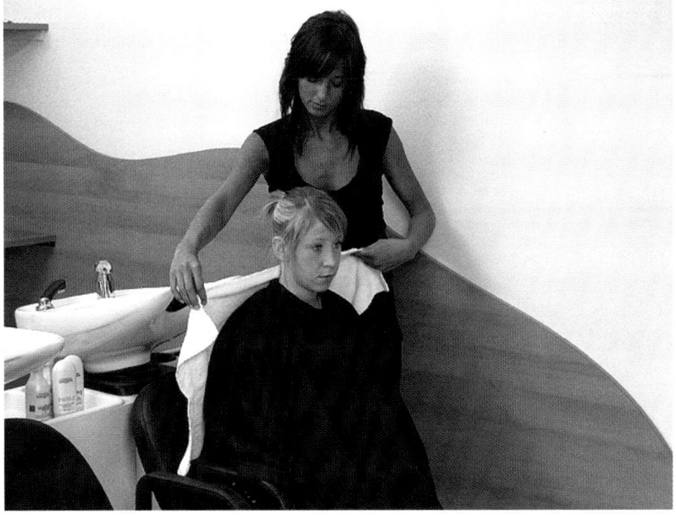

Figure 8.4 Placing a towel around the client's neck

Client comfort at the basin

If you are using a forward facing basin offer the client a face cloth or a folded towel to protect the eyes during the service. When using a backwash basin manoeuvre or support the client's head over the basin. Make sure that the client's neck feels comfortable at all times. Towels should be below the basin neckline. This prevents water seeping into the towels and soaking the client's clothes. If any product splashes into the client's eye, bathe the eye with cool water and seek medical advice.

Definition

Manoeuvre: To move.

Safety first

If any product splashes into the client's eye, bathe the eye with cool water and seek medical advice.

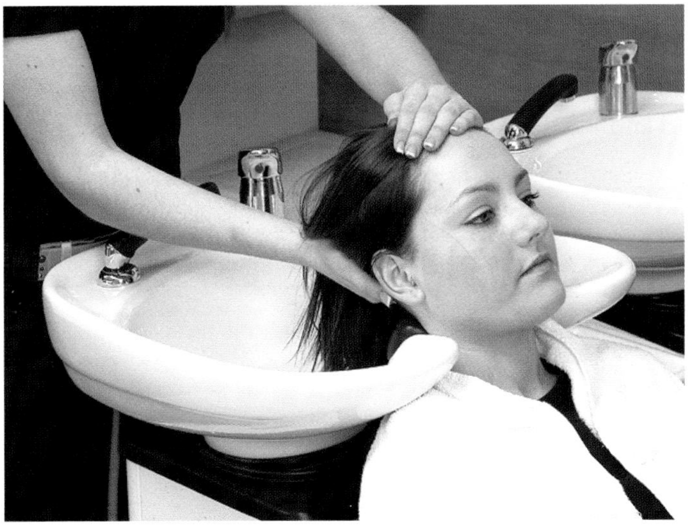

Figure 8.5 Supporting the client's head

Correct posture

Key information

The most common effect of a bad posture is fatigue.

Definition

Fatigue: Extreme tiredness.

When standing at the washbasin, stand with your weight evenly distributed throughout your body. Wear flat, comfortable shoes as this will help weight distribution. Do not bend over the basin; extend the arms from the shoulders. Do not lean across the client. Walk around to the other side to work. All of these points help to minimise the effects of bad posture on the body. The most common effect of a bad posture is fatigue.

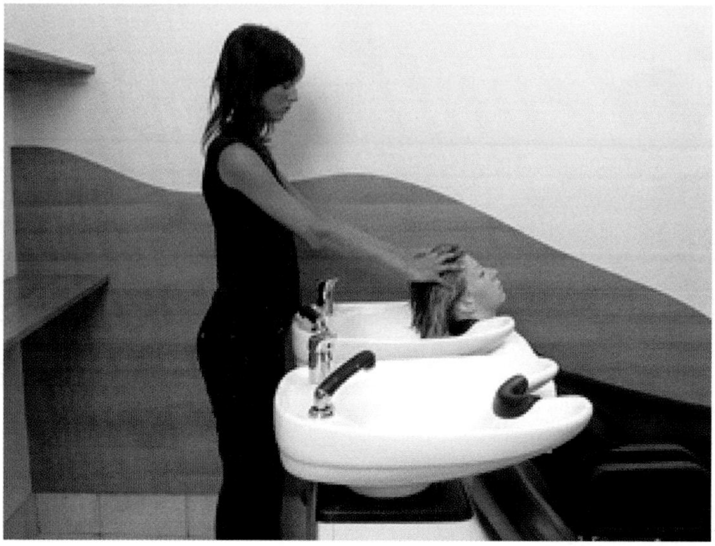

Figure 8.6 Correct posture

Control of Substances Hazardous to Health Regulations 2002 (COSHH)

These are commonly called the COSHH regulations and they lay down the essential requirements for controlling exposure to hazardous substances and for protecting people who may be affected by them. A substance is considered to be hazardous if it can cause harm to the body. It only poses a risk if it is:

- inhaled (breathed in)
- ingested (swallowed)
- in contact with the skin
- absorbed through the skin
- injected into the body
- introduced into the body via cuts etc.

www

The associated learning screen for this part is interactive

For more information about the COSHH regulations refer to Chapter 2.

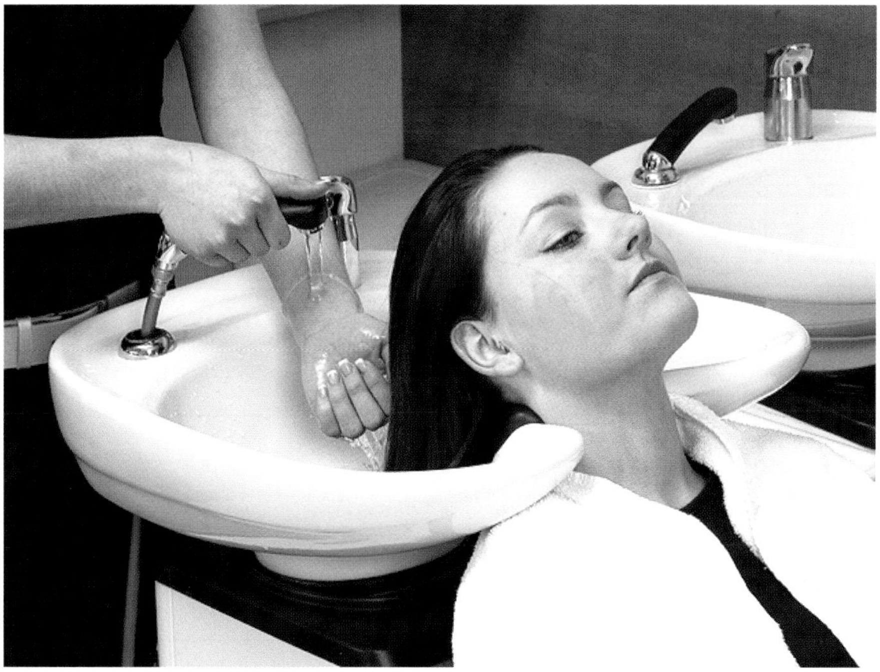

Figure 8.7 Regular wet work can cause dermatitis

Dermatitis

This is a very common skin disease in hairdressers and is caused by hands being exposed to certain products and carrying out wet work regularly. Dermatitis can be prevented by:

- ensuring shampoo and conditioner are rinsed from your hands
- drying hands thoroughly
- moisturising regularly
- wearing disposable gloves.

Figure 8.8 Wearing disposable gloves can help prevent dermatitis

Electricity at Work Regulations 1989

These regulations state that you must:

- Always check electrical equipment before using it. Look for loose wires and that the plug is not cracked or damaged in any way. Check that the cord is not frayed or cracked.
- Never use electrical equipment when your hands are wet.
- Electrical equipment should be maintained regularly and checked by a suitably qualified person. Once checked the equipment should have a certificate or label acknowledging it.
- Faulty electrical equipment in the workplace must be removed, labelled as faulty and reported to the relevant person.

Definition

Faulty: Does not work.

Online activity 8.2

Correct selection

Products and record keeping

Key information

If you notice that products are running low, ensure that you inform the relevant person according to your salon's policy.

Make sure that you read manufacturers' instructions before using products. If you notice that products are running low, ensure that you inform the relevant person according to your salon's policy. Do this without delay as running out of stock would have very negative consequences for your salon's reputation. Equally, do not waste products as this will not be cost effective for the salon. Make a note on the client's record card of any products that you use. Ensure that records are updated regularly, clear and correct.

Figure 8.9 Read the manufacturer's instructions

Suggested service times

Commercially viable times for shampooing, conditioning and/or treating hair are as follows (excluding any development times):

Table 8.2 Suggested service times

Length of hair	Time
Above shoulders	10 minutes
Below shoulders	15 minutes

8.2 Shampoo hair and scalp

It is essential to cleanse the hair and scalp to remove dirt, oil and any product build up that may act as a barrier to future services. This section covers the shampooing technique and the products that should be used depending on the client's hair and scalp.

> **Key information**
>
> It is essential to cleanse the hair and scalp to remove dirt, oil and any product build up that may act as a barrier to future services.

pH, acidity and alkalinity

The pH of a product is measured on a scale of 0 to 14. Water has a pH of 7 and is said to be neutral. Products with a pH of less than 7 are described as acid and they close the cuticles. Products with a pH of more than 7 are described as alkaline and they open the cuticles. Shampoos and conditioners are usually 5.5-6 on the pH scale.

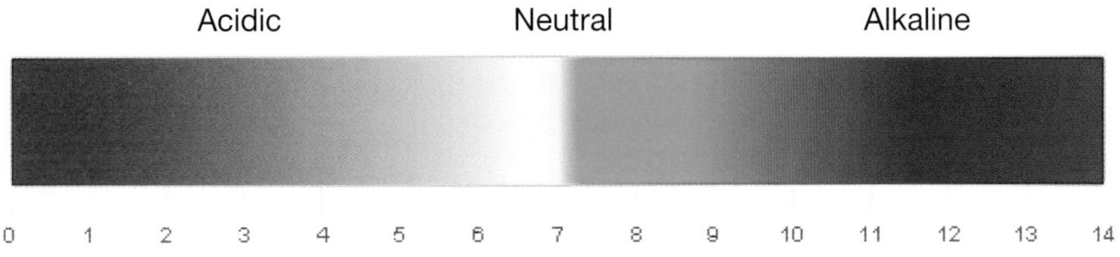

Figure 8.10 pH colour scale

Shampooing products

Choice of shampoo is determined by:

- type, texture and condition of the hair and scalp
- purpose of the shampoo
- treatment after the shampoo.

Figure 8.11 A selection of shampoos

Types of shampoos and ingredients

There are many shampoos used for the different hair or scalp types. The table below shows the ingredients that may be contained in the relevant shampoo.

Table 8.3 Types of shampoo and their ingredients

Type	Ingredients
Normal hair	Rosemary Soya
Dry/damaged hair	Almond oil Coconut Lanolin
Oily hair	Lemon Egg white
Dandruff	Coal tar Zinc pyrithione Selenium sulphide

Online activity 8.3

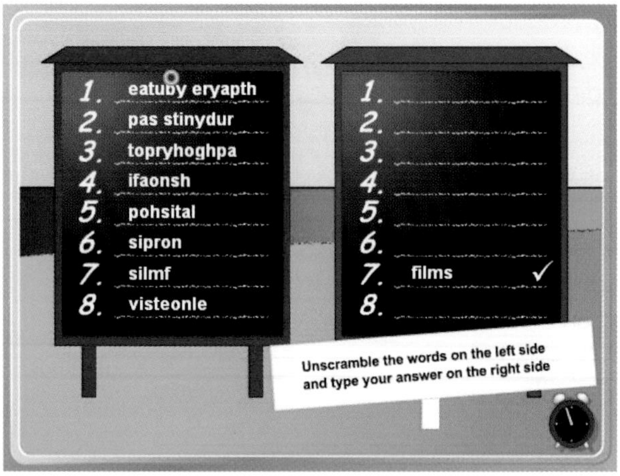

Scrambled words

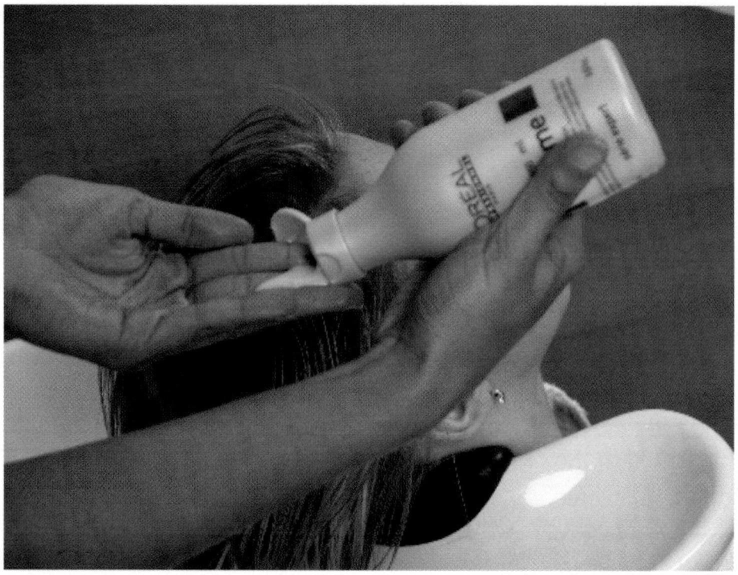

Figure 8.12 Dispensing shampoo

Figure 8.13 Pre-perm shampoo

Key information

Using the wrong shampoo can cause problems for any further treatments, particularly chemical processes such as perming.

Definition

Hair shaft: The part of the hair that is above the skin.

Purpose of the shampoo

The purpose of the shampoo is to:

- cleanse the hair
- remove any products
- prepare the hair for the next service.

Service after shampoo

Ensure you know which service the client is going to have done to their hair after the shampoo. Using the wrong shampoo can cause problems for any further treatments, particularly chemical processes such as perming. Pre-perm shampoo is a soapless detergent shampoo that contains no additives. If a shampoo that contains additives is used before a perm it will coat the hair and prevent the perm solution from entering the hair shaft. This will act as a barrier.

How shampoos work – shampoo and its relationship with water

The detergent molecules of the shampoo have a head and a tail. The head is hydrophilic which means it attracts water and the tail is hydrophobic which means it repels water. The hydrophobic end of the molecule is attracted to dirt on the hair. It surrounds the dirt and suspends it in the water. This action is aided by agitation from the massage.

When the hair is rinsed the hydrophilic heads pull the dirt or oil from the hair and carry it away with the flow of water. During the shampooing process the detergent acts as an emulsifying agent because it holds the oil and water together.

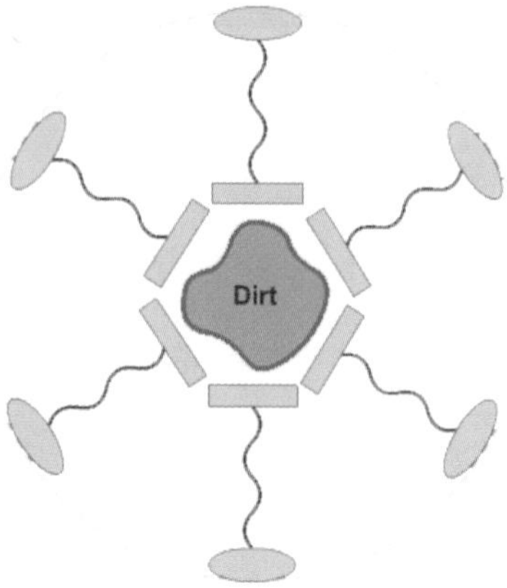

Figure 8.14 Shampoo molecules surrounding the dirt

Hard water in the salon

Hard water can be a problem in the salon, causing the spray jets to become blocked. The basins may become stained and look unsightly.

Figure 8.15 Basins can become stained

Massage techniques

The following techniques for massaging are used when shampooing hair:

- effleurage
- rotary.

Effleurage massage is a gentle, smooth, stroking movement using the palms of the hands. It is mainly used on long, dense hair to avoid tangling and ensure thorough cleaning. Rotary massage uses the pads of the fingers in quick, circular movements.

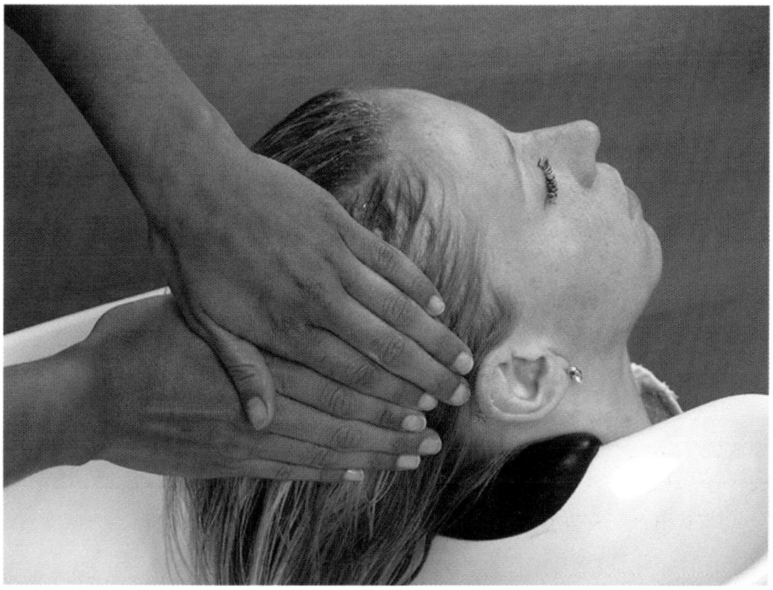

Figure 8.16 Be careful when massaging

Definition

Seborrhoea: Condition in which excess sebum is produced from the sebaceous gland.

Client care

Some clients are more sensitive to pressure than others. When massaging, be aware of the client's tolerance levels. Look for warning signs that you may be massaging too vigorously. Do not overstimulate the scalp if the client suffers from seborrhoea, dizziness or high blood pressure.

WWW Online activity 8.4

Round the board

Shampooing procedure

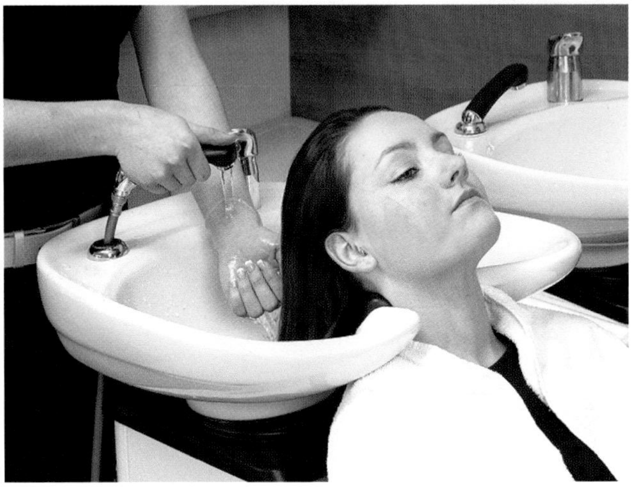

Figure 8.17 After the client has been gowned correctly and is sitting comfortably at the washbasin the temperature of the water should be tested on the inside of the shampooist's wrist. This is to prevent scalding the client.

Figure 8.18 Check the temperature with the client, which may vary. Some clients may require the water cooler or warmer. Apply water to hair.

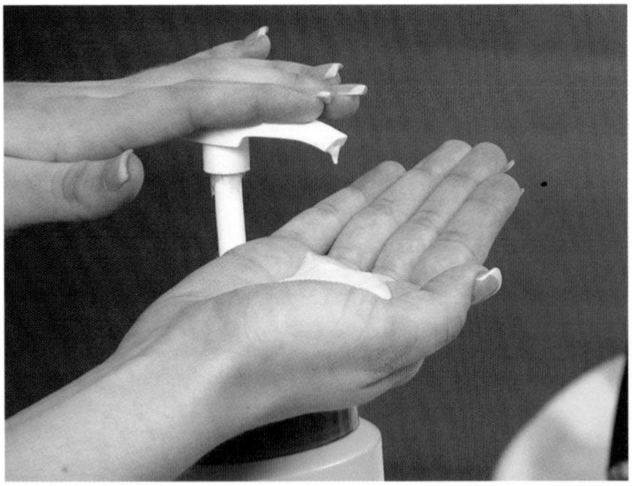

Figure 8.19 Dispense the shampoo into the palm of the hand. Gently rub both hands together to evenly distribute the shampoo through the hair. Shampoo that is applied to one area of the scalp is difficult to distribute evenly. Use the amount of shampoo recommended by the manufacturer. Do not use more than the recommended amount.

Figure 8.20 The shampoo is applied using effleurage massage (online video).

Online activity

You can see a video of the massage techniques online

Website

www.atthairdressing.com

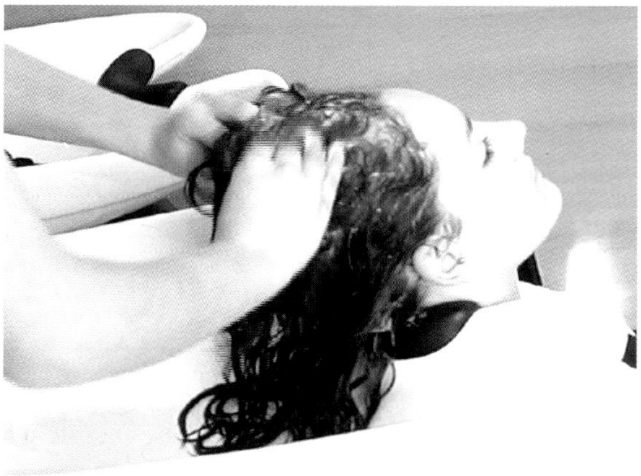

Figure 8.21 The second massage movement used during shampooing is rotary. Begin at the front hairline and work towards the ears. Repeat this action several times. Pay particular attention to the hairline of female clients as this is where residuals of make-up and face creams are found.

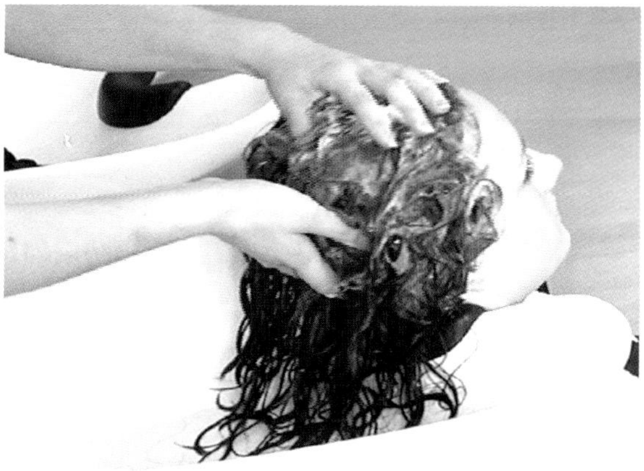

Figure 8.22 Then move the fingers from the front hairline over the crown and down towards the nape. Next move the hands over the sides of the head continuing the massage movement. Repeat this formation several times. Make sure that all of the scalp area is covered thoroughly. Pay attention to the nape area particularly when shampooing at a backwash basin. It may be necessary to repeat this process to remove a build up of products.

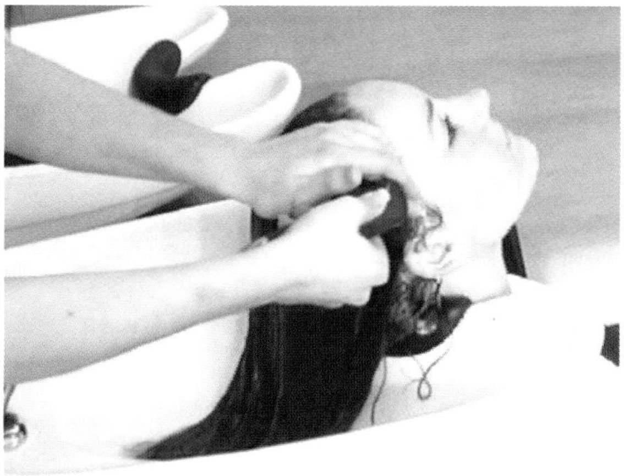

Figure 8.23 Rinse the hair thoroughly, so that it is completely free of shampoo. Start rinsing from the front hairline if using a backwash or from the nape of the neck if using a forward basin, and work through the rest of the head. Remove excess moisture with a towel and comb through.

Online activity 8.5

Drag into correct order

Key information

Dispense the shampoo into the palm of the hand. Gently rub both hands together to evenly distribute the shampoo through the hair.

Definition

Immiscible: Liquids that are incapable of mixing together.

Safety first

If a client's hair has poor porosity, and this is ignored, you may damage the hair further by applying chemicals, e.g. colour or tint.

Shampooing oily hair

If the hair is oily, apply the shampoo directly to dry hair. Oil and water are immiscible substances and the detergent of the shampoo is needed to emulsify the oil. It is recommended to use the effleurage technique of massage so that the scalp is not stimulated as this can produce more oil.

Rinse the hair thoroughly. Continue the process as with any other shampoo. This process can also be used to remove heavy hair products such as wax.

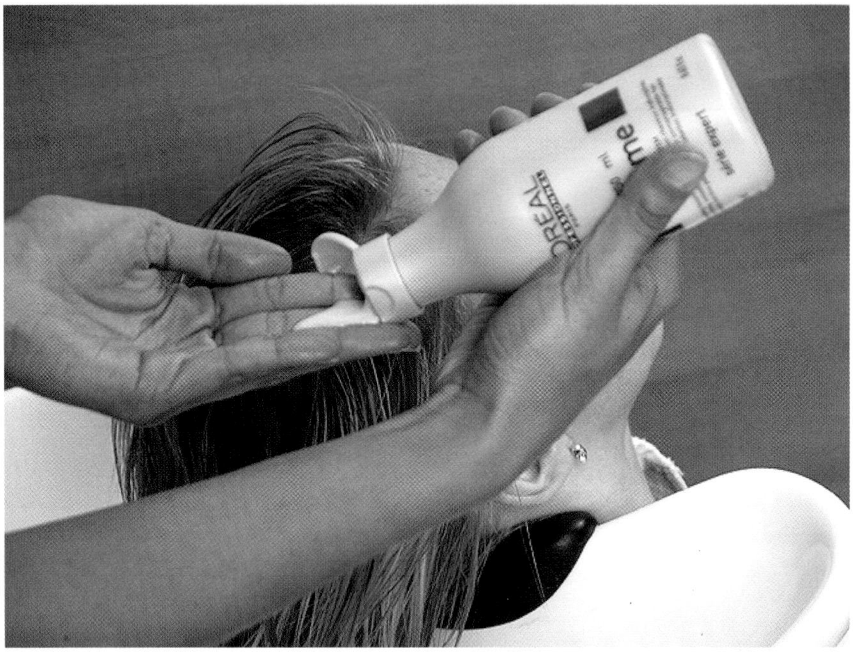

Figure 8.24 Applying shampoo to dry hair

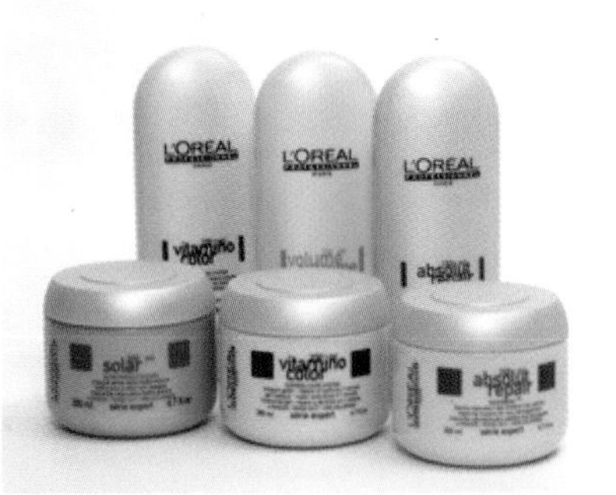

Figure 8.25 Selection of conditioners

8.3 Condition and treat the hair and scalp

It is essential to look after the client's hair so that it is kept in the best possible condition. If a client's hair has poor porosity, and this is ignored, you may damage the hair further by applying chemicals, e.g. colour or tint. Conditioners and conditioning treatments will improve the condition and allow the hair to be controlled effectively.

Types of conditioners

Conditioners work by closing the hair cuticle. This will make it easier to comb the hair through. The types of conditioner are:

- surface conditioners
- penetrating conditioners
- scalp treatments.

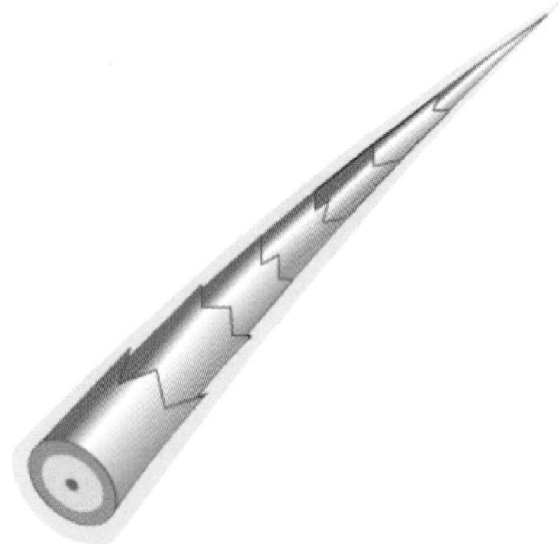

Figure 8.26 Conditioners coat the hair

Surface conditioners

These work on the surface layer of the hair, coating the hair shaft and filling any gaps in the cuticle layer that have been caused by previous treatments.

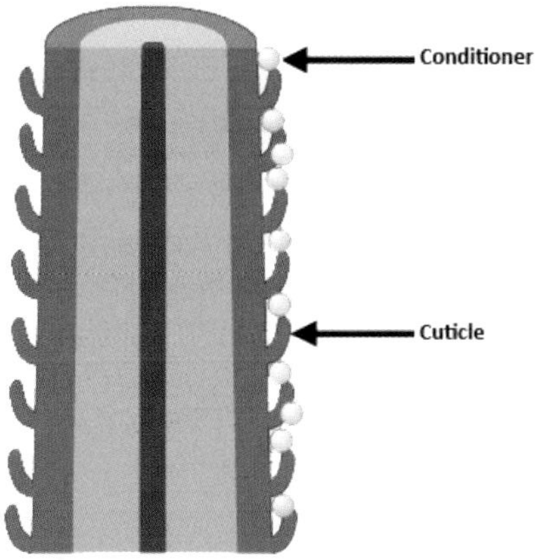

Figure 8.27 Surface conditioner

Penetrating conditioners

These conditioners penetrate the cuticle and help to repair damage by adding protein. As these conditioners add protein to the hair they are known as substantive products and will strengthen the hair structure.

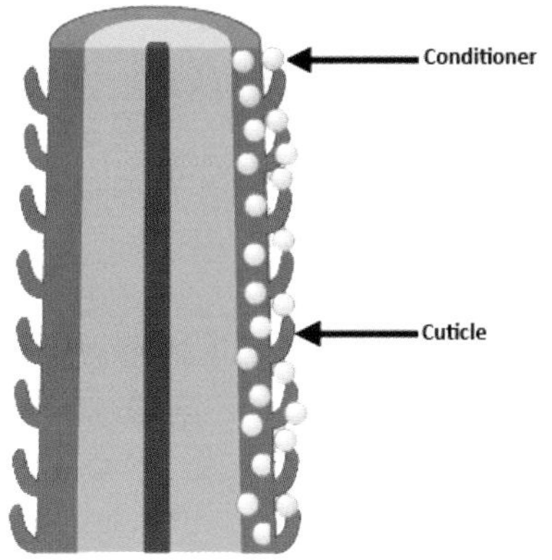

Figure 8.28 Penetrating conditioner

Scalp treatments

Scalp treatments can be used for dry or oily scalps. There are many products on the market to choose from.

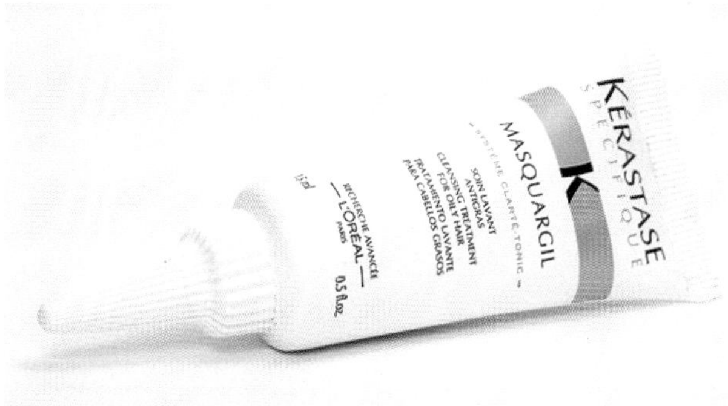

Figure 8.29 Example of a scalp treatment

Massage techniques

The following techniques for massaging are used when conditioning hair:

- effleurage
- petrissage.

Effleurage massage is a gentle, smooth, stroking movement using the palms of the hands. It is used more on long, dense hair to avoid tangling and ensure thorough cleaning.

Petrissage massage movements are performed using the pads of the fingers in slow, circular, kneading movements around the hairline and over the scalp. It is a firm massage which improves the circulation, relaxes the client and helps to break down any fatty adhesions to the scalp. If the hair is sparse be very careful to avoid 'pulling the hair'.

Definitions

Adhesions: Scar tissue.

Sparse: Not dense. Thin.

Online activity 8.6

Five in a row

Figure 8.30 Effleurage massage

Figure 8.31 Petrissage massage

Application of surface and penetrating conditioners

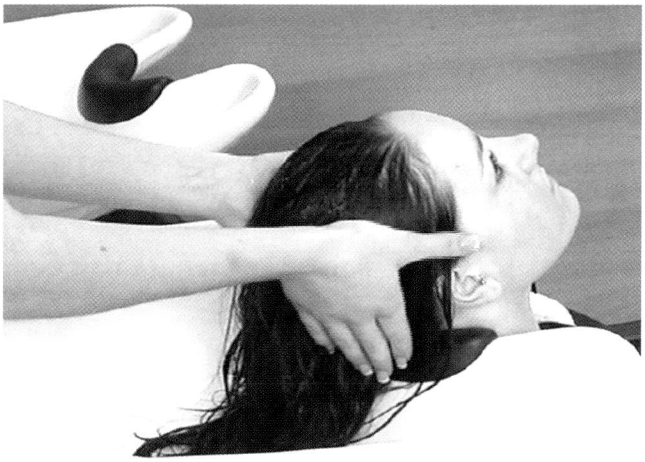

Figure 8.32 Most conditioners are applied at the basin after the hair has been shampooed and towel dried. The product is evenly distributed through the hair using the effleurage massage technique.

Figure 8.33 The product is then massaged through the hair and into the scalp using the petrissage technique.

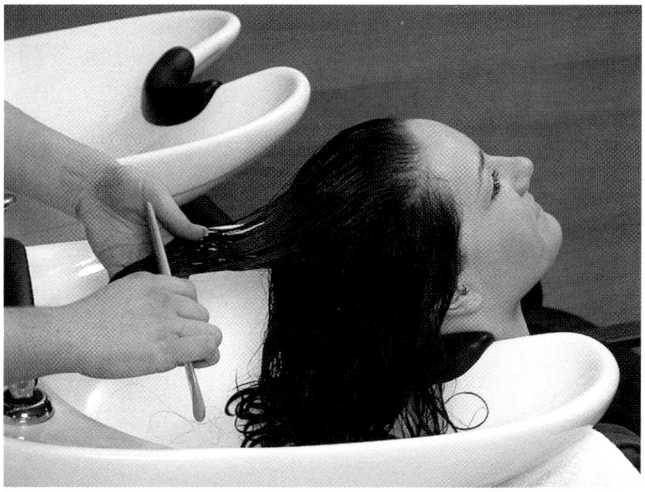

Figure 8.34 Comb through from ends to roots.

Figure 8.35 Surface conditioners are rinsed off straight away. Penetrating conditioners are left in the hair for the recommended time, which is approximately 5–10 minutes. Ensure all products have been rinsed out. Remove any excess moisture and comb the hair.

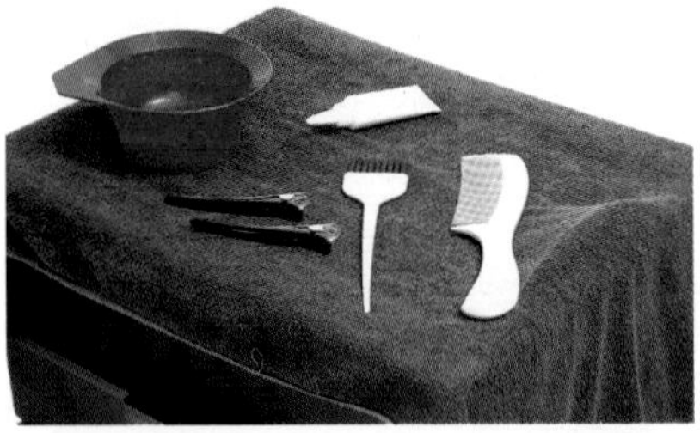

Figure 8.36 Equipment needed for scalp treatment

Preparing equipment for scalp treatment

Prepare the equipment and products before starting the treatment. It will save time.

For conditioning you will need the following equipment, tools and products:

- sterile large tooth comb
- tint brush
- bowl for the product
- clips
- scalp treatment product.

Key information

Prepare the equipment and products before starting the treatment as it will save time.

WWW Online activity 8.7

Correct boxes

Application of scalp treatment

Figure 8.37 Dispense the product into the bowl directly from the tube.

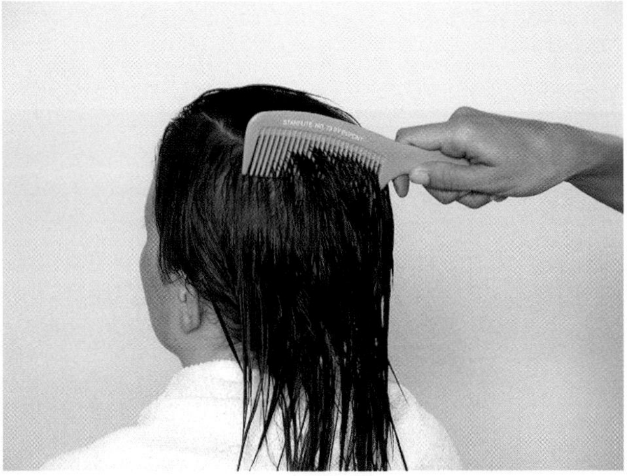

Figure 8.38 The hair is shampooed prior to applying a conditioning treatment. Comb the hair to remove any tangles.

Figure 8.39 Section the hair from forehead to nape. Section the hair from ear to ear over the crown.

Figure 8.40 Starting at the nape area of the back sections, sub-divide the larger section and apply the conditioner to the partings.

Figure 8.41 Repeat this process for all four sections, finishing at the front hairline.

Figure 8.42 Comb the product through the hair. For a dry scalp it is recommended to massage the hair for 10 minutes using the petrissage method. For an oily scalp you would not massage the scalp.

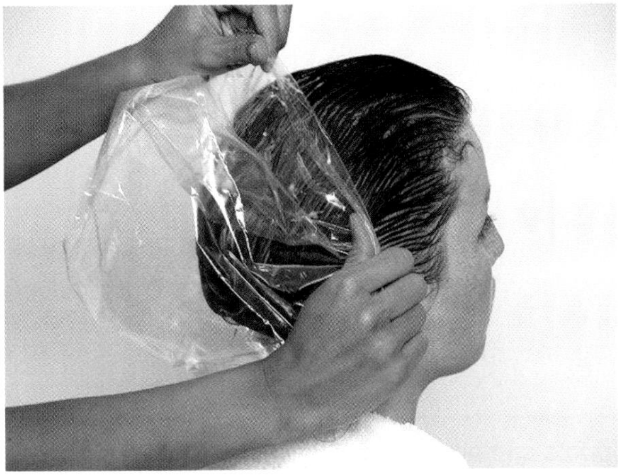

Figure 8.43 Place protective covering over the hair.

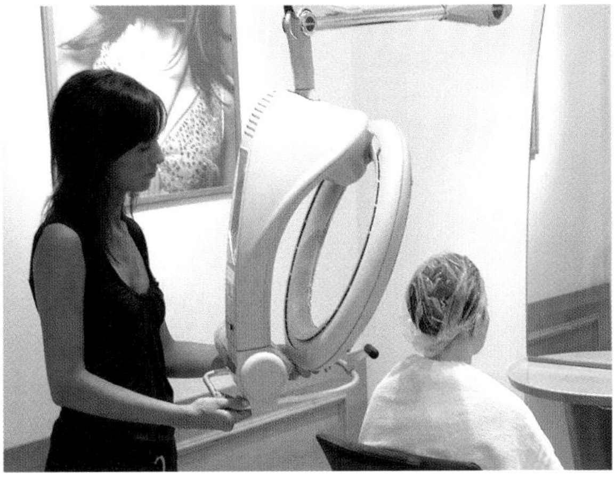

Figure 8.44 Apply heat if required for 5-10 minutes.

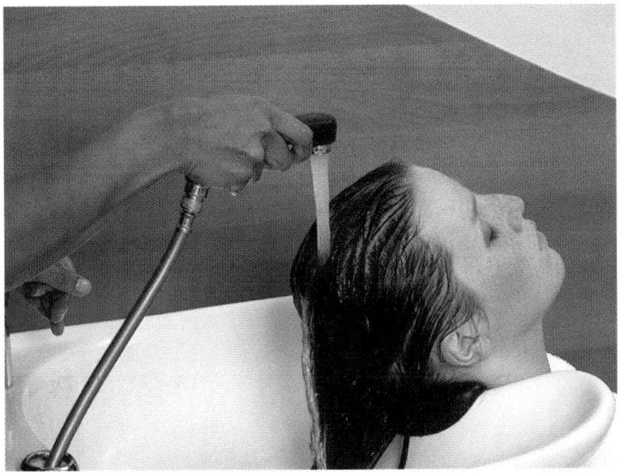

Figure 8.45 When rinsing the scalp check that the temperature of the water will not irritate the client's skin (particularly if it is sensitive). Remove excess moisture from the hair. Comb the hair through in preparation for the next service.

Online activity 8.8 WWW

Drag into correct order

Safety first

Always follow manufacturers' instructions.

Figure 8.46 Advise on use of products

8.4 Provide aftercare advice

An important part of this service is to give the client aftercare advice. This advice includes the use of products and showing the client the correct way to brush and comb their hair after shampooing, conditioning and treating.

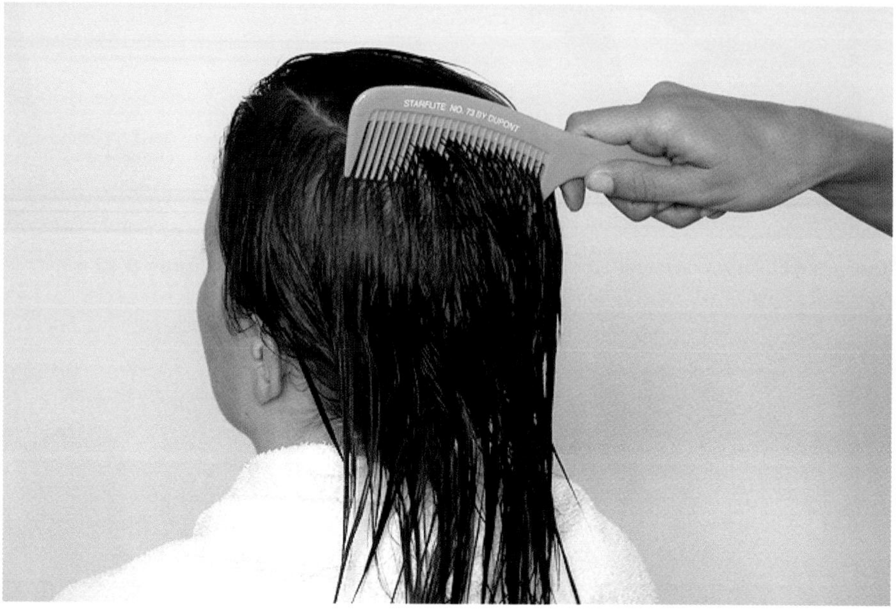

Figure 8.47 Advise client on how to comb their hair

Safety first

Explain when to use particular products, always following the manufacturer's instructions.

Products

Advise the client which products can be used at home. This should be based on the type and condition of the client's hair and scalp. Explain when to use particular products, always following the manufacturer's instructions. Refer to Chapter 6 for more information.

Figure 8.48 Advise the client on products for use at home

Use of brushes and combs

Explain to the client that it is advisable to use a large tooth comb when combing wet hair. They should comb through from ends to roots. It is not recommended to use a brush on wet hair as this may cause damage.

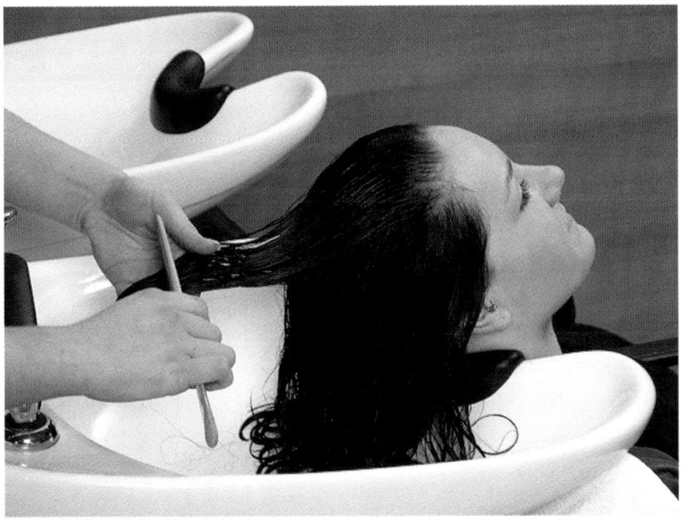

Figure 8.49 Comb from ends. . .

Figure 8.50 . . . to roots

Online activity 8.9 WWW

Round the board

WORKSHEETS

8.5 Worksheets

You can carry out the worksheets during your study of a chapter or unit, or at the end. An example is presented here and there are more online. If your college or company is registered with ATT Training, lots more are available. Write your answers directly in the book, but only if you own it of course – if it is a library or college book, use a separate piece of paper!

8.5.1 Condition of hair

What might cause different hair conditions? Complete this table by filling in the right hand column:

Table 8.4 Hair condition and causes

Hair condition	Main causes
Chemically damaged	
Heat damaged	
Environmentally damaged	
Product build up	

8.6 Assessment

Well done! If you have studied all the content of this unit you may be ready to test your knowledge.

Check out the 'Preparing for assessments' section in Chapter 1 if you have not already done so, and always remember:

- You can only do your best if you have. . .
  - studied hard
  - completed the activities
  - completed the worksheets
  - practised, practised, practised
  - and then revised!

Now carry out the online multiple-choice quiz

. . . and good luck in the final exam, which will be arranged by your tutor/assessor.

CHAPTER 9

Style and finish hair

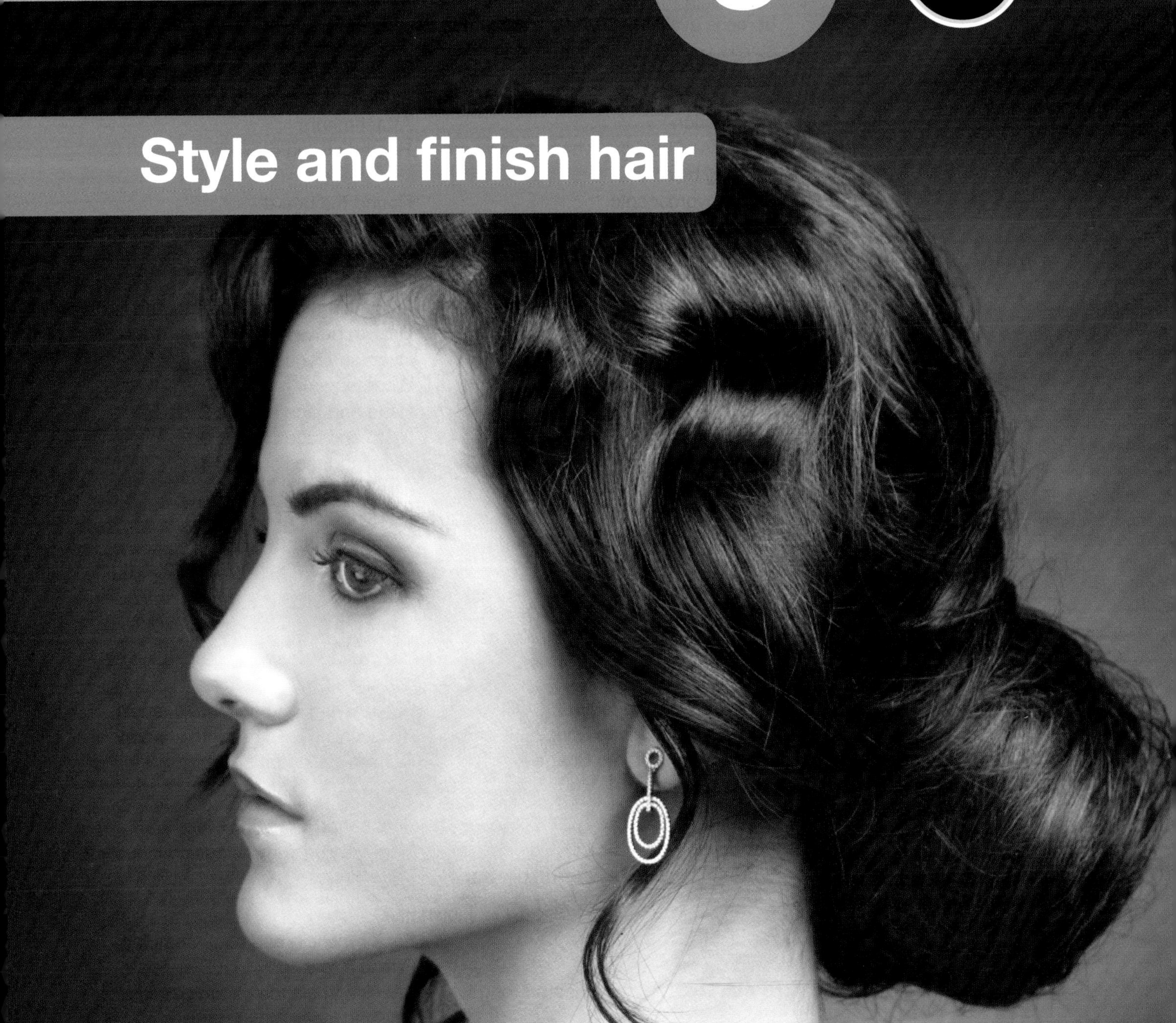

This chapter covers the NVQ/SVQ unit GH10, Style and finish hair and part of the VRQ unit 209, The art of dressing hair.

After every service the client will have their hair styled and finished. This unit covers the techniques of both blow-drying and finger-drying.

In this chapter you will learn about:

- maintaining effective and safe methods of working when styling and finishing hair
- blow-drying hair into shape
- finishing hair
- providing aftercare advice.

Website
www.atthairdressing.com

CHAPTER 9 STYLE AND FINISH HAIR: CONTENTS, SCREENS AND ACTIVITIES

Key:
Sections from the book are set in this colour
Screens available online are set in this colour
Online activity screens are set in this colour

Working safely

Introduction
Methods of working when styling and finishing hair
Hair is hygroscopic
Products used during styling and finishing
Select correct box
Mousses
Serums
Lotions
Creams
Gels
Heat protectors
Hairsprays
Five in a row
COSHH
Blow-drying tools and equipment
Brushes
Hand dryers
Attachments
Heated styling equipment
Round the board
Electricity at Work Regulations 1989
Consultation
Influencing factors - haircut and texture
Growth patterns
Head and face shapes 1
Wordsearch
Head and face shapes 2
Head and face shapes 3
Head and face shapes 4
Five in a row
Preparing client for styling
Comfort during styling
NVQ times for styling and finishing

Blow-dry hair

Introduction
Controlling styling tools
Blow-drying Hair into Shape 1
Blow-drying Hair into Shape 2
Round the board
Blow-drying hair into shape using a variety of brushes
Blow-drying long hair into shape 1
Blow-drying long hair into shape 2
Correct selection

Finger dry hair into shape

Introduction
Finger drying curly hair using diffuser 1
Finger drying curly hair using diffuser 2

Finish hair

Introduction
Finishing products
Electrical equipment - heated tongs
Hair straighteners
Back brushing and back combing
Five in a row
Checking balance of completed style
Finished looks

Provide aftercare advice

Introduction
Products and heated styling equipment
Worksheet – head and face shapes
Online multiple choice quiz
Worksheet – growth patterns
Worksheet – finish hair

9.1 Working safely

When styling hair, you will use many different products, tools and equipment. This section covers health and safety requirements necessary for their use and other areas necessary for styling including consultation and preparation. Chapter 2 covers health and safety working methods in more detail. Refer to this unit if needed.

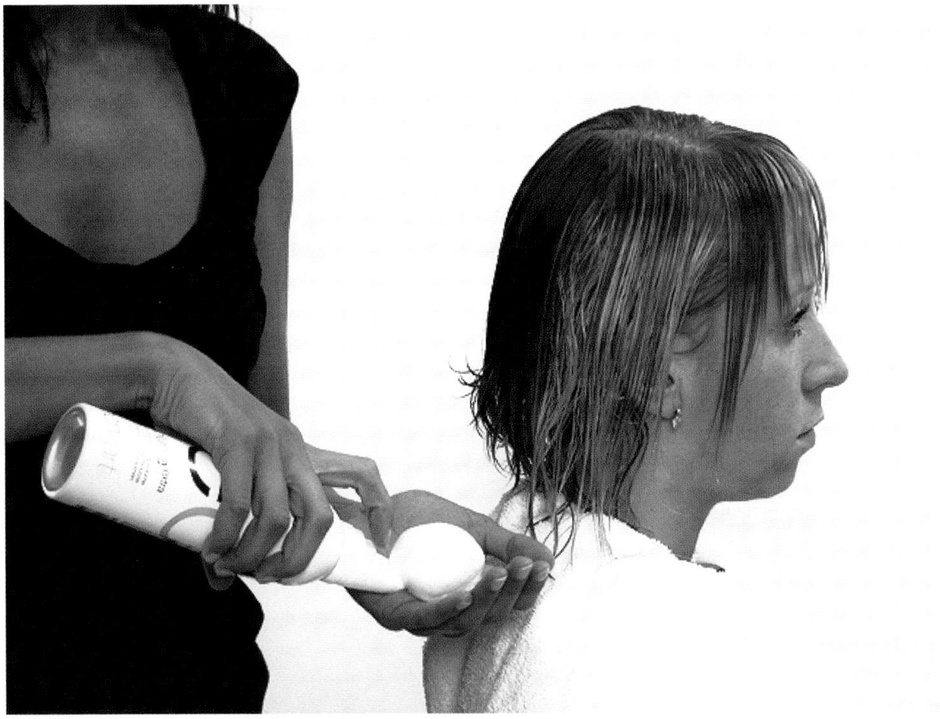

Figure 9.1 Styling requires you to work with products

Hair is hygroscopic

This means that it has the ability to absorb moisture.

Wet hair can be stretched nearly double its normal length. This is called elasticity. Wet hair in its stretched state is called the 'beta keratin'. When it is in the natural state (un-stretched), the hair is called the 'alpha keratin'. The reason why hair stretches is because the hydrogen bonds are broken down by water. It is these properties that allow us to alter the shape of hair. When heat is applied the hydrogen bonds can be re-formed into a new shape. The humidity in the air will affect the structure of the hair by making the hair feel damp. This will take the hair back to its natural state.

WWW

View the online video to learn more about the hair in its various states

WWW **Website**

www.atthairdressing.com

Definitions

Alpha keratin: Hair in its natural un-stretched state.

Beta keratin: The stretched (wet) state of hair.

Products used during styling and finishing

These include:

- mousses
- serums
- lotions
- creams
- gels
- heat protectors
- sprays.

To prevent wastage of products, only use the amount needed according to manufacturers' instructions.

Figure 9.2 A selection of products

Figure 9.3 A range of mousse products

WWW **Online activity 9.1**

Select correct box

Mousses

Mousses are available in different strengths. They are applied to wet hair with the hands and will hold the style in place and achieve a soft effect.

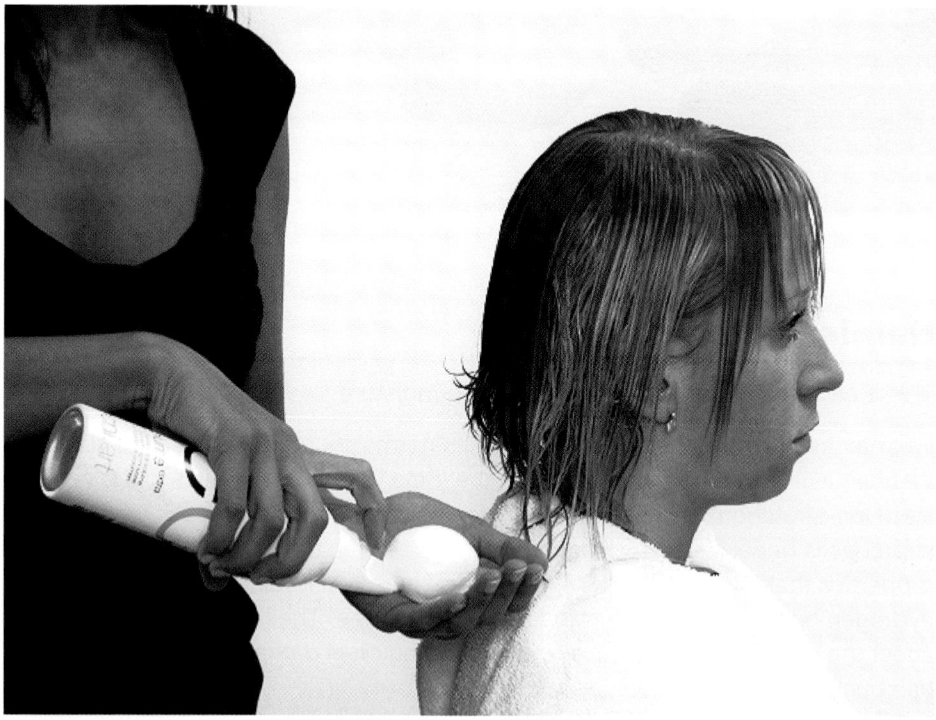

Figure 9.4 Mousse is applied to wet hair

Serums

Hair serum will make hair look shiny and in better condition. This product must be used sparingly as it is very concentrated and can make hair appear lank or greasy.

Figure 9.5 A range of serums

Figure 9.6 Use sparingly!

Lotions

Lotions are used on wet hair and are produced as a light cream or liquid. They help to maintain the style for longer.

Figure 9.7 Different types of lotion

Figure 9.8 Applying lotion

Creams

Creams can be used on wet or dry hair and should be used sparingly. They are used to give moisture to the hair and curl definition.

Figure 9.9 Creams

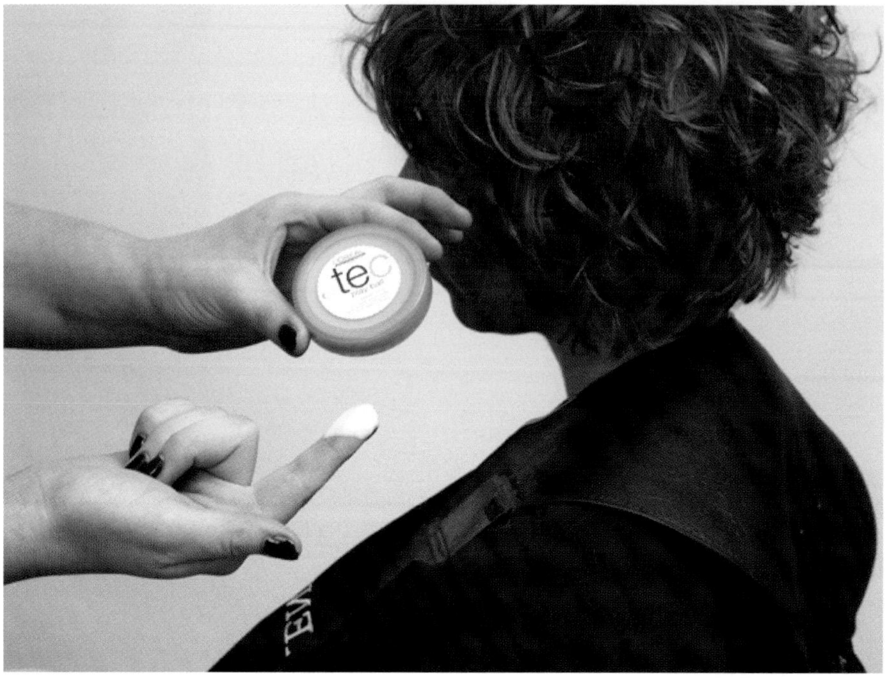

Figure 9.10 Applying cream

Gels

Gels are designed to be used on either wet or dry hair. They complement and give definition to the style.

Figure 9.11 Gels

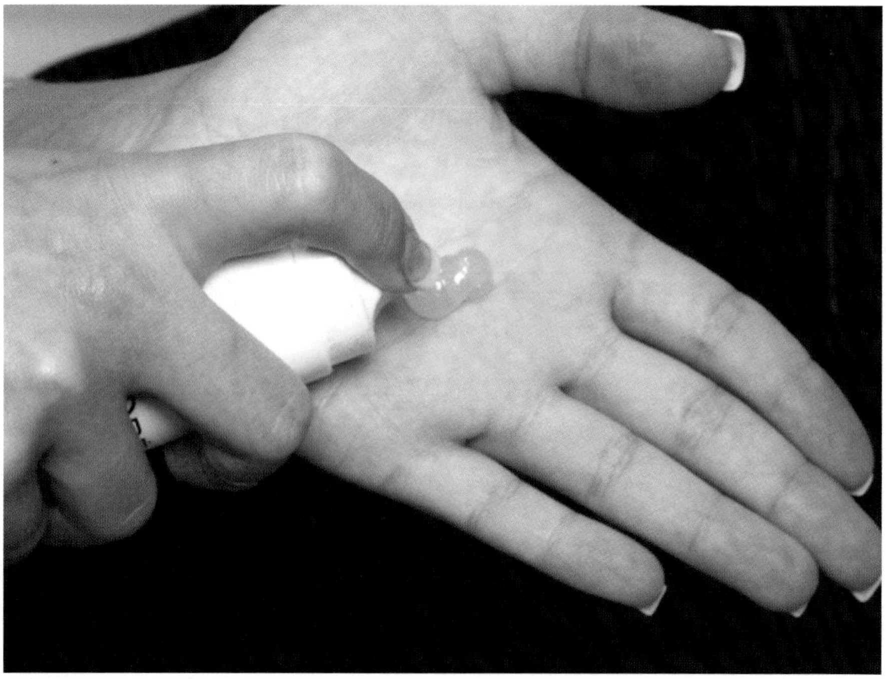

Figure 9.12 Applying gel

Heat protectors

These products protect the hair from damage caused by using heated styling equipment. When such equipment is used frequently, the hair structure can become damaged as the cuticle swells and raises. When heat protectors are applied, they form a shield around the hair which acts as a barrier and absorbs the heat.

Figure 9.13 Heat protectors

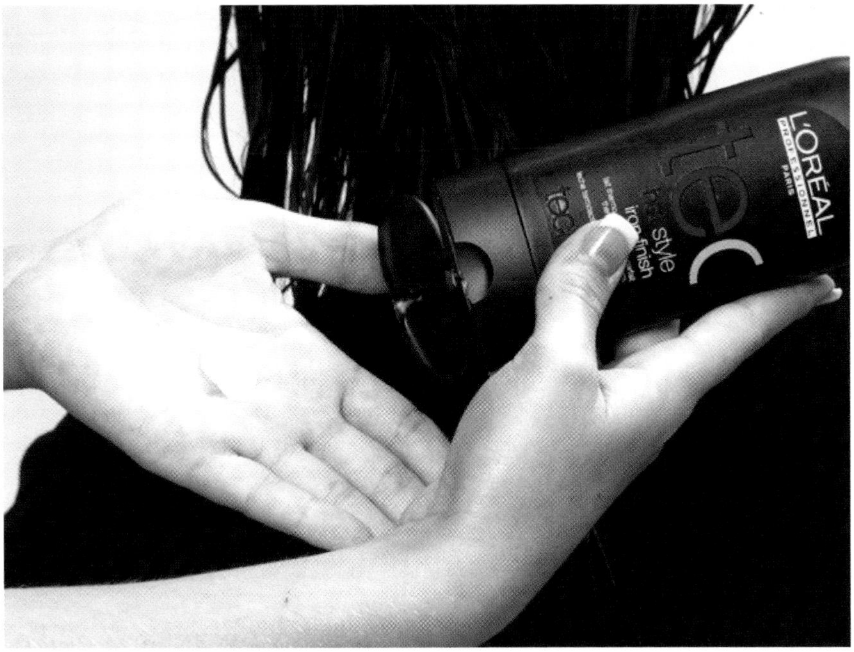

Figure 9.14 Applying heat protector

Hairsprays

Hairspray holds the hair in place and protects the hair from the weather and humidity. It comes in different strengths and it is easily removed from the hair by brushing or wetting as most hairsprays are water soluble. Application of hairspray should be done away from the client's face. This can be achieved by standing in front of your client when you are applying the product. It should be held at approximately 10-12 inches from the head.

Figure 9.15 Hairsprays

Figure 9.16 Spray 10-12 inches from the head

Online activity 9.2

Five in a row

Control of Substances Hazardous to Health Regulations 2002 (COSHH)

These are commonly called the COSHH regulations and they lay down the essential requirements for controlling exposure to hazardous substances and for protecting people who may be affected by them. A substance is considered to be hazardous if it can cause harm to the body. It only poses a risk if it is:

- inhaled (breathed in)
- ingested (swallowed)
- in contact with the skin
- absorbed through the skin
- injected into the body
- introduced into the body via cuts etc.

Safety first

For more information about the COSHH regulations refer to Chapter 2.

www

The associated learning screen for this part is interactive

Blow-drying tools and equipment

Tools and equipment used for blow-drying hair include:

- brushes
- hand dryers
- diffusers
- nozzles.

Figure 9.17 Range of blow-drying equipment

Key information

Keep all tools and equipment clean and sterilised at all times to minimise products from building up and causing sticky areas.

Keep all tools and equipment clean and sterilised at all times to minimise products from building up and causing sticky areas. As the tools and equipment are used, the hair may become attached to these areas and become damaged.

Brushes

It is essential to have different sized circular brushes so that you can produce appropriate sized curls according to the client's wishes. For longer hair, large circular brushes are used. Flat brushes are used to straighten hair.

Figure 9.18 Small circular brush

Figure 9.19 Large circular brush

Figure 9.20 Flat brush

Hand dryers

There are many different types of hand dryer. You should be able to change the temperature and speed. It will be used for long periods of time and so should be durable. The hand dryer should also be easy to use and lightweight.

Figure 9.21 Hand dryer

Attachments

Diffusers and nozzles can be attached to the hand dryer. The diffuser is attached to the end of the hand dryer. When switched on this disperses air evenly to the hair. It enables the hair to be dried gently and is suitable for creating curls that are soft on all lengths. The nozzle enables the air from the hand dryer to be distributed to one particular area. It is suitable for blow-drying the hair into shape.

Figure 9.22 Hand dryer with attachments

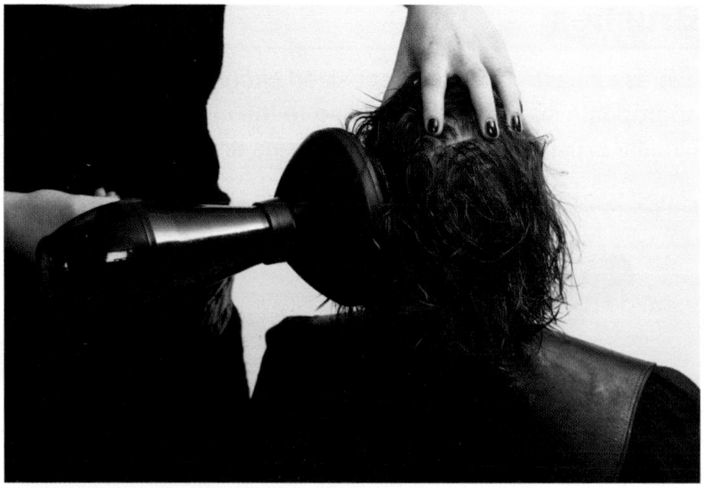

Figure 9.23 A diffuser distributes air evenly

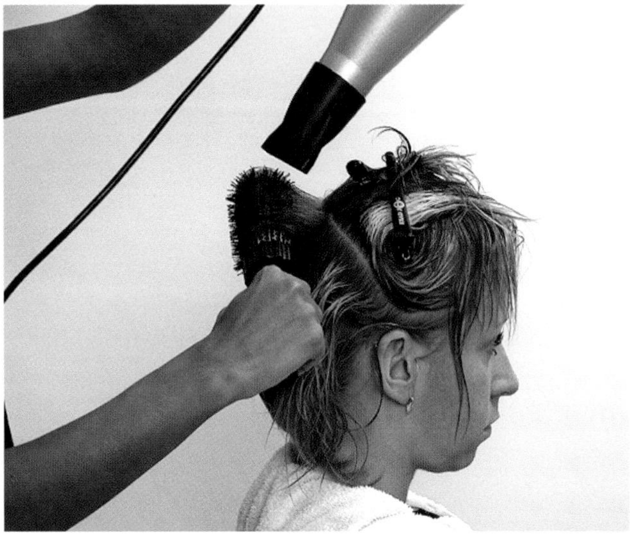

Figure 9.24 A nozzle distributes air to a particular area

Heated styling equipment

These include hair straighteners and curling tongs. The temperature of heated styling equipment should be checked throughout the service and never held on the hair for longer than necessary. Do not hold too close to the client's scalp. This may result in burning the client.

Figure 9.25 Straighteners

Figure 9.26 Curling tongs

Online activity 9.3 WWW

Round the board

Electricity at Work Regulations 1989

These regulations state that you must:

- Always check electrical equipment before using it. Look for loose wires and that the plug is not cracked or damaged in any way. Check that the cord is not frayed or cracked.
- Never use electrical equipment when your hands are wet.
- Electrical equipment should be maintained regularly and checked by a suitably qualified person. Once checked the equipment should have a certificate or label acknowledging it.
- Faulty electrical equipment in the workplace must be removed, labelled as faulty and reported to the relevant person.

Figure 9.27 Check equipment before using

Consultation

Before any service begins the hairdresser must determine the client's expectations. The consultation is used to ensure the client's wishes are interpreted accurately and the desired look achieved. It is essential to be factual, honest, tactful, sincere, direct and clear. The consultation will give the opportunity to decide on products, the service that is carried out and the equipment that is used.

Definition

Tactful: To show skills in sensing the correct way to deal with others.

Figure 9.28 Find out the client's expectations

Growth patterns

You must understand growth patterns to see which way the hair naturally falls. Hair growth patterns include:

Cowlick – A cowlick is usually found on the front hairline across the forehead. The roots of the hair grow backwards and the mid-lengths and ends of the hair are forwards, causing the hair to spring up.

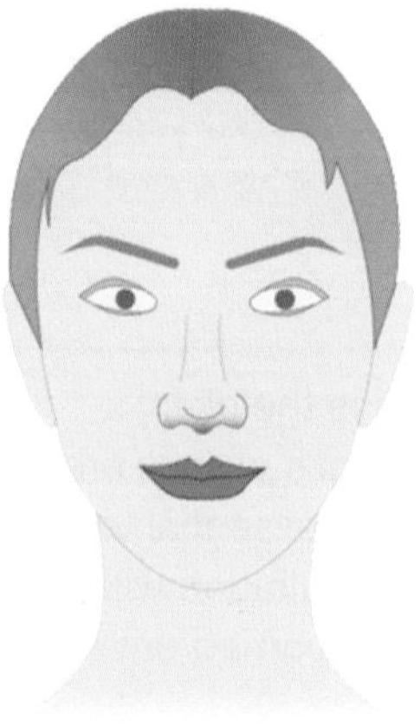

Figure 9.29 Cowlick

Crowns – A crown is a circular movement of the hair (whorl) positioned towards the back, on top of the head. It is important to identify the crown area because it can be a very strong movement or in some cases a double crown or two crowns are present, moving in different directions. This may restrict styling.

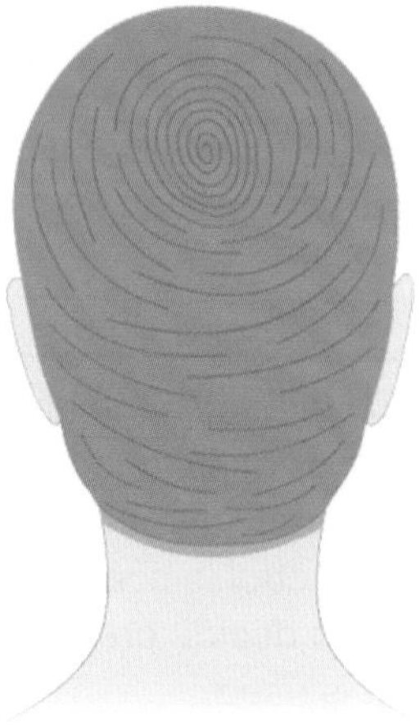

Figure 9.30 Crown

Inward and upward nape – This describes the movement of the hair in the nape area which is below the occipital bone. Some hair grows from the outside of the hairline into the middle and in some cases the hair grows from the middle of the nape area towards the hairline. In extreme cases the hair grows and lies in one direction only.

Natural partings – A natural parting is where the hair falls in a dividing line. It can be in the centre of the front sections, to the left or to the right. It is advisable to work with a natural parting and adapt any style. It is difficult to maintain a style that goes against a natural parting.

Widow's peak – A widow's peak is a very strong centre forward growth on the front hairline.

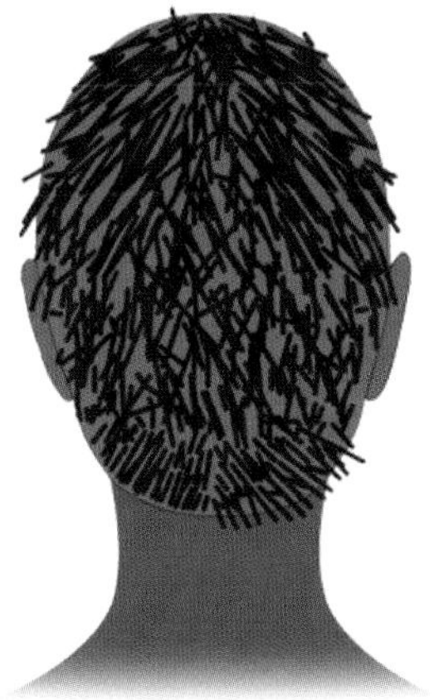

Figure 9.31 Inward and upward nape

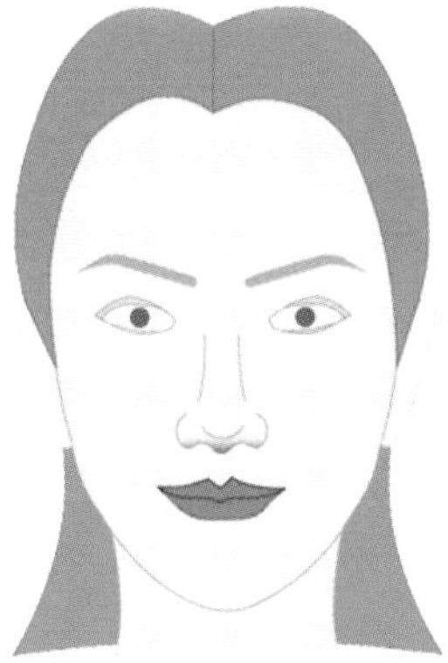

Figure 9.32 Natural parting

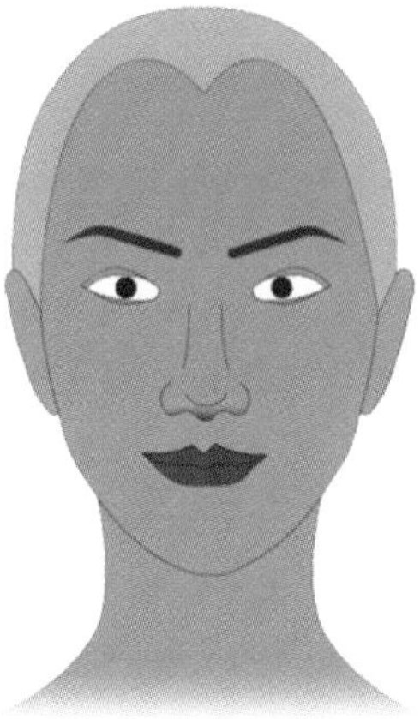

Figure 9.33 Widow's peak

Head and face shapes

The client may have the following head or face shape:

- oval
- round
- long
- square
- heart
- pear.

The oval shaped face is considered to be the perfect shape that suits any style. However, people have differing features and it is therefore important to choose the hairstyle to suit both features and face shape.

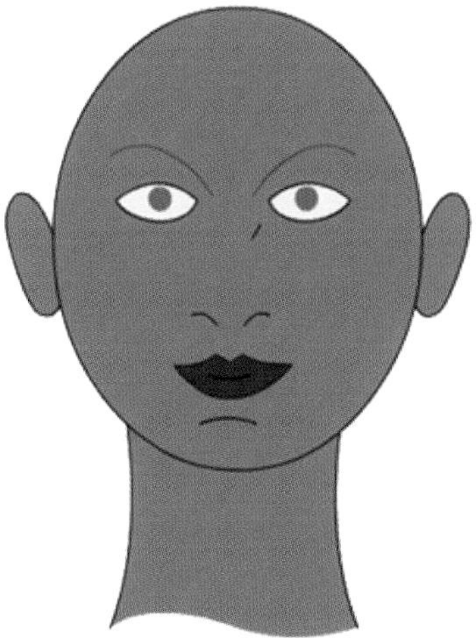

Figure 9.34 An example of a round face

Online activity 9.4 WWW

Wordsearch

If your client has a round face, a hairstyle will be needed that is flat at the sides and high on the top. This will enhance the client's features.

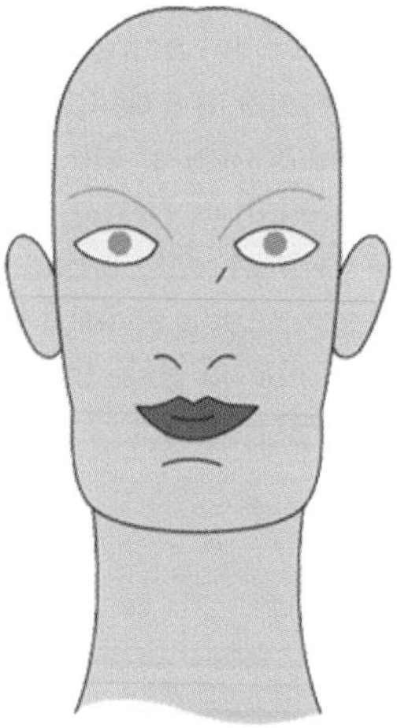

Figure 9.35 An example of a narrow or long face

If the client has a narrow or long face, the hairstyle needs to be fuller at the sides and flatter on top.

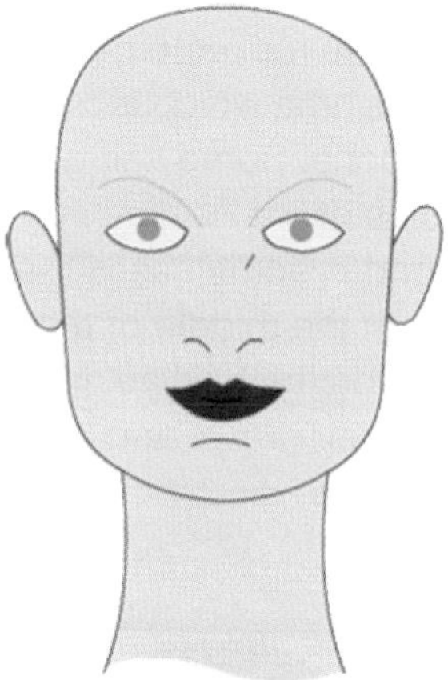

Figure 9.36 An example of a square shaped face

If a client has a square or angular jawline, the hairstyle will need to be softer in style and covering part of that area. This will flatten the face.

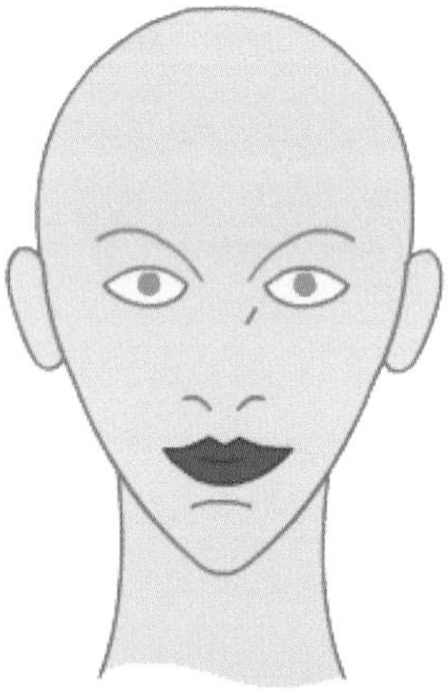

Figure 9.37 An example of a heart shaped face

A client with a heart shaped face will usually be very wide around the eyes and cheek-bones. They may also have a very wide forehead. A fringe would help to narrow the forehead and also hair will need to be brought onto the face to create more fullness between the jaw and the bottom of the ear.

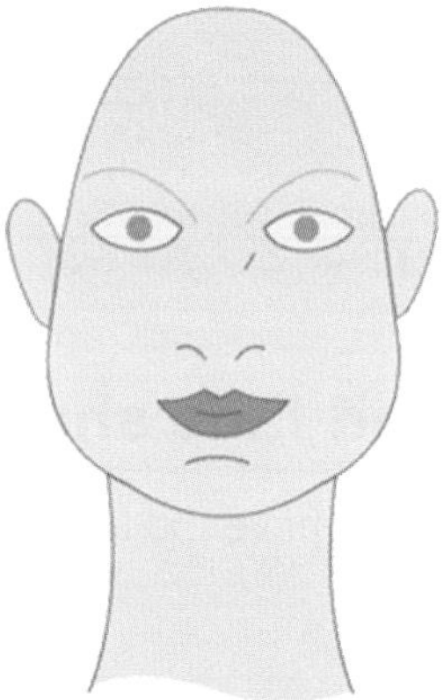

Figure 9.38 An example of a pear shaped face

If a client has a pear shaped face, the hairstyle will have to be flat around the jawline but have lots of volume and fullness around the temples. This will narrow the appearance of the face.

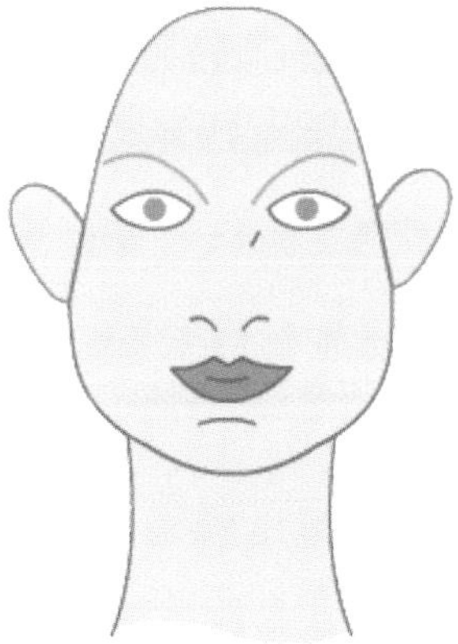

Figure 9.39 Large ears

Large ears that protrude need to be covered for a flattering effect.

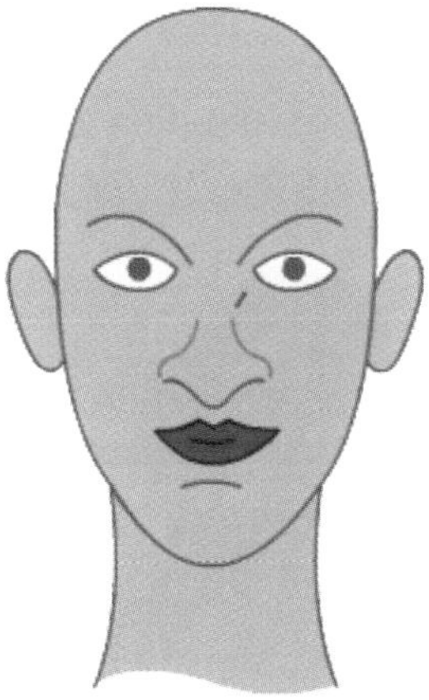

Figure 9.40 Large nose

If the client has a big nose or broken nose a centre parting will exaggerate this. Choose an asymmetric style. This will be more flattering.

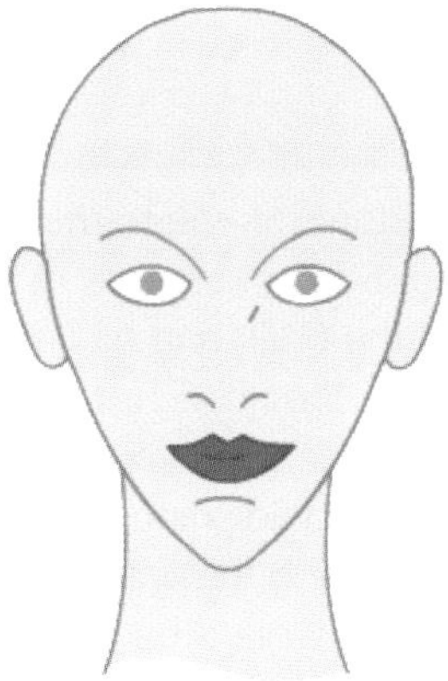

Figure 9.41 High forehead

A fringe will achieve the best effect for a client with a high forehead or receding hairline.

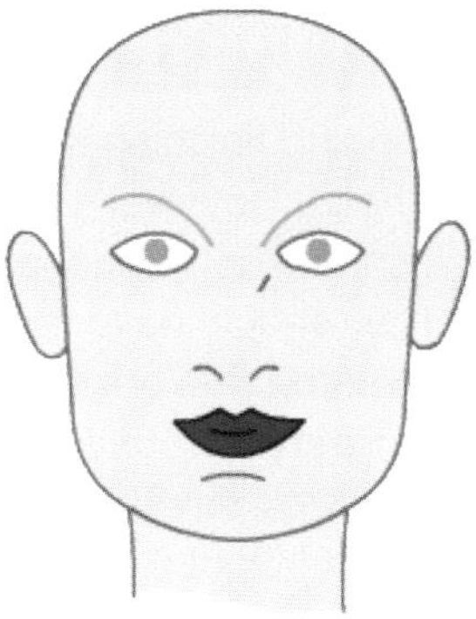

Figure 9.42 Short neck

A short, stocky neck requires a softer hairstyle which is more flattering to the client.

Online activity 9.5 WWW

Five in a row

Preparing client for styling

Assist the client to put on a suitable sized gown to protect his or her clothing while in the salon. After the hair is shampooed, it is combed through to detangle.

Figure 9.43 Gown the client to protect their clothing

Comfort during styling

Whilst styling and finishing the client's hair, it is important for you to move around the client's head. However, the client's comfort should be considered at all times. Their back should be positioned right to the back of the chair and as flat as possible. They should have both feet on the footrest or the floor. Not only will this be a more comfortable position for the client but it also enables you to create a balanced hairstyle. Your own comfort during styling and finishing should be considered as well. Check your posture is correct, ensuring that your client's seat is at the correct height for you to work. Ensure that your work area is tidy and free from clutter.

Key information

The client's comfort should be considered at all times.

Figure 9.44 Incorrect posture

Figure 9.45 Correct posture

Suggested times for styling and finishing

Commercially viable times for blow-drying and finishing are as follows:

Table 9.1 Suggested service times

Length of hair	Time
Above shoulders	35 minutes
Below shoulders	45 minutes

9.2 Blow-dry hair

The blow-drying technique is performed using a hand-held dryer with an attached nozzle. Wet hair is then dried into shape. The consultation will allow you to agree a style with the client. Check the client is happy with the style you are creating before and during the service. Ensure the hair does not dry out naturally as this will stop you from achieving the desired look that is created through drying.

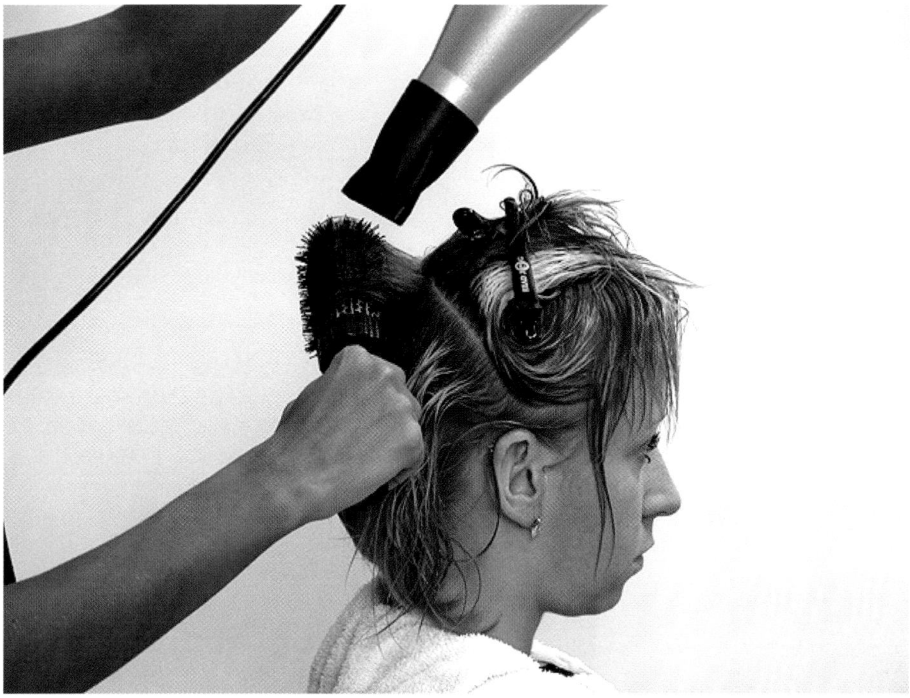

Figure 9.46 Always be gentle

Controlling styling tools

When using any brush, it is important to be gentle otherwise the hair could become tangled or damaged. This is also uncomfortable for the client. An even tension should be kept at all times to avoid overstretching the hair. When drying, the angle of the brush determines how much root movement (lift or bounce) is achieved. Long hair will not allow much root lift because of the length and weight of the hair.

Definition

Root lift: Creating volume at the root.

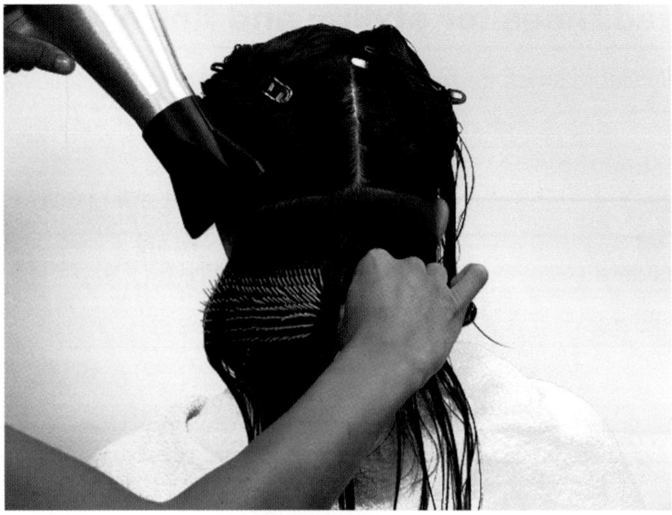

Figure 9.47 There will be little root lift with long hair

Blow-drying hair into shape

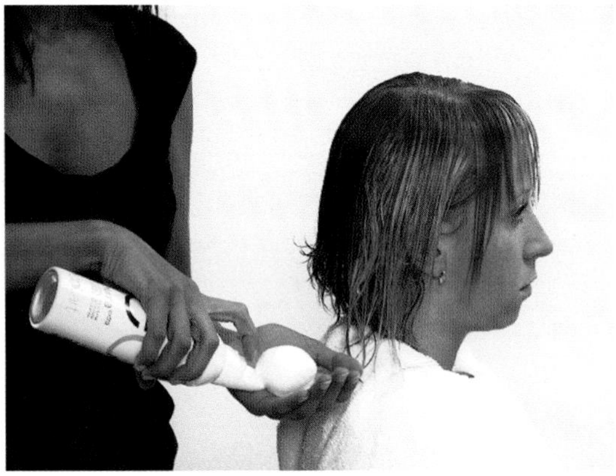

Figure 9.48 Apply products suitable for the client's hair type. Section the hair before drying.

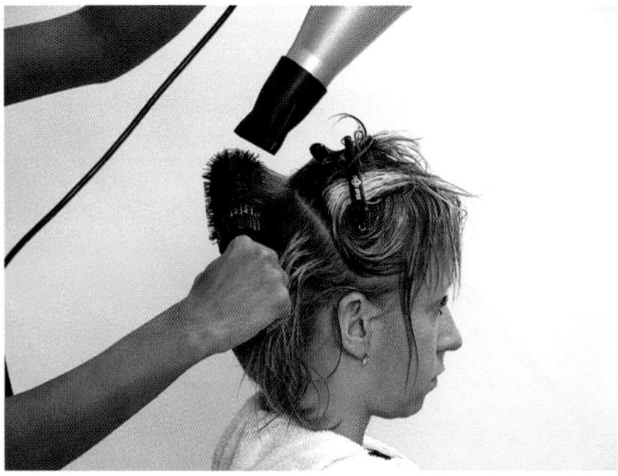

Figure 9.49 Starting at the nape area, dry the hair by curling around the brush. Use a small, medium or large circular brush for the required curl strength. When drying curly or long hair into shape on a client, the position of the head is very important. When working at the nape area, the head has to be angled forward for efficient operation.

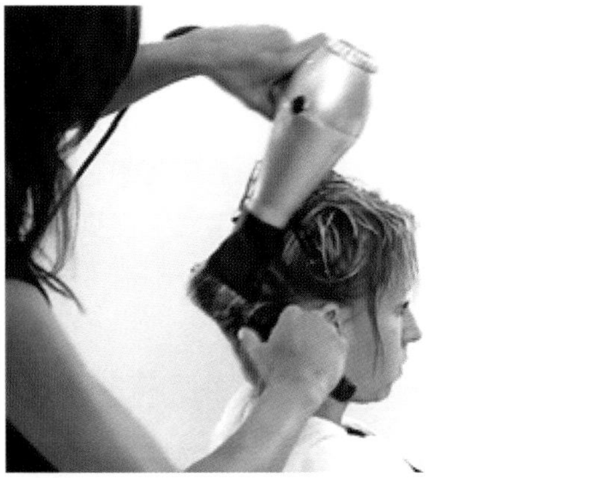

Figure 9.50 When placing the hand dryer over the hair keep the nozzle of the hand dryer moving to prevent the hair and scalp being burnt. The direction of the air flow from the hand dryer must be directed along the hair shaft from roots to ends and in the same direction as the brush strokes. This will ensure an even and smoother finish.

Figure 9.51 Work methodically through each section ensuring root lift and smoothness of curl formation until the hair is dry.

Online activity 9.6 WWW

Round the board

WWW **Website**

www.atthairdressing.com

Blow-drying hair into shape using a variety of brushes

Figure 9.52 Section the hair after application of product. Starting at the nape area, dry the hair by curling the hair around the brush. Use a small, medium or large spiral brush for the required curl strength (online video).

Figure 9.53 Work methodically through each section (online video).

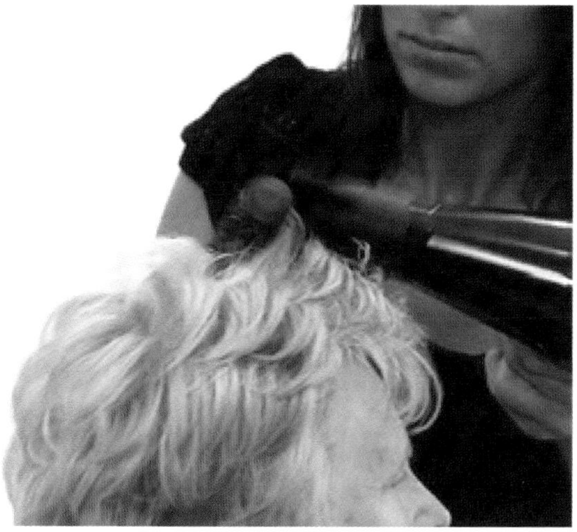

Figure 9.54 Ensure root lift and smoothness of curl formation until the hair is dry (online video).

Blow-drying long hair into shape

Figure 9.55 After applying a suitable product, section the hair and secure the hair not to be dried at this time with clips.

Figure 9.56 To achieve a smooth effect a flat or a very large circular brush can be used. Create neat sections and dry the hair from roots to ends ensuring each section is thoroughly dry before going on to the next section.

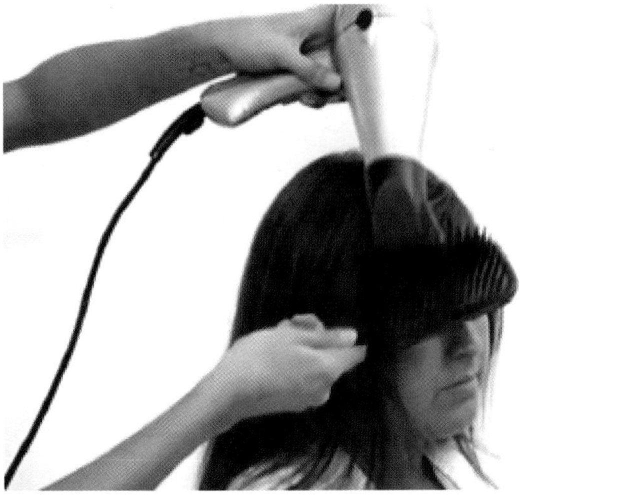

Figure 9.57 As the hairdresser works up the head in sections, the head will need to be altered to a more upright position. This will assist the hairdresser.

WWW **Online activity 9.7**

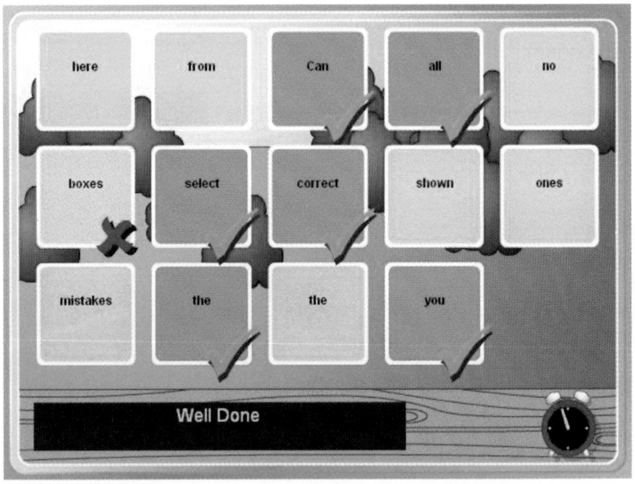

Correct selection

9.3 Finger-dry hair into shape

This technique involves using manual dexterity to direct the hair into the required style. The consultation will allow you to agree on a style with the client. Check the client is happy with the style you are creating before and during the service. Ensure the hair is kept damp during styling because if the hair dries out you will not be able to achieve the desired look.

Definition

Dexterity: To perform tasks with the hands, using skill.

Finger-drying curly hair using diffuser

Figure 9.58 Apply product to damp hair following the manufacturer's instructions. You may need to ask the client to lean her head back depending on the length of her hair. Starting in the nape of the neck, support the head with the fingers.

Figure 9.59 The diffuser on the hand held dryer is used to dry the hair into curls using circular movements.

Figure 9.60 The fingers direct the hair, creating volume and curl for the desired look.

9.4 Finish hair

Key information

If the hair is not COMPLETELY dry it will return to its natural state and so the style you wish to create will not be possible.

This section looks at the techniques used to finish hair styles. The use of heated styling equipment to aid finishing hair is included as is using back combing and back brushing techniques. Ensure that, before finishing the hair, it is completely dry. If not the hair will return to its natural state and so the style you wish to create will not be possible.

Finishing products

Before and after finishing hair, products can be applied. These include hairsprays, serums, gels and creams. Heat protectors are used beforehand to protect the hair from heated styling equipment.

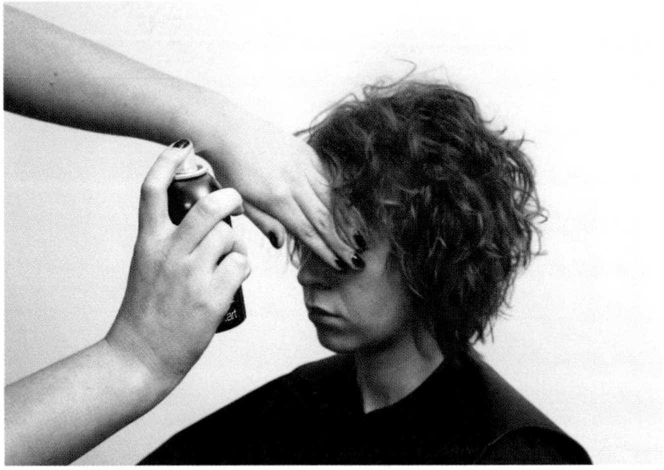

Figure 9.61 Applying hairspray when style is complete

Safety first

Never place heated tongs too close to the scalp as they may burn the client.

Electrical equipment – heated tongs

Heated tongs are used to give the hair curl. To achieve a spiral look, wind the hair around the tongs from roots to ends. Starting at the ends of the hair, wind towards the roots to give a conventional curl. Never place them too close to the scalp as this may burn the client.

Figure 9.62 Creating a spiral curl (online video)

Figure 9.63 Creating a conventional curl (online video)

Hair straighteners

Straighteners will straighten hair. Smooth the hair from roots to ends, starting from the nape and working towards the front of the head, incorporating all sections of the hair. As with heated tongs, never place them too close to the scalp as this may burn the client.

Safety first

As with heated tongs, never place straighteners too close to the scalp as this may burn the client.

Figure 9.64 Smooth hair from root to ends

Back brushing and back combing

To add height to the hair, it can be back combed or back brushed. Back brushing achieves a softer effect but will 'fluff' the hair with more bounce. Back combing achieves a stiffer style. Take a section of hair and pull the comb through it towards the roots. Apply hairspray as needed.

Figure 9.65 Back brushing achieves a softer effect

Figure 9.66 Back combing creates a stiffer style

Online activity 9.8

Five in a row

Checking balance of completed style

Check the balance of the hairstyle, using the front mirror to ensure that the profile shape of the hairstyle and the finish is appealing to the client and reinforce this by confirming with the client. Use a back mirror from behind, angling the position so both you and the client can see the finished result from the back.

Figure 9.67 Check the balance

Figure 9.68 Use a back mirror to show your client the finished result

Key information

Ensure the client is aware that if the hair becomes damp through weather conditions, it is likely to drop or revert back to its natural state.

Key information

Throughout the service you must explain to the client what you are doing. Do this fully and accurately, repeating yourself if needed.

9.5 Provide aftercare advice

An important part of this service is to give the client aftercare advice. The client should be able to recreate the look that you have given them. Ensure the client is aware that if the hair becomes damp through weather conditions, it is likely to drop or revert back to its natural state.

The client's lifestyle must be taken into consideration when creating a style that the client can maintain. For example an important factor for some would be a style that can be managed with minimum effort due to career and home life demands. Throughout the service you must explain to the client what you are doing. Do this fully and accurately, repeating yourself if needed.

Products and heated styling equipment

When explaining to the client the use of heated styling equipment, take care giving health and safety advice. Continual use will damage the hair. Therefore regular conditioning and using heat protectors are advisable.

Figure 9.69 Give health and safety instructions for using heated styling equipment

Advise the client which products can be used at home. This should be based on the factors that influence the service. Refer to Chapter 6 for more information.

WORKSHEETS

9.6 Worksheets

You can carry out the worksheets during your study of a chapter or unit, or at the end. An example is presented here and there are more online. If your college or company is registered with ATT Training, lots more are available. Write your answers directly in the book, but only if you own it of course – if it is a library or college book, use a separate piece of paper!

9.6.1 Growth patterns

The natural hair-fall and the hair growth patterns are particularly important for you to be aware of before starting any haircut. Some growth patterns may prevent you from cutting the hair in a particular style.

Below are definitions of five growth patterns. Label each one with the title that you think best matches the definition.

A circular movement of hair (whorl) positioned towards the back, on the top of the head. It is important to identify the crown area because it can be a very strong movement or in some cases a double crown or two crowns are present, moving in different directions. May restrict styling.

A very strong centre forward growth on the front hairline.

The hair falls in a dividing line. It can be in the centre of the front sections, to the left or to the right. It is advisable to work with a natural parting and adapt any style. It is difficult to maintain a style that goes against a natural parting.

This is usually found on the front hairline across the forehead. The roots of the hair grow backwards and the mid-lengths and points of the hair are forward, causing the hair to spring up. It is difficult to control when cut into a fringe.

This describes the movement of the hair in the nape area which is below the occipital bone. Some hair grows from the outside of the hairline into the middle and in some cases the hair grows from the middle of the nape area towards the hairline. In extreme cases the hair grows and lies in one direction only.

9.7 Assessment

Well done! If you have studied all the content of this unit you may be ready to test your knowledge.

Check out the 'Preparing for assessments' section in Chapter 1 if you have not already done so, and always remember:

- You can only do your best if you have. . .
  - studied hard
  - completed the activities
  - completed the worksheets
  - practised, practised, practised
  - and then revised!

Now carry out the online multiple-choice quiz

. . . and good luck in the final exam, which will be arranged by your tutor/assessor.

CHAPTER 10

Set and dress hair

This chapter covers the NVQ/SVQ unit GH11, Set and dress hair and part of the VRQ unit 209, The art of dressing hair.

This chapter focuses on setting and dressing techniques to creative a variety of effects. Setting techniques are important to master at this stage as they can be used to produce many different creative styles and so will help you progress within the hairdressing industry. You will be using many different tools, equipment and products so using them all safely is essential.

In this chapter you will learn about:

- maintaining effective and safe methods of working when setting and dressing hair
- setting hair
- dressing hair
- providing aftercare advice.

Website
www.atthairdressing.com

CHAPTER 10 SET AND DRESS HAIR: CONTENTS, SCREENS AND ACTIVITIES

Key:
Sections from the book are set in this colour
Screens available online are set in this colour
Online activity screens are set in this colour

Working safely

Introduction
Safe methods of working when setting and dressing hair
Round the board
Hygroscopic
Products used during setting and dressing
Scrambled Words
Tools and equipment
COSHH
Rollers
Pins
Combs
Brushes
Drag the pictures
Heated equipment
Drying hair using hood dryer
Electricity at Work Regulations
Consultation
Influencing factors - haircut and texture
The occasion
Growth patterns
Head and face shapes 1
Wordsearch
Head and face shapes 2
Head and face shapes 3
Head and face shapes 4
Five in a row
Preparing clients for setting
Comfort during setting
Suggested NVQ times for setting and dressing

Set hair

Introduction
Products used during setting
Setting lotions
Round the board
Mousses
Gels
Creams
Wet setting techniques
Pin curling
Roller setting 1
Roller setting 2
Drag into correct order
Considerations
Brickwork
Directional wind
Correct selection
Testing for dry hair
Spiral curling 1
Spiral curling 2
Spiral curling 3
Round the board
Dry setting techniques

Dress hair

Introduction
Products used during dressing
Check it
Hairsprays
Wax
Serums
Brushing set hair into style
Back brushing and back combing
Roll
Dressing spiral set
Electrical equipment
Checking balance of completed style
Five in a row

Provide aftercare advice

Introduction
Removal of hairstyle
Products and heated styling equipment
Worksheet – hygroscopic
Worksheet – tools and equipment
Worksheet – heated equipment
Worksheet – the occasion
Online multiple choice quiz

10.1 Working safely

Many of the tools and equipment used for setting and dressing hair will come in lots of different sizes. It is important to note here that the choice of tool or equipment will depend on the style that the customer wishes to have. Always remember health and safety issues for your client and yourself when styling hair. Chapter 2 covers health and safety working methods in more detail. Refer to this unit if needed.

Online activity 10.1 WWW

Round the board

Hair is hygroscopic

This means that it has the ability to absorb moisture. Wet hair can be stretched nearly double its normal length. This is called elasticity. Wet hair in its stretched state is called the 'beta keratin'. When it is in the natural state (un-stretched), the hair is called the 'alpha keratin'. The reason why hair stretches is because the hydrogen bonds are broken down by water. It is these properties that allow us to alter the shape of hair. When heat is applied the hydrogen bonds can be re-formed into a new shape. The humidity in the air will affect the structure of the hair by making the hair feel damp. This will take the hair back to its natural state.

WWW **Website**

www.atthairdressing.com

WWW

View the online video to learn more about the hair in its various states

Products

Products used during setting and dressing include:

- setting lotions
- mousses
- gels
- creams
- sprays
- serums
- waxes.

To prevent wastage of products, only use the amount needed as according to manufacturers' instructions.

Figure 10.1 A selection of products used for setting and dressing

Online activity 10.2 WWW

Scrambled words

Figure 10.2 Tools and equipment

Tools and equipment

These include:

- rollers
- pins
- combs
- brushes
- heated equipment.

Keep tools and equipment clean at all times to minimise products from building up and causing sticky areas. As the tools and equipment are used, the hair may become attached to these areas and become damaged.

Activity

The associated learning screen for this part is interactive.

Control of Substances Hazardous to Health Regulations 2002 (COSHH)

These are commonly called the COSHH regulations and they lay down the essential requirements for controlling exposure to hazardous substances and for protecting people who may be affected by them. A substance is considered to be hazardous if it can cause harm to the body. It only poses a risk if it is:

- inhaled (breathed in)
- ingested (swallowed)
- in contact with the skin
- absorbed through the skin
- injected into the body
- introduced into the body via cuts etc.

For more information about the COSHH regulations refer to Chapter 2.

Figure 10.3 Rollers

Rollers

The various sizes of roller create volume, root lift, curl and direction to the hair.

Pins

Fine pins can be used to secure pin curls, and also for dressing hair when putting hair up. Straight pins are stronger than fine pins and used on long hair up-style and holding rollers in place. Plastic setting pins for securing rollers are more gentle on the hair and scalp. Double pronged metal clips are used for securing pin curls. Hair grips are used on long hair work for securing chignons. Section clips are used for sectioning hair.

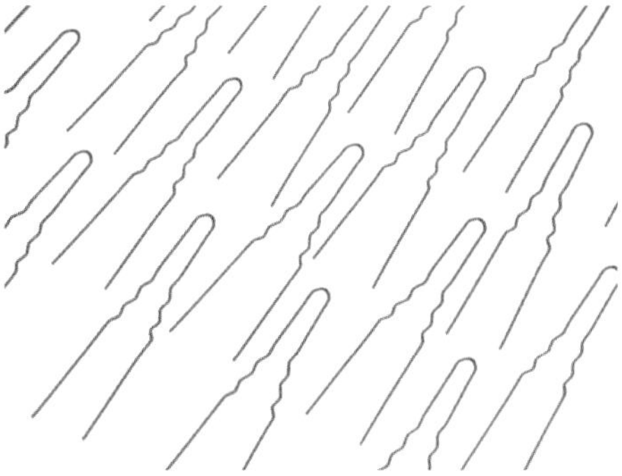

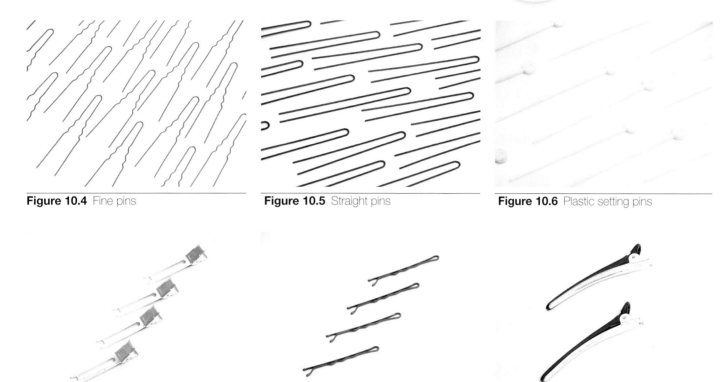

Figure 10.4 Fine pins

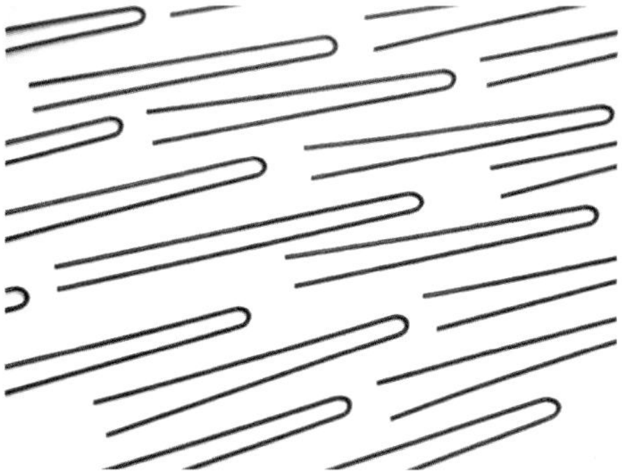

Figure 10.5 Straight pins

Figure 10.6 Plastic setting pins

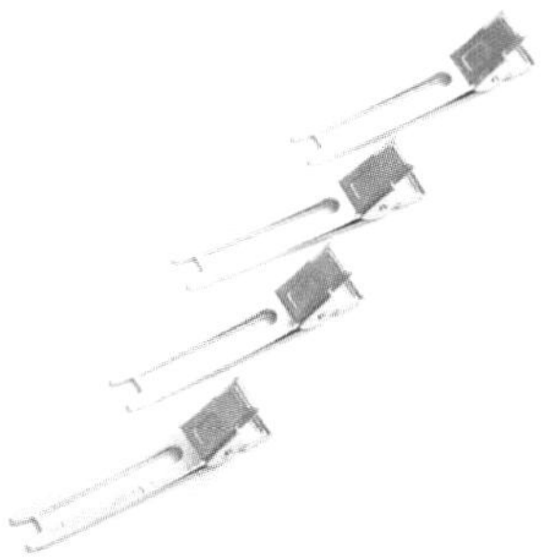

Figure 10.7 Double pronged pins

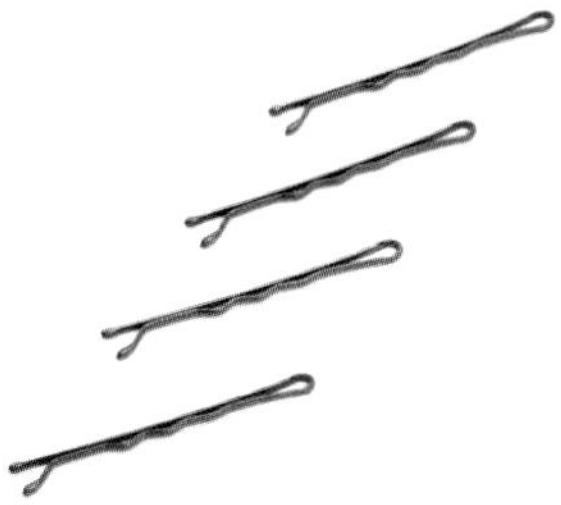

Figure 10.8 Hair grips

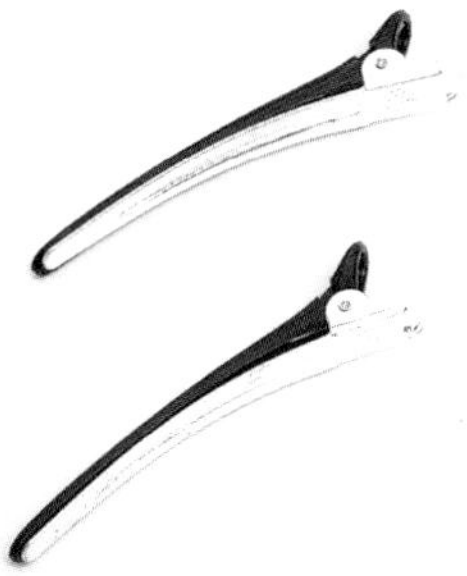

Figure 10.9 Section clips

Combs

A tail comb is used to help sectioning when setting. A setting comb is used for finger-waving or dressing hair.

Figure 10.10 Tail comb

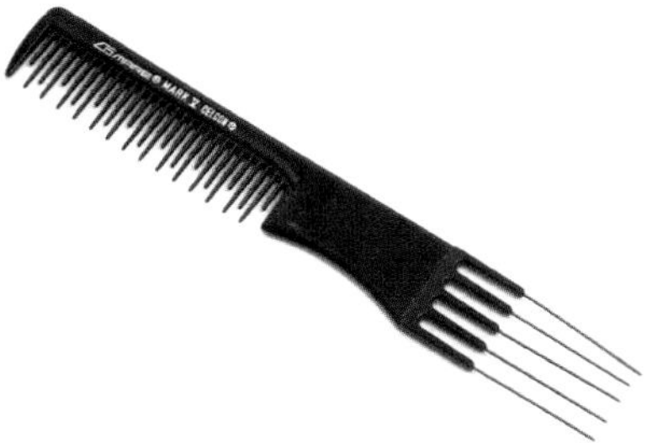

Figure 10.11 Setting tail

Brushes

Vent brushes will achieve a broken up casual effect on the hair. Circular brushes (small, medium and large) can be used in setting to loosen out the set using the hair dryer to achieve a softer look. A Denman brush is a firm brush ideal for a thorough brush when the rollers have been removed prior to styling the hair. A dressing out brush is used for gentle brushing and can be used for back brushing and dressing hair.

Figure 10.12 Vent brush

Figure 10.13 Circular brush

Figure 10.14 Denman brush

Figure 10.15 Dressing out brush

WWW Online activity 10.3

Drag the pictures

Heated equipment

For setting and dressing hair the following heated equipment will be used:

- electronically heated rollers
- curling tongs
- straighteners.

The temperature of heated styling equipment should be checked throughout the service and never held on the hair for longer than necessary. Do not hold too close to the client's scalp. This may result in burning the client.

Safety first

The temperature of heated styling equipment should be checked throughout the service and never held on the hair for longer than necessary.

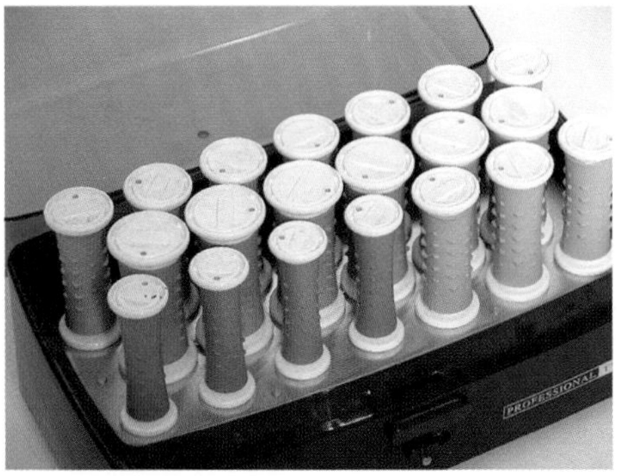

Figure 10.16 Electronically heated rollers

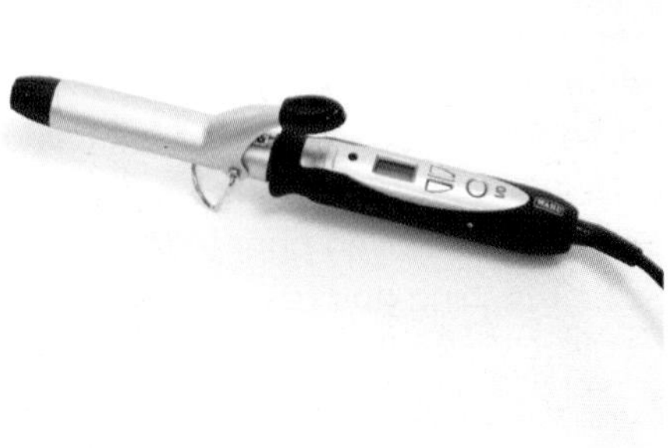

Figure 10.17 Curling tongs

Figure 10.18 Straighteners

Drying hair using hood dryer

Direct the client to the hood dryer. Offer support if necessary to an incapacitated or infirm client. Ensure that there are no obstacles in the way of the client. The hairdresser's hands must be dry when positioning the dryer over the client and switching it on.

Figure 10.19 Hands must be dry when positioning the dryer

Safety first

The hairdresser's hands must be dry when positioning the dryer over the client and switching it on.

Electricity at Work Regulations 1989

These regulations state that you must:

- Always check electrical equipment before using. Look for loose wires and that the plug is not cracked or damaged in any way. Check that the cord is not frayed or cracked.
- Never use electrical equipment when your hands are wet.
- Electrical equipment should be maintained regularly and checked by a suitably qualified person. Once checked the equipment should have a certificate or label acknowledging it.
- Faulty electrical equipment in the workplace must be removed, labelled as faulty and reported to the relevant person.

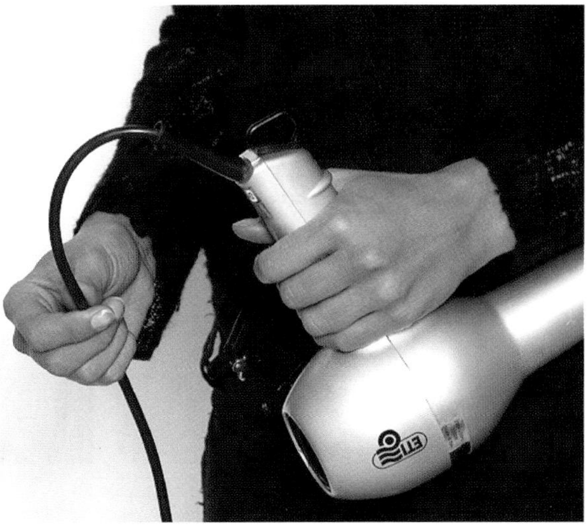

Figure 10.20 Check equipment for damage

Figure 10.21 Label faulty equipment appropriately

Consultation

Before any service begins the hairdresser must determine the client's expectations. The consultation is used to ensure the client's wishes are interpreted accurately and the desired look achieved. It is essential to be factual, honest, tactful, sincere, direct and clear. The consultation will give the opportunity to decide on products, the service that is carried out and the equipment that is used.

Influencing factors – haircut and texture

Check the client's current haircut as this will influence the way that you style it. Taking a look at how the client wears her hair beforehand helps if she would like to wear it in the same way. Also, look to assess the texture of the hair. There are three types of hair: fine, medium and coarse.

Figure 10.22 Ask what the client requires

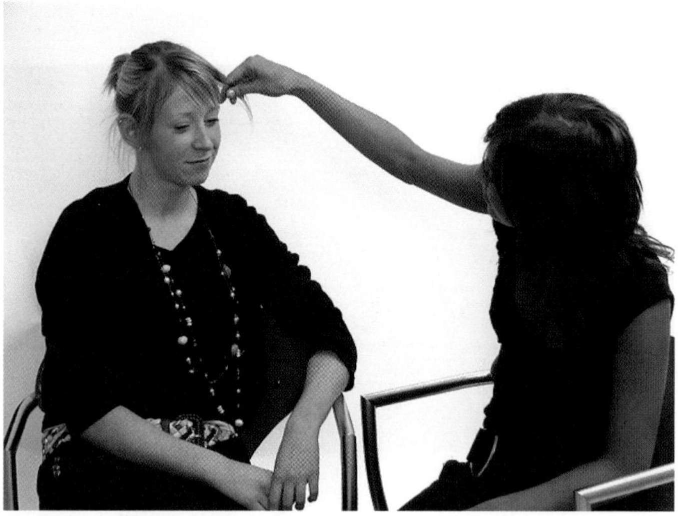

Figure 10.23 Check the texture of the client's hair

The occasion

Most of the time, a client who has their hair set and dressed will want it for a special occasion. These occasions amongst others include:

- weddings
- parties
- proms/balls.

Make sure you find out the occasion and match the look to this. Ask the client what outfit they will be wearing and match accordingly. If the hair is to be styled for a wedding, make sure that you ask the bride to collect many different visual aids of the look that she wishes to achieve. Ask her to bring in a picture of the dress that she will be wearing and any themes that may be running through her forthcoming wedding. This helps you to form a clear picture of the look that she wishes to have.

Key information

Make sure you find out the occasion and match the look to this. Ask the client what outfit they will be wearing and match accordingly.

Figure 10.24 Magazines can help when selecting a style

Growth patterns

For more information about growth patterns and head and face shapes, refer to Chapter 9.

You must understand growth patterns to see which way the hair naturally falls. Hair growth patterns include:

- widow's peak
- crowns
- cowlick
- natural partings
- inward and upward nape.

Head and face shapes

The client may have the following head or face shape:

- oval
- round
- long
- square
- heart
- pear.

The oval shaped face is considered to be the perfect shape that suits any style. However, people have differing features and it is important to choose the hairstyle to suit both features and face shape.

If your client has a round face, a hairstyle will be needed that is flat at the sides and high on the top. This will enhance the client's features.

If the client has a narrow or long face, the hairstyle needs to be fuller at the sides and flatter on top.

If a client has a square or angular jawline, the hairstyle will need to be softer in style and covering part of that area. This will flatten the face.

A client with a heart shaped face will usually be very wide around the eyes and cheek-bones. They may also have a very wide forehead. A fringe would help to narrow the forehead and also hair will need to be brought onto the face to create more fullness between the jaw and the bottom of the ear.

If a client has a pear shaped face, the hairstyle will have to be flat around the jawline but have lots of volume and fullness around the temples. This will narrow the appearance of the face.

Large ears that protrude need to be covered for a flattering effect.

If the client has a big nose or broken nose a centre parting will exaggerate this. Choose an asymmetric style. This will be more flattering.

A fringe will achieve the best effect for a client with a high forehead or receding hairline.

A short stocky neck requires a softer hairstyle which is more flattering to the client.

WWW **Online activity 10.4**

Five in a row

Preparing client for setting

Assist the client to put on a suitable sized gown to protect his or her clothing while in the salon. After the hair is shampooed, it is combed through to untangle.

Figure 10.25 Gown the client

Comfort during setting

Whilst setting and finishing the client's hair, it is important for you to move around the client's head. However, the client's comfort should be considered at all times. Their back should be positioned right to the back of the chair and as flat as possible. They should have both feet on the footrest or the floor. Not only will this be a more comfortable position for the client but it also enables you to create a balanced hairstyle. Your own comfort during setting and finishing should be considered as well. Check your posture is correct, ensuring that your client's seat is at the correct height for you to work. Ensure that your work area is tidy and free from clutter.

Definition

Posture: Working position of the body.

Figure 10.26 Incorrect position

Figure 10.27 Correct position

Suggested times for setting and dressing

Commercially viable times for setting and dressing hair are as follows (times do not include drying):

Table 10.1 Suggested service times

Length of hair	Time
Above shoulders	35 minutes
Below shoulders	45 minutes

10.2 Set hair

Setting is the way in which hair is moulded into shape by holding it in position. It can be set either wet or dry. This section will cover the following techniques:

- roller setting
- spiral curling
- pin curling.

The consultation will allow you to agree on a style with the client. Check the client is happy with the style you are creating before and during the service.

Key information

Check the client is happy with the style you are creating before and during the service.

Products used during setting

These include:

- setting lotions
- mousses
- gels
- creams.

Safety first

Check manufacturers' instructions before applying products.

Setting lotions

Setting lotion is applied sparingly onto wet hair to ensure an even application and then massaged into the hair. This helps to hold the set in place and puts a film to protect from weather and humidity. It gives lots of body to fine or limp hair.

www Online activity 10.5

Round the board

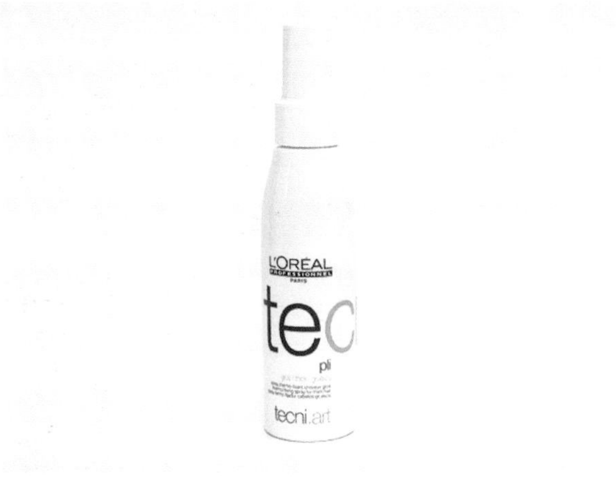

Figure 10.28 Setting lotion

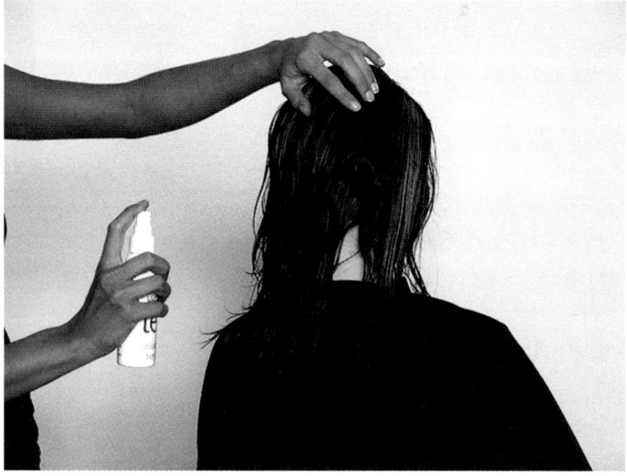

Figure 10.29 Applying setting lotion

Mousses

Mousses are available in different strengths. They are applied to wet hair with the hands and will hold style in place and achieve a soft effect.

Figure 10.30 A selection of mousses

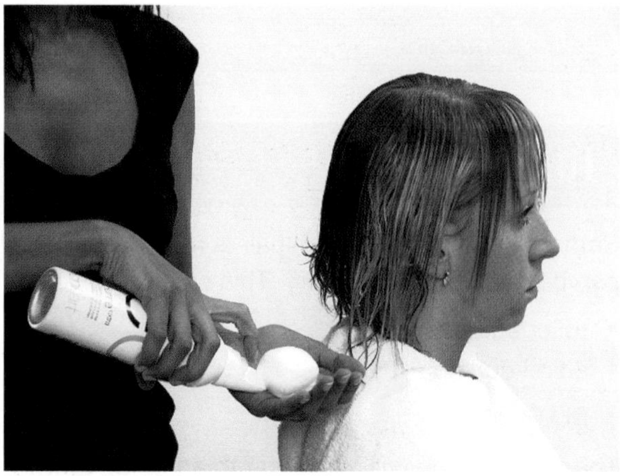

Figure 10.31 Applying mousse

Gels

Gels are designed to be used on wet or dry hair and should also be used sparingly. Used to give moisture to the hair and curl definition.

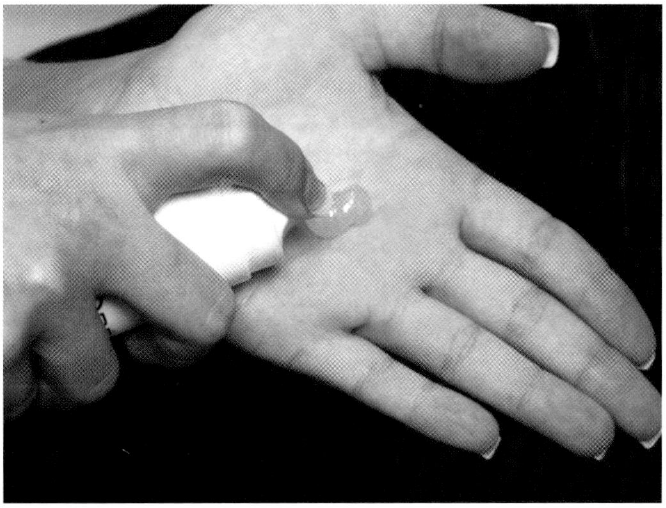

Figure 10.32 Applying gel

Figure 10.33 Different gels

Creams

Creams can be used on wet or dry hair and should be used sparingly. They are used to give moisture to the hair and curl definition.

Figure 10.34 Creams

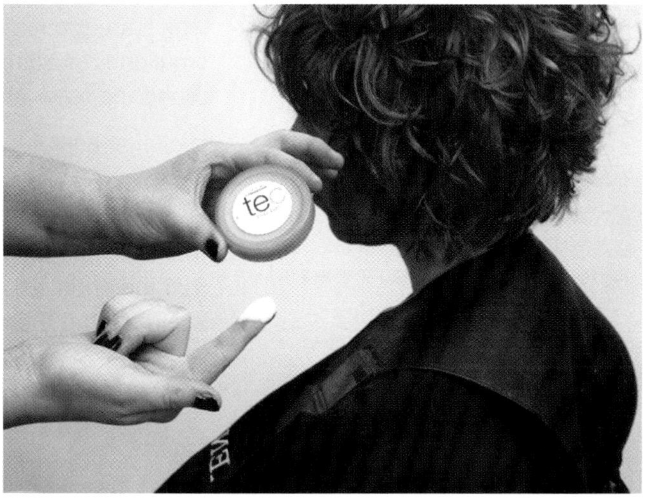

Figure 10.35 Applying cream

Wet setting techniques

Setting involves placing the hair into chosen positions and keeping it there while it forms a shape. The techniques that can be used include curling, rollering and spiral curling.

Key information

Setting involves placing the hair into chosen positions and keeping it there while it forms a shape.

Pin curling

There are three main types of pin curling effects:

- Barrel curls are used on hair that is too short to insert rollers but the same result is achieved.

- Open centred pin curls are loose, soft pin curls which sit off-base and are usually used in the nape or the sides of the head where a loose, flatter effect needs to be achieved.
- Clock spring pin curls are used to create very tight curls or wave movements.

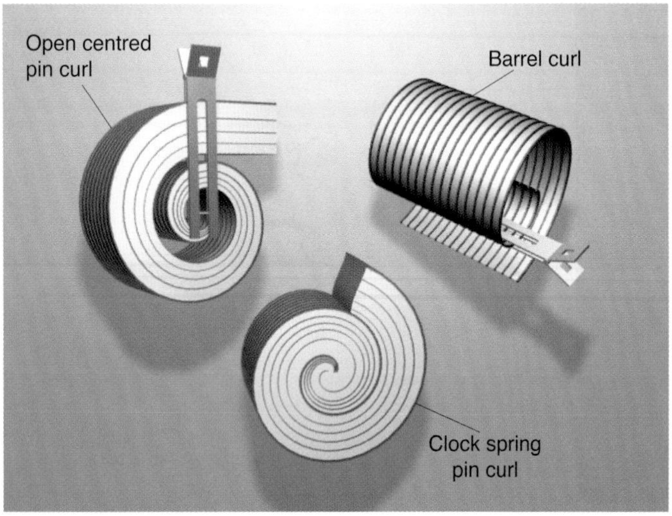

Figure 10.36 Open centred pin curl, barrel curl and clock spring pin curl

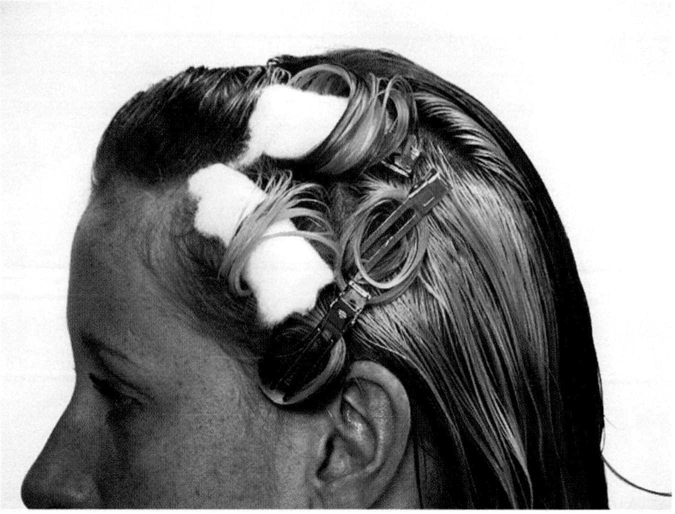

Figure 10.37 Barrel curl (with cotton wool) and open centred pin curls

Roller setting

Comb the client's hair to assess size of rollers and setting direction of hair. Choosing the correct style is important but choice of rollers is crucial. Rollers which are too large will not hold in the hair or hold the style. If the rollers are too small the resulting curl will be too tight. A good rule is that the hair should go round the roller at least one and a half times.

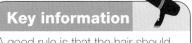

Key information

A good rule is that the hair should go round the roller at least one and a half times.

Rollers are inserted in a direction determined by the style. Section the hair mesh and use the width and length of a setting roller to determine the size of your section. Lift up and forward. Comb the hair at a 45 degree angle and using both thumbs and fingers wind the ends of the hair carefully around the roller. Ensure that the ends are not buckled. Holding at an even tension, wind down to the scalp so that the roller is sitting exactly on its base and secure with a pin.

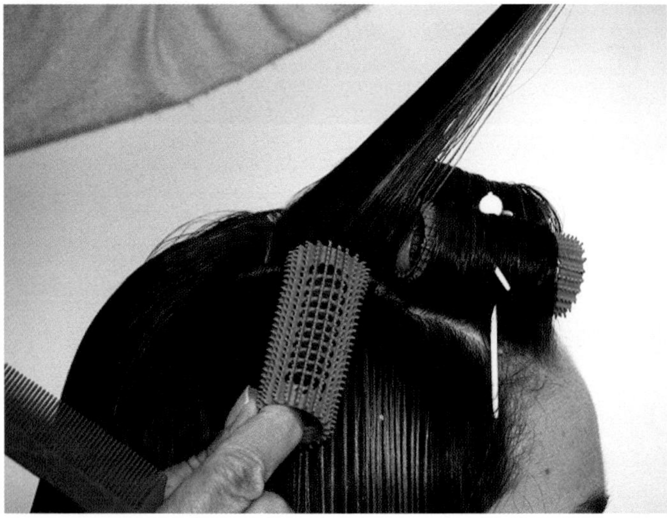

Figure 10.38 Choice of roller is crucial

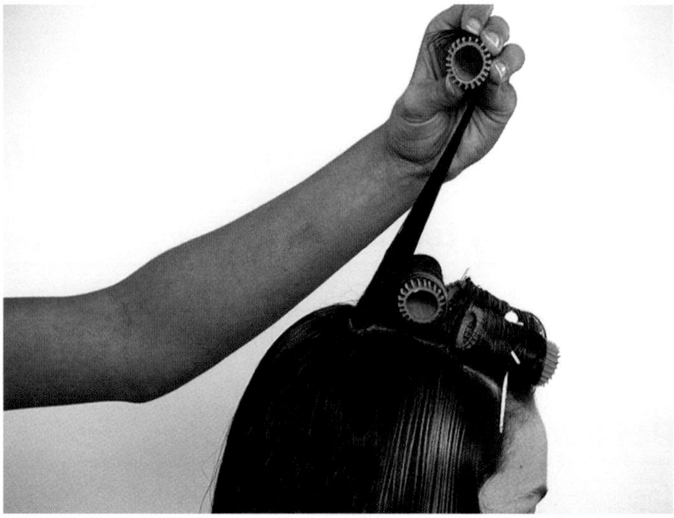

Figure 10.39 Use width and length of roller to determine size of section

Figure 10.40 Wind hair carefully around roller ensuring ends are not buckled

Figure 10.41 Hold at an even tension and wind down to scalp

Online activity 10.6 WWW

Drag into correct order

Considerations

Take care when inserting rollers. Bear in mind:

- Insertion of too many rollers will cause a bunching effect.
- Insertion of too few rollers will create gaps and partings.

When inserting the rollers on base, root lift can be achieved by ensuring that the roller sits squarely on the section giving maximum lift at the roots. When setting rollers 'off-base', little root lift is achieved. The roots are dragged to achieve volume at the ends with very little lift at the roots. Do not allow the hair to dry out whilst you are inserting rollers, otherwise the desired style will not be achieved.

Key information

Do not allow the hair to dry out whilst you are inserting rollers, otherwise the desired style will not be achieved.

Figure 10.42 Rollers sitting squarely to give root lift

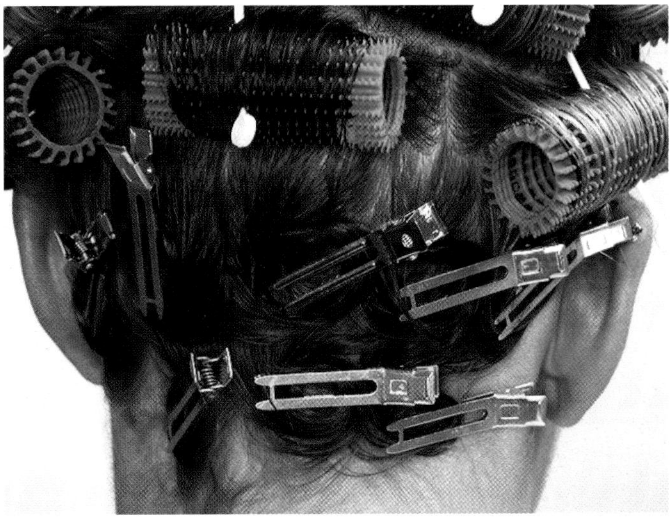

Figure 10.43 The roller sits 'off-base' for this style

Brickwork

Brickwork is a term used in setting for positioning rollers in the shown illustration. They follow the format like tiles in a roof. This method will ensure that no 'tram lines' or partings show when brushing out the hair for the finished look.

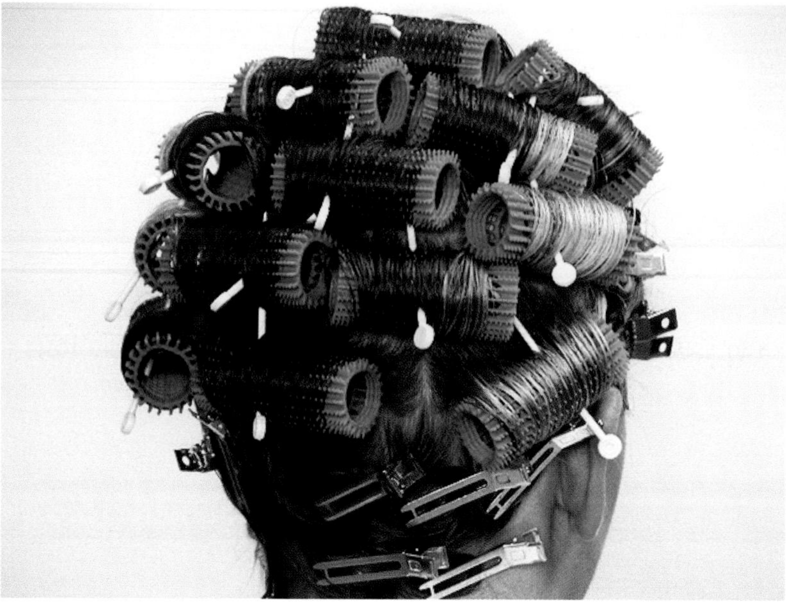

Figure 10.44 Brickwork positioning

Directional wind

The rollers follow the look of the finished style. When hair is set up in rollers or pin curls it is called the 'pli'.

Website www

www.atthairdressing.com

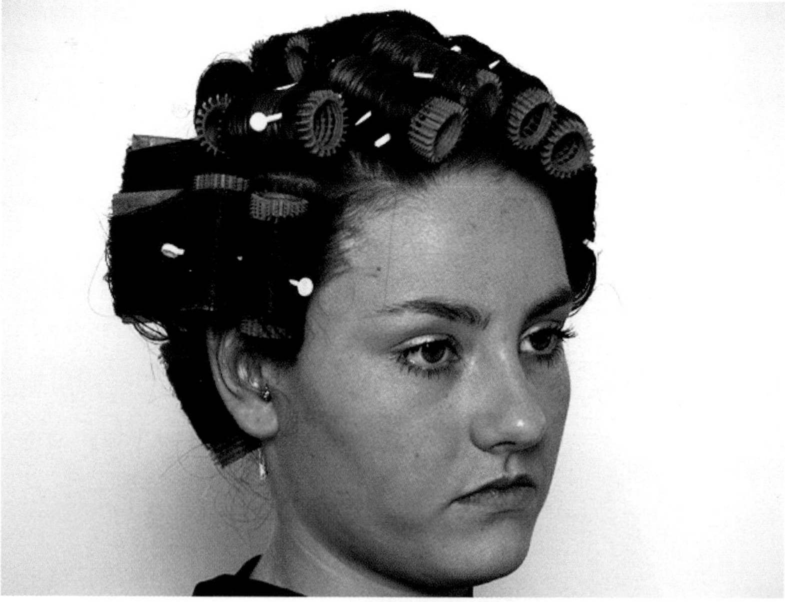

Figure 10.45 The rollers vary in position to follow the style

www Online activity 10.7

Correct selection

Testing for dry hair

To ensure that the hair is dry, run the hair through the fingers. If the curl springs back and does not droop, this will indicate that the hair is dry. When removing the rollers it is important to ensure that the meshes are not disturbed. On longer hair this will cause the set to drop. Take care not to cause discomfort to the client when removing rollers and pins. Check that the client is happy with the effect of the curls.

Figure 10.46 If the curl springs back and does not droop, this will indicate that the hair is dry

Spiral curling

Figure 10.47 After combing the hair, section for ease of work. Start at the nape area.

Figure 10.48 Take small sections of hair and comb through. Keeping the hair damp, wind the hair from roots to points around the foam rod. An even tension should be maintained. Using the end of a tail comb, tuck the points of the hair in to avoid fish hooks (online video).

Figure 10.49 Take sections from the left to right ear.

Figure 10.50 As you move up to the next section, wind the sections in the opposite direction i.e. from right to left ear. The technique of winding will give maximum root lift.

Figure 10.51 When the hair is completely dry, remove the foam rods, taking care not to cause any discomfort to the client.

Online activity 10.8

Round the board

Key information

A temporary set will not last as long as a wet set and will drop quickly.

Dry setting techniques

Dry setting is a temporary set. The hair is not wet but the hair can be altered temporarily with heated rollers. A temporary set will not last as long as a wet set and will drop quickly.

Figure 10.52 Dry setting is a temporary set

10.3 Dress hair

After the hair has been set, dressing is the way in which the hair is finished using curling and smoothing techniques, rollers, back combing and back brushing. Ensure that, before dressing the hair, it is completely dry. If not the hair will return to its natural state and the style you wish to create will not be possible. Products and heated equipment can be used to aid the dressing technique.

Key information

After the hair has been set, dressing is the way in which the hair is finished using curling and smoothing techniques, rollers, back combing and back brushing.

Products used during dressing

These include:

- hairspray
- waxes
- serums.

Check manufacturers' instructions before applying products.

Online activity 10.9 WWW

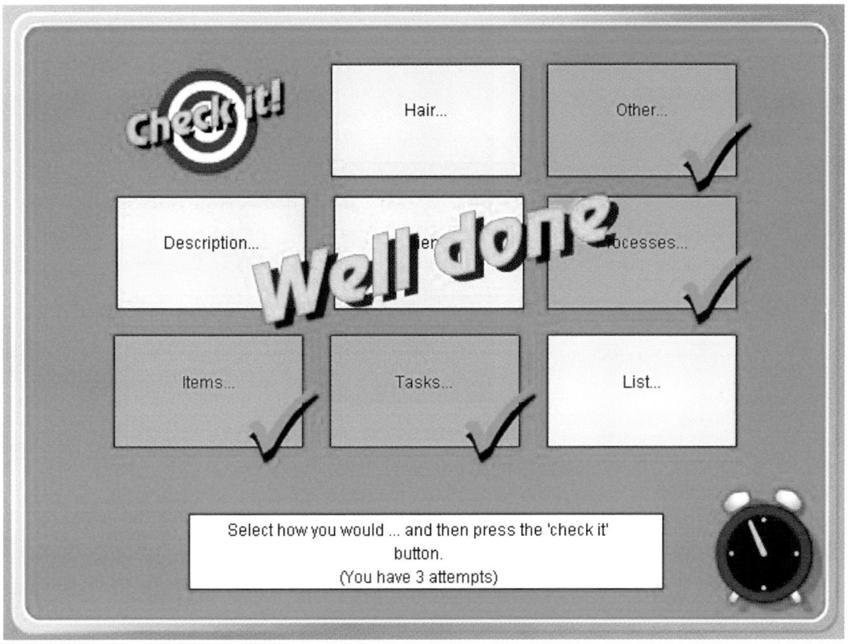

Check it

Hairspray

Hairspray holds the hair in place and protects the hair from the weather and humidity. It comes in different strengths, and it is easily removed from the hair by brushing or wetting as most hairsprays are water soluble. Application of hairspray should be pointed away from the client's face. This can be achieved by standing in front of your client when you are applying the product. It should be held at approximately 10-12 inches from the head.

Figure 10.53 Hairsprays

Figure 10.54 Applying hairspray

Definitions

Humidity: The dampness in the air.

Water soluble: Dissolves in water.

Waxes

Wax is used on dry hair to separate curls and give definition to the hair.

Figure 10.55 Wax

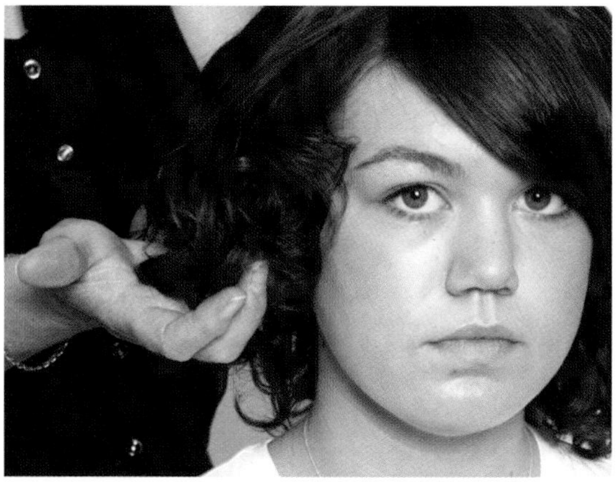

Figure 10.56 Applying wax

Serums

Hair serum will make hair look shiny and in better condition. This product must be used sparingly as it is very concentrated and can make hair appear lank or greasy.

Figure 10.57 Hair serums

Figure 10.58 Applying serums

Brushing set hair into style

Using the palm of the hand and a brush, the hairdresser should thoroughly brush the hair to eliminate any roller marks before styling.

Figure 10.59 Finished style after brushing out (online video)

Website

www.atthairdressing.com

Back brushing and back combing

Back brushing achieves a softer effect but will 'fluff' the hair with more bounce. Back combing achieves a stiffer style. The hairdresser will determine the method by how stiff or full the client requires the hairstyle. Continue to comb out and apply hairspray if required.

Key information

Back brushing achieves a softer effect but will 'fluff' the hair with more bounce. Back combing achieves a stiffer style.

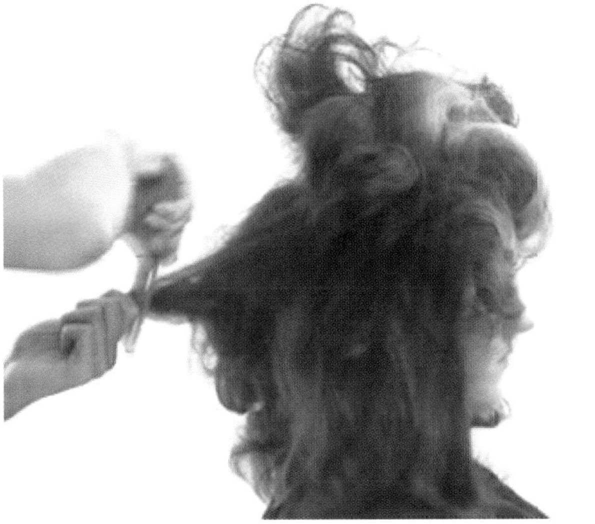

Figure 10.60 Back combing the hair

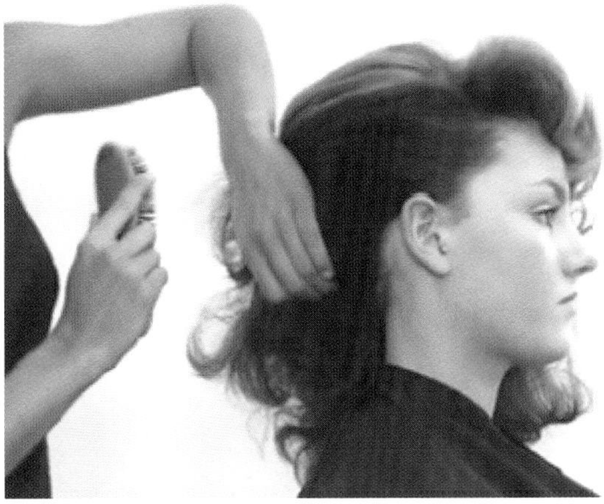

Figure 10.61 Brush out the hair to complete the style

Roll

This consists of a fold of hair usually at the back of the head. It is most commonly used on long hair but short hair can be made into a roll.

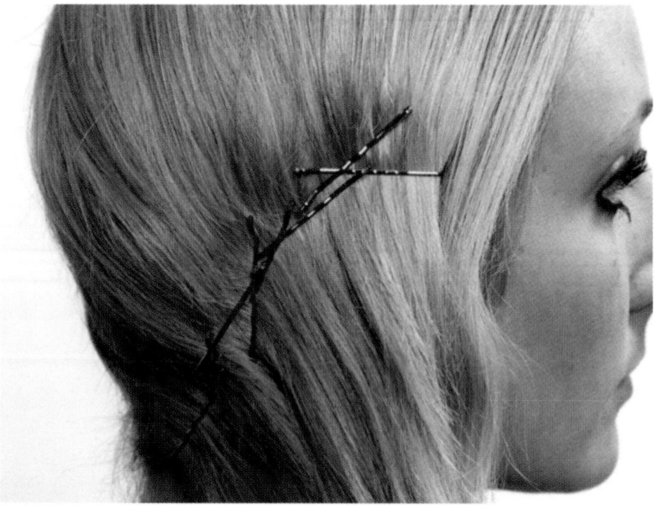

Figure 10.62 Back brush the hair if appropriate. Comb the hair to one side and using hair grips, secure from nape to the ear, using a crossover method.

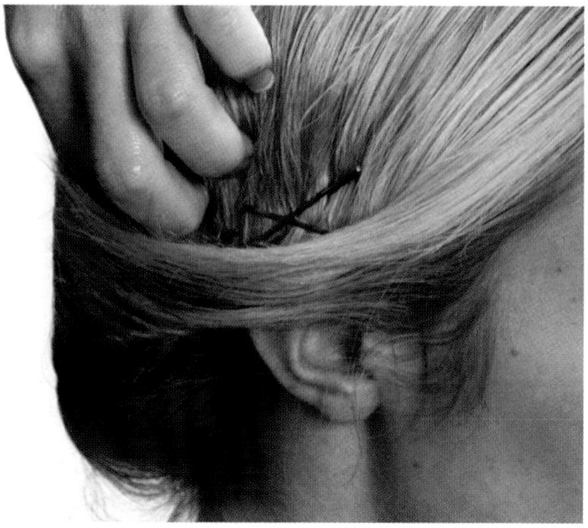

Figure 10.63 Fold the hair over in a roll and finish with fine hair pins to keep the finished style in place. Use hairspray to hold the style in place.

Figure 10.64 Finished roll

Key information

It is most commonly used on long hair but short hair can be made into a roll.

Dressing a spiral set

To dress out a spiral wind, use your fingers and not brushes or combs. This will maintain the curl.

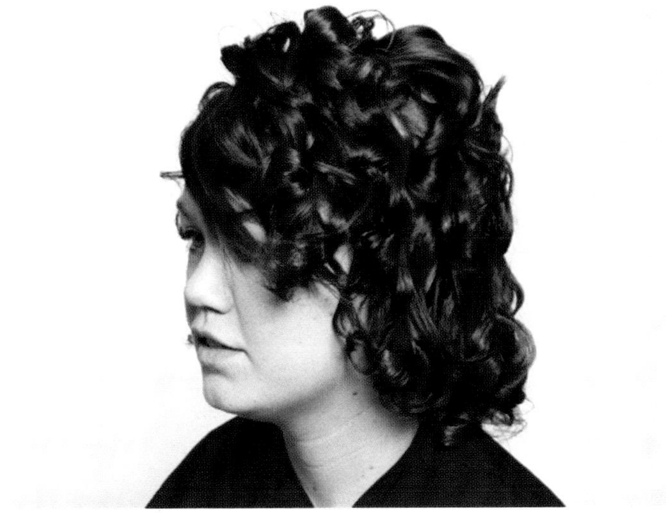

Figure 10.65 A spiral set ready to be dressed

Figure 10.66 Use your fingers to maintain the curl

Electrical equipment

Curling tongs and straighteners can be used to personalise the finished style. Curling tongs can be used to loosen the curl that has been set if required. Straighteners can be used to smooth and straighten a fringe area.

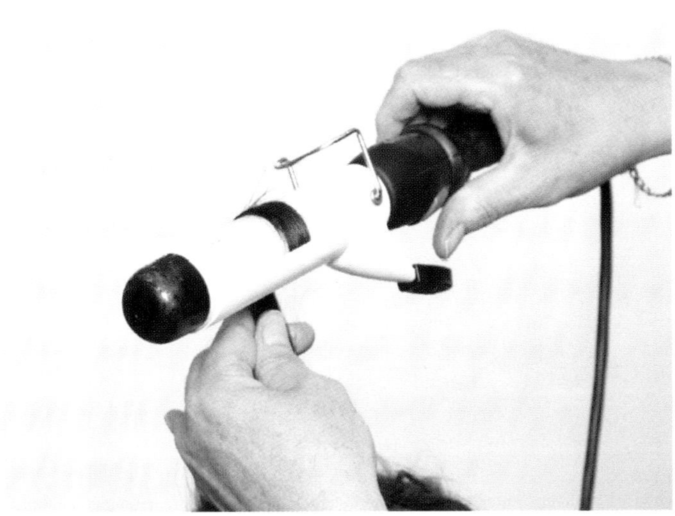

Figure 10.67 Use curling tongs to loosen a set curl

Figure 10.68 Using straighteners to smooth the fringe area

Checking balance of completed style

Check the balance of the hairstyle, using the front mirror to ensure that the profile shape of the hairstyle and the finish are appealing to the client, and reinforce this by confirming with the client. Use a back mirror from behind, angling the position so both you and the client can see the finished result from the back. Ensure that the client is happy with the finished style.

Definition

Reinforce: To make information sink in. To confirm.

Figure 10.69 Check the balance

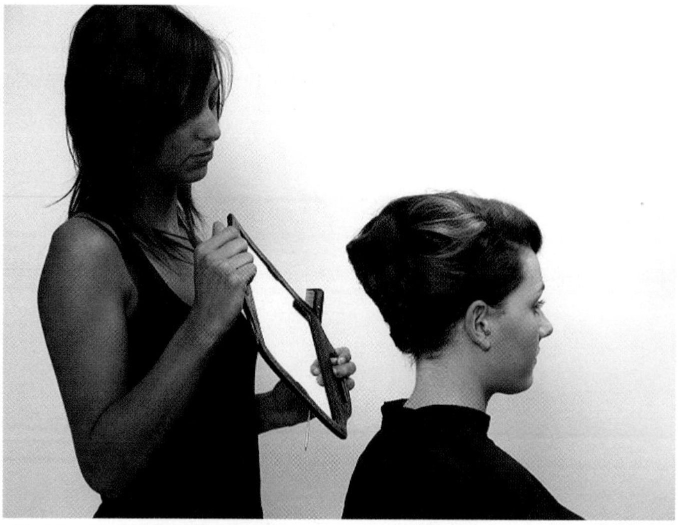

Figure 10.70 Use back mirror so that client can see the completed style

Online activity 10.10

Five in a row

10.4 Provide aftercare advice

Key information

The client's lifestyle must be taken into consideration when creating a style that the client can maintain.

An important part of this service is to give the client aftercare advice. Ensure the client is aware that if the hair becomes damp through weather conditions, it is likely to drop or revert back to its natural state. The client's lifestyle must be taken into consideration when creating a style that the client can maintain. Throughout the service you must explain to the client what you are doing. Do this fully and accurately, repeating yourself if necessary.

Figure 10.71 Explain to the client what you are doing throughout the service

Removal of hairstyle

Explain to the client the way in which the hairstyle is taken down. Pins and grips must be removed carefully before brushing the hair.

Figure 10.72 Explain how to remove the pins and grips

Products and heated styling equipment

When explaining to the client the use of heated styling equipment, take care giving health and safety advice. Continual use will damage the hair. Therefore regular conditioning and using heat protectors are advisable. Advise the client which products can be used at home. This should be based on the factors that influence the service. Refer to Chapter 6 for more information.

Figure 10.73 Give advice on using heated styling equipment

Figure 10.74 Give advice on products to use at home

WORKSHEETS

10.5 Worksheets

You can carry out the worksheets during your study of a chapter or unit, or at the end. An example is presented here and there are more online. If your college or company is registered with ATT Training, lots more are available. Write your answers directly in the book, but only if you own it of course – if it is a library or college book, use a separate piece of paper!

10.5.1 Hygroscopic

Hair is hygroscopic. This means that it has the ability to absorb moisture. Wet hair can be stretched nearly double its normal length. This is called elasticity. Wet hair in its stretched state is called 'beta keratin'. When it is in the natural state (unstretched), the hair is called 'alpha keratin'. The reason why hair stretches is that the hydrogen bonds are broken down by water. It is these properties that allow us to alter the shape of the hair. When heat is applied the hydrogen bonds can be re-formed into a new shape. The humidity in the air will affect the structure of the hair by making the hair feel damp. This will take the hair back to its natural state.

State 5 treatments carried out in your salon that involve the above process.

1 ______________________________

2 ______________________________

3 ______________________________

4 ______________________________

5 ______________________________

10.6 Assessment

Well done! If you have studied all the content of this unit you may be ready to test your knowledge.

Check out the 'Preparing for assessments' section in Chapter 1 if you have not already done so, and always remember:

- You can only do your best if you have. . .
  - studied hard
  - completed the activities
  - completed the worksheets
  - practised, practised, practised
  - and then revised!

Now carry out the online multiple-choice quiz

. . . and good luck in the final exam, which will be arranged by your tutor/assessor.

CHAPTER 11

Cutting hair

This chapter covers the NVQ/SVQ unit GH12, Cut hair using basic techniques and the VRQ unit 206, Cut women's hair.

In this chapter you will be learning the skills you need to cut hair into a range of styles and effects. This will include styles for curly, wavy and straight hair.

In this chapter you will learn about:

- maintaining effective and safe methods when cutting hair
- cutting hair to achieve a variety of looks
- providing aftercare advice.

Website

www.atthairdressing.com

CHAPTER 11 CUTTING HAIR: CONTENTS, SCREENS AND ACTIVITIES

Key:

Sections from the book are set in this colour

Screens available online are set in this colour

Online activity screens are set in this colour

11.1 Working safely

Safety is the key issue when cutting hair. The tools that you use must allow you to perform the haircut that the client wishes to have. Be careful not to damage your tools as you work. Chapter 2 covers health and safety working methods in more detail. Refer to this unit if needed.

Scissors

These come in a variety of materials such as stainless steel, with metal or plastic handles. They also come in a variety of designs and prices. Picking scissors up and holding them is the best way to see if they are suitable. It is important that they feel comfortable. Scissors should always be clean and sharp. Before sterilising remember to remove all loose hairs.

Key information

Scissors should always be clean and sharp.

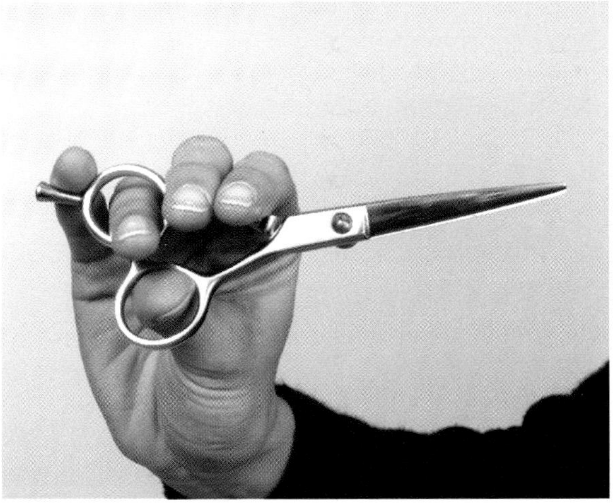

Figure 11.1 Hold scissors to see if they are suitable

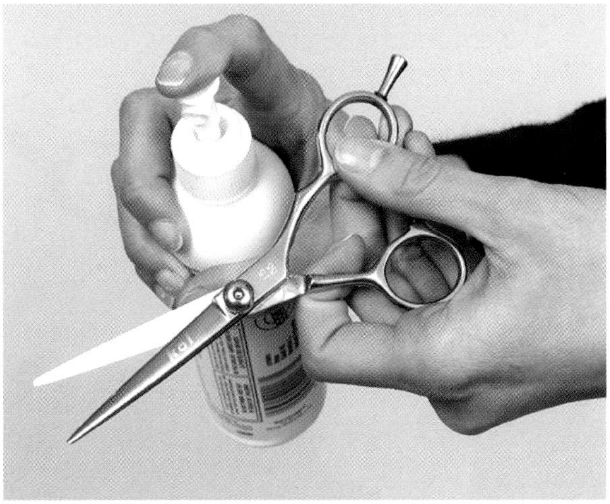

Figure 11.2 Sterilise scissors

Thinning scissors

These are scissors specifically designed for thinning the hair. They have one or possibly two blades that look like the teeth on a comb. The teeth of the blades are sharp and cut the hair. The gaps between the teeth just allow the hair to pass through without removing any hair at all. The size of the gap determines how much hair is removed.

Key information

The size of the gap determines how much hair is removed.

Figure 11.3 Thinning scissors with one serrated blade

Figure 11.4 Thinning scissors with two serrated blades

Online activity 11.1

Correct selection

Razors

A safety razor is designed to prevent accidental cuts to the person using it or to the client. The disadvantage of this type of razor is that it does not allow the stylist to clean or mark out the hairline as it will not cut hair against the skin. It is used on mid-lengths to ends for reducing length and volume. Razors have a disposable blade. Some razors have a protecting handle.

Key information

Razors can only be used on wet hair; when used on dry hair they tear and shred the cuticle leaving the cortex frayed and exposed.

Razors can only be used on wet hair; when used on dry hair they tear and shred the cuticle leaving the cortex frayed and exposed. It is also uncomfortable for the client. Salons using razor blades must dispose of them in a container such as a sharps box.

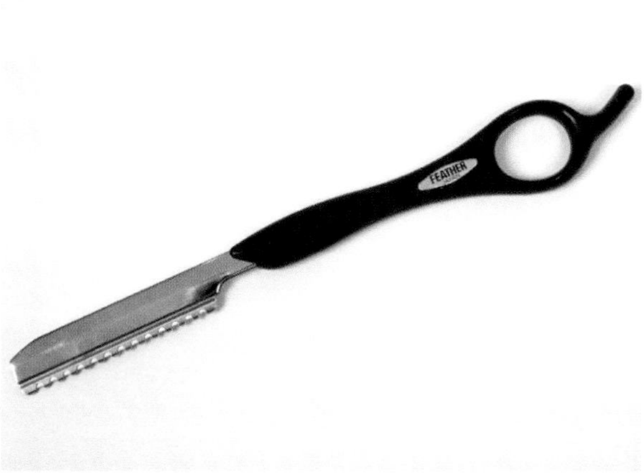

Figure 11.5 Safety razor

Figure 11.6 Sharps box

Clippers

Safety first

When using electric clippers all repairs should be carried out by a qualified electrician.

Electric clippers can be used with or without attachments. When in use the bottom blade remains still whilst the top blade moves across it very quickly to cut the hair. Do not use electric clippers when your hands are wet and remember to oil them using clipper oil after every use. When using electric clippers all repairs should be carried out by a qualified electrician.

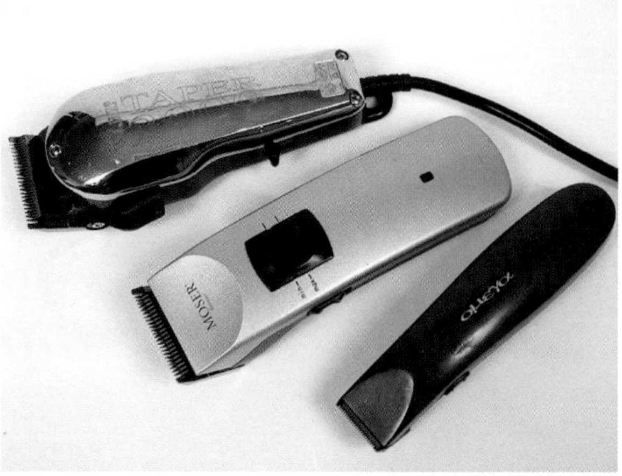

Figure 11.7 Clippers

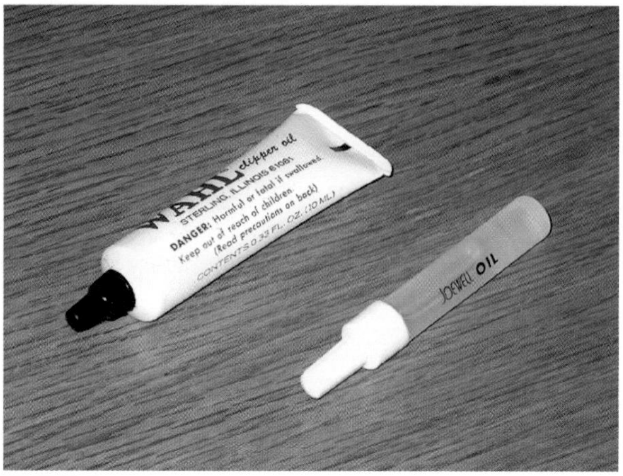

Figure 11.8 Clipper oil

Towels and gowns

All towels and gowns should be clean and sterile for each client to prevent cross infection of parasitic, viral, fungal and bacterial diseases.

These include:

- pediculosis capitis
- herpes simplex
- tinea capitis
- impetigo.

Safety first

All towels and gowns should be clean and sterile for each client to prevent cross infection of parasitic, viral, fungal and bacterial diseases.

Preparing the client for a haircut

It is important to gown the client effectively prior to cutting the hair. This is to protect the client's clothes and to ensure that the client is comfortable. Hair cuttings are extremely prickly when they go down the back of the neck; cuttings are also very difficult to remove from clothes. Do not have too much bulk from clothes and towels around the neck; this restricts the accuracy when cutting and in some cases the mobility of the client's neck.

WWW Website

www.atthairdressing.com

Figure 11.9 Gown the client effectively

Online activity 11.2 WWW

Round the board

Consultation

Before any service begins the hairdresser must find out what the client wants or needs. The consultation is used to ensure the client's wishes are interpreted accurately and the desired look achieved. It is essential to be factual, honest, tactful, sincere, direct and clear.

Figure 11.10 Find out what the client wants

Analyse hair and scalp

Key information

Prior to all hairdressing tasks it is necessary to analyse the hair and scalp.

Prior to all hairdressing tasks it is necessary to analyse the hair and scalp. This includes a visual examination and a physical examination. The natural hair-fall and the hair growth patterns are particularly important for you to be aware of before starting any haircut. Some growth patterns, face shapes and other factors may prevent you from cutting the hair in a particular style.

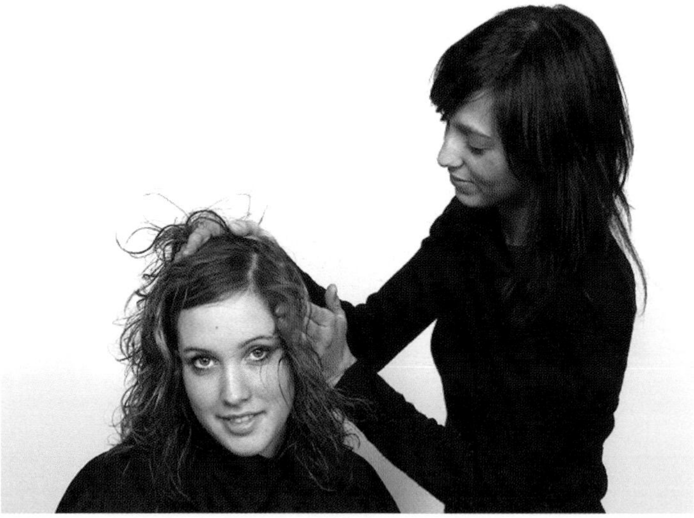

Figure 11.11 Look at the hair and scalp

Definitions

Contraindications: A condition preventing a treatment.

Infestation: A group of parasites.

Infection: A disease caused by micro-organisms.

During the analysis prior to cutting the hair other contraindications need to be taken into account. These can be divided into two distinct areas:

- infestations or infections including pediculosis capitis (head lice)
- tinea capitis (ringworm of the scalp).

Comfort during cutting

Whilst cutting the client's hair, it is important for you to move around the client's head. However, the client's comfort should be considered at all times. Their back should be positioned right to the back of the chair and as flat as possible. They should have both feet on the footrest or the floor. Not only will this be a more comfortable position for the client but it also enables you to create a balanced hairstyle. Your own comfort during cutting should be considered as well. Check your posture is correct, ensuring that your client's seat is at the correct height for you to work. Ensure that your work area is tidy and free from clutter.

Figure 11.12 Incorrect posture

Figure 11.13 Correct posture

After cutting always remember to sweep up the hair cuttings off the floor and dispose of them in the appropriate place.

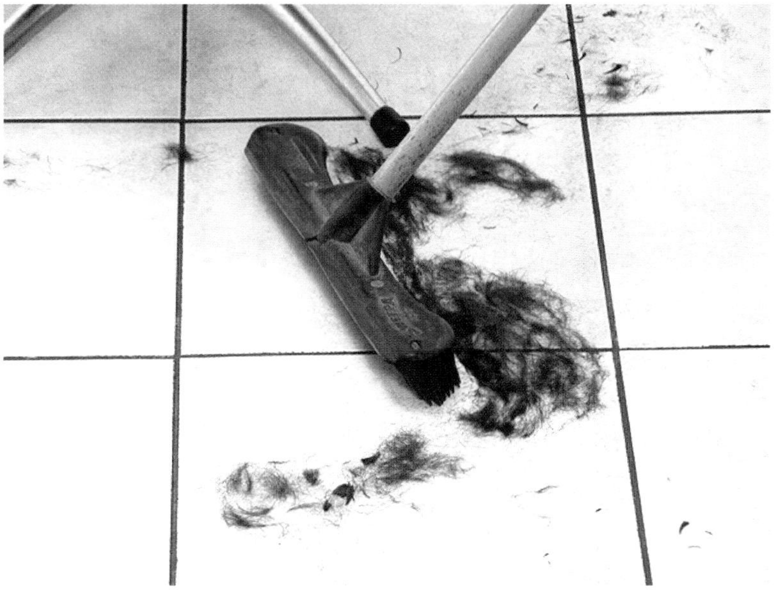

Figure 11.14 Sweep up hair cuttings

Suggested times for cutting

A commercially viable time for cutting is 45 minutes. This is for the haircut only.

11.2 Cut hair to achieve a variety of looks

In this section you will learn how to perform several haircuts using basic cutting techniques whilst keeping in mind any important factors, for example head and face shapes.

Growth patterns

The natural hair-fall and the hair growth patterns are particularly important for you to be aware of before starting any haircut. Some growth patterns may prevent you from cutting the hair in a particular style. There is more information about growth patterns in Chapter 4.

Hair growth patterns include:

- widow's peak
- crowns
- cowlick
- natural partings
- inward and upward nape.

WWW Online activity 11.3

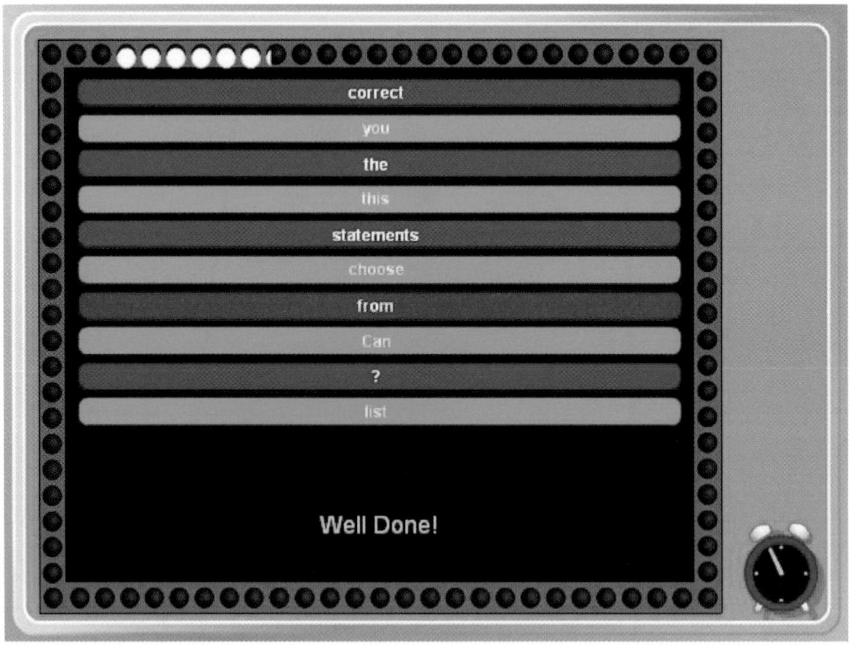

Select correct boxes

Head and face shapes

The client may have the following head or face shape:

- The oval shaped face is considered to be the perfect shape that suits any style. However, people have differing features and it is important to choose the hairstyle to suit each client's face shape and features.

- If your client has a round face, a hairstyle will be needed that is flat at the sides and high on the top. This will enhance the client's features.
- If the client has a narrow or long face, the hairstyle needs to be fuller at the sides and flatter on top.
- If a client has a square or angular jawline, the hairstyle will need to be softer in style and covering part of that area. This will flatten the face.
- A client with a heart shaped face will usually be very wide around the eyes and cheekbones. They may also have a very wide forehead. A fringe would help to narrow the forehead and hair will need to be brought onto the face to create more fullness between the jaw and the bottom of the ear.
- If a client has a pear shaped face, the hairstyle will have to be flat around the jawline but have lots of volume and fullness around the temples. This will narrow the appearance of the face.
- Large ears that protrude need to be covered for a flattering effect.
- If the client has a big nose or broken nose a centre parting will exaggerate this. Choose an asymmetric style. This will be more flattering.
- A fringe will achieve the best effect for a client with a high forehead or receding hairline.
- A short, stocky neck requires a softer hairstyle which is more flattering to the client.

Key information

For more information about head and face shapes, refer to Chapter 4.

Hair texture

There are three types of hair. These will need different strengths of products:

- Fine textured hair requires firm hold.
- Medium and coarse textured hair will need normal strength hold.

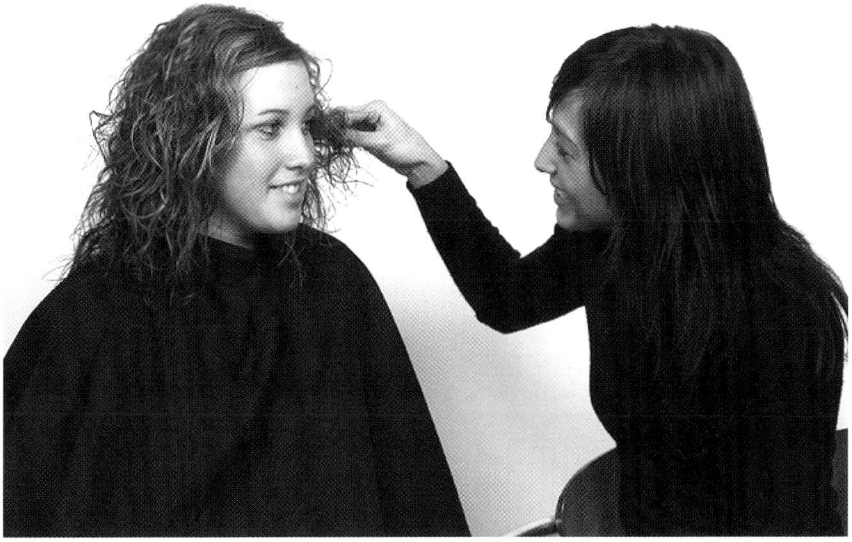

Figure 11.15 Check hair texture

Hair density

This refers to the amount of hair that the client has on his or her head. If a client has dense hair this means that you will not be able to see the client's scalp. If you can see the client's scalp then they have a low density of hair on their head.

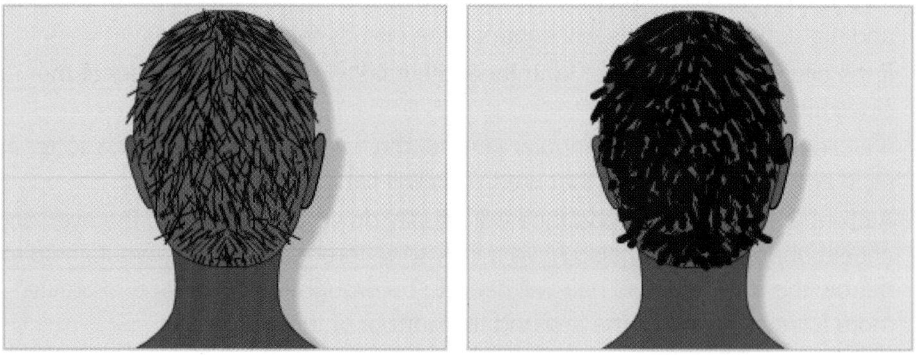

Figure 11.16 Low density of hair shown on the left, dense hair shown on the right

WWW Online activity 11.4

Round the board

Elasticity

Key information

The elasticity test assesses the extent of damage to the cortex of the hair.

This test assesses the extent of damage to the cortex of the hair. It measures the ability of the hair to be stretched. Hold a single strand of hair firmly at each end with finger and thumb. Pull back gently and see how much the hair stretches and springs back. A hair in good condition can stretch up to a third of its length and return to its original length. If the hair snaps it indicates that the hair has a weak cortex.

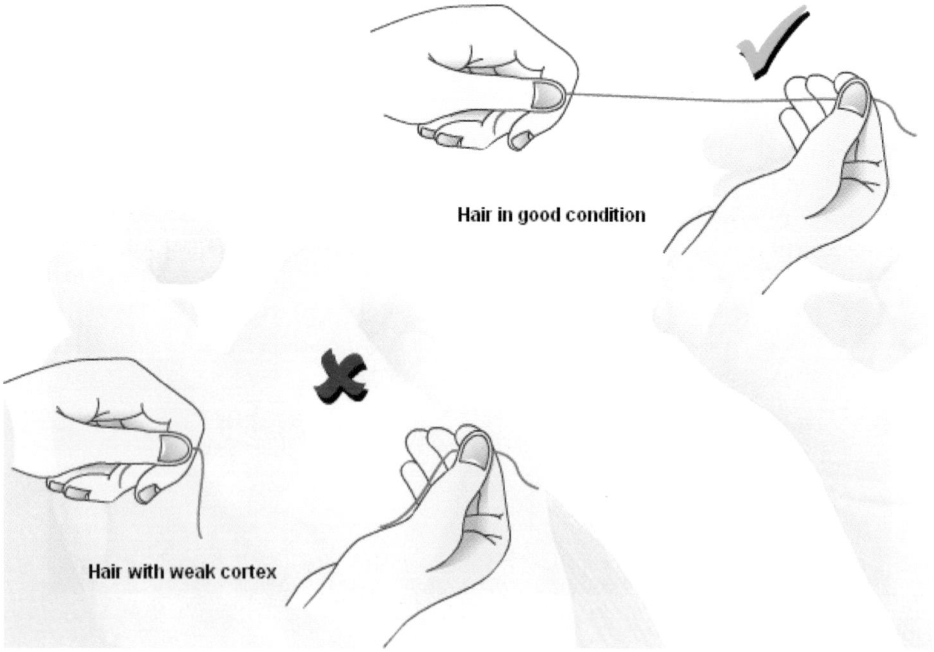

Figure 11.17 Diagram showing elasticity test

Website WWW

www.atthairdressing.com

One length cutting

The hair is cut completely on the base or perimeter line, i.e. a 'bob'. There is no graduation.

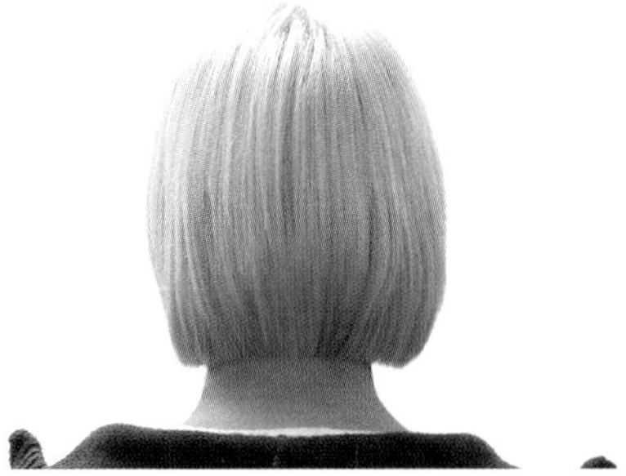

Figure 11.18 One length haircut

Graduation

The hair is cut in such a way as to produce an internal shape, blending different lengths and angles without leaving steps or lines. It is used to produce a style where the inner length is longer than the outside or perimeter length.

Figure 11.19 A graduated style

Club cutting

Each section of hair is cut straight across bluntly, usually done with scissors but can also be achieved with clippers. The hair mesh is cut straight across to produce level ends.

Figure 11.20 Club cutting

Tapering

Involves a method of tapering the hair to remove bulk or volume alone, or to remove length and volume at the same time. Can also be known as feathering. The hair is cut to produce a tapered point.

Figure 11.21 Tapering

Pointing

The points of the scissors are used to break up the point of the hair. This will create texture in hair that has been club cut. Another technique for texturing is called brick cutting.

Online activity 11.5 WWW

Correct selection

Figure 11.22 Pointing

Figure 11.23 Scissor over comb technique

Scissor over comb

Used when the hair is required to be very short and finely graduated. When using this cutting method a smooth flowing movement is required to avoid 'steps' in the hair. Keep the head up in a sitting position. Use the points of the scissors to lift a section of hair. Place a comb under the section of hair. Glide the comb in an upward direction. Follow the comb with the scissors and carefully cut the hair to the required length. Open and close the scissors rapidly clipping away at the length.

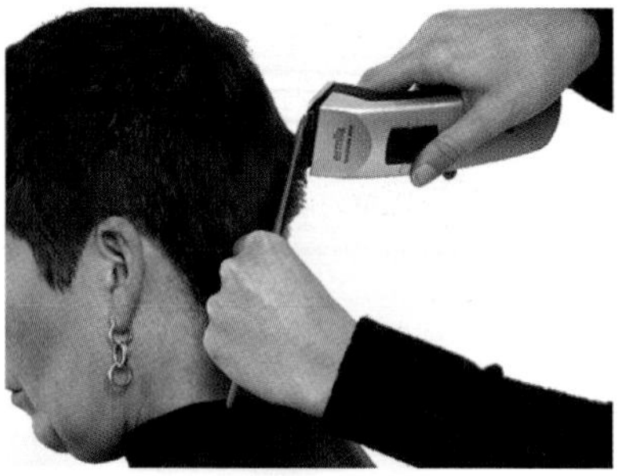

Figure 11.24 Clipper over comb technique

Clipper over comb

This eliminates the hard work from the scissor over comb technique. Place the comb and hold at the appropriate angle under a section of hair. Glide the clippers across the comb. Repeat this until the required length is achieved.

Figure 11.25 Thinning hair using thinning scissors

Thinning

Many cutting techniques can be used for thinning the hair, not only the use of thinning scissors. It can be carried out on wet or dry hair.

Figure 11.26 Slice cutting (online video)

Slice cutting

This is where the scissors are used like a razor. The hair is held between the fingers for support and the open scissors are slid down the hair shaft. This removes length and tapers the ends of the hair. It allows very steep graduation to be cut into long hair.

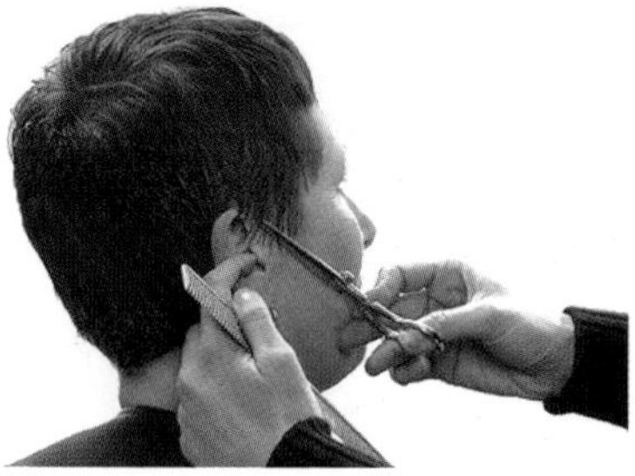

Figure 11.27 Freehand cutting

Freehand cutting

This is mainly used when creating a one-length look on straight hair. Comb the hair into place and then cut freehand without using tension on the hair. By not using tension on the hair when dry, it gives a better indication of where the hair will sit.

WWW Online activity 11.6

Shoot the target

A one-length haircut on straight hair

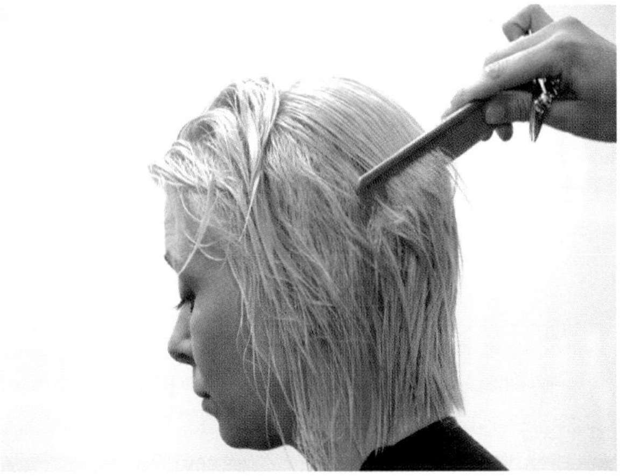

Figure 11.28 Comb to untangle the hair.

Figure 11.29 Section the hair from forehead to nape using a centre parting. Using the centre parting as a guide, comb approximately 1.5 cm of hair from both sides of the centre section.

Figure 11.30 Cut the baseline to the required length. When cutting the hair in the centre sections at the back of the head, the head should be positioned and held slightly forward.

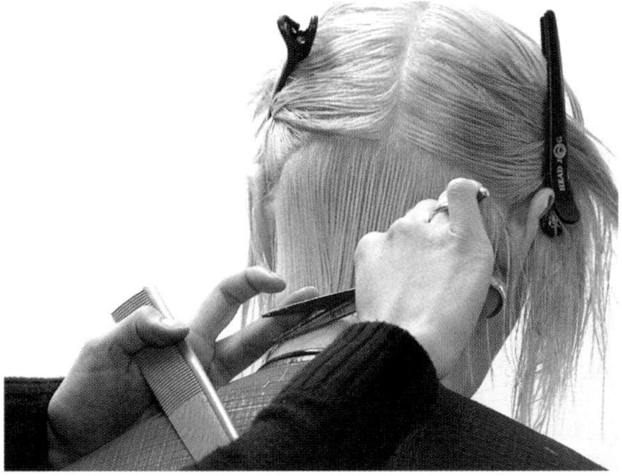

Figure 11.31 Comb down the second section. This section should be fine enough for you to see the baseline through it, so it can be used as a cutting guide. Checking for finger position and hair tensions, cut off required amount of hair.

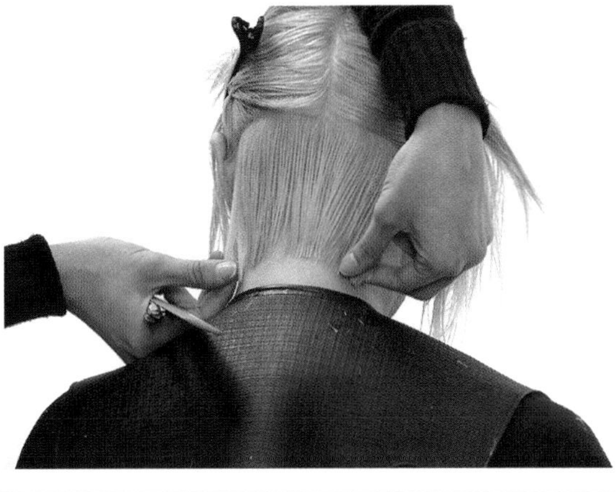

Figure 11.32 Take two strands of hair from the outside of this section and pull gently into the middle under the centre partings to check that they are the same length. This will indicate whether you have cut the hair in a straight line.

Figure 11.33 Take another section and using the previously cut section as a guideline continue cutting the hair in a straight line.

Figure 11.34 Continue bringing small sections from either side of the centre parting and cutting to the guideline.

Figure 11.35 When the sections have reached to the top of the ear, bring the head into a natural sitting position. This discourages the hair being cut shorter by mistake. Check that your cutting line is straight and to your guideline.

Figure 11.36 When the sections at the back are level with the hair over the top of the ears, introduce the hair from the front sections to the back sections and work in horseshoe sections around the head.

Figure 11.37 Cutting the sides of the hair with the back sections will create uniform graduation and makes it easier to blend in the sides at the correct length.

Figure 11.38 When all sections have been cut to the guideline, comb the hair into shape.

Figure 11.39 Check each side of the hair, making sure both sides are the same length.

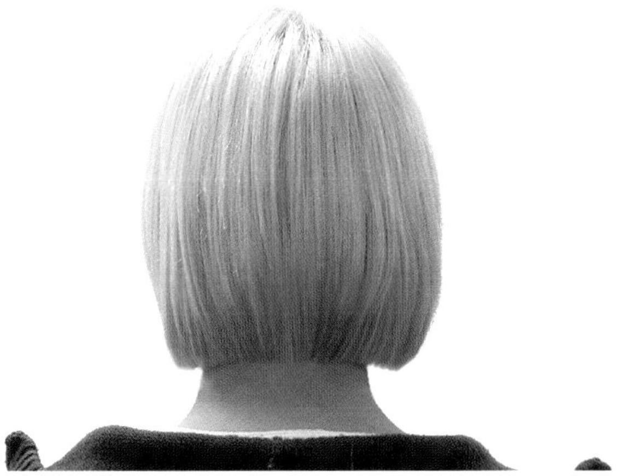

Figure 11.40 Dry or finish hair as required.

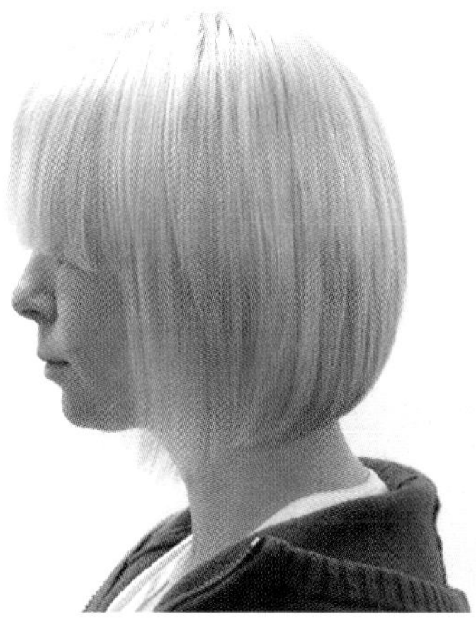

Figure 11.41 A side view.

Online activity 11.7

Five in a row

Uniform layer

Uniform layers produce a style where the inside length is the same length as the perimeter hair length.

Figure 11.42 Comb to untangle the hair. Section the hair from forehead to nape using a centre parting. Using the centre parting as a guide, comb approximately 1.5 cm of hair from both sides of the centre section.

Figure 11.43 Cut the baseline to the required length.

Figure 11.44 Working in vertical sections from the centre of the nape, hold the hair out from the scalp at 90 degrees. Cut hair to this guideline. Do not cut into the baseline, cut to it or from it.

Figure 11.45 Comb down the second section. Working in vertical sections from the centre of head, again hold the hair out at 90 degrees and cut to the guideline. Continue working around the head.

Figure 11.46 The sides of the hair are joined in by working in vertical sections from the back of the ear to the front of the hairline.

Figure 11.47 The hair is cut throughout the head at various angles. This creates inside shape and movement within the style; it also creates fullness. Layers can be left at any length depending on the required style.

Figure 11.48 Dry or finish hair as required.

Figure 11.49 Back view.

WWW **Online activity 11.8**

Drag into correct order

Cutting in a fringe

Figure 11.50 Section the hair. Determine the length of the front perimeter line. Negotiate the length of the fringe with the client.

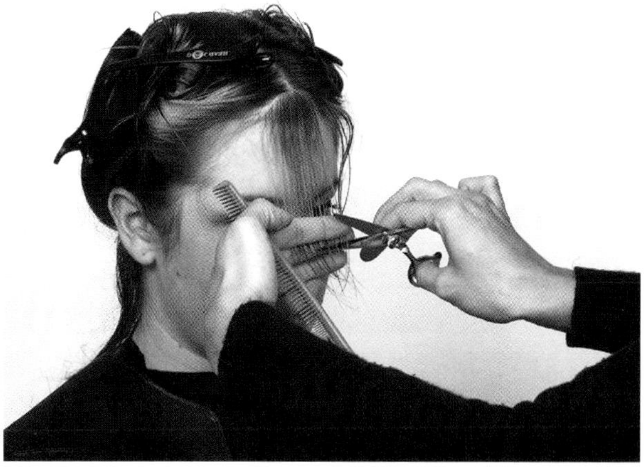

Figure 11.51 No matter what length the front perimeter line is being cut to, the width of the first section should be no wider than the arch of the eyebrow to the arch of the eyebrow.

Key information

If the front perimeter line is cut too wide across the forehead it will result in too little hair left in the recession areas and weaker sides to the hair design.

Long layer haircut

Figure 11.52 Section the hair, and comb down a section around the hairline and pull forward. Cut to the desired length to form the guideline. Cut both sides the same.

Figure 11.53 For a general guide for long layer hair cut with a fringe, rest the fingers on the bridge of the nose, and adjust the graduation accordingly.

Figure 11.54 Unclip the hair on the top of the head and comb from the middle parting. Bring each section of hair forward and cut to the guideline.

Figure 11.55 The angle of the fingers that are supporting the hair to be cut, will determine the length of the layers. This gradient will leave length. Take sections from the crown, comb down and cut to the guideline.

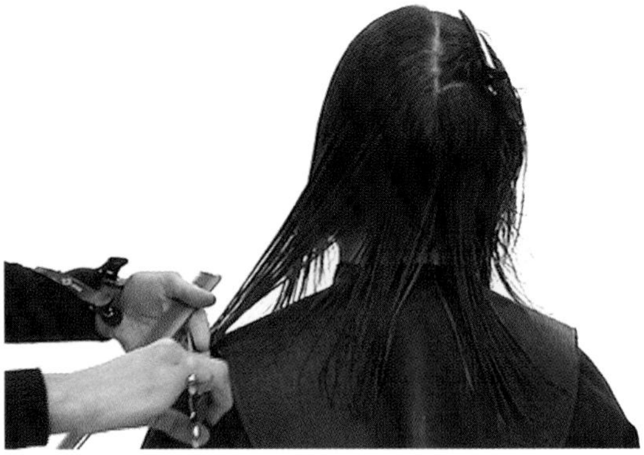

Figure 11.56 Check the hair length at the back following your guideline that has been created from the sides.

Figure 11.57 Working from the centre parting take a section from crown to front hairline. The front hairline is the guideline to be used. Lift and angle the hair and cut to the guideline. The sharper the angle the longer the hair will be left. Follow the sections down to the top of the ears.

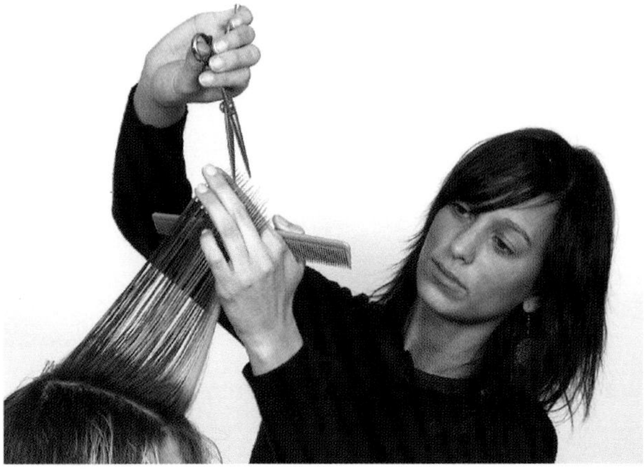

Figure 11.58 Once the sides have all been cut, move on to the crown using the same method.

Figure 11.59 Starting from the centre crown, lift a section of hair and angle towards the guideline to produce the crown layers. This produces a band of layers from the crown to the nape (don't forget to move around your client as you work).

Figure 11.60 Once the layers have been cut throughout the hairstyle, cross check through the hair making sure that all of the layers are even.

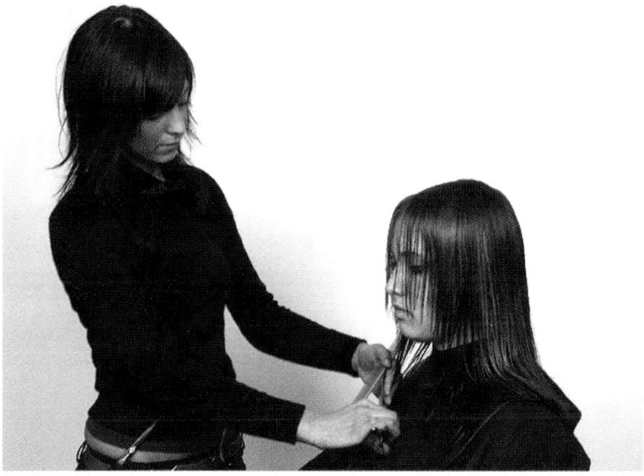

Figure 11.61 Return to the front perimeter line and double check that the front hair and the sides are the required length.

Figure 11.62 Style as required.

Online activity 11.9 WWW

Scrambled words

Graduation haircut on curly hair

When cutting this type of hair, always allow for the natural curl. The tighter the curl, the shorter the hair will be when dry.

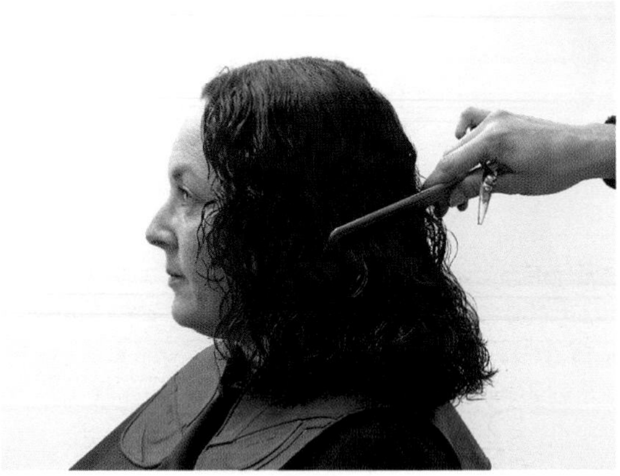

Figure 11.63 Comb hair to untangle.

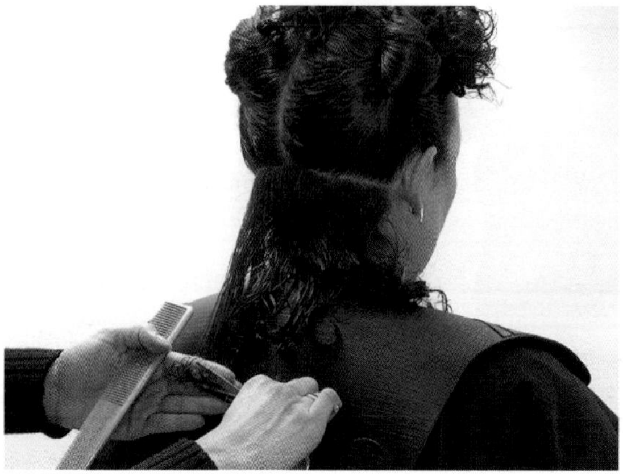

Figure 11.64 After sectioning from forehead to nape, twist and secure hair to top of the head. Comb down approximately 1.5cm of hair from both sides. Cut the baseline to the required length.

Figure 11.65 Comb down the second section. This section should be fine enough for you to see the baseline through it, so it can be used as a cutting guide. Cut off the required amount of hair.

Figure 11.66 Take another section and using the previously cut section as a guideline, continue cutting the hair in a straight line. Continue bringing sections from either side of the centre parting and cutting to the guideline.

Figure 11.67 When the sections have reached the top of the ear, take a section from ear to hairline.

Figure 11.68 This new guideline will introduce a graduation.

Figure 11.69 Continue to bring sections down working towards the crown of the head. Repeat on the other side of the head.

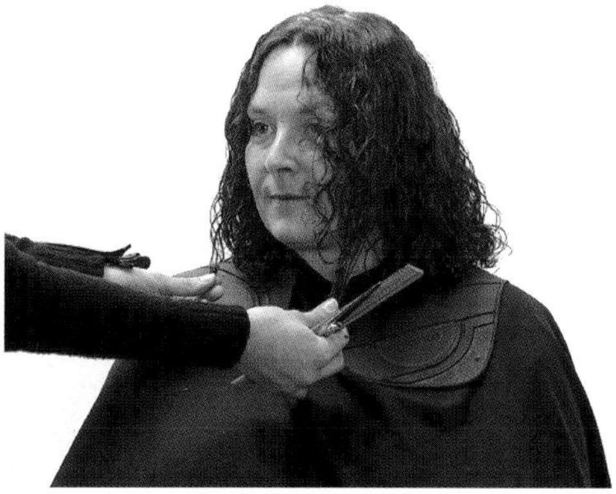

Figure 11.70 Check the sides of the haircut to make sure they are the same length.

Figure 11.71 Square layers will create a graduation on the crown and front sections of the hair to complement the haircut. Take a section of the hair from the crown, lifting it to 180 degrees. Cut straight across. This creates the guideline for the next section.

Figure 11.72 Working towards the front hairline, take the next section and cut to the guideline. Continue to cut sections of the hair until you reach the front hairline.

Figure 11.73 The degree of curl will determine the finished length of the style as illustrated by this graduated cut.

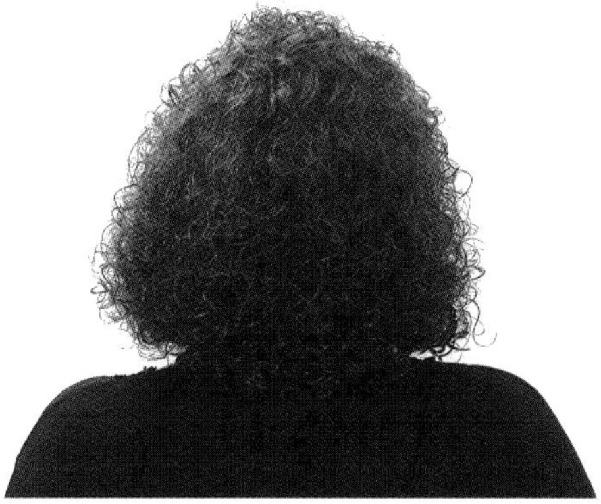

Figure 11.74 Back view.

Online activity 11.10

Round the board

Key information

Check with the client that they are happy with the finished look.

Client care

After cutting, remove any loose clippings of hair from neck and/or shoulders. You can then dry the hair into the required shape. Check with the client that they are happy with the finished look.

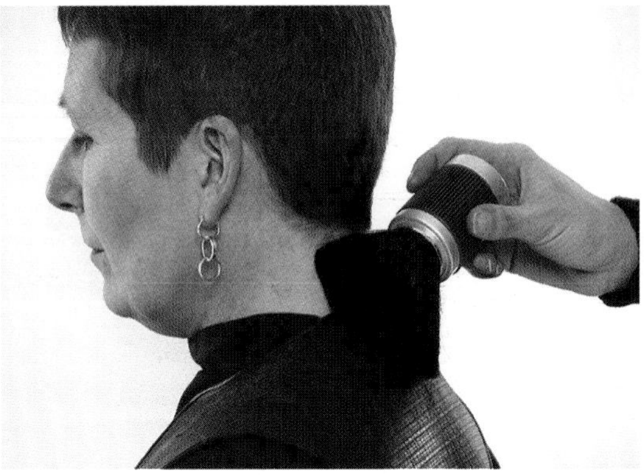

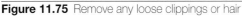

Figure 11.75 Remove any loose clippings or hair

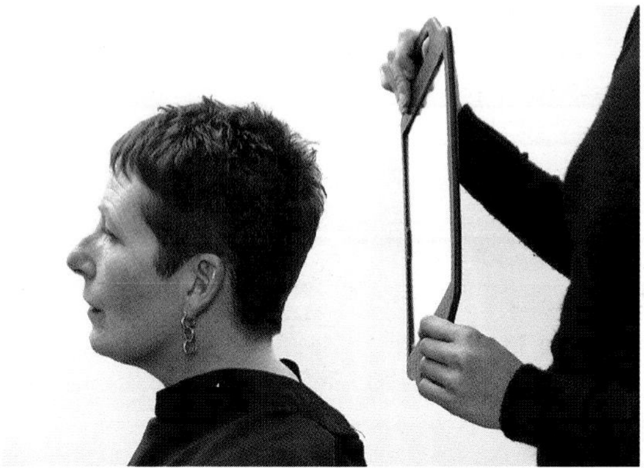

Figure 11.76 Check that the client is happy

Online activity 11.11

Correct selection

11.3 Provide aftercare advice

Key information

An important part of this service is to give the client aftercare advice.

An important part of this service is to give the client aftercare advice. You should explain to the client how often they should return to the salon to maintain their haircut. This will depend on the length of the client's hair. For example, short hair may need to be cut more often than a long hairstyle.

Products

Advise the client on which products can be used at home. This should be based on the factors that influence the service. Refer to Chapter 6 for more information.

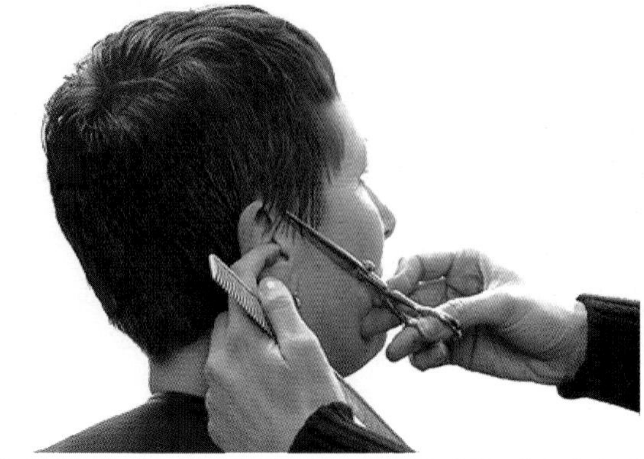

Figure 11.77 Short hair may need more regular maintenance

Figure 11.78 Give customer advice

11.4 Worksheets

WORKSHEETS

You can carry out the worksheets during your study of a chapter or unit, or at the end. An example is presented here and there are more online. If your college or company is registered with ATT Training, lots more are available. Write your answers directly in the book, but only if you own it of course – if it is a library or college book, use a separate piece of paper!

11.4.1 Equipment for cutting

Safety is the key issue when cutting hair. The tools that you use must allow you to perform the haircut that the client wishes to have. Be careful not to damage your tools as you work.

Scissors

These come in a variety of materials such as stainless steel or ceramic, with metal or plastic handles. They also come in a variety of designs and prices. Picking scissors up and holding them is the best way to see if they are suitable. It is important that they feel comfortable. Scissors should always be clean and sharp. Before sterilising remember to remove all loose hairs.

Make a note of different types and brands of scissors that you have come across. Also say which scissors you have and why.

Thinning scissors

These are scissors specifically designed for thinning the hair. They have one or possibly two blades that look like the teeth on a comb. The teeth of the blades are sharp and cut the hair. The gaps between the teeth just allow the hair to pass through without removing any hair at all. The size of the gap determines how much hair is removed.

Make a note of different types and brands of thinning scissors that you have come across. Also say which thinning scissors you have and why.

Razors

A safety razor is designed to prevent accidental cuts to the person using it or to the client. The disadvantage of this type of razor is that it does not allow the stylist to clean or mark out the hairline as it will not cut hair against the skin. It is used on mid-lengths to points for reducing length and volume. Razors can only be used on wet hair; when used on dry hair they tear and shred the cuticle leaving the cortex frayed and exposed. It is also uncomfortable for the client. Salons using razor blades must dispose of them in a container such as a sharps box.

Make a note of different types and brands of razor that you have come across.

What does the sharps box or razor disposal container look like in your salon and where can it be found?

Clippers

Electric clippers can be used with or without attachments but should only be used on dry hair. When in use the bottom blade remains still whilst the top blade moves across it very quickly to cut the hair. Do not use electric clippers when your hands are wet and remember to oil clippers using clipper oil after every use. When using electric clippers all repairs should be carried out by a qualified electrician.

Describe the attachments that you could find with electric clippers, and state their purpose.

Why should you avoid using electric clippers when your hands are wet? What would be the effect if you did use them with wet hands?

Why should you oil clippers after every use?

11.5 Assessment

Well done! If you have studied all the content of this unit you may be ready to test your knowledge.

Check out the 'Preparing for assessments' section in Chapter 1 if you have not already done so, and always remember:

- You can only do your best if you have. . .
  - studied hard
  - completed the activities
  - completed the worksheets
  - practised, practised, practised
  - and then revised!

Now carry out the online multiple-choice quiz

. . . and good luck in the final exam, which will be arranged by your tutor/assessor.

CHAPTER 12

Colour hair

This chapter covers all aspects of the NVQ/SVQ unit GH9, Change hair colour, GB2, Change men's hair colour, and the VRQ unit 207, Colour and lighten hair. Some extra application techniques for men's colouring can be accessed online.

This chapter introduces you to the techniques of colouring. You will learn about the different products available and the effects these may have on the hair along with the various methods used for colouring hair.

In this chapter you will learn about:

- maintaining effective and safe methods of working when colouring and lightening hair
- preparing for colouring and lightening hair
- colouring and lightening hair
- providing aftercare advice.

Website

www.atthairdressing.com

CHAPTER 12 COLOURING HAIR: CONTENTS, SCREENS AND ACTIVITIES

Key:
Sections from the book are set in this colour
Screens available online are set in this colour
Online activity screens are set in this colour

Working safely

Introduction
Maintain effective and safe methods
Round the board
COSHH
Precautions
Protecting the client
Posture and deportment
Record keeping
Data Protection Act
NVQ application times
Shoot the targets

Prepare for colouring and lightening

Introduction
Understanding colour
The colour star
Correct selection
Natural colour
Choosing colour
Semi-permanent colour 1
Semi-permanent colour 2
Quasi-permanent colour 1
Quasi-permanent colour 2
Permanent colour
Hydrogen peroxide
Diluting hydrogen peroxide
Five in a row
Bleach 1
Drag into correct order
Bleach 2
Toning
Preparation - consultation
Viability to colouring or lightening
Check it
Contraindications
Tests - skin test
Porosity test
Elasticity test
Incompatibility test
Test cutting
Colour test
Round the board
Record the results
Recommendations
Preparing client for colouring and lightening
Preparing colouring products

Colour and lighten hair

Introduction
Processing time and temperature
Application of semi-permanent colour 1
Application of semi-permanent colour 2
Drag into correct order
Application of quasi colour 1
Application of quasi colour 2
Application of quasi colour 3
Drag into correct order
Application of colour to re-growth hair 1
Application of colour to re-growth hair 2
Application of colour to re-growth hair 3
Application of colour to re-growth hair 4
Round the board
Application of colour to re-growth hair 5
Full head application of permanent colour 1
Full head application of permanent colour 2
Full head application of permanent colour 3
Full head application of permanent colour 4
Full head application of permanent colour 5
Create highlight and lowlight effects
Wordsearch
Application of weaved highlights and lowlights 1
Application of weaved highlights and lowlights 2
Application of weaved highlights and lowlights 3
Application of weaved highlights and lowlights 4
Drag into correct order
Application of weaved highlights and lowlights 5
Application of weaved highlights and lowlights - foils
Pull through lowlights and highlights - plastic strips
Confirming with the client and record results
Dealing with problems

Provide aftercare advice

Introduction
Post colouring treatments
Check it
Client's lifestyle
Use of heated styling equipment
Worksheet – dealing with problems
Worksheet – the colour star
Worksheet – preparing for colouring/lightening
Online multiple choice quiz

12.1 Safe working methods when colouring and lightening hair

Effective and safe methods

When colouring and lightening hair it is very important that you keep in mind that you are working with chemicals. This section will cover the health and safety issues to protect yourself and your client from the dangers from colouring and lightening hair.

Safety first

Chapter 2 covers health and safety working methods in more detail. Refer to this chapter if needed.

Online activity 12.1 WWW

Round the board

Control of Substances Hazardous to Health Regulations 2002 (COSHH)

These lay down the essential requirements for controlling exposure to hazardous substances and for protecting people who may be affected by them. A substance is considered to be hazardous if it can cause harm to the body. It only poses a risk if it is:

- inhaled (breathed in)
- ingested (swallowed)
- in contact with the skin or eyes
- absorbed through the skin
- injected into the body
- introduced into the body via cuts etc.

Safety first

A substance is considered to be hazardous if it can cause harm to the body.

WWW

The associated learning screen for this part is interactive

Precautions

- Follow manufacturers' instructions.
- Always wear personal protective equipment (PPE).
- Avoid chemical contact with skin, eyes and face.
- Do not use on sensitive or damaged skin.
- Always use a non-metallic bowl to avoid rapid decomposition of the product.
- Store the product in a cool, dry place away from sunlight or other sources of heat. Make sure containers are properly sealed when not in use.
- Store the product in the container and replace the cap immediately after use.
- Never mix products unless recommended by the manufacturer.
- Take extra care not to inhale any powder bleach when mixing.
- Rotate stock.
- Keep products, especially aerosols, away from naked flames or heat.

Safety first

Take extra care not to inhale any powder bleach when mixing.

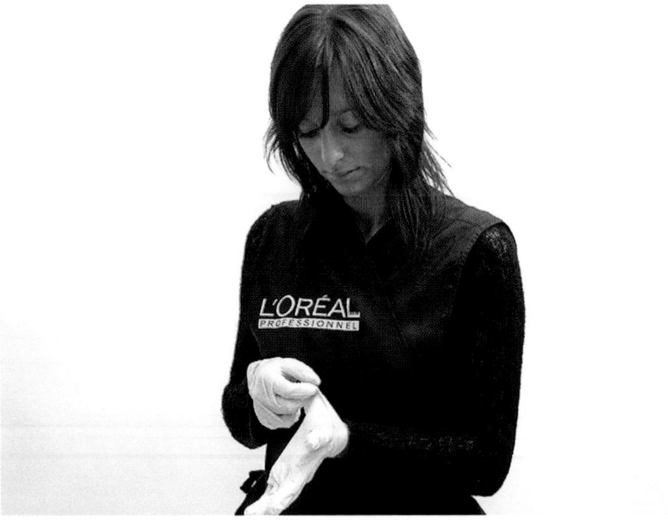

Figure 12.1 Always wear PPE (Personal Protective Equipment)

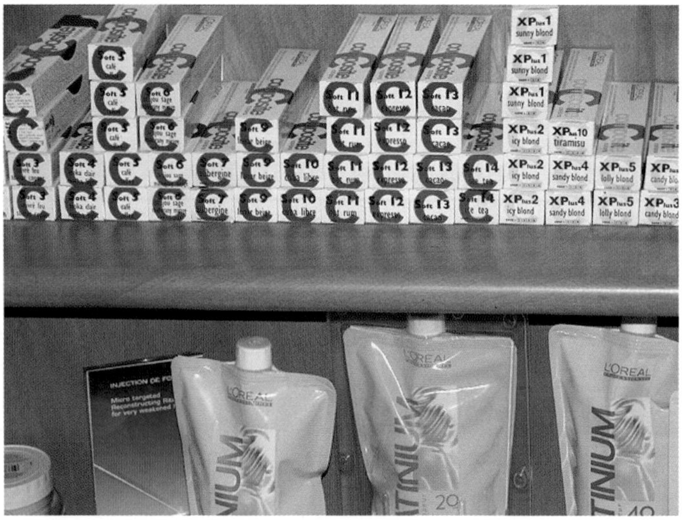

Figure 12.2 Colouring products

Safety first

Keep all products, but especially aerosols, away from naked flames or heat.

Website

www.atthairdressing.com

Protecting the client during the colouring and lightening process

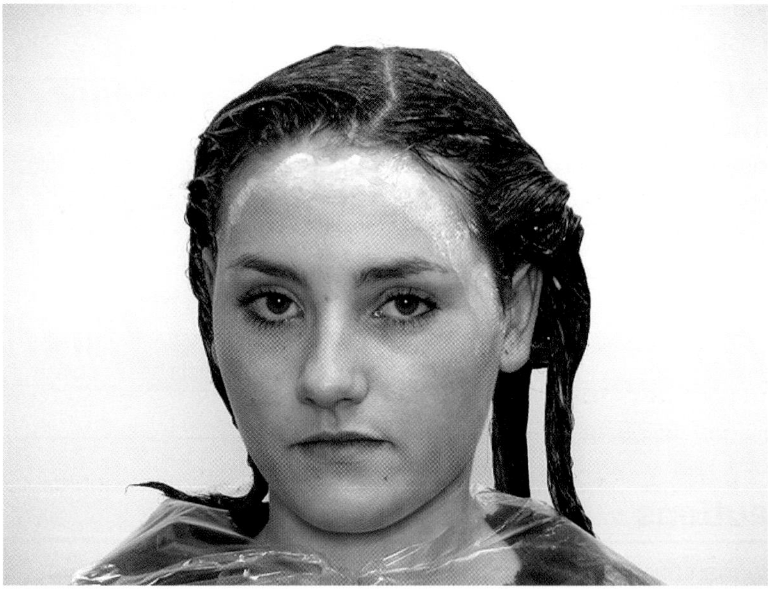

Figure 12.3 Barrier cream can be used

Care should be taken not to come into contact with the scalp surrounding skin as colouring (especially semi-permanent) will stain the skin and scalp. A barrier cream should be used around the hairline and at the tops of the ears. Extra care should be taken with very fine hair. Since bleaching will remove colour from fabric, it is important to protect the client's clothes from any damage through accidental spillage of products. Make sure that the client is comfortable throughout the colouring process.

Key information

Make sure that the client is comfortable throughout the colouring process.

Posture and deportment

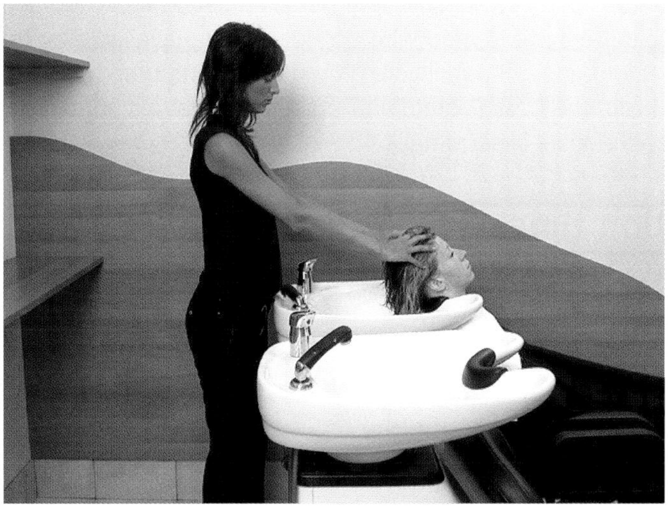

Figure 12.4 A good working posture

Make sure you check your posture during the colouring and lightening process to avoid injury. The back should be kept straight, bend from the knees, feet apart with weight evenly distributed. If the spine is bent the back will have excess strain and the body will tire. The lungs will also be constricted; this lowers the intake of oxygen, which induces tiredness.

Safety first

Make sure you check your posture during the colouring and lightening process to avoid injury.

Record keeping

It is important to record consultation details and information regarding all services carried out on a client including the following:

- date of skin test
- choice of colour
- date of last service
- documented evidence in case of litigation
- salon's professional image.

For this purpose all hairdressing salons have a system of client record keeping and the hairdresser must take great care in record entry.

Figure 12.5 Record all details accurately

Definition

Data Protection Act: A United Kingdom Act of Parliament which defines UK law on the processing of data on identifiable living people. It is the main piece of legislation that governs the protection of personal data in the UK.

Key information

To fulfil the Data Protection Act all client details must be recorded accurately.

Data Protection Act

To fulfil the Data Protection Act all client details must be recorded accurately. They must be current, be treated with confidence and available for the client to access their information. If details are stored on a computer, the company must be registered with the Data Protection Register and have a named person who will access confidential client details.

Application times

Table 12.1 shows times to complete each colour and/or lightening application.

Table 12.1 Application times

Preparation, mix colour and apply	Time (minutes)
Re-growth permanent colour	25
Full head pulled through highlights/lowlights	35
At least 20% of the head pulled through highlights/lowlights	15
Full head woven highlights/lowlights	75

Online activity 12.2

Shoot the target

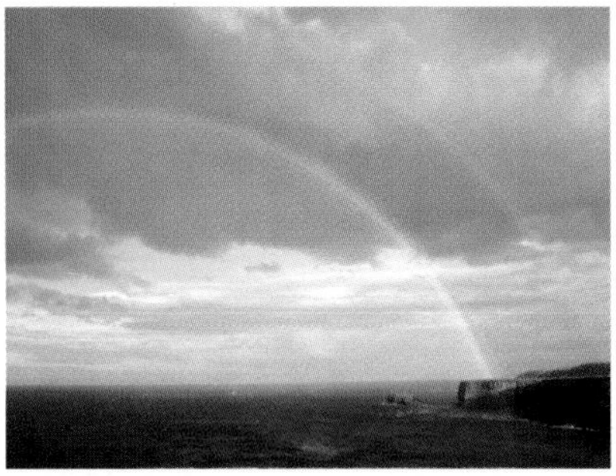

Figure 12.6 A rainbow of colours

Activity

Associated learning screen is online.

Definition

White light is a mixture of colours.

12.2 Prepare for colouring and lightening

Introduction

This preparation involves carrying out a consultation to find out the client's colour requirements. When the client is choosing a colour shade, it is essential that you understand the colouring principles so that you can help them make an informed decision. Tests must be carried out before colouring and lightening to ensure the client's hair and scalp are suitable for the process.

Understanding colour

White light is a mixture of colours. This is shown when rain falls on sunlight and a rainbow appears. In hairdressing you will need to distinguish the primary and secondary colours.

The colour star

The achievement of a desired colour can be explained by the concept of a colour star. All colours are made up from the primary shades yellow, blue and red. Secondary shades are produced by mixing the primary shades together. Other colours can be made by mixing the primary and secondary colours together. The various possible colour combinations are achieved by differing the proportions of the primary and secondary colours.

- Red, yellow and orange are the warm colours on the colour star.
- Blue, green and violet are the cool colours.
- Opposite colours on the colour star will neutralise each other. For example, if a colour appears to look too green it can be neutralised using a warm shade.

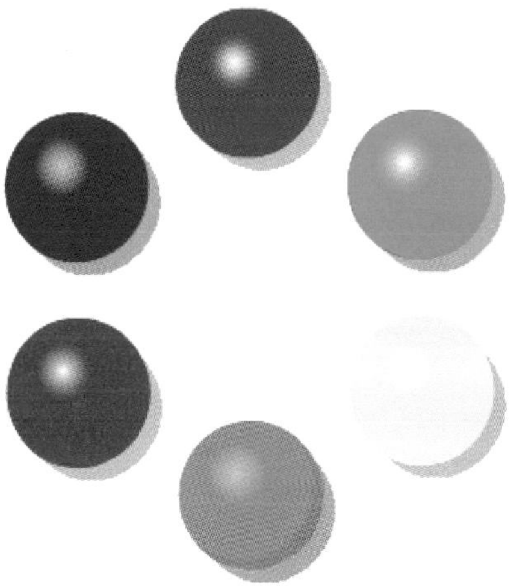

Figure 12.7 The colour star

Online activity 12.3 WWW

Correct selection

Key information

All colours are made up from the primary shades yellow, blue and red.

Natural colour

- Natural colouring pigment in the hair is called melanin and is found in the cortex.
- Pheomelanin are the red and yellow colouring pigments.
- Eumelanin are the black and brown pigments.
- White hair is hair without pigment (colourless hair is called canities).
- Grey hair is a mixture of natural coloured hair and white hair, often expressed as a percentage.
- Colour depth is a term used to describe the natural lightness and darkness of the hair.

Definition

Pheomelanin: Is found in hair and skin and is present both in lighter-skinned humans and darker-skinned humans. Pheomelanin imparts a pink to red hue and, thus, is found in particularly large quantities in red hair.

Definition

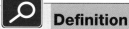

Eumelanin: The two types are black eumelanin and brown eumelanin. Black eumelanin is present mostly in non-Europeans and aged Europeans, while brown eumelanin is present in mostly young Europeans.

A small amount of black eumelanin in the absence of other pigments causes grey hair. A small amount of brown eumelanin in the absence of other pigments causes yellow (blonde) colour hair.

Choosing colour

Figure 12.8 Checking the client's base colour

Definition

ICC: International Colour Code.

Figure 12.9 Semi-permanent colour molecules are deposited in the cuticle

Key information

Semi-permanent colours are collectively called nitro-dyes.

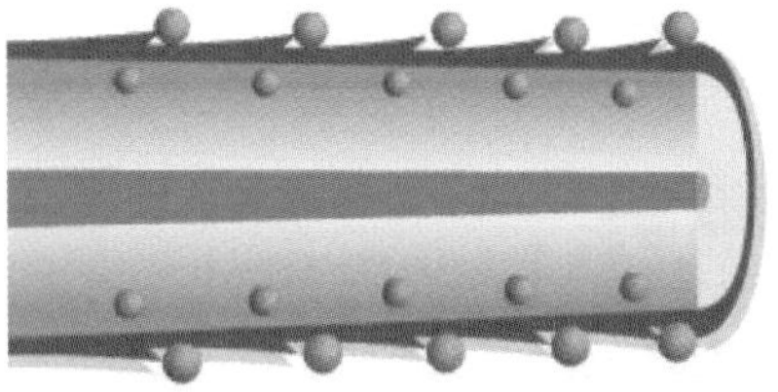

Figure 12.10 Quasi-permanent colour does not penetrate as far into the cortex as permanent tint

Key information

Quasi-permanent colour lasts longer than a semi-permanent colour but not as long as a permanent tint.

Definition

Quasi: A combining form meaning resembling, having some, but not all of the features of something. It is used in the formation of compound words such as quasi-colour!

Key information

Quasi-colours are popular because of the variety of fashion shades to choose from as well as natural shades.

When selecting a target colour, you must first use a shade chart to select the client's base colour. All shade charts use a system which is similar to the international coding system ICC (International Colour Code). Base colour describes the natural lightness and darkness of the hair (depth) and will be from 1 (black) - 10 (lightest blonde). This will be the first number on the chart. Any following numbers describe the tone of the colour.

Semi-permanent colour

Small colour molecules are deposited in the hair cuticle or wedged under the open cuticle. The number of colour molecules is reduced a little each time the hair is shampooed. This causes a gentle fading of the colour. Semi-permanent colours are collectively called nitro-dyes. The dyes will darken the hair, add strong colour tones, blend in white hair, and achieve a subtle colour change. The colour lasts between 6 and 8 washes.

Quasi-permanent colour

Quasi-permanent colour lasts longer than a semi-permanent colour but not as long as a permanent tint. The colour molecules do not penetrate as far into the cortex as the permanent tint. Unlike the semi-permanent colour it fades over a longer period of time and will lighten, colour and tone the hair. Like permanent tint there is usually a regrowth line.

Figure 12.11 Squeezing tint into a bowl

Figure 12.12 Measuring out hydrogen peroxide

Most quasi-colours are mixed with their own developers containing a low percentage of hydrogen peroxide. The colour molecules are oxidised by the oxygen from hydrogen peroxide. Quasi-colours are popular because of the variety of fashion shades to choose from as well as natural shades. They are more effective and are longer lasting than semi-permanent colours. They are not so harsh on the hair, add shine and have conditioning properties.

Permanent colour

With this type of colour the molecules penetrate the cuticle and are absorbed into the cortex. The colour molecules are oxidised by the hydrogen peroxide and it remains permanently deposited in the cortex.

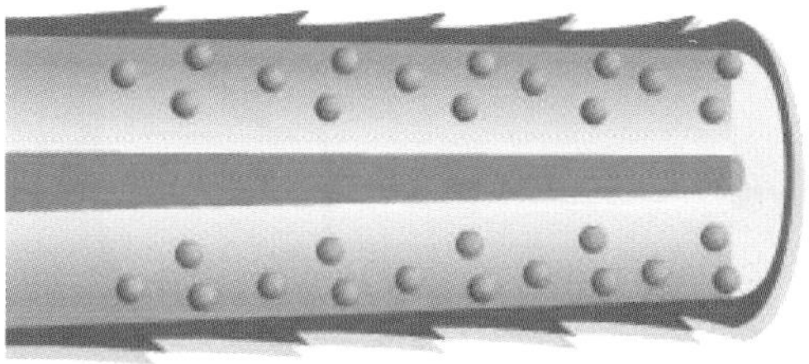

Figure 12.13 Permanent colour molecules penetrate the cuticles and are absorbed into the cortex

Key information

With a permanent colour, the molecules penetrate the cuticles and are absorbed into the cortex.

Hydrogen peroxide

Tint remains in the hair until it is cut out and will darken or lighten and add tone to the hair. Hydrogen peroxide is required to be mixed with the tint in order to activate it. On the basis of the choice of tint, the strength of hydrogen peroxide required is determined by whether the hair is to be tinted darker or lighter. In general hair being tinted lighter will require a peroxide of 30 volume (9%) while hair being tinted darker, or within its base colour depth, will require a strength of 20 volume (6%).

Figure 12.14 Squeezing out tint into a bowl

Definition

Peroxide: Short for hydrogen peroxide, especially when used for bleaching hair. Peroxide actually means a compound having lots of oxygen attached.

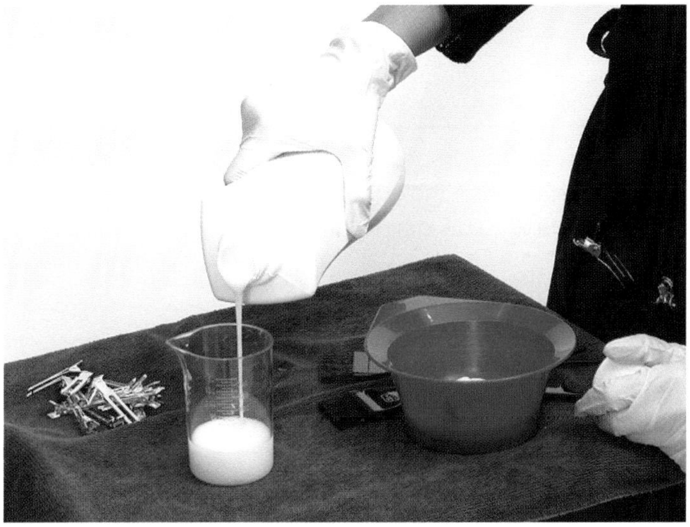

Figure 12.15 Measuring out hydrogen peroxide

Figure 12.16 Mixing

Key information

Tint remains in the hair until it is cut out and will darken or lighten the hair and add tone.

Diluting hydrogen peroxide

Should you need to dilute hydrogen peroxide use water in the correct ratio shown in Table 12.2:

Table 12.2 Diluting hydrogen peroxide

Current strength	Ratio - water: peroxide	Dilutes to
20 vol (6%)	1:1	10 vol (3%)
30 vol (9%)	2:1	10 vol (3%)
30 vol (9%)	1:2	20 vol (6%)
40 vol (12%)	1:1	20 vol (6%)
40 vol (12%)	1:3	30 vol (9%)

WWW Online activity 12.4

Five in a row

Bleach

When bleach is mixed with hydrogen peroxide, oxygen is released. The product penetrates the cuticle and then the cortex. Oxygen mixes with the melanin in the cortex creating oxymelanin. This oxymelanin is colourless.

The oxygen forms with the different colour pigments in a certain order:

- black
- brown
- red
- orange
- orange yellow
- yellow
- pale yellow.

Definition

Oxymelanin: The by-product of the bleaching process.

Key information

When bleach is mixed with hydrogen peroxide, oxygen is released.

Bleach remains within the hair until it is cut out. See online screen for more information.

Online activity 12.5 WWW

Drag into correct order

Figure 12.17 Emulsion oil cream or gel bleach is one example of a bleaching product

Bleaching products

The two most commonly used types of bleaches are:

- powder bleach used for highlights (most powder bleachers are not recommended for use on the scalp)
- emulsion oil cream or gel bleach used for full head treatment.

In general hair being bleached will require a peroxide of 30 volume (9%).

Toning

It may be necessary to remove the yellow tones from the hair after bleaching. Violet may be used to neutralise. If used, toner should be applied to damp hair, starting at the roots and working towards the mid-lengths and ends. The products should be used according to the manufacturers' instructions.

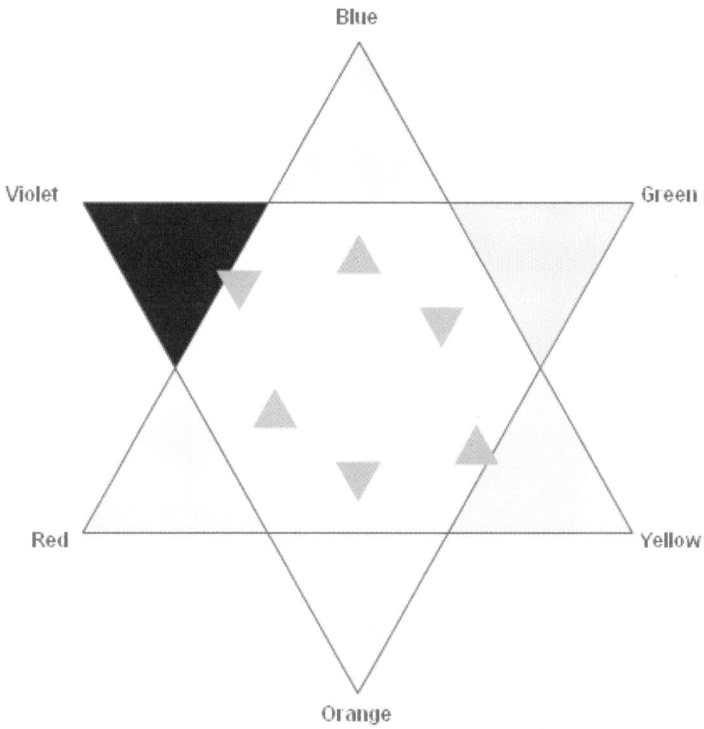

Figure 12.18 Toner guide

Preparation for colouring/lightening – consultation

A consultation is carried out to establish the client's ideas about colour and to discuss a target colour they wish to have. Any questions they may have should be answered, for example how it is possible to achieve the target colour. Establish the client's natural hair colour by examining the hair for previous treatments.

Key information

A consultation is carried out to establish the client's ideas about colour and to discuss a target colour they wish to have.

Figure 12.19 Discuss the client's ideas during the consultation

Viability of colouring or lightening

Before colouring and/or lightening the client's hair, you must check that it is viable to do so. You can do this by:

- checking the client's records to see if they have had any previous allergic reactions to colouring products
- asking the client during the consultation if they have had any adverse effects from colouring
- visually checking the client's hair and scalp
- carrying out skin and hair tests, referring to manufacturers' instructions at all times.

Ensure that any responses or results are recorded for future use.

Figure 12.20 Checking the hair

Online activity 12.6 WWW

Check it

Contraindications to the colouring and/or lightening service

These include:

- medical reasons
- allergies to any products
- skin disorders
- incompatibility to products
- damage to the hair.

Figure 12.21 Checking the client's hair for contraindications

Tests – skin test

This is conducted to see if a client will develop an allergic reaction to the chemicals contained in colouring products. They are usually carried out before tinting and semi-permanent services. About one in twenty five clients develops a positive reaction to the test; under no circumstances should the service be completed. Colouring companies recommend this method to comply with legal requirements.

Gown the client and prepare a solution of the chemical to be used in the salon service. Cleanse behind the ear with cotton wool and alcohol. Place a penny sized smear of the chemical on the cleansed area. To protect the area from water it may be covered with collodion. Ask the client to return after 48 hours. Redness, swelling or irritation would indicate a positive reaction and the treatment should not be supplied. Colouring companies recommend this method to comply with legal requirements.

Safety first

A skin test is conducted to see if a client will develop an allergic reaction to the chemicals contained in colouring products.

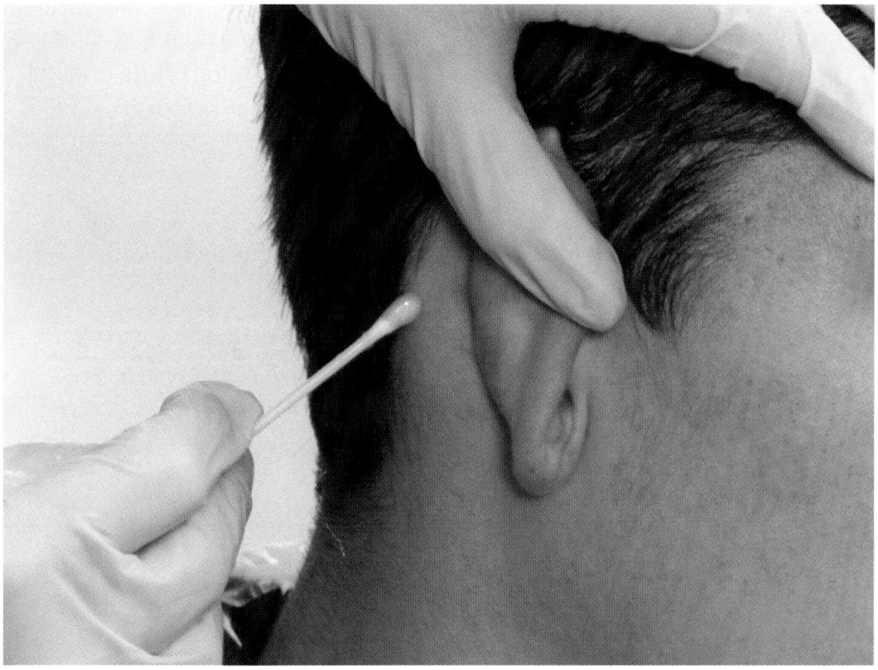

Figure 12.22 Carry out a skin test

Definition

Porosity: The condition of being porous but also the ratio of the volume of all the pores (spaces) in a material to the volume of the whole.

Porosity test

The porosity test assesses the degree of damage to the cuticle. A damaged cuticle absorbs more moisture, which makes the hair feel rougher.

Hold a few strands of the hair at the end and slide your fingers towards the root. If it feels rough the cuticles are raised and this indicates the condition of the hair is poor. If it feels smooth the cuticles are flat and the condition of the hair is good.

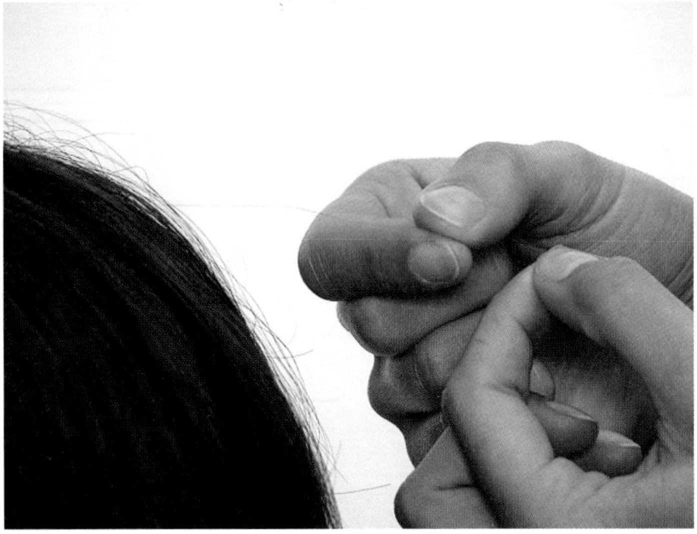

Figure 12.23 The porosity test

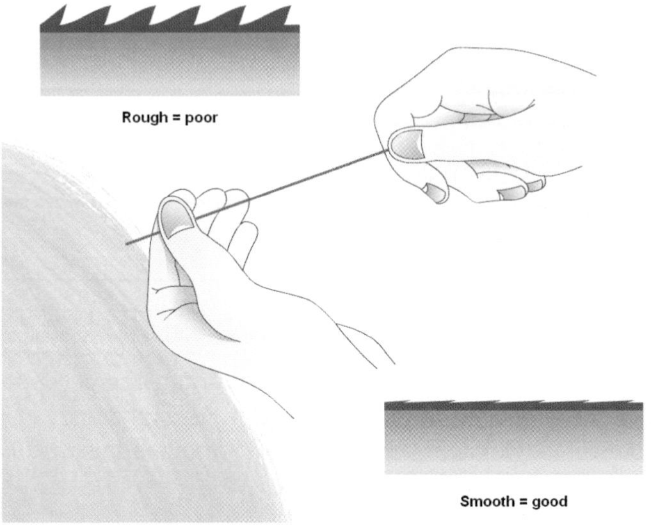

Figure 12.24 Porosity test method

Definition

Cuticles: A term used for any of a variety of tough but flexible, non-mineral outer coverings of an organism, or parts of an organism, that provide protection.

Elasticity test

This test assesses the extent of damage to the cortex of the hair. It measures the ability of the hair to be stretched.

Hold a single strand of dry hair firmly at each end with finger and thumb. Pull back gently and see how much the hair stretches and springs back. A hair in good condition can stretch up to a third of its length and return to its original length. If the hair snaps it indicates that the hair has a weak cortex.

Figure 12.25 Elasticity test

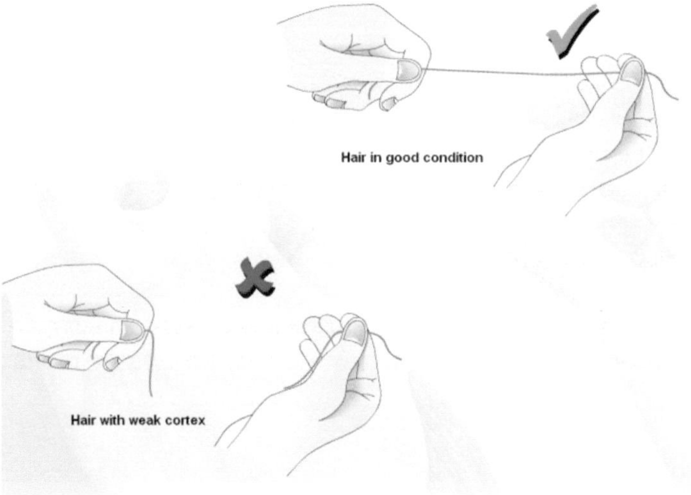

Figure 12.26 Elasticity test results

Incompatibility test

The hairdresser should make sure that any products that have been used previously on the hair do not react unfavourably with products that the hairdresser intends to use. This incompatibility test detects metallic salts used in colour preparations, so-called 'hair colour restorers'.

Prepare a solution of twenty parts hydrogen peroxide and one part ammonia. Sellotape together a small group of hairs taken from the client's head, at the root end. Immerse the hairs in the solution for 30 minutes. A positive reaction will show the presence of bubbles, give off heat (the beaker gets warmer), or the hair will change colour.

Figure 12.27 Incompatibility test

Test cutting

This method can be used to assess the effects of an application before the whole head is treated.

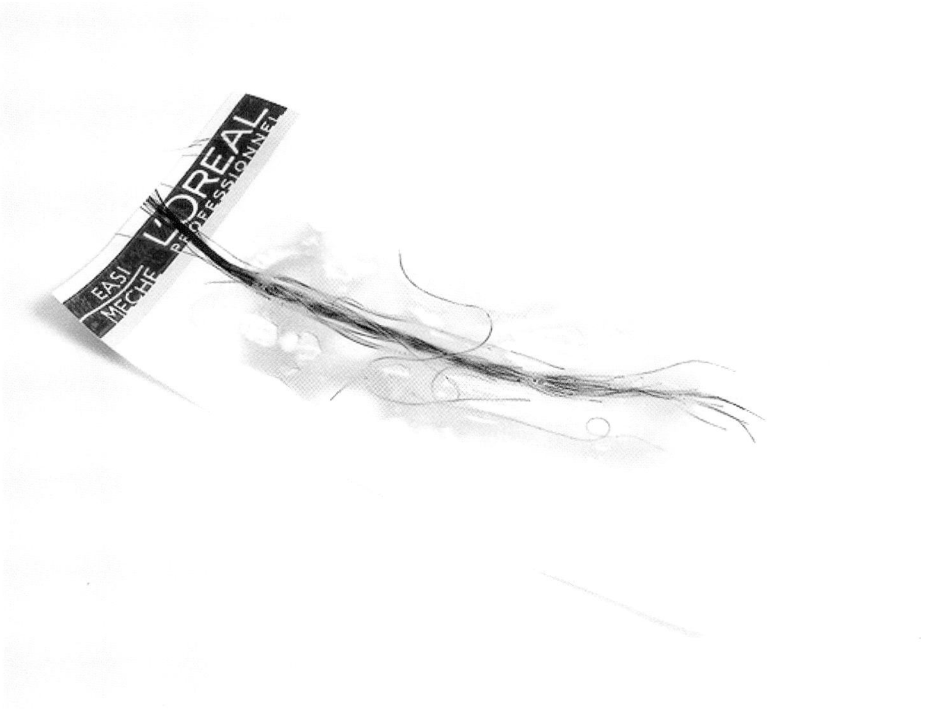

Figure 12.28 Test cutting

Cut a few strands of hair and Sellotape them at the roots. Immerse the strands of hair in the intended products and process according to the manufacturer's instructions. Examine the results for colour effects. Uneven colouring will indicate damaged hair and whether it can take further chemical treatment.

Key information

Sellotape: Clear sticky tape – other brands are available!

Safety first

Uneven colouring will indicate damaged hair and whether it can take further chemical treatment.

Colour/strand test

This test monitors the colour development along a strand of hair during processing. This should be done before the colorant is rinsed from the hair.

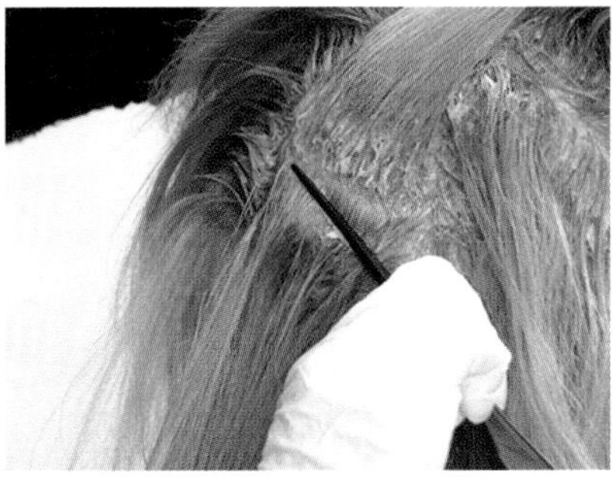

Figure 12.29 Colour/strand test

Remove the colorant from a small mesh of hair. Check to see if the target shade has been reached. If not, leave the colour to develop further. If it has, then remove colour.

WWW Online activity 12.7

Round the board

Record the results

Figure 12.30 Seeking assistance

Record all the results from the tests you have carried out. If you have any doubts about whether to carry out the service, consult with the relevant person, e.g. your manager.

Recommendations

Figure 12.31 Making your recommendations to the client

Once you have carried out the consultation and the relevant tests you should make your recommendations to the client. The basis of this recommendation will be the effect that you believe the hair will achieve. The colour should enhance the client's skin colour. Use shade charts to ensure you are both in agreement before starting the service. Explain clearly to the client how long the service will take and how much it will cost.

Definition

Enhance: To improve something.

Key information

Hair colour should enhance the client's skin colour.

Preparing client for colouring and lightening

Gown the client appropriately for the colouring process. You can apply barrier cream around the hairline if required.

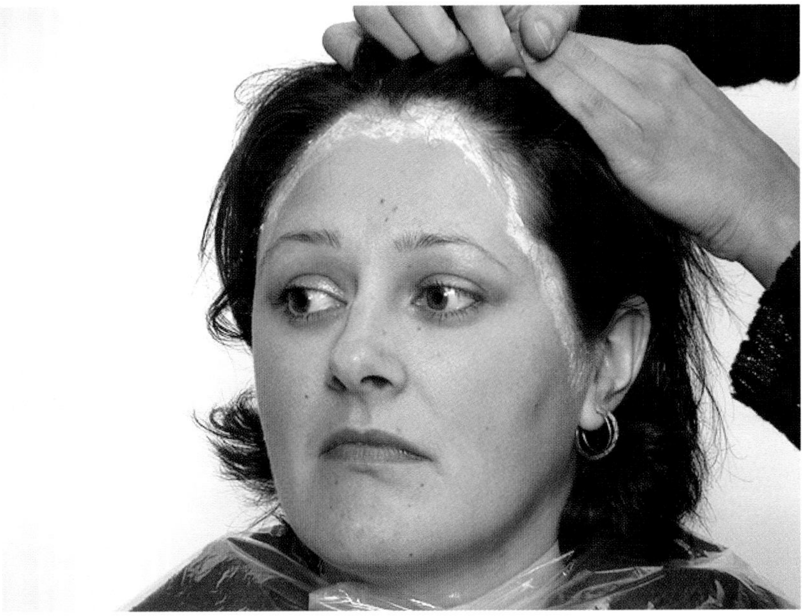

Figure 12.32 Apply barrier cream if required

Preparing colouring products

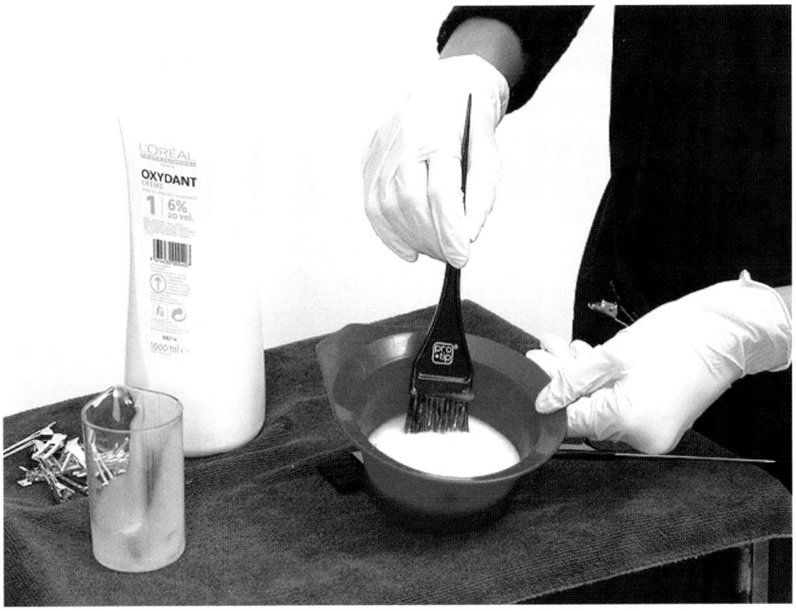

Figure 12.33 Preparing colour

Safety first

Before preparing and/or mixing colour, always read the manufacturer's instructions carefully.

Definition

Lighteners: A product used to lighten the hair to the desired shade.

Before preparing and/or mixing colour, always read the manufacturer's instructions carefully. Measure out products accurately, making sure you have knowledge of the correct volume of hydrogen peroxide to use. Always wear the correct PPE.

12.3 Colour and lighten hair

This section covers the methods of application for both colour and lighteners to the hair. Before commencing the colouring and/or lightening service, confirm with the client the colour that they wish to achieve. This is to ensure that there are no surprises once the colour/lightener has developed.

Processing time and temperature

Processing time can be affected by temperature in the following ways:

- A warm salon will need less processing time than a cool salon.
- If the salon is cool then extra heat can be applied but check the manufacturer's instructions first before applying.

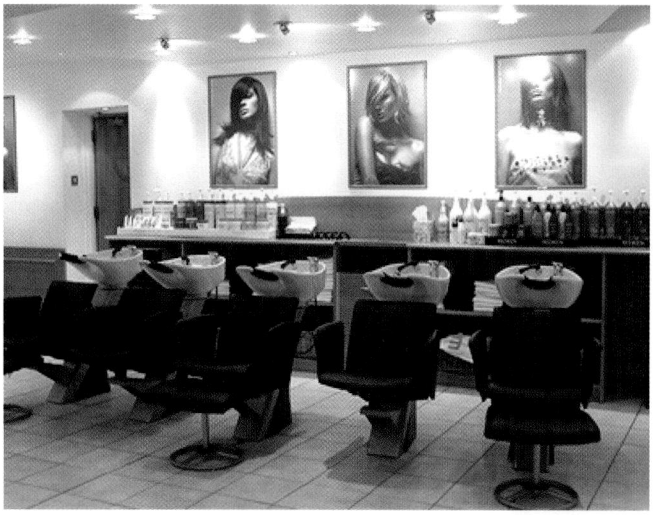

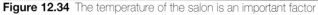

Figure 12.34 The temperature of the salon is an important factor

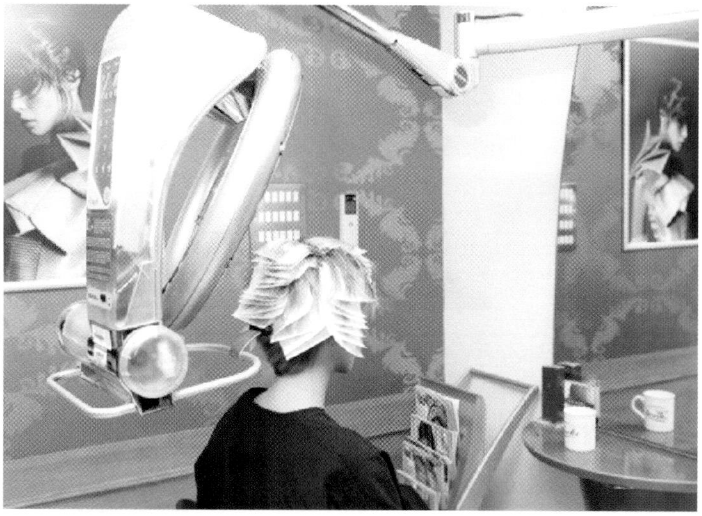

Figure 12.35 Applying heat to the head

Safety first

Ensure that you are wearing the correct PPE when applying colour.

Application of semi-permanent colour

The hair is shampooed and towel dried. Make sure that you and your client are wearing the correct PPE and apply the colour using the product applicator. Take small sections of hair (approximately 3 – 4 cm) taking care the product is distributed evenly all over the head.

Monitor the development according to the manufacturer's instructions. This usually takes 20 – 30 minutes. Rinse the colour out, testing the water to ensure the correct temperature. Dry and style hair into shape.

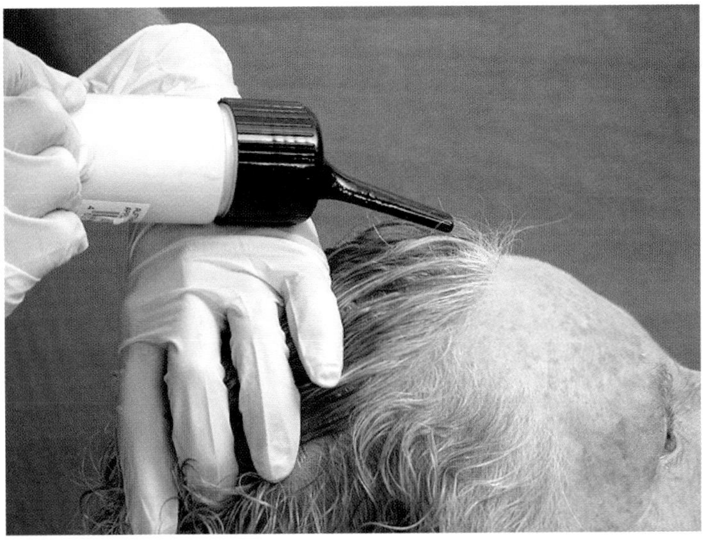

Figure 12.36 Application of semi-permanent colour (online video)

Figure 12.37 Dry and style hair into shape

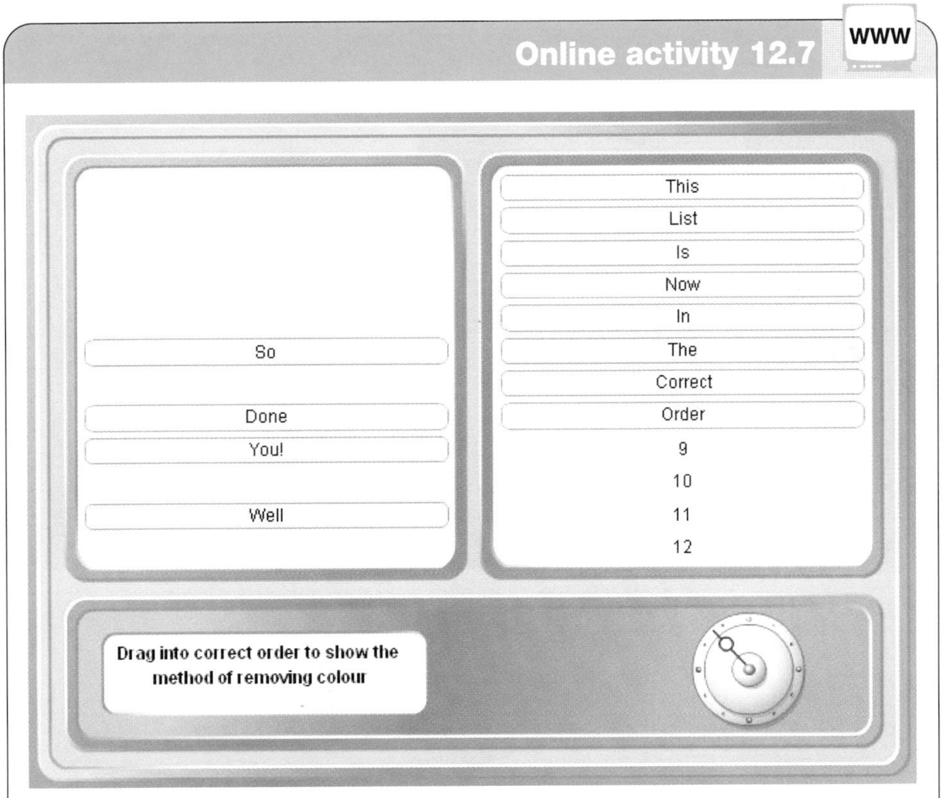

Drag into correct order

Application of quasi-colour

Gown the client and then carry out the following procedure:

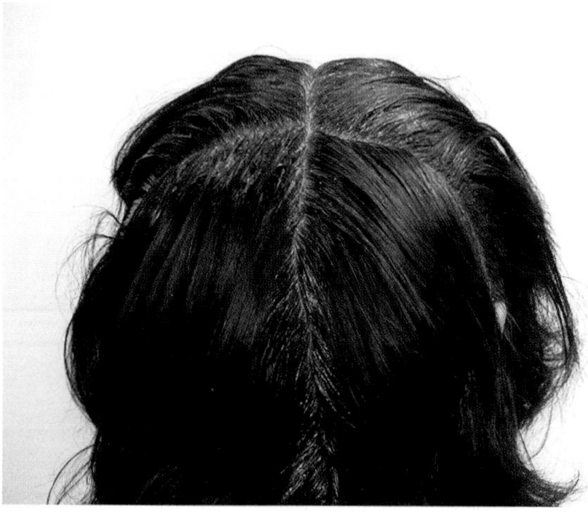

Figure 12.38 After the client is gowned, start at the roots and divide the hair into four using the hot cross bun method.

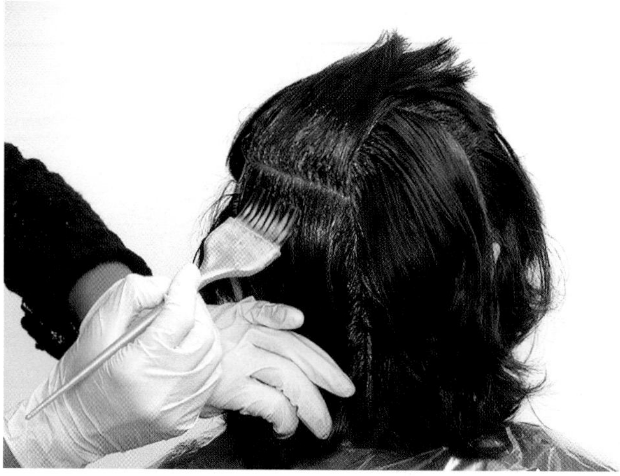

Figure 12.39 Apply to the roots of the hair in each section, ensuring you are wearing the correct PPE. Development time for this colour is approximately 20 minutes.

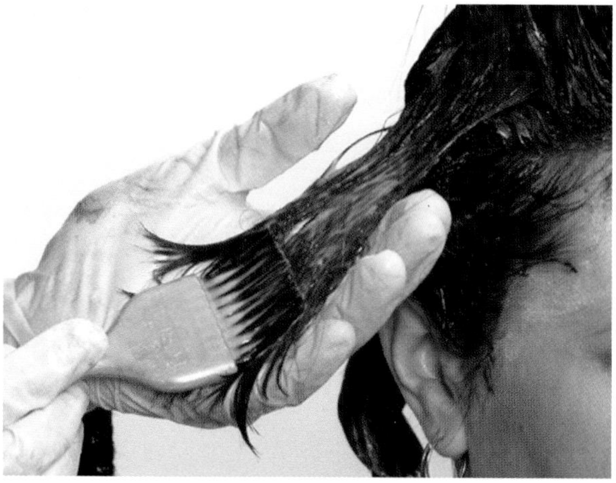

Figure 12.40 Take through to the middle lengths and ends.

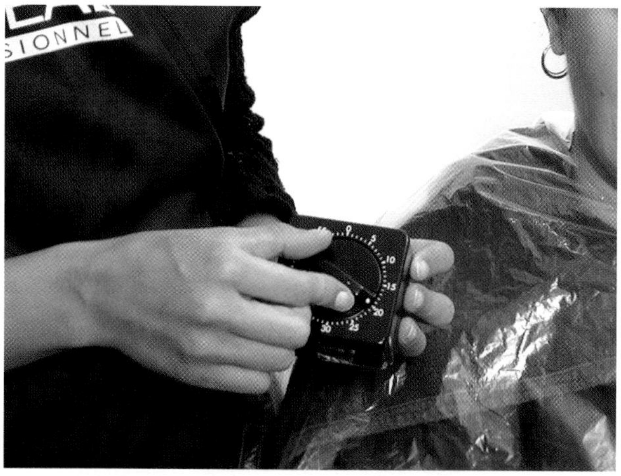

Figure 12.41 Rinse off colour after development time and massage around the hairline to emulsify the colour.

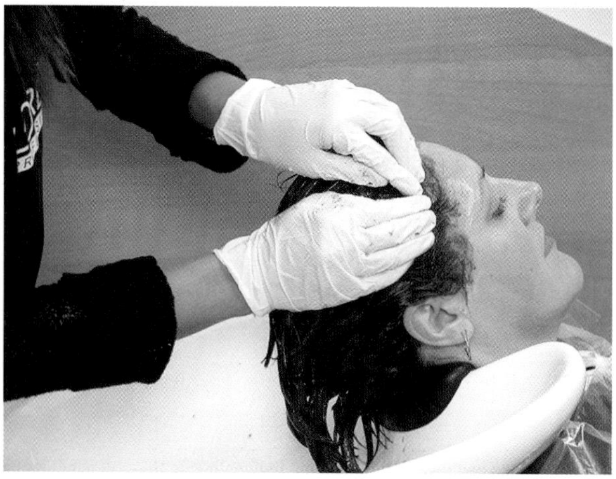

Figure 12.42 Leave to develop.

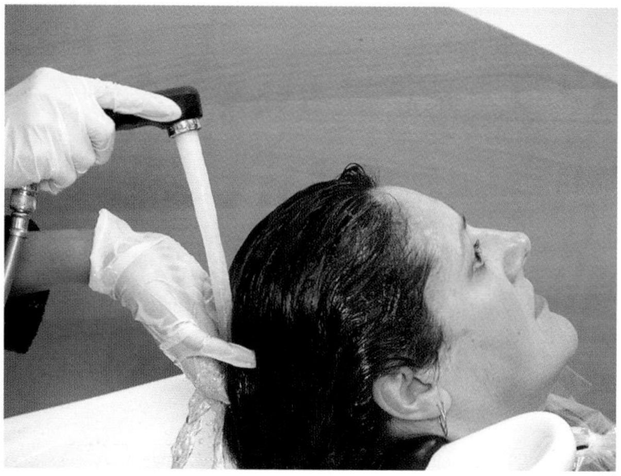

Figure 12.43 Continue to rinse the colour out of the hair.

Figure 12.44 Dry and style hair into shape.

Online activity 12.9 WWW

Drag into correct order

WWW **Website**

www.atthairdressing.com

Application of colour to re-growth hair

Figure 12.45 Once the client has been gowned, the hair is divided into four sections. Clip the sections with large sectioning clips.

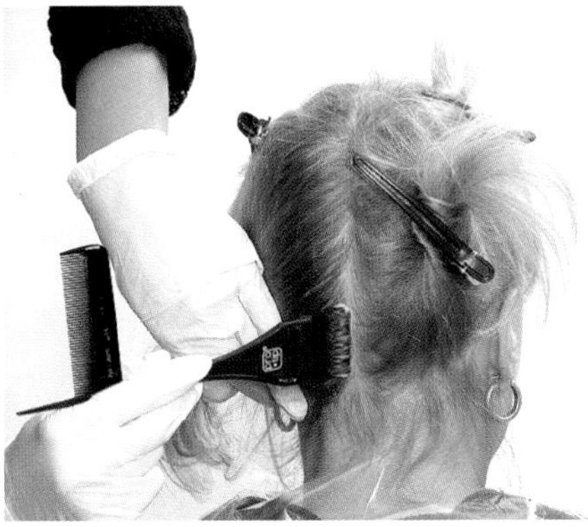

Figure 12.46 Wearing the correct PPE, begin the application by working from the back section starting at the nape. Apply colour using a brush.

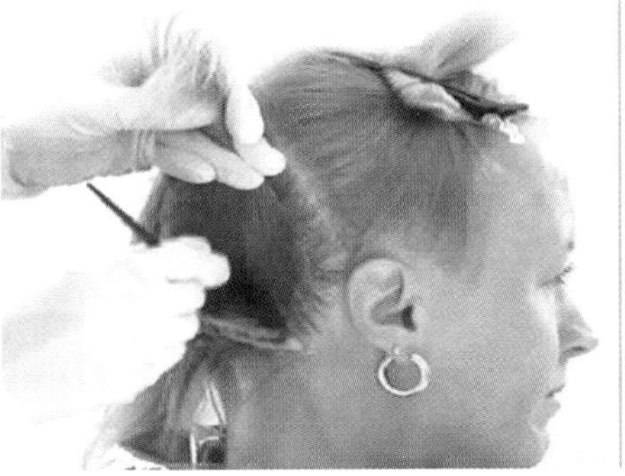

Figure 12.47 Take small sections of hair (approximately 1 cm) and apply the product working towards the front section (see online video).

Figure 12.48 The product should be applied evenly over the head taking care to cover only the re-growth (hair that has grown through from the previous tint). Ends may require colour bath.

Monitor the development according to the manufacturer's instructions. If the hair has faded it will be necessary to refresh the hair colour to the ends of the hair. The product is applied to the ends of the hair for the last 5 – 10 minutes of processing time.

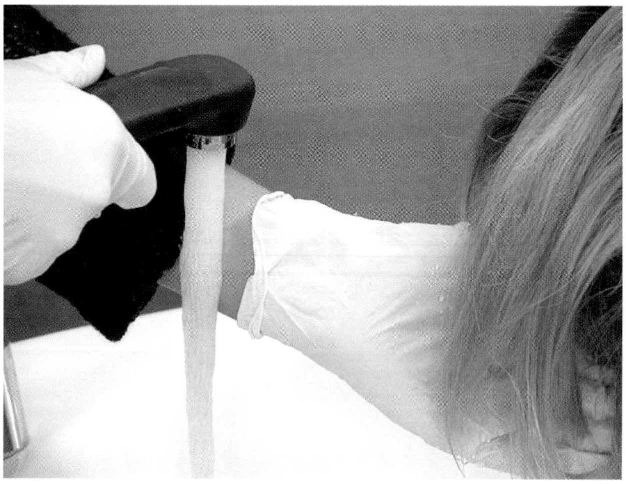

Figure 12.49 Wearing the correct PPE, test the temperature of the water on your wrist. Check the temperature with the client.

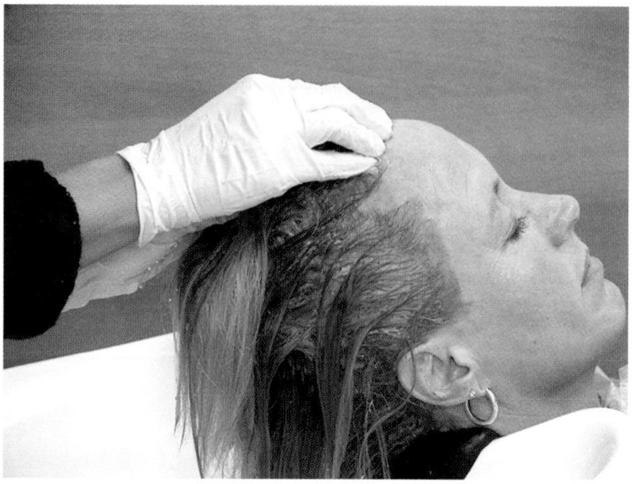

Figure 12.50 Apply water to the client's head and gently massage around the hairline. This process is called emulsifying. Take care to remove all colour traces around the hairline using gentle massage movements.

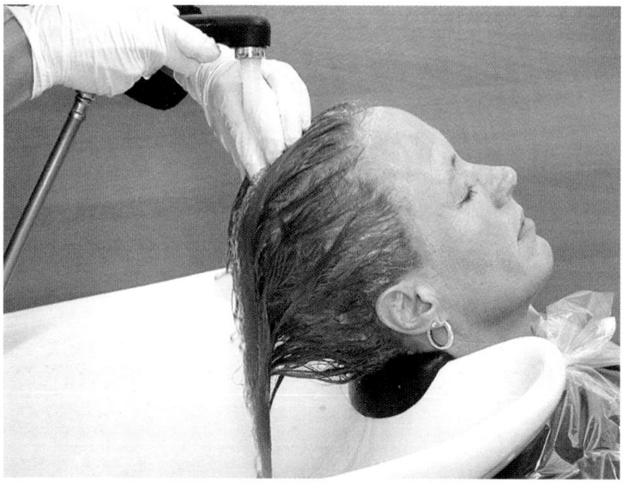

Figure 12.51 Rinse to remove all surplus traces of the product. When removing chemicals from the hair, the water temperature should be cooler as the scalp may be sensitive.

Figure 12.52 Dry and style hair into shape.

Safety first

When removing chemicals from the hair, the water temperature should be cooler as the scalp may be sensitive.

WWW Online activity 12.10

Round the board

Full head application of permanent colour

It is important to bear in mind the length of the hair, porosity and body heat as this will affect how long the colour will need to be developed for:

- Mid-lengths are the most resistant to colour.
- Hair that is porous, mainly at the ends, will develop more quickly than hair that is non-porous.
- Roots will develop faster than the ends due to body heat from the scalp.

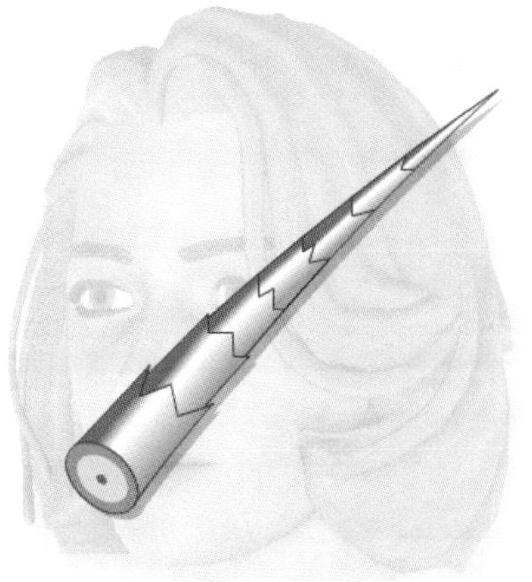

Figure 12.53 Heat affects the development time (see online animation).

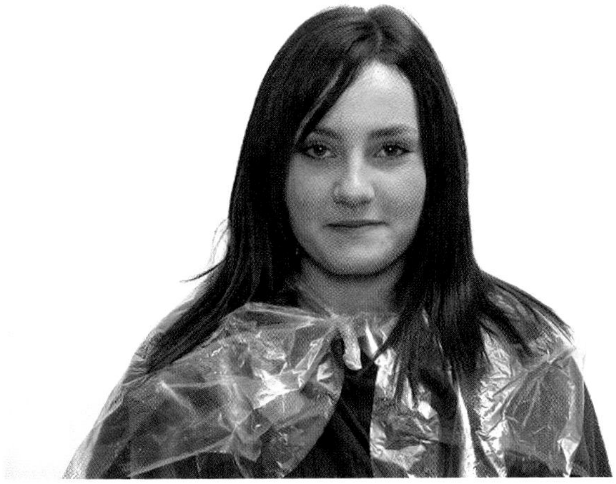

Figure 12.54 Gown the client in the appropriate way and apply barrier cream if necessary.

Figure 12.55 Before applying the tint, section the hair.

Figure 12.56 Begin the application at the nape of the neck, applying the product from the mid-lengths to the ends of each hair mesh.

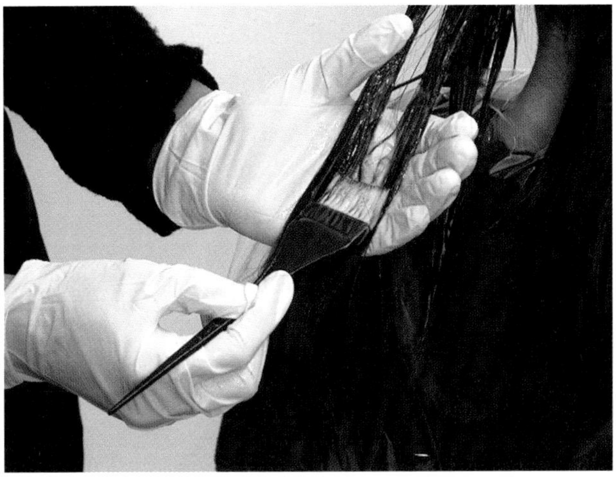

Figure 12.57 Colour is applied to small sections (1-2 cm). Work through the entire head. The tint is allowed to process for twenty minutes or as recommended by the manufacturer's instructions.

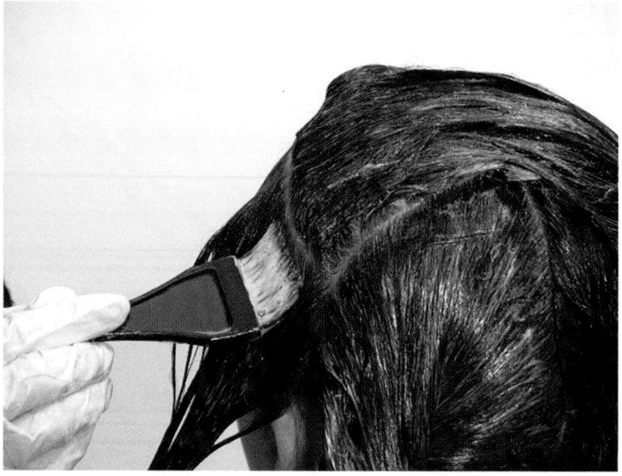

Figure 12.58 The roots should be treated when the mid-lengths and ends have reached the required colour depth. Take small sections of the hair (approximately 1 cm) and apply the product working towards the front section.

Figure 12.59 The product should be applied evenly over the head.

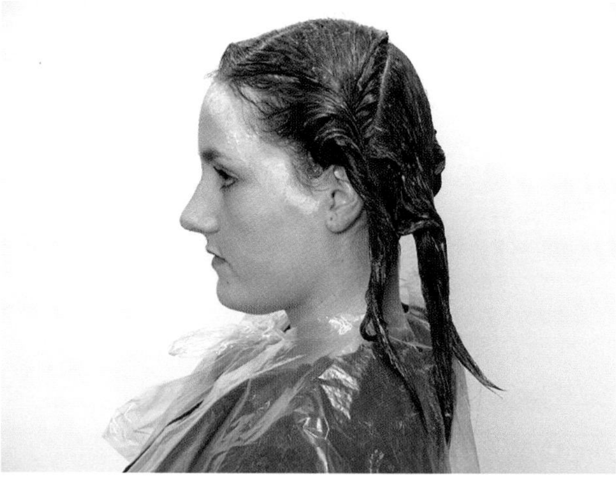

Figure 12.60 Monitor the development time according to the manufacturer's instructions. A colour/strand test will enable you to check colour development.

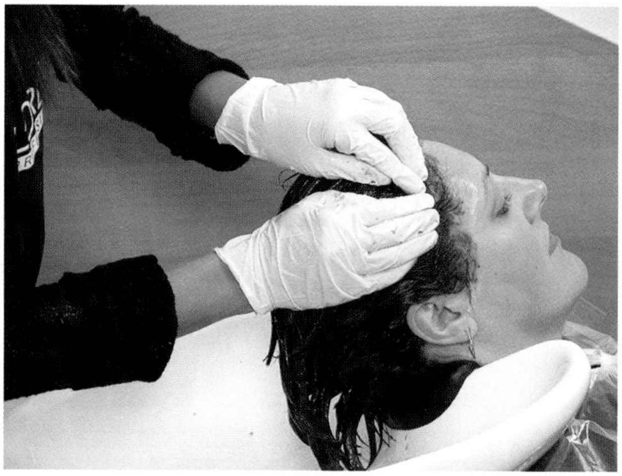

Figure 12.61 Rinse off the product and use the emulsifying technique around the hairline. Condition as appropriate.

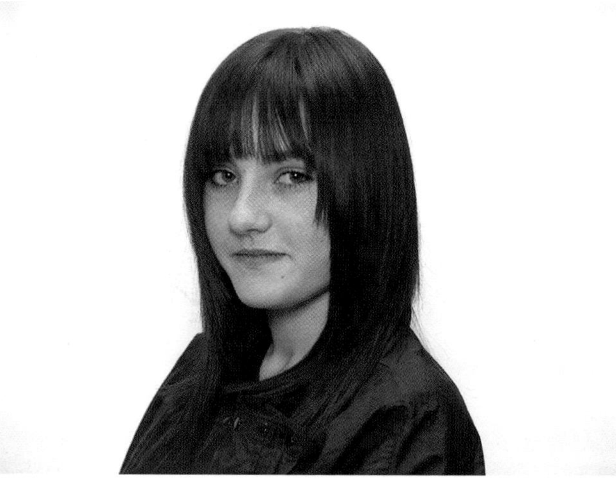

Figure 12.62 Dry and style hair into shape.

Figure 12.63 The finished colour.

Create highlight and lowlight effects in hair

Partial colouring can be achieved using weaving or the pull through method. Meshes or foils are suitable for full head weaving. When carrying out the foil/ mesh method small sections of hair are weaved evenly throughout the head. The sections are placed on foil. The chosen product is then applied to produce the desired effect. Tinting caps or plastic strips can be used for the pull through method. Strands of hair are evenly pulled through using a crochet hook. The hair is treated with the selected product to produce highlights or lowlights.

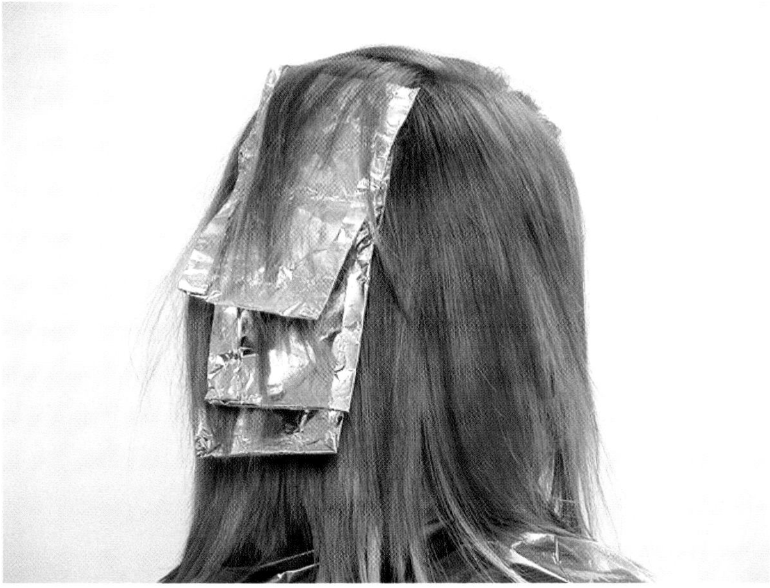

Figure 12.64 Foil method

Figure 12.65 Cap method

Figure 12.66 Mesh method

Online activity 12.11 WWW

Wordsearch

Key information

Highlights and lowlights can be achieved using weaving or the pull through method.

Application of weaved highlights and lowlights

Figure 12.67 Section the hair and place first mesh in the hair around the nape area.

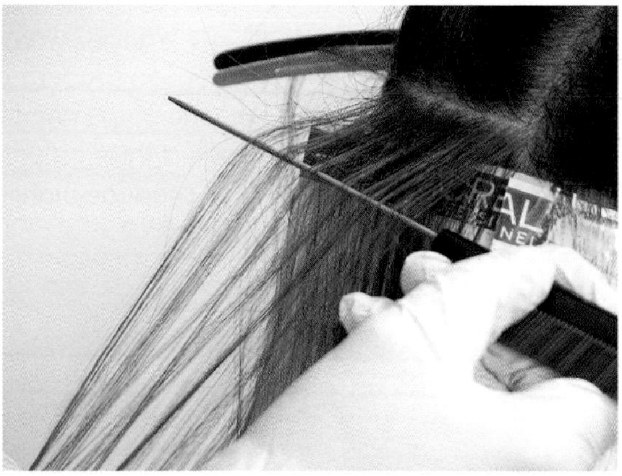

Figure 12.68 Evenly weave the required amount of hair for each packet to produce the desired look.

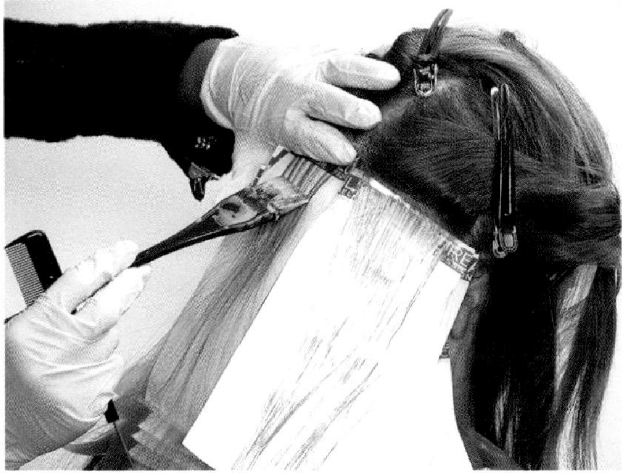

Figure 12.69 Care must be taken to prevent the product from coming into contact with the scalp when applying the product to the mesh. Avoid disturbing the packets during application and removal. Seepage and leakage from packets will cause colour to develop on the hair you do not want coloured. This is referred to as spotting. Close up the packet.

Figure 12.70 Monitor the development time according to the manufacturer's instructions.

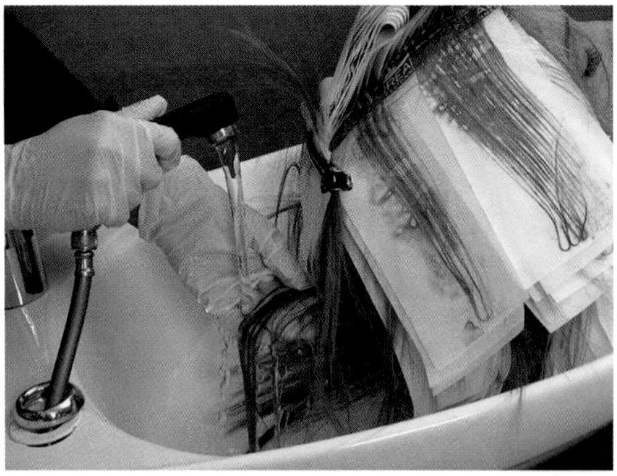

Figure 12.71 Rinse and shampoo to remove the product, checking the water temperature with the client. Acid balanced shampoo should be used for restoring the hair's pH. Rinse the hair until the water runs clear. Condition the hair if necessary.

Figure 12.72 Dry and style hair into shape.

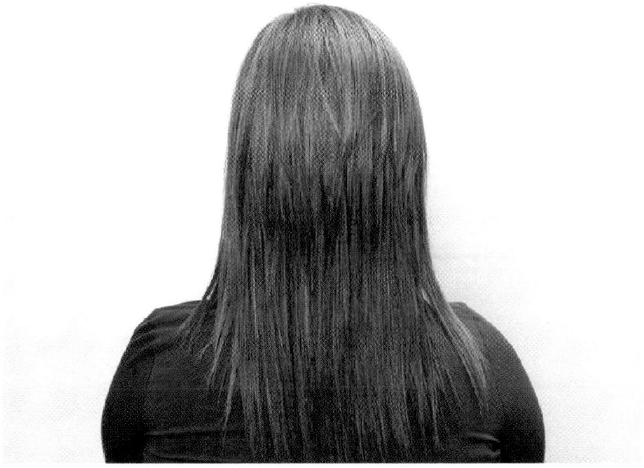

Figure 12.73 The final shape and colour.

Online activity 12.12 WWW

Drag into correct order

Key information

Colour developing on the hair you do not want coloured is referred to as spotting.

Application of weaved highlights and lowlights using foils

The method of weaving using foils is the same as for meshes. The product is applied to the hair and the foils closed up. The hair is monitored for the correct length of time according to the manufacturer's instructions.

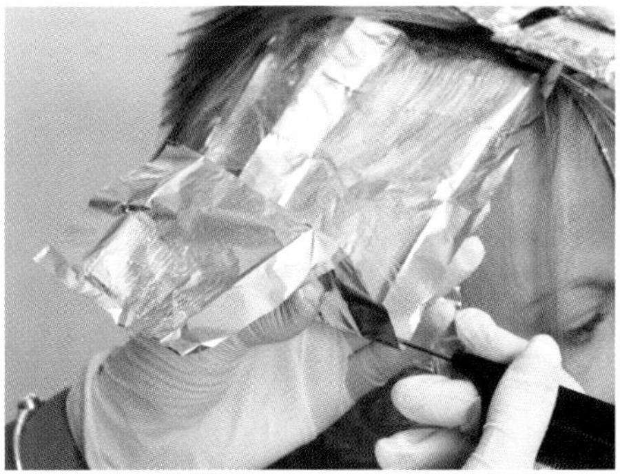

Figure 12.74 Fold in half.

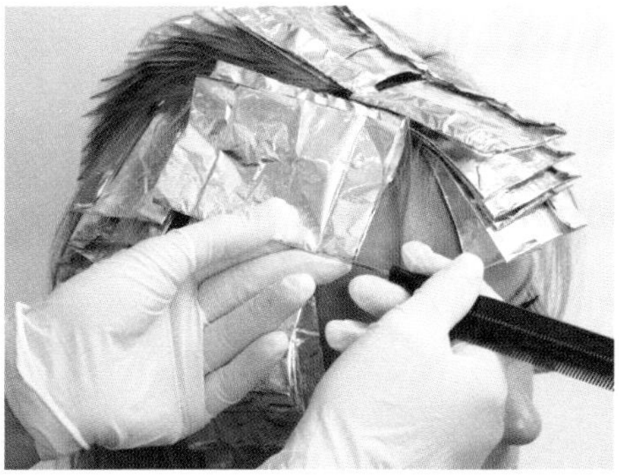

Figure 12.75 Seal foil.

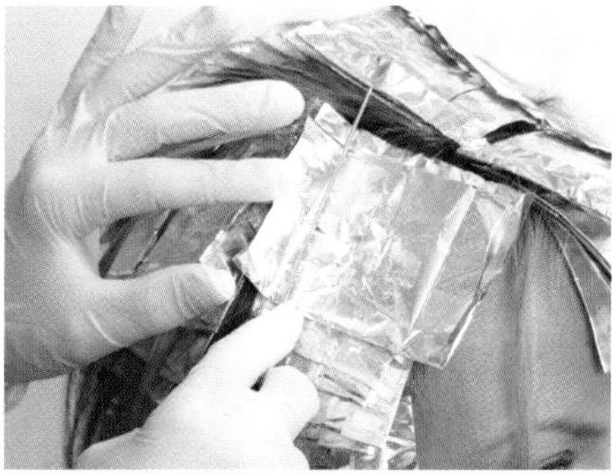

Figure 12.76 Fold over ends.

Pull through highlights/lowlights using plastic strips

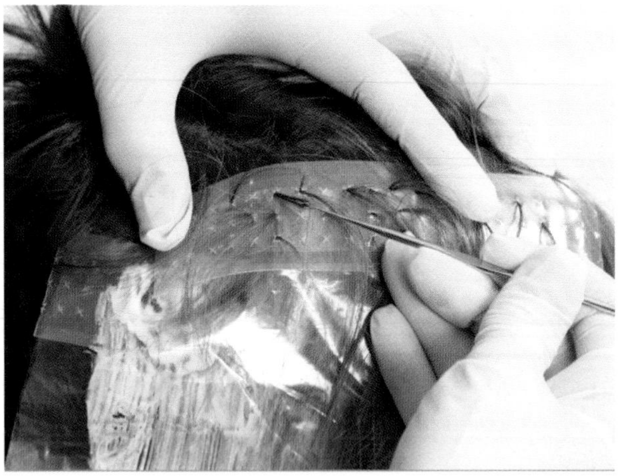

Figure 12.77 Place the plastic strips on the head in the direction of the hairstyle. Holding the strip in place with one hand, pull the required amount of hair through the holes in the strip with a crochet hook.

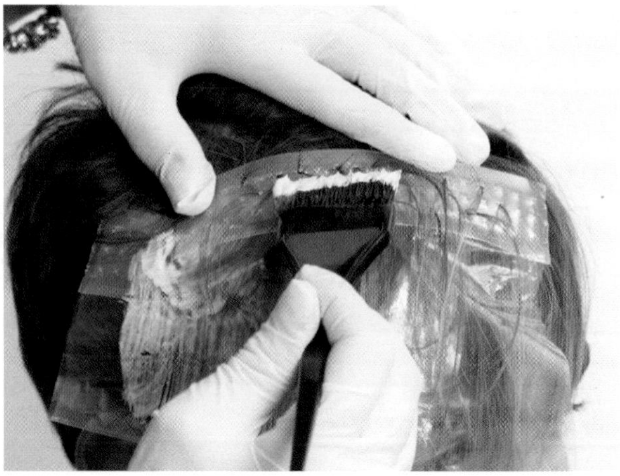

Figure 12.78 Apply the product to the pulled through hair. Take care to apply the correct amount.

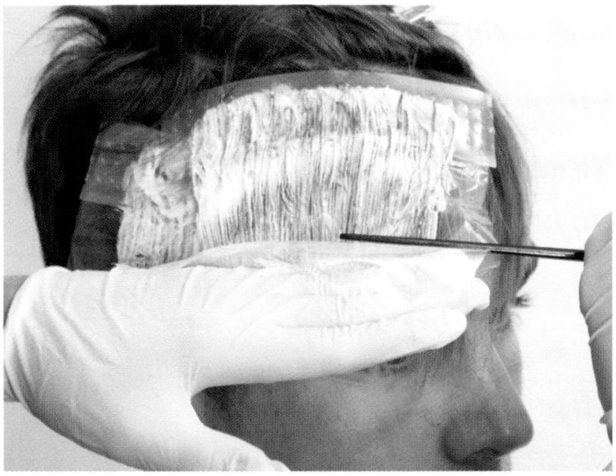

Figure 12.79 Using the end of the brush to hold in place. . .

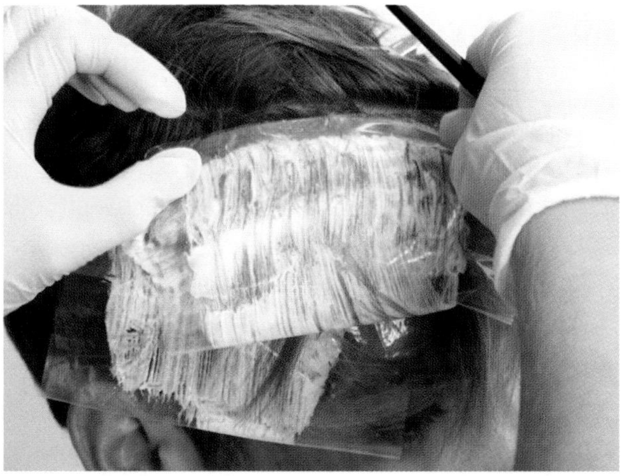

Figure 12.80 . . .pull over the plastic strip to close.

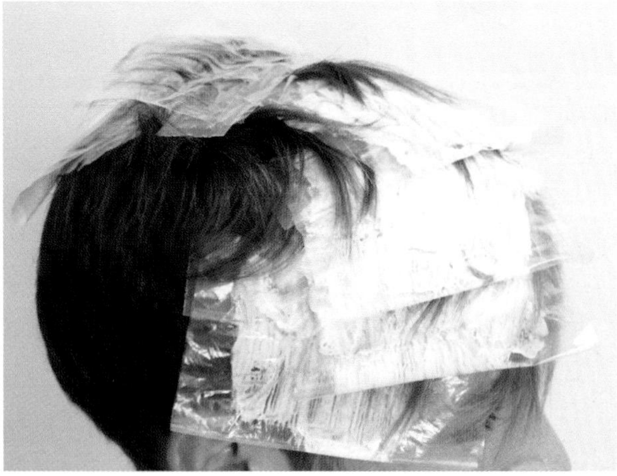

Figure 12.81 Monitor the development time according to the manufacturer's instructions.

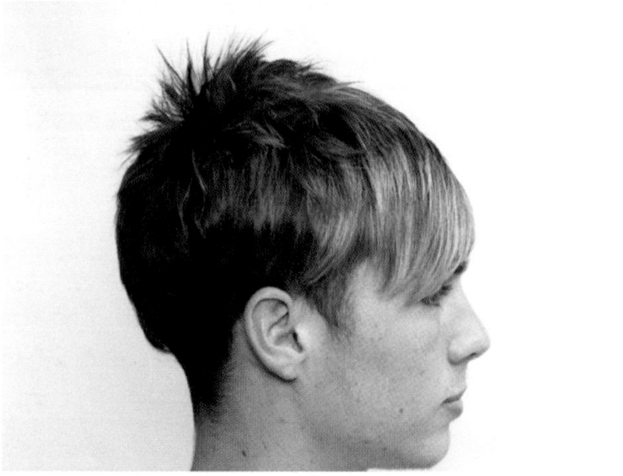

Figure 12.82 Finished look.

Confirming with the client and record results

Make sure that the client is happy with the end result. The results of any colouring process, the product used and the development time must be recorded on a client record card or computerised system.

Figure 12.83 Record all results

Dealing with problems

Table 12.3 shows you what certain problems are caused by and what action you should take in the event of this happening. Study it carefully. If you cannot resolve a colour problem, talk to your manager straight away.

Table 12.3 Colouring problems and how to deal with them

Problem	Caused by	Action to take
Stains on the skin	Applying too much product Sloppy application Failing to emulsify during removal	Use a stain remover
Poor hair condition	Colour left on for too long Incorrect strength of peroxide Unsuitable product used	Use a penetrating conditioning treatment to strengthen the hair
Overprocessing of product	Incorrect strength of peroxide Product left on for too long	Use a penetrating conditioning treatment to strengthen the hair
Underprocessing of product	Incorrect strength of peroxide Lack of product applied Product not left to develop for recommended time	Re-apply bleach or colour if the hair is strong enough

(Continued)

Problem	Caused by	Action to take
Patchy result	Application uneven Porosity uneven	Spot colour where appropriate
Seepage during highlighting	Foils and mesh incorrectly used Poor application of product	Spot colour where appropriate
Yellow overtones	Bleach not left on for long enough Incorrect product used Natural (base) hair too dark	Use a violet toner
Faded colour	Sunlight Porous hair	Cover hair during sun exposure A course of restructuring conditioning treatment to strengthen the hair

12.4 Provide aftercare advice

An important part of this service is to give the client aftercare advice. You should explain to the client how often they should return to the salon to maintain their colour. This will depend on the type of colour. A client that has had a full head colour should be recommended to return to the salon after 4-5 weeks whereas those with highlights/lowlights could return after 4-5 months.

Figure 12.84 This client may need to return to the salon more frequently.

Figure 12.85 This client will not have to visit as often.

Post-colouring treatments

Post-colouring treatments will:

- prevent colour fade
- prevent loss of moisture
- close cuticles
- restore hair pH balance.

Figure 12.86 Post-colouring conditioners

Online activity 12.13 WWW

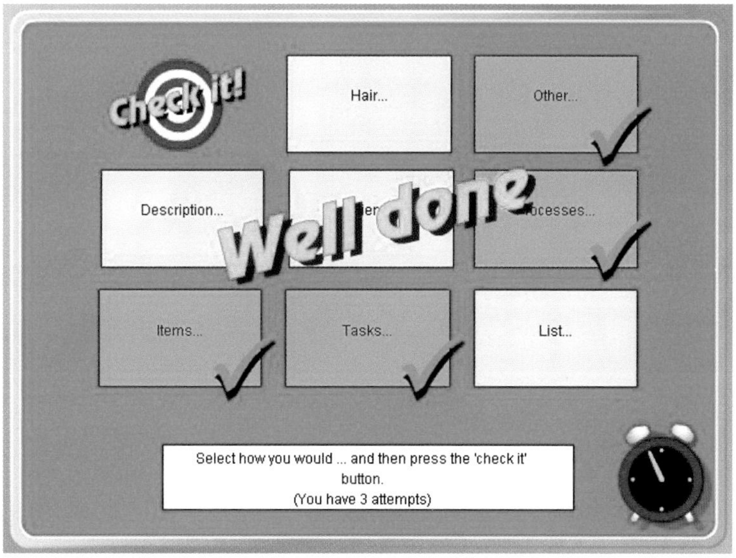

Check it

Client's lifestyle

Ensure that the home care products that you recommend to the client will be appropriate to their lifestyle. For example, for those with a busy lifestyle, a leave-in conditioner may be considered. The client's lifestyle may also affect the durability of the colour. For example a regular swimmer may find the colour may fade faster.

Figure 12.87 Ensure products are suitable to the client's lifestyle.

Definition

Durability: The ability to endure, to last.

Use of heated styling equipment

Continual use of heated styling equipment will damage the hair. Therefore regular conditioning and using heat protectors are advisable.

Figure 12.88 Using heated styling equipment.

12.5 Worksheets

WORKSHEETS

You can carry out the worksheets during your study of a chapter or unit, or at the end. An example is presented here and there are more online. If your college or company is registered with ATT Training, lots more are available. Write your answers directly in the book, but only if you own it of course – if it is a library or college book, use a separate piece of paper!

12.5.1 The colour star

What are the three primary colours?

What are the three secondary colours?

How are secondary colours made?

How are other colours made?

Label the warm and cool shades on the colour star:

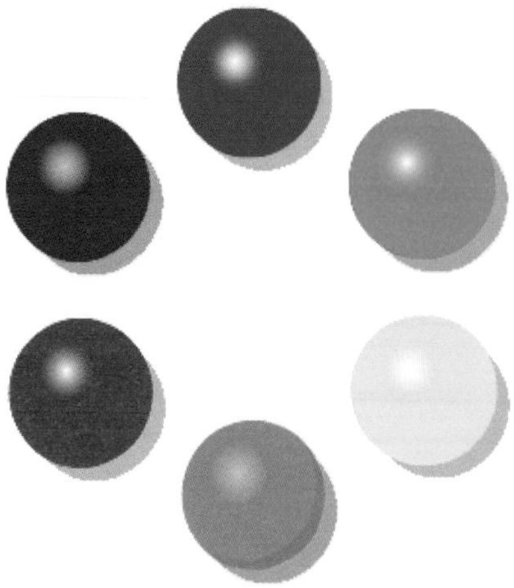

Describe which colours neutralise each other and give examples here:

12.6 Assessment

Well done! If you have studied all the content of this unit – you may be ready to test your knowledge.

Check out the 'Preparing for assessments' section in Chapter 1 if you have not already done so, and always remember:

- You can only do your best if you have. . .
  - studied hard
  - completed the activities
  - completed the worksheets
  - practised, practised, practised
  - and then revised!

Now carry out the online multiple-choice quiz

. . . and good luck in the final exam, which will be arranged by your tutor/assessor.

CHAPTER 13

Perm and neutralise hair

This chapter covers the NVQ/SVQ unit GH14, Perm and neutralise hair and the VRQ unit 208, Perm and neutralise hair.

Perming can be defined as the method of curling hair by altering the structure using chemicals. Neutralising keeps the structure of the hair in position after the change from perming.

In this chapter you will learn about:

- safe methods of working when perming and neutralising hair
- preparing for perming and neutralising
- perming and neutralising hair
- providing aftercare advice.

Website WWW

www.atthairdressing.com

CHAPTER 13 PERM AND NEUTRALISE HAIR: CONTENTS, SCREENS AND ACTIVITIES

Key:

Sections from the book are set in this colour

Screens available online are set in this colour

Online activity screens are set in this colour

Working safely

Introduction	Working environment
Maintain effective and safe methods when perming	Prepare for the practical work - perming
Layers in a strand of hair	Neutralising
Correct selection	Select correct boxes
Chemical changes during perming 1	Preparing clients for perming and neutralising
Chemical changes during perming 2	Gowning
COSHH	Comfort during perming
Precautions to take when handling chemicals	NVQ times for perming

Prepare for perming and neutralising

Carry out tests for perming and neutralising	Record the results
Elasticity test	Round the board
Wordsearch	pH, acidity and alkalinity
Porosity test	Pre-chemical and post-chemical treatment
Incompatibility test	Neutralisers
Pre-perm test curl	Barrier cream
Development test curl	

Perm and neutralise hair

Introduction	Neutralise hair 4
Pre-perm shampoo	Neutralise hair 5
Winding technique	Neutralise hair 6
Check it	Neutralise hair 7
Nine-section winding technique 1	Applying conditioner
Nine-section winding technique 2	Five in a row
Applying perm lotion	Problems with perming and neutralising 1
Processing	Problems with perming and neutralising 2
Unwinding	Problems with perming and neutralising 3
Drag into correct order	Problems with perming and neutralising 4
Neutralise hair 1	Problems with perming and neutralising 5
Neutralise hair 2	Check it
Neutralise hair 3	Problems with perming and neutralising 6

Provide aftercare advice

Introduction	Worksheet – precautions to take when handling chemicals
Products, heated styling equipment and lifestyle	Worksheet – ph, acidity and alkalinity
Worksheet – chemical changes during perming	Online multiple choice quiz

13.1 Working safely

Before you learn how to perm clients' hair, it is useful to know how the process affects the structure of the hair. As you will be using chemicals throughout perming it is important to be aware of the health and safety issues. More information can be found in Chapter 2.

Safety first

As you will be using chemicals throughout perming it is important to be aware of the health and safety issues.

Hair structure and texture

Figure 13.1 shows the three layers of a strand of hair: cuticle, cortex and medulla.

The cuticle is translucent (the hair colour shows through it) and has a protective function. It is made up of layers of scales. There are more layers around the base of the hair due to wear and tear at the tip. The cortex forms the bulk of the hair. In this part of the hair the chemical changes of bleaching, tinting, perming and straightening take place. Melanin and pheomelanin are found in the cortex, which gives the hair its colour. The medulla is the centre of the hair shaft.

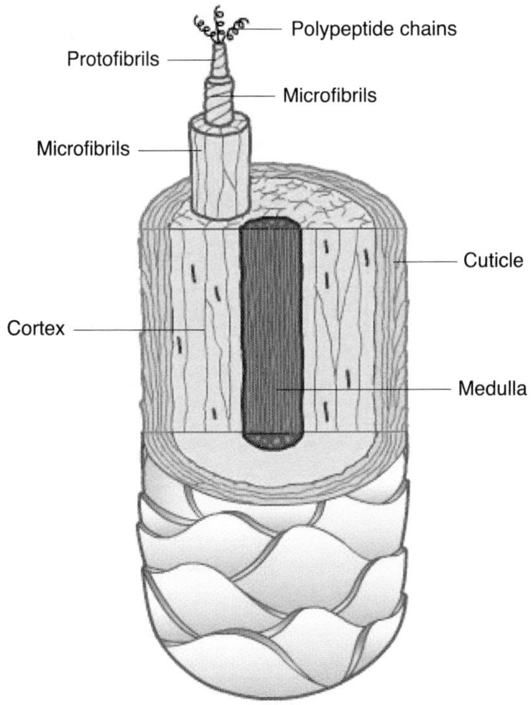

Figure 13.1 Hair structure

Online activity 13.1 WWW

Correct selection

Chemical changes during perming

During perming chemical changes take place to the structure of the hair. It is the cortex which is most affected by the chemicals.

Key information

It is the cortex which is most affected by the chemicals.

Website
www.atthairdressing.com

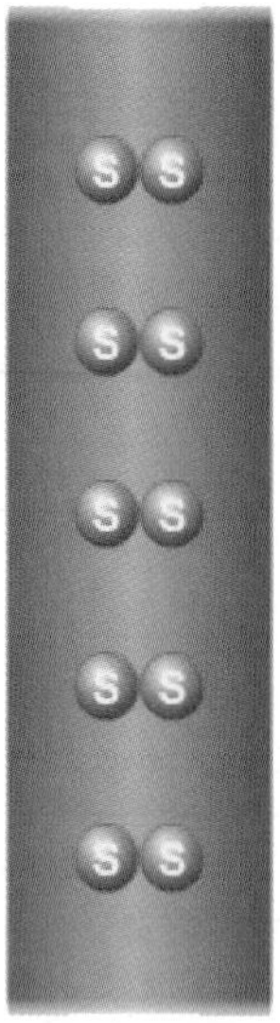

Figure 13.2 Cystines are composed largely of sulphur

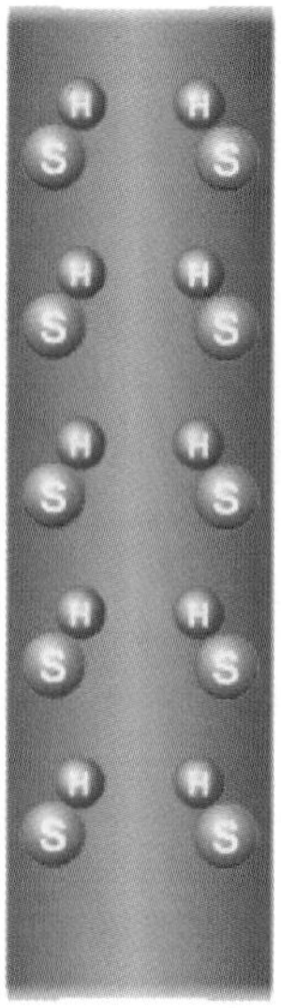

Figure 13.3 Sulphur aligned with hydrogen

The cortex is made up of proteins. Proteins are formed from amino acids, in this case an amino acid called cystine. Cystines are composed largely of sulphur and bonded together by different types of bonds, including di-sulphide bonds.

The permanent wave lotion breaks the di-sulphide bonds by the addition of hydrogen. The breaking of the bonds allows the hair to be 're-shaped'. For this purpose the perm rods are inserted. Because the perm rods have forced the hair into a new shape, the sulphurs are aligned with different partners.

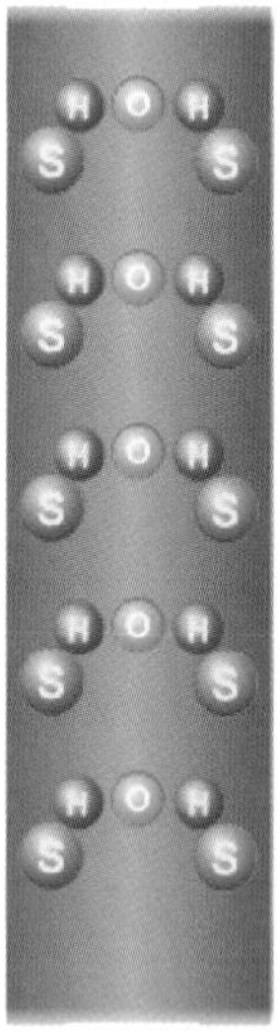

Figure 13.4 Oxygen from the neutralising agent attaches itself to the hydrogen molecules

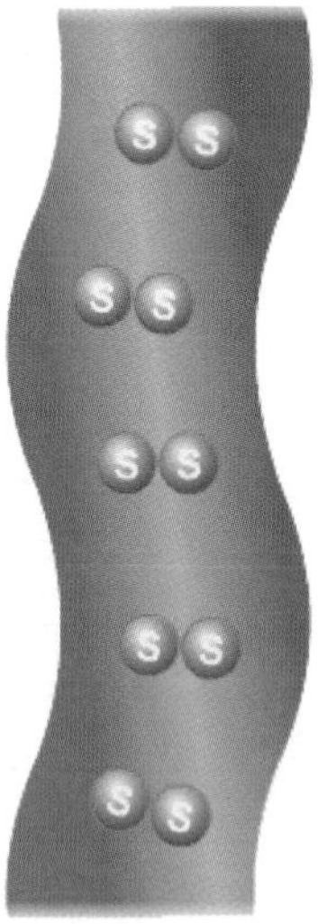

Figure 13.5 This process fixes the curl

During neutralising (oxidation process) chemical changes take place to the hair which the hairdresser should understand. Again, in neutralising, the cortex is the most affected by chemicals. The neutralising lotion enables the sulphur bonds to join back together, making the new shape permanent. The oxygen from the neutralising agent (e.g. hydrogen peroxide) attaches itself to the hydrogen molecules supplied by the perm agent. The addition of oxygen to hydrogen forms water.

During this process the amino acid returns to cystine. This process fixes the curl. Hydrogen peroxide can cause hair colour to fade.

Control of Substances Hazardous to Health Regulations 2002 (COSHH)

These are commonly called the COSHH regulations and they lay down the essential requirements for controlling exposure to hazardous substances and for protecting people who may be affected by them. A substance is considered to be hazardous if it can cause harm to the body. It only poses a risk if it is:

- inhaled (breathed in)
- ingested (swallowed)
- in contact with the skin
- absorbed through the skin
- injected into the body
- introduced into the body via cuts etc.

For more information about the COSHH regulations refer to Chapter 2.

Working environment

Make sure the working environment is clean and dry at all times, which includes clothing, work areas and all equipment. Floors should be kept clean; clean up any perm lotion or neutraliser straight away. If floors are wet, notices should be left to warn clients and other staff. Towels should be washed after each client in order to prevent cross infection. Place them into a closed bin after use.

Figure 13.6 Clean work surfaces

Safety first

Precautions to take when handling chemicals:

- Always wear protective gloves.
- Avoid contact of the chemical with the eyes and face.
- Do not use on sensitive or damaged skin.
- Always use a non-metallic bowl to avoid rapid decomposition of the product.
- Store the product in a cool, dry place away from sunlight or other sources of heat.
- Store the product in the container and replace the cap immediately after use.
- Always read manufacturers' instructions.

Prepare for the practical work – perming

Get your equipment and products ready before you start the treatment. It will save time. For perming you will need the following equipment, tools and products:

- sectioning clips
- pin tail comb
- perm rod of size to be used to measure section
- barrier cream
- perming lotion
- cotton wool
- record card
- gloves
- end papers
- large tooth comb
- perm towel.

Figure 13.7 Equipment needed for perming

Neutralising

For neutralising you will need the following equipment, tools and products:

- non-metallic bowl
- cotton wool
- towels
- large tooth comb
- protective gloves
- neutralising agent.

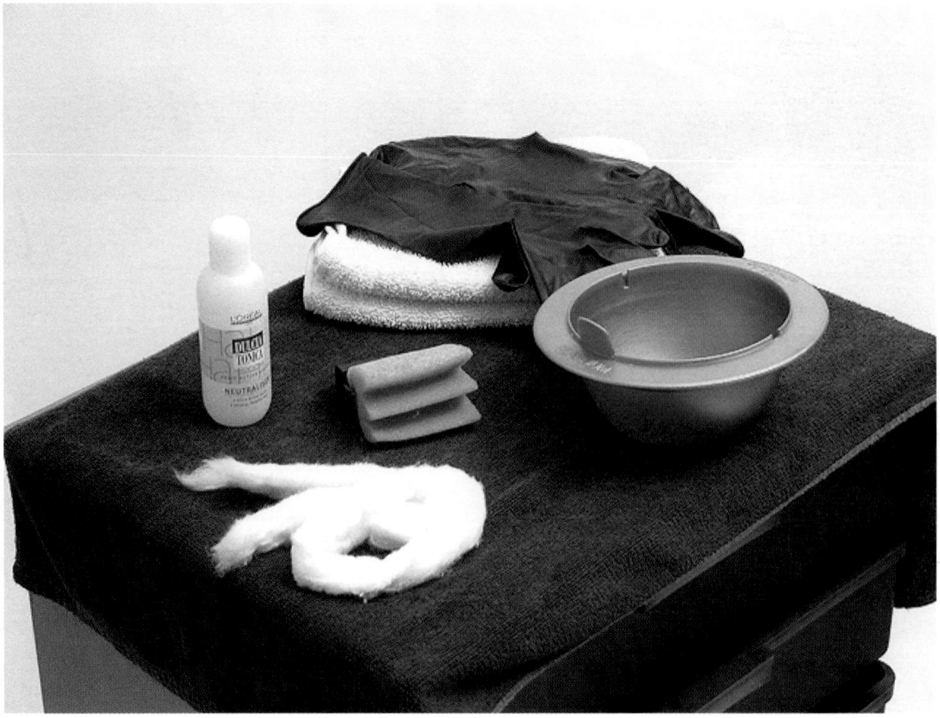

Figure 13.8 Equipment needed for neutralising

Online activity 13.2 WWW

Select correct boxes

Preparing clients for perming and neutralising – consultation

Before any service begins the hairdresser must find out what the client wants or needs. This will require obtaining information from the client such as details of previous treatments or lotions that the client uses. The results of the diagnosis and consultation must be recorded on a client record card or computerised system.

Key information

The results of the diagnosis and consultation must be recorded on a client record card or computerised system.

Gowning

It is important to protect the client's clothes from any damage through accidental spillage of products. Always choose a suitably sized gown to ensure that all the client's clothes are covered. Assist the client to put on a gown to protect his or her clothing while in the salon.

Safety first

It is important to protect the client's clothes from any damage through accidental spillage of products.

Figure 13.9 Gowning the client before perming

Comfort during perming

Check that your client is comfortable throughout the perming process. Also do not forget your own comfort. Check your posture is correct at all times.

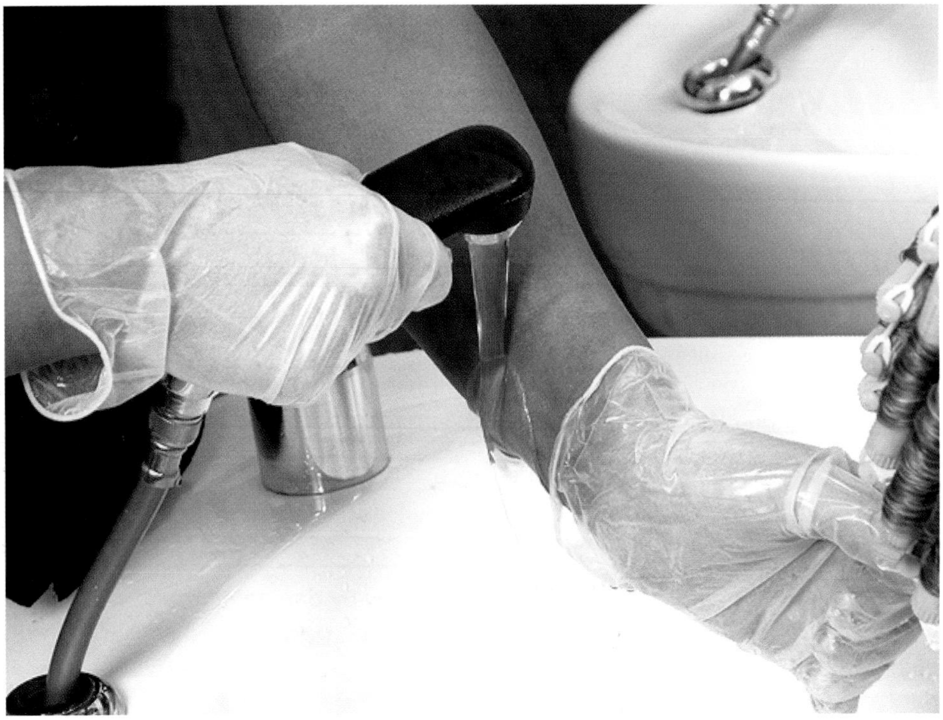

Figure 13.10 Ensure client comfort at all times

Suggested service time for perming

The time allocating for perming is 45 minutes. This is for the winding only.

13.2 Preparing for perming and neutralising

Carry out tests for perming and neutralising

It is important to decide whether or not you should perm a client's hair. The consultation you have carried out will tell you if the client has had any previous treatments or is sensitive to perming lotions. Once you have recorded these details, you must determine whether or not the hair should be permed at all. Refer to the manufacturer's instructions for performing a skin test. Also, it is essential you determine the correct products to use when perming a client's hair.

Safety first

Also, it is essential you determine the correct products to use when perming a client's hair.

Elasticity test

This test assesses the extent of damage to the cortex of the hair. It measures the ability of the hair to be stretched. Hair that is wet or treated with perm wave lotion will have increased elasticity.

Hold a single strand of dry hair firmly at each end with finger and thumb. Pull back gently and see how much the hair stretches and springs back. A hair in good condition can stretch up to a third of its length and return to its original length. If the hair snaps it indicates that the hair has a week cortex.

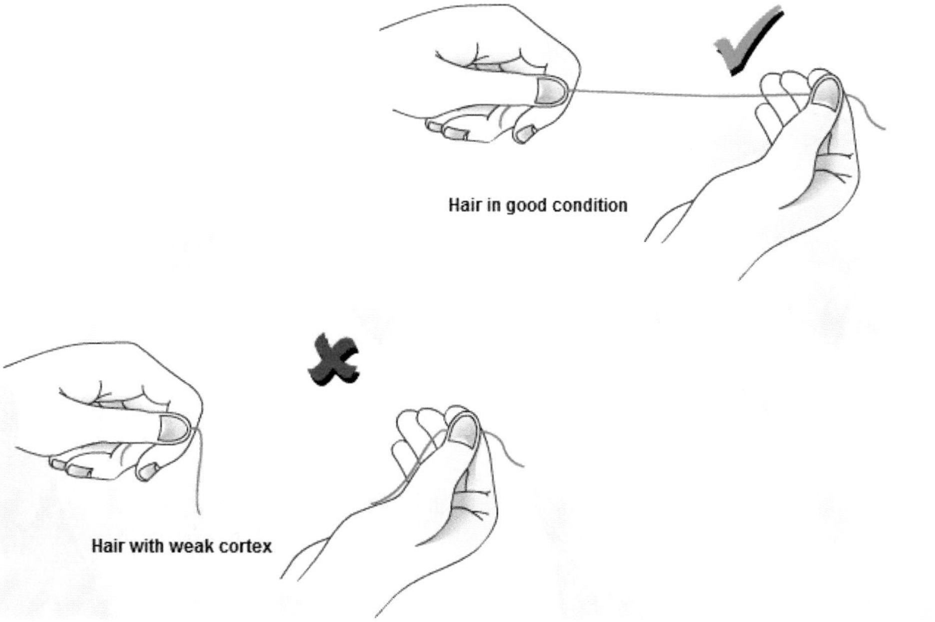

Figure 13.11 Elasticity test results

Online activity 13.3 WWW

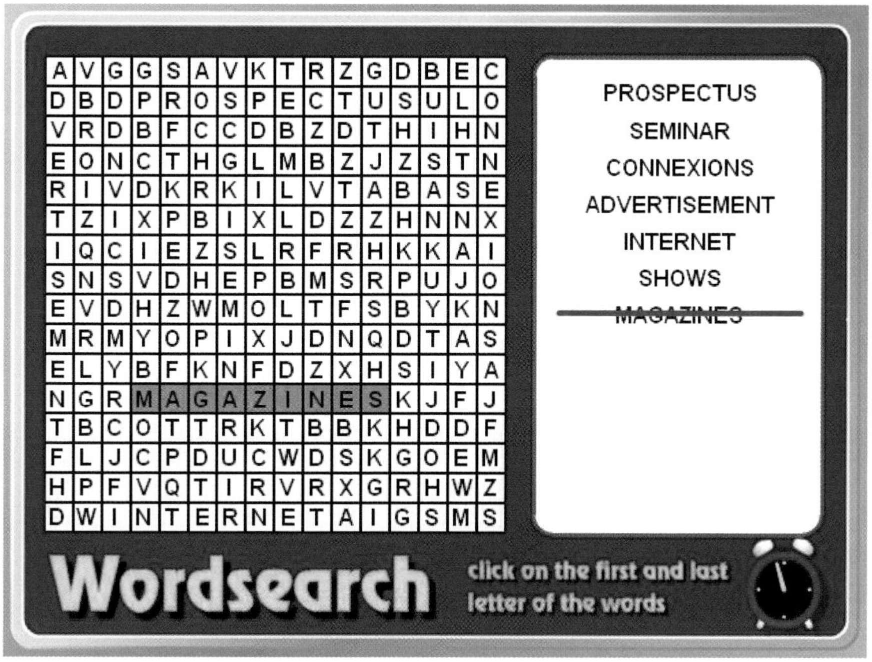

Wordsearch

Porosity test

The porosity test assesses the degree of damage to the cuticle. A damaged cuticle absorbs more moisture, which makes the hair feel rougher.

Hold a few strands of hair at the end and slide your fingers towards the root. If it feels rough the cuticles are raised and this indicates the condition of the hair is poor. If it feels smooth the cuticles are flat and the condition of the hair is good.

Key information

A damaged cuticle absorbs more moisture, which makes the hair feel rougher.

Definition

Cuticles: Outer layer of the hair shaft.

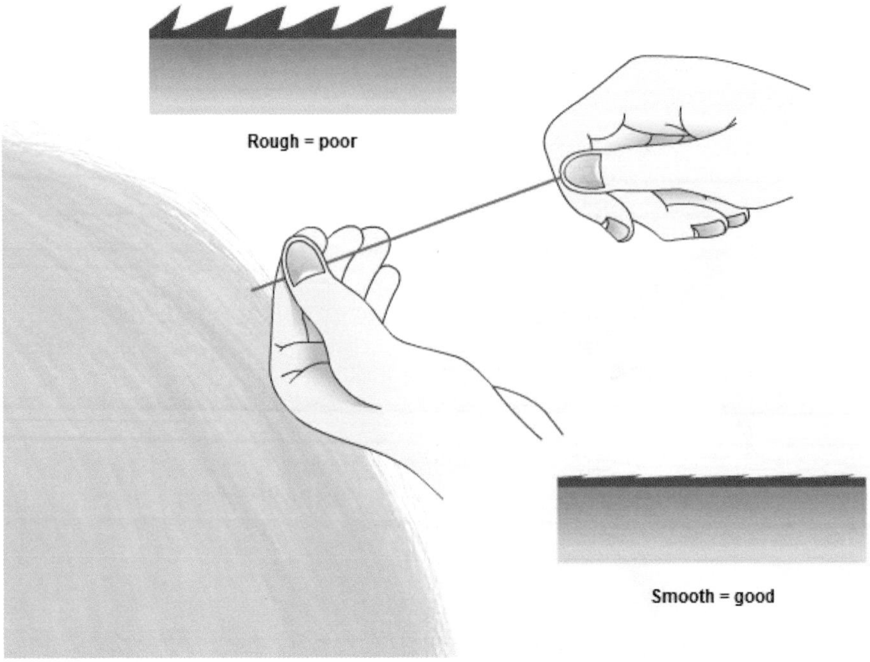

Figure 13.12 Raised and flat cuticles

Incompatibility test

The hairdresser should make sure that any products that have been used previously on the hair do not react unfavourably with products that the hairdresser intends to use. This incompatibility test detects metallic salts used in colour preparations, so-called 'hair colour restorers'.

Prepare a solution of twenty parts hydrogen peroxide and one part ammonia. Sellotape together a small group of hairs taken from the client's head, at the root end. Immerse the hairs in the solution for 30 minutes. A positive reaction will show the presence of bubbles, give off heat (the beaker gets warmer), or the hair will change colour.

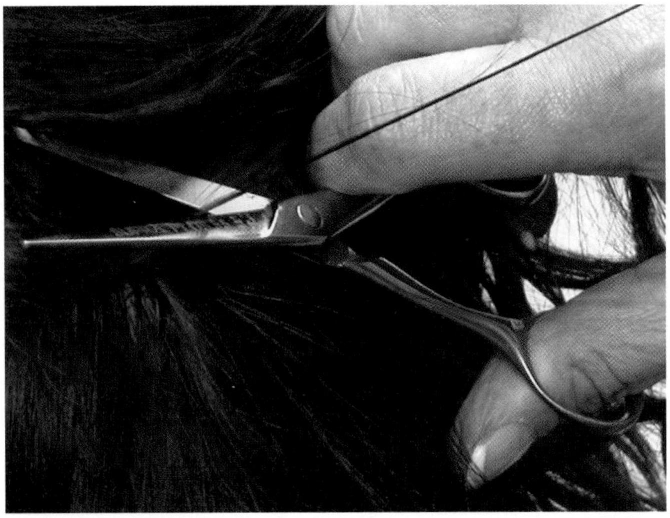

Figure 13.13 Take hairs from the root

Figure 13.14 Immerse hair in solution for 30 minutes

Pre-perm test curl

If the hair has been damaged through perming or colouring, a sample of hair should be tested to find out if the full head can be permed.

Take a cutting from the hair, apply perm lotion and wind around a perm rod. Leave the hair to develop and neutralise. Dry the hair and test the elasticity strength. If the results are satisfactory, the hairdresser can continue with the perm. If the result is unsatisfactory, do not perm.

Figure 13.15 Pre-perm test curl

Safety first

If the result is unsatisfactory, do not perm.

Development test curl

After a perm lotion has been on the hair for a certain length of time, this test can be carried out to see if the hair has reached the correct development.

Unwind four rods in different sections to check development. The curl should show an 'S' shaped bend, separation of the strands and the hair should look shiny. The curl should be checked after five minutes. Gloves must always be worn when carrying out this test.

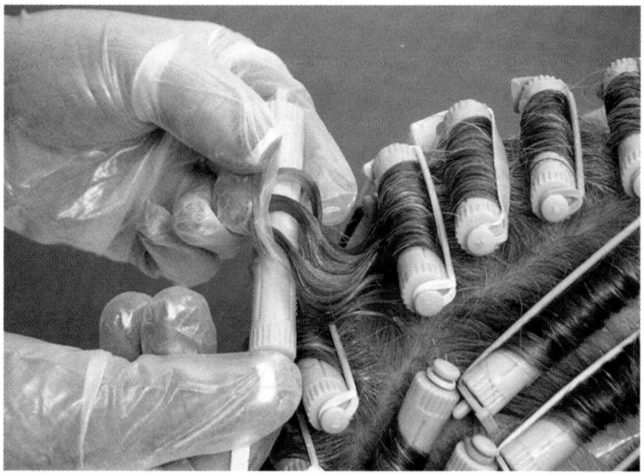

Figure 13.16 An 'S' curl

Key information

After a perm lotion has been on the hair for a certain length of time, this test can be carried out to see if the hair has reached the correct development.

Safety first

Gloves must always be worn when carrying out this test.

Record the results

Once the tests have been carried out, you can decide whether to carry out the perm. If there are any problems with the tests or any contraindications, you must ask for help from your supervisor/manager.

Definition

Contraindications: A condition preventing a treatment.

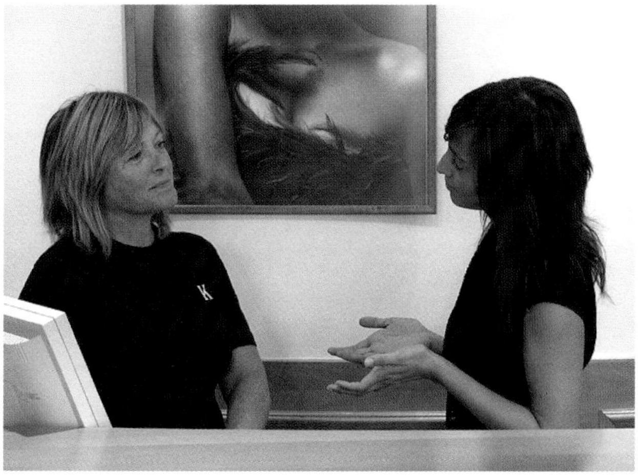

Figure 13.17 Ask for help if you feel it is needed

www Online activity 13.4

Round the board

pH, acidity and alkalinity

The pH of a product is measured on a scale of 0 – 14. Water has a pH of 7 and is said to be neutral. Products with a pH of less than 7 are described as acid and they close the cuticle. Products with a pH of more than 7 are described as alkaline and they open the cuticle.

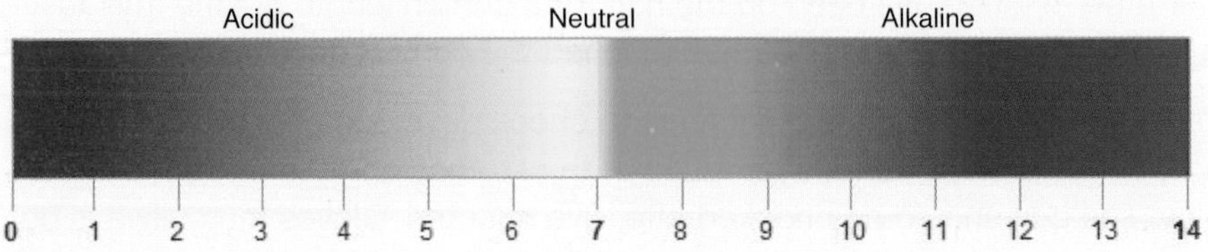

Figure 13.18 pH colour scale

Definition

Porosity: Ability to absorb moisture.

Pre-chemical and post-chemical treatment

Pre-chemical (protective) treatments even out porosity of the hair. They are applied before a perm ensuring that the perm solution is absorbed evenly into the hair shaft, producing an even curl. Post-chemical (corrective) treatments restore the hair to the correct acidity level after an alkaline chemical process such as perming. This improves the condition.

Figure 13.19 Pre-chemical treatment

Neutralisers

The chemical used for the neutralisation process usually contains hydrogen peroxide which is a hazardous substance. It is an irritant to skin and eyes.

Figure 13.20 Neutraliser

Barrier cream

Barrier cream should be applied around the hairline to prevent damage to the skin from hazardous substances, e.g. perming lotions and neutralisers.

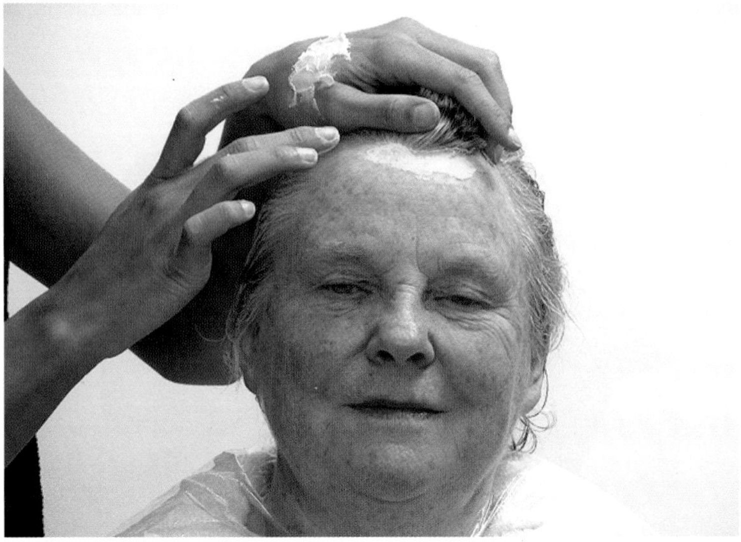

Figure 13.21 Applying barrier cream

13.3 Perm and neutralise hair

Once you have carried out the consultation and the tests to see if the client can actually have their hair permed, you are ready to begin. This section will show you how to perform the different winding techniques, apply the perm lotion and then explain the neutralising procedure. This will enable you to carry out a perm from start to finish.

Use a pre-perm shampoo that does not contain additives. Read the manufacturer's instructions as some permanent wave lotions have their own shampoo. Excess moisture can dilute the strength of perming lotion. For bleached and tinted hair use a pre-wrap lotion to even out the porosity of the hair.

Definition

Winding: Technique to change the shape of hair.

Safety first

For bleached and tinted hair use a pre-wrap lotion to even out the porosity of the hair.

Figure 13.22 Read manufacturer's instructions

Winding techniques

These include:

- nine-section winding
- brick winding
- directional winding.

See online screen for more details.

Online activity 13.5 WWW

Check it

Nine-section winding technique

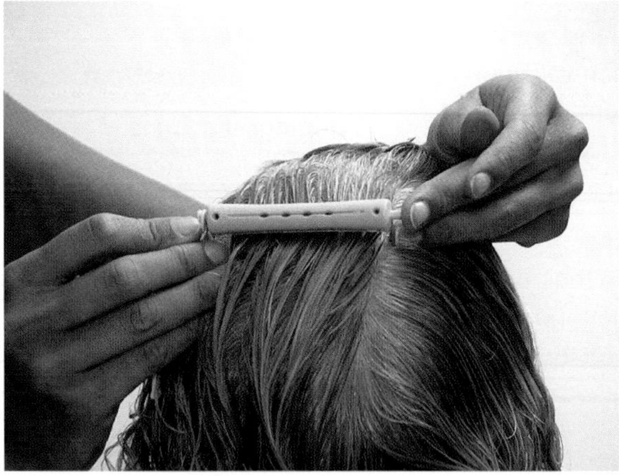

Figure 13.23 Use the perm rod to determine the width of the section. Holding the hair on top of the head, twist and secure with a sectioning clip. Divide the hair from ear to ear over the top part of the head. Divide the hair into six sections ready for winding.

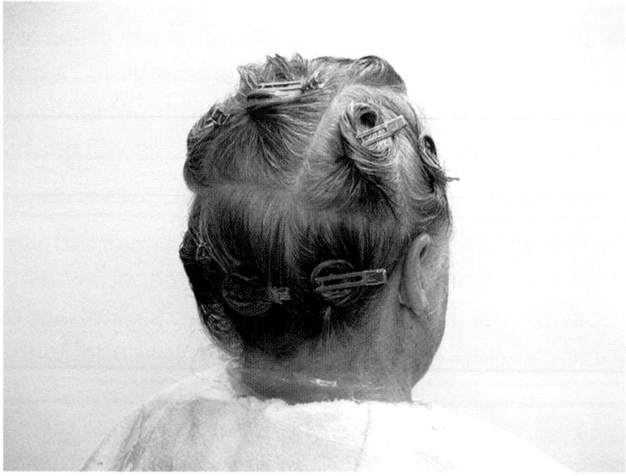

Figure 13.24 The back hair is divided into nape and back sections. The sides are divided from the top front section at eyebrow level. Position the client's head for ease of winding.

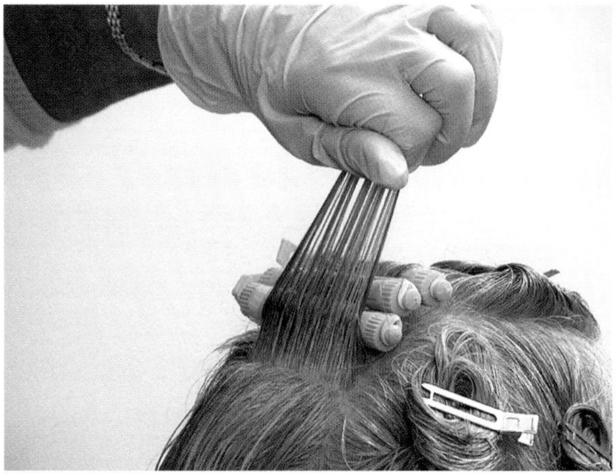

Figure 13.25 Comb the section to be wound around the perm rod neatly from roots to ends. Hold the hair firmly to ensure even tension. Direct the hair up and out from the head to approximately 150 degrees. The hair ends should be level with the section centre.

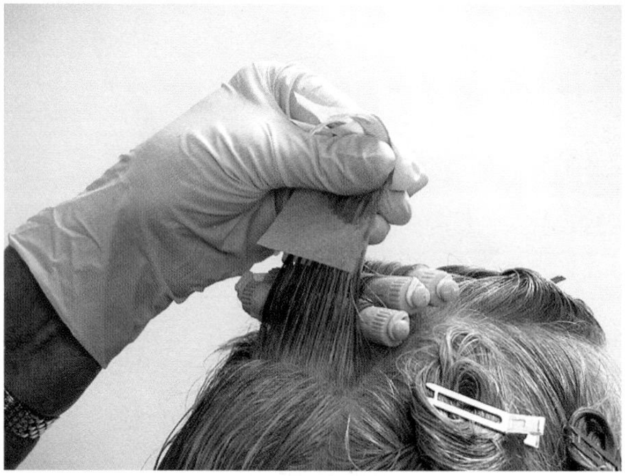

Figure 13.26 Using an 'end' paper, cover the ends of the hair.

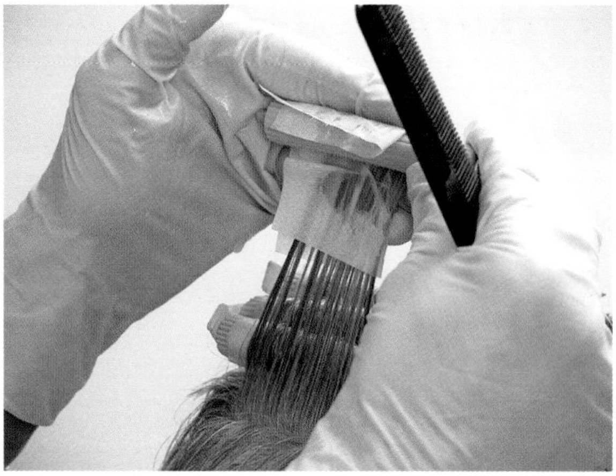

Figure 13.27 Place the hair in the middle of the perm rod. Using a turning twisting action direct the hair round and under the perm rod.

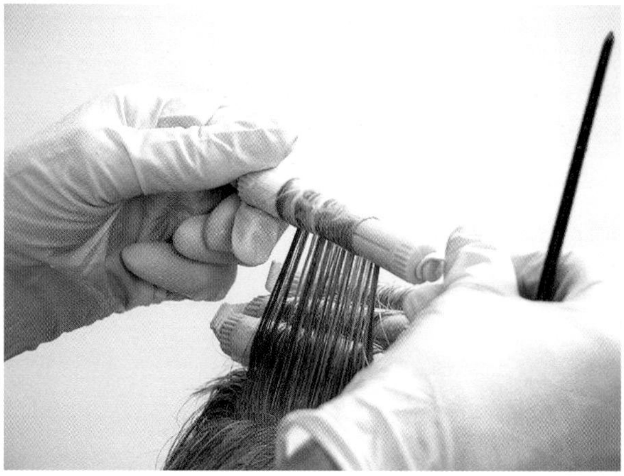

Figure 13.28 Wind the rod down towards the scalp so that the rod sits securely on the base.

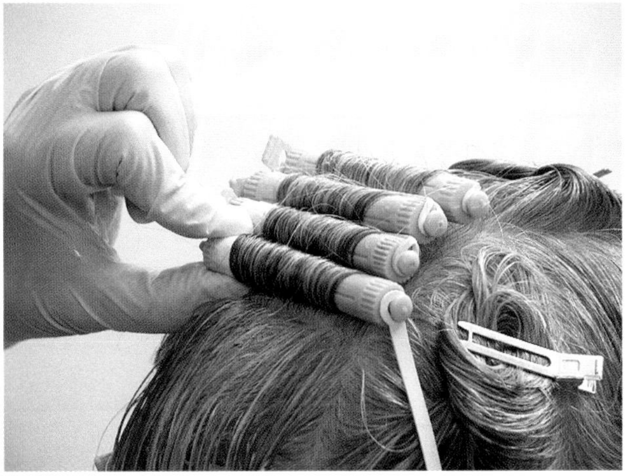

Figure 13.29 Fasten the band to secure the rod, taking great care to sit the band on top.

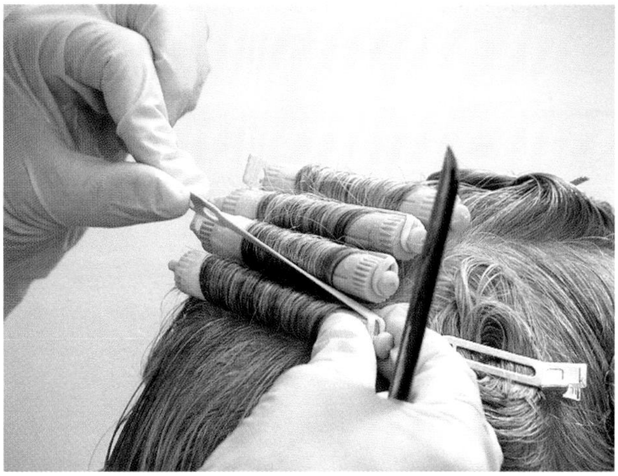

Figure 13.30 Make sure the band does not lie across the root of the mesh or that it is not twisted.

Applying perm lotion

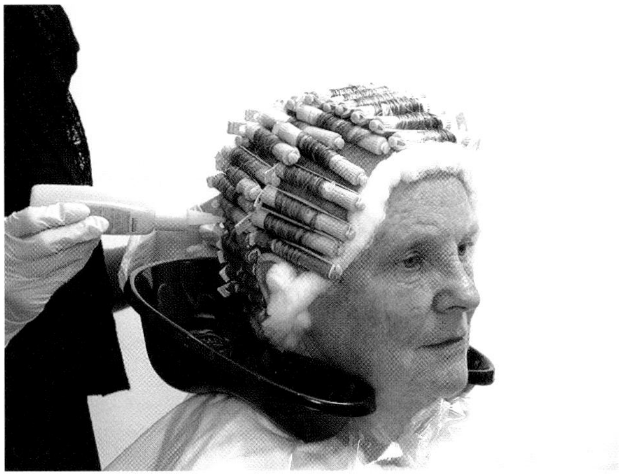

Figure 13.31 Apply barrier cream around the hairline if this has not already been done. The hairdresser must wear protective gloves to apply perm solution. When applying the lotion start at the nape and work systematically over the head. Take care not to miss any rods. Apply the lotion evenly to each of the wound rods. Use a piece of cotton wool to absorb any drips. The first application will swell the cuticle. This will enable the hair to absorb the second application and avoid a tendency to drip. The hair readily absorbs the required amount of lotion needed to penetrate to the ends of the hair.

Figure 13.32 Process for the required time making reference to the manufacturer's instructions. The processing time is assisted by heat from a climazone or a plastic cap applied over the wound curlers. The perming process is one of the more expensive treatments. Ensure the comfort and attend to the needs of your client e.g. ask if the client would like something to read or a cup of coffee.

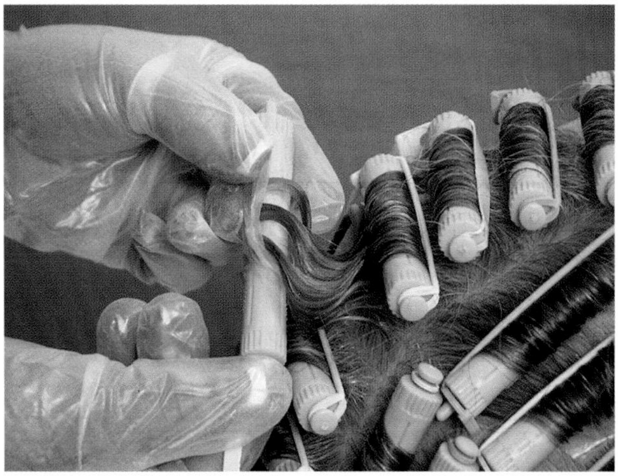

Figure 13.33 Check the process after the first 5 minutes. Unwind four rods in different sections to check development. The curl should show an 'S' shaped bend, separation of the strands and the hair should look shiny. Check the hair every 5 minutes until the curl has developed. The time may vary depending on the hair type and product. Check the manufacturer's instructions.

Key information

The curl should show an 'S' shaped bend and separation of the strands and the hair should look shiny.

Key information

If neutralising is not carried out correctly and not timed accurately the hair will straighten in a short period of time.

Website

www.atthairdressing.com

Online activity 13.6

Drag into correct order

Neutralise hair

Neutralising means fixing the curl after permanent waving or returning the hair to its original state after a chemical process. If neutralising is not carried out correctly and timed accurately the hair will straighten in a short period of time. Other names for the process of neutralising include normalising, rebonding, oxidising and fixing.

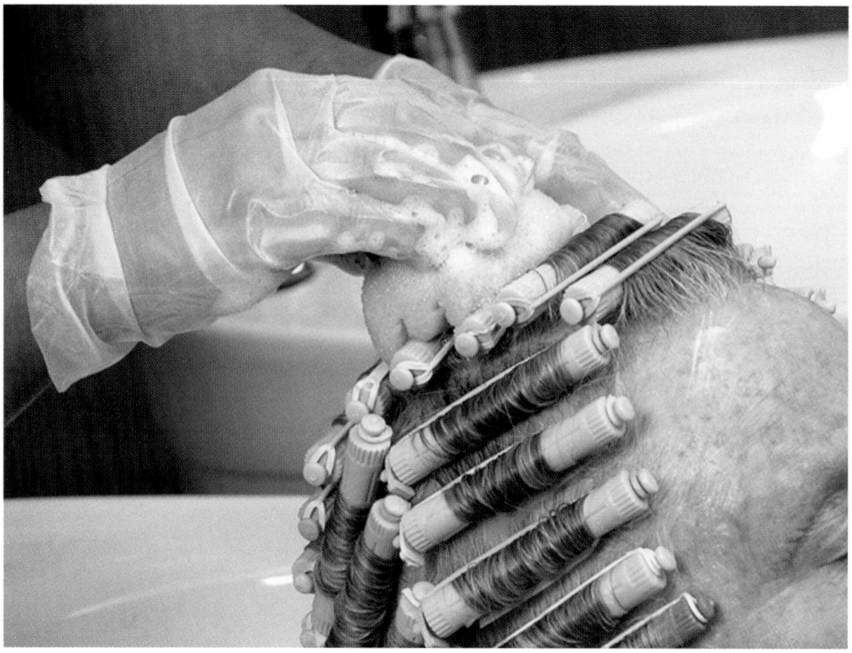

Figure 13.34 Neutralising hair

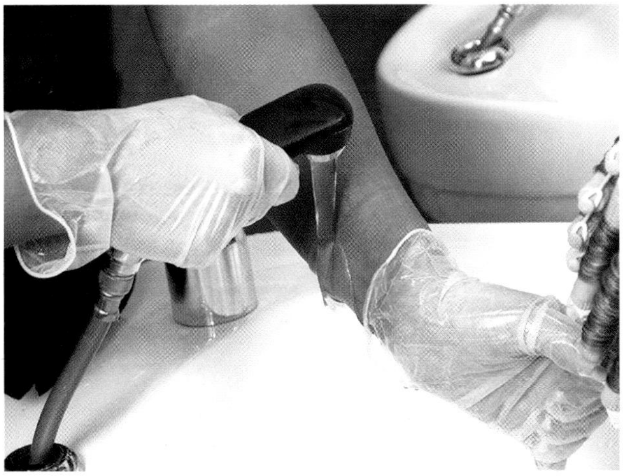

Figure 13.35 The temperature of the water should be tested on the inside of the hairdresser's wrist before placing the water spray on the client. Always make sure that you ask the client if the water temperature is comfortable and adjust accordingly.

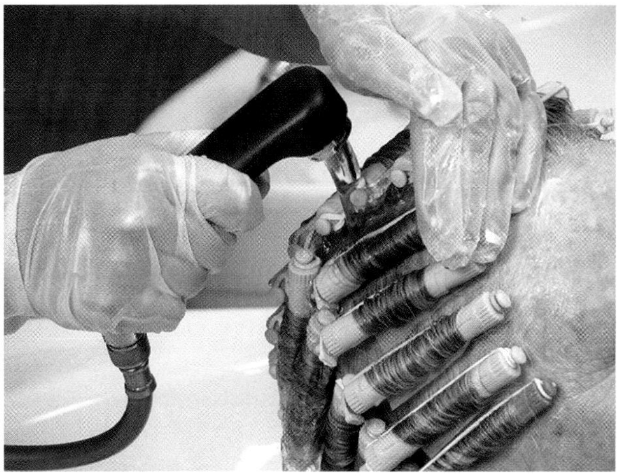

Figure 13.36 Rinse the perm rods and hair thoroughly for 5 minutes. It is the rinsing that removes the perm lotion and therefore prevents the perm from continuing to process the hair. When removing chemicals from the hair, the water temperature should be cooler as the scalp may be sensitive. The pressure of the water should not be so strong that it will disturb the perm rods.

Safety first

When removing chemicals from the hair, the water temperature should be cooler as the scalp may be sensitive.

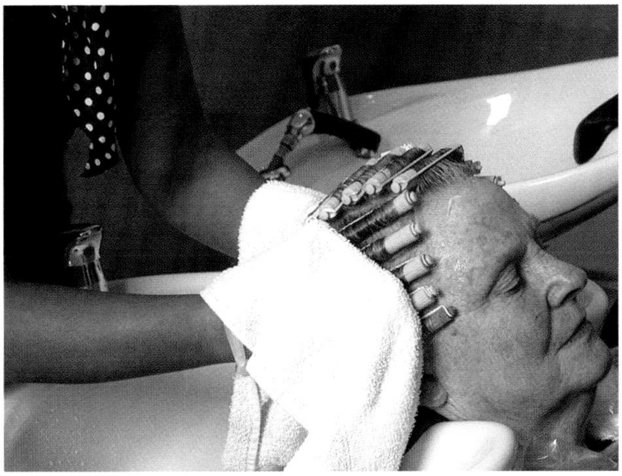

Figure 13.37 Blot the hair dry with towels and cotton wool to remove any excess water. It is important to remove any excess moisture left in the hair because it can weaken the effect of the neutraliser.

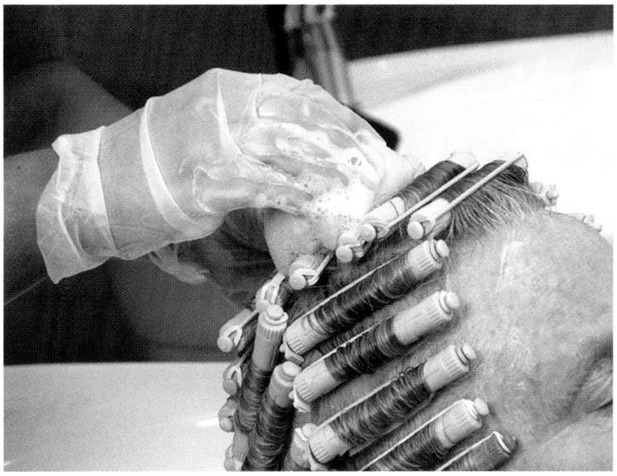

Figure 13.38 Before applying the neutraliser read the manufacturer's instructions and then apply the correct amount. Do not miss any perm rods. Leave the neutraliser on the hair for the time recommended by the manufacturer, usually 5 minutes. If the neutraliser is left on too long the hair can be seriously weakened. This can be harmful to the condition of the hair (online video).

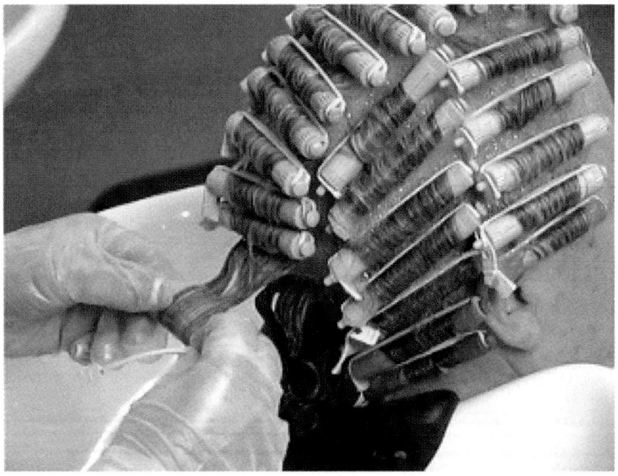

Figure 13.39 Beginning at the nape, take out the perm rods by unwinding each curl gently into itself. Take care not to pull the hair at this stage as the curl has not been completely fixed.

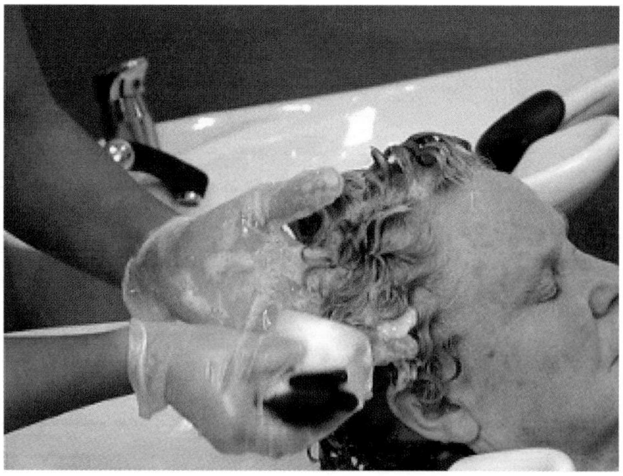

Figure 13.40 After the rods have been removed, work the neutraliser well into the ends of the hair, gently and evenly. Do not flatten the curl.

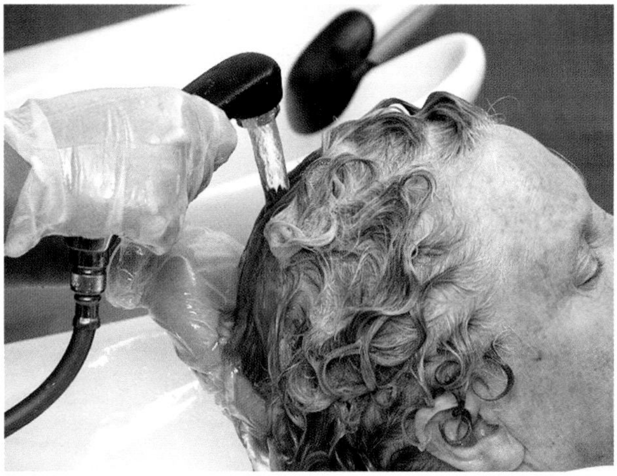

Figure 13.41 Leave the neutraliser on for the time recommended by the manufacturer. After this time has elapsed the hair will be permanently fixed. Rinse the hair thoroughly to remove all traces of neutraliser from the hair.

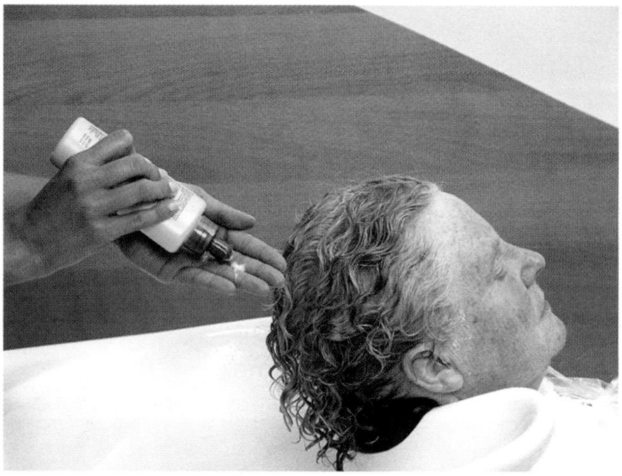

Figure 13.42 It may be necessary to apply a conditioner, particularly if the neutraliser did not contain one. Seek advice from your supervisor if you are not sure.

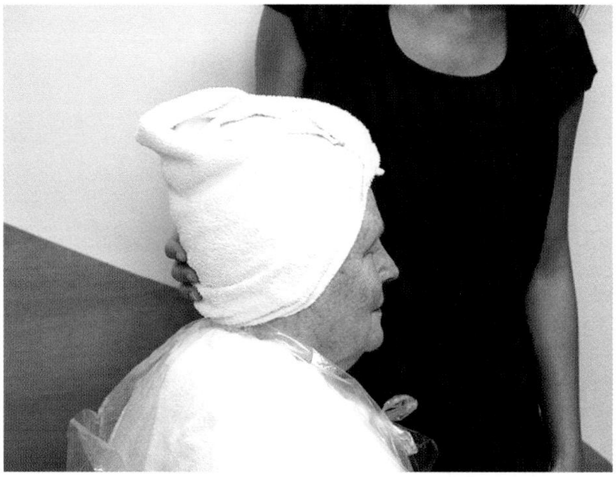

Figure 13.43 Wrap the client's hair in a towel.

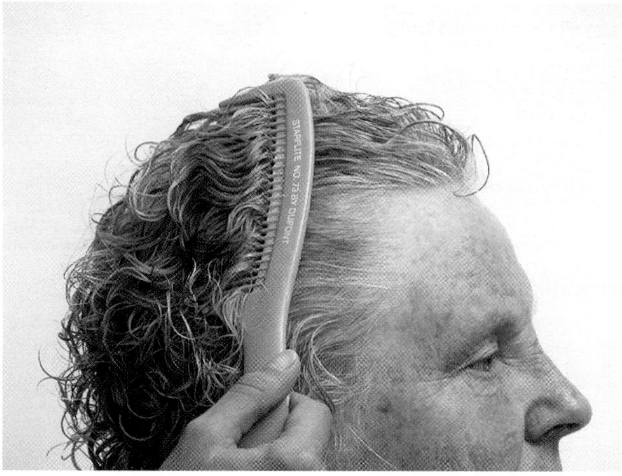

Figure 13.44 Gently comb the hair using a large tooth comb.

Figure 13.45 The finished perm.

> **Safety first**
>
> If the neutraliser is left on too long the hair can be seriously weakened.

Online activity 13.7 www

Five in a row

Problems with perming and neutralisation – hairline and scalp irritation

This can be caused by any of the following:

- cotton wool was left on for too long
- cuts and abrasions around the hairline or on the scalp
- too much perm lotion applied.

Rinse the hair straight away with cool water.

> **Safety first**
>
> Seek medical advice if necessary.

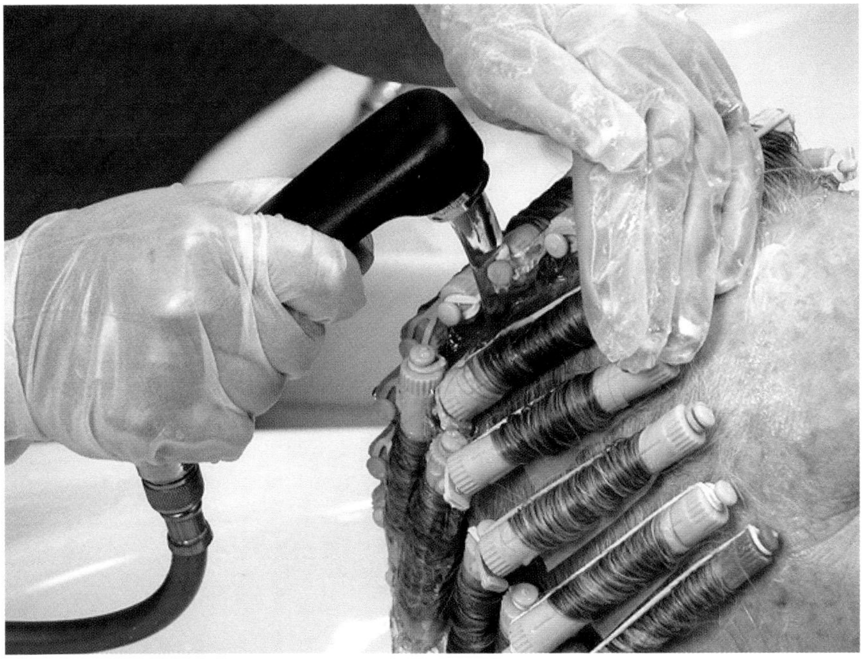

Figure 13.46 Rinse hair if irritation occurs

Hair breakage

Can be caused by:

- too much tension when winding
- rubbers placed incorrectly
- overprocessing.

Use a restructurant or deep penetrating conditioner if these occur.

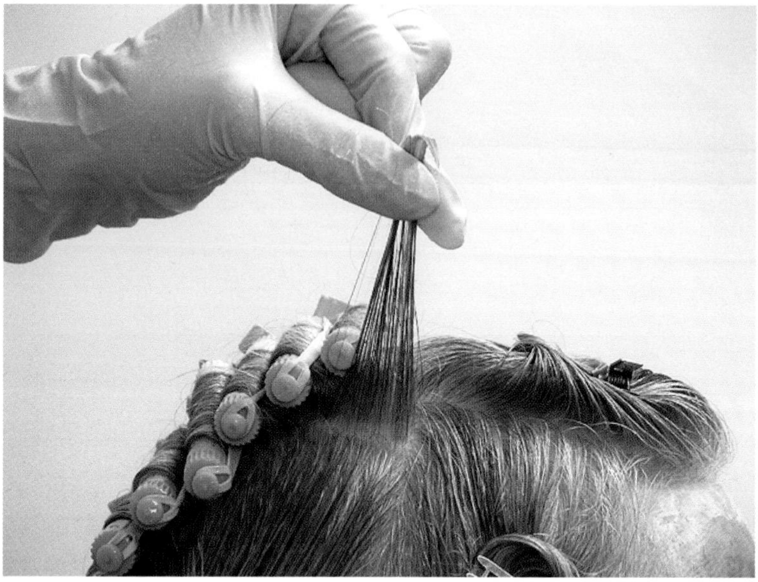

Figure 13.47 Ensure the correct tension to avoid hair breakage

Straight pieces

These can be caused by:

- perm lotion applied unevenly
- neutraliser applied unevenly
- rods wound unevenly.

Correct by re-perming if condition permits.

Figure 13.48 Rods wound unevenly

Fish hooks

These are caused by:

- hair ends buckled when winding
- hair bent during winding.

They can be removed by cutting.

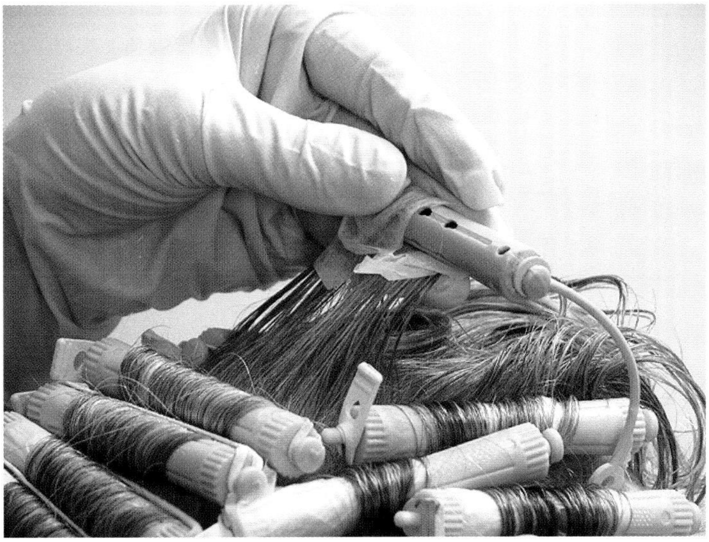

Figure 13.49 Hair wound like this will cause fish hooks

Frizz

This is caused by:

- overprocessing when perming
- the perm lotion too strong
- the perming rods too small.

It can be remedied by:

- cutting if possible
- using a restructurant or deep penetrating conditioner.

Figure 13.50 Perming rods that are too small will cause frizz

Online activity 13.8

Check it

Creeping oxidation

This is caused by chemicals remaining within the hair, which may continue working within the cortex. An anti-oxidant conditioner will prevent this happening. It is caused by not rinsing the hair thoroughly enough after neutralising or not using a pH balanced conditioner on completion of neutralising.

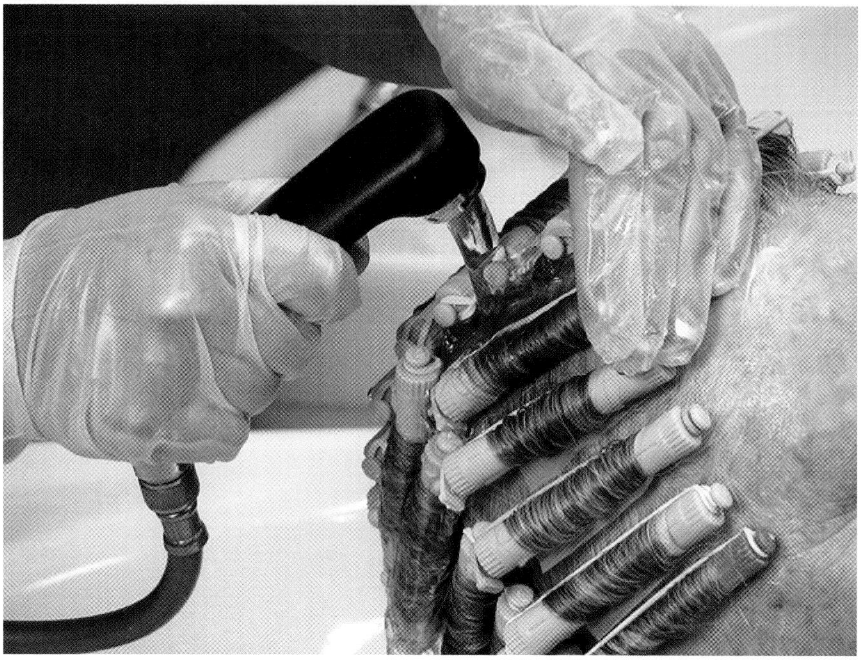

Figure 13.51 Ensure you rinse perm lotion thoroughly

13.4 Provide aftercare advice

Key information

The client should be recommended to leave their hair for 2 – 3 days before shampooing.

An important part of this service is to give the client aftercare advice. The client should be recommended to leave their hair for 2 – 3 days before shampooing. The reason for this is to allow the hair to harden. You should explain to the client how often they should return to the salon to maintain their perm. A haircut after a few weeks will revitalise the hair. The hair can be permed again after approximately 4 months or once the old perm has been cut out. If any further chemical services are asked for the stylist must always check the condition of the hair.

Products, heated styling equipment and lifestyle

The stylist should recommend shampoos and conditioners that are suited to permed hair. Shampoos that should be avoided are those not suited to chemically treated hair. Continual use of heated styling equipment will damage the hair. Therefore regular conditioning and using heat protectors are advisable. The client's lifestyle may affect the condition of the hair once it has been permed.

For example a regular swimmer may need to return to the salon for conditioning treatments.

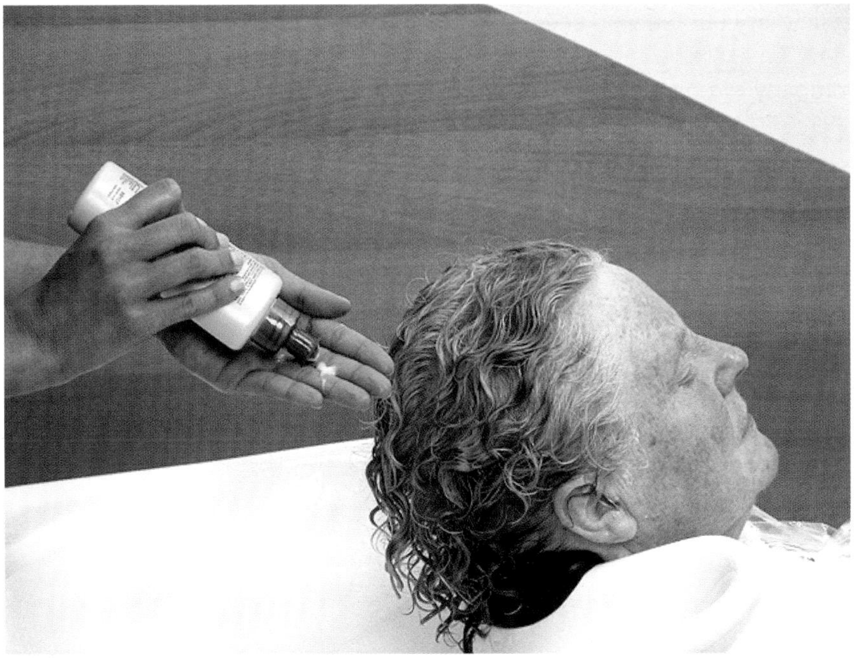

Figure 13.52 Explain which products are suitable for permed hair

WORKSHEETS

13.5 Worksheets

You can carry out the worksheets during your study of a chapter or unit, or at the end. An example is presented here and there are more online. If your college or company is registered with ATT Training, lots more are available. Write your answers directly in the book, but only if you own it of course – if it is a library or college book, use a separate piece of paper!

13.5.1 Precautions to take when handling chemicals

Read the precautions stated below. Next to each, state what might/will happen if you do not take these precautions.

1 Always wear protective gloves.

2 Avoid contact of the chemical with eyes and face.

3 Do not use on sensitive or damaged skin.

4 Always use a non-metallic bowl to avoid rapid decomposition of the product.

5 Store the product in a cool, dry place away from sunlight or other sources of heat.

6 Store the product in the container supplied and replace the cap immediately after use.

7 Always read the manufacturer's instructions.

13.6 Assessment

Well done! If you have studied all the content of this unit – you may be ready to test your knowledge.

Check out the 'Preparing for assessments' section in Chapter 1 if you have not already done so, and always remember:

- You can only do your best if you have. . .
  - studied hard
  - completed the activities
  - completed the worksheets
  - practised, practised, practised
  - and then revised!

Now carry out the online multiple-choice quiz

. . . and good luck in the final exam, which will be arranged by your tutor/assessor.

CHAPTER 14

Plait and twist hair

This chapter covers the NVQ/SVQ unit GH13, Plait and twist hair and the VRQ unit 105, Plaiting and twisting hair

Plaiting and twisting techniques have been popular for many years as many different looks can be achieved. Manual skill is needed for the methods but once the basic plaits and twists are mastered, you can create other ways of showing them.

In this chapter you will learn about:

- maintaining effective and safe methods of working when plaiting and twisting
- plaiting and twisting hair
- providing aftercare advice.

Website
www.atthairdressing.com

CHAPTER 14 PLAIT AND TWIST HAIR: CONTENTS, SCREENS AND ACTIVITIES

Key:
Sections from the book are set in this colour
Screens available online are set in this colour
Online activity screens are set in this colour

Working safely

Introduction	Gels
Safe methods of working when plaiting and twisting	Coshh
Tools and equipment	Preparing clients for plaiting and twisting
Select correct picture	Round the board
Products	Comfort during plaiting and twisting
Hairsprays	The effects of plaiting and twisting on the hair
Serums	

Plait and twist hair

Introduction	French plait 2
Consultation	Fishtail plait
Influencing factors – haircut and texture	Cornrows
Head and face shapes 1	Creating multiple cornrows 1
Wordsearch	Creating multiple cornrows 2
Head and face shapes 2	Twists
Head and face shapes 3	Flat twists 1
Head and face shapes 4	Flat twists 2
Five in a row	Drag into correct order
Plaiting hair	Two strand twists
French plait 1	Checking balance of completed style

Provide aftercare advice

Introduction	Worksheet – prepare the client for a haircut
Round the board	Worksheet – the effects of plaiting and twisting on the hair
Products	Worksheet – plaiting hair
Removal of hairstyle	Online multiple choice quiz

14.1 Working safely

When plaiting and twisting hair, you will use different products, tools and equipment. This section covers health and safety requirements necessary for their use and other areas including consultation and preparation. Chapter 2 covers health and safety working methods in more detail. Refer to this unit if needed.

Key information

Chapter 2 covers health and safety working methods in more detail. Refer to this unit if needed.

Tools and equipment

You may need the following tools and equipment when plaiting and twisting hair:

- dressing comb and tailcomb
- wide tooth comb (for wet hair)
- hairbrush (for dry hair)
- hairbands
- accessories if required.

Online activity 14.1 www

Select correct picture

Products

Products used during plaiting and twisting include:

- spray
- serum
- gel.

Key information

To prevent wastage of products, only use the amount needed according to the manufacturer's instructions.

Hairspray

Hairspray holds the hair in place and protects the hair from the weather and humidity. It comes in different strengths and is easily removed from the hair by brushing or wetting as most hairsprays are water soluble. Application of hairspray should be made so that the direction of the spray is pointed away from the client's face. This can be achieved by standing in front of your client when you are applying the product. It should be held at approximately 10 – 12 inches from the head.

Figure 14.1 Hairsprays

Figure 14.2 Applying hairspray

Safety first

Application of hairspray should be made so that the direction of the spray is pointed away from the client's face.

Serums

Hair serum will make hair look shiny and in better condition. This product must be used sparingly as it is very concentrated and can make hair appear lank or greasy.

Figure 14.3 A range of serums

Figure 14.4 Use sparingly!

Gels

Gels are designed to be used on either wet or dry hair. They complement and give definition to the style.

Figure 14.5 Gels

Figure 14.6 Applying gel

Control of Substances Hazardous to Health Regulations 2002 (COSHH)

These are commonly called the COSHH regulations and they lay down the essential requirements for controlling exposure to hazardous substances and for protecting people who may be affected by them. A substance is considered to be hazardous if it can cause harm to the body. It only poses a risk if it is:

- inhaled (breathed in)
- ingested (swallowed)
- in contact with the skin
- absorbed through the skin
- injected into the body
- introduced into the body via cuts etc.

For more information about the COSHH regulations refer to Chapter 2.

Safety first

A substance is considered to be hazardous if it can cause harm to the body.

Preparing clients for plaiting and twisting

Assist the client to put on a suitable sized gown to protect his or her clothing while in the salon. After the hair is shampooed, it is combed through to detangle.

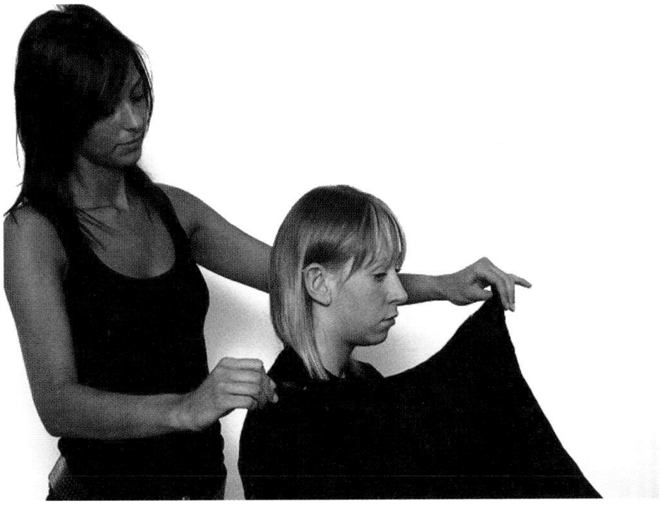

Figure 14.7 Gown the client

Online activity 14.2 WWW

Round the board

Comfort during plaiting and twisting

Whilst plaiting and twisting the client's hair, it is important for you to move around the client's head. However, the client's comfort should be considered at all times. Their back should be positioned right to the back of the chair and as flat as possible. They should have both feet on the footrest or the floor. Not only will this be a more comfortable position for the client but also enables you to create a balanced hairstyle. Your own comfort during plaiting and twisting should be considered as well. Check your posture is correct, ensuring that your client's seat is at the correct height for you to work. Ensure that your work area is tidy and free from clutter.

Figure 14.8 Incorrect posture

Figure 14.9 Correct posture

Definitions

Traction alopecia: A condition in which the hair falls out due to excessive pulling.

Follicle: Sac containing the hair shaft in the epidermis.

The effects of plaiting and twisting on the hair

Take care to use the correct tension when plaiting and twisting. Too much pulling will damage the hair follicle. Be aware of traction alopecia, a condition where the hair has fallen out in places due to excessive pulling. It is a more common condition in those who have cornrows or hair weaves due to the tightness of the plait or twist. These types of styles are also kept in the hair for longer than basic plaits. Always check with the client that you are not exerting too much pressure on their head and that they feel comfortable throughout.

Figure 14.10 Take care to use the correct tension

14.2 Plait and twist hair

This section covers the plaiting and twisting techniques in detail. There are many different options for plaits and twists depending on the client's wishes. If required, hair length can be extended using added hair.

Figure 14.11 Plait

Consultation

Before any service begins the hairdresser must find out what the client wants or needs. The consultation is used to ensure the client's wishes are interpreted accurately and the desired look achieved. It is essential to be factual, honest, tactful, sincere, direct and clear. Ensure that the client is aware that the longer lasting plaits and twists take longer to create and so they should be clear on time and cost of the service.

Key information

Ensure that the client is aware that the longer lasting plaits and twists take longer to create and so they should be clear on time and cost of the service.

Figure 14.12 Consultation with the client

Influencing factors – haircut and texture

Key information

If you do notice the signs of traction alopecia you should avoid styles that create further tension on the hair.

Check the client's current haircut as this will influence the way that you style it. Taking a look beforehand at how the client wears their hair helps if they would like to wear it in the same way. Also, look to assess the texture of the hair. There are three types of hair: fine, medium and coarse.

Look for any previous signs of traction alopecia during the consultation. You may notice some thinning or absent hair which could be around the hairline. If you do notice the signs of this, then avoid styles that create further tension on the hair.

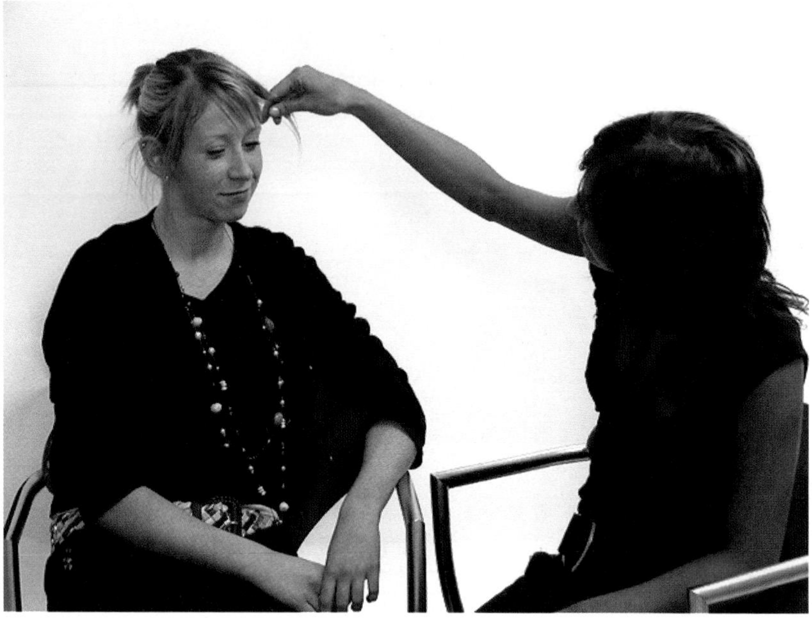

Figure 14.13 Look at the client's hair

Head and face shapes

Key information

For more information about head and face shapes, refer to Chapter 4.

The client may have the following head or face shape:

- oval
- round
- long
- square
- heart
- pear.

WWW Online activity 14.3

Wordsearch

The oval shaped face is considered to be the perfect shape that suits any style. However, many people have differing features and it is important to choose the hairstyle to suit both features and face shape.

If your client has a round face, a hairstyle will be needed that is flat at the sides and high on the top. This will enhance the client's features.

If the client has a narrow or long face, the hairstyle needs to be fuller at the sides and flatter on top.

If a client has a square or angular jawline, the hairstyle will need to be softer in style and covering part of that area. This will flatten the face.

A client with a heart shaped face will usually be very wide around the eyes and cheek-bones. They may also have a very wide forehead. A fringe would help to narrow the forehead and also hair will need to be brought onto the face to create more fullness between the jaw and the bottom of the ear.

If a client has a pear shaped face, the hairstyle will have to be flat around the jawline but have lots of volume and fullness around the temples. This will narrow the appearance of the face.

Large ears that protrude need to be covered for a flattering effect.

If the client has a big nose or broken nose a centre parting will exaggerate this. Choose an asymmetric style. This will be more flattering.

A fringe will achieve the best effect for a client with a high forehead or receding hairline.

A short, stocky neck requires a softer hairstyle which is more flattering to the client.

Online activity 14.4 WWW

Ring the bell by clicking true or false. You must get five in a row correct. If you answer one incorrectly you must start again.
Colours and lighteners are chemical free.
True
False

Five in a row

Plaiting hair

Plaiting is the method of intertwining sections of hair. Three or more strands are used when carrying out this technique. A variety of woven effects can be created depending on the client's desired look. If the client wishes the look for an occasion, then decoration can be applied. This could include flowers, silks, beads and added hair. The following plaits will be created:

Website
www.atthairdressing.com

- French plait/scalp plait
- fishtail plait
- cornrows.

Figure 14.14 Added hair may be used

French plait

Once this technique is mastered, then many different looks can be created. For example if larger sections are taken, the look will be softer. Hair can be either wet or dry when creating a French plait. Always remember to use less tension if the hair is wet, as it will stretch more and tighten up when dry.

Figure 14.15 French plait

Figure 14.16 Brush and/or comb the hair to detangle. Tilt the head backwards and divide the hair at the front of the head into three sections. The outer section is placed over the centre section at one side. This is then repeated on the other side.

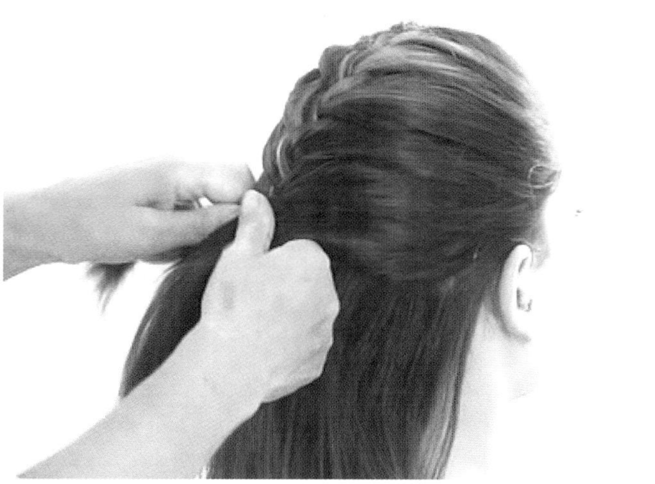

Figure 14.17 A fourth section is then taken and included with the next outer section to be plaited. Repeat on the opposite outer section. When you run out of hair to add, continue plaiting the ends of the hair and secure with a band, ribbon or thread. Spray with finishing spray if required.

Fishtail plait

The hair is brushed to detangle and divided into two sections. The section at the right is sectioned again into two. Cross the outer section over so that it is in the centre. This is repeated to the ends of the hair. The hair is secured with a band, ribbon or thread. Apply finishing spray if required.

Figure 14.18 Fishtail plait (online video)

Cornrows

This technique is popular due to cornrows being long lasting and having a dramatic effect. They are fairly easy to maintain but should have products applied regularly. Cornrows originate from Africa and are a type of three-stem plait that is interwoven close to the scalp. Many different patterns can be achieved; therefore it can be a very creative technique. Added hair can be interwoven to add length if desired.

Key information

Cornrows originate from Africa and are a type of three-stem plait that is interwoven close to the scalp.

Cornrows can be applied to the hair for up to 6 weeks and then they must be removed. They could be applied to the whole head or a partial head.

Figure 14.19 Cornrows

Creating multiple cornrows

After the hair is washed and conditioned, it is dried straight.

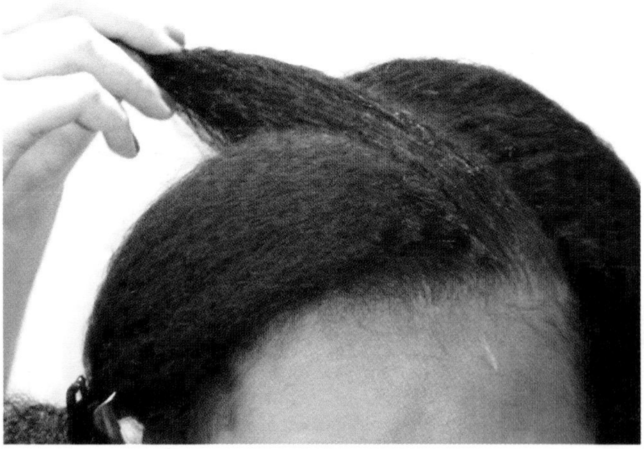

Figure 14.20 The hair is divided into tidy sections. A channel of hair is sectioned using a tailcomb. This will create the course of the design. Gel is applied to the section of hair.

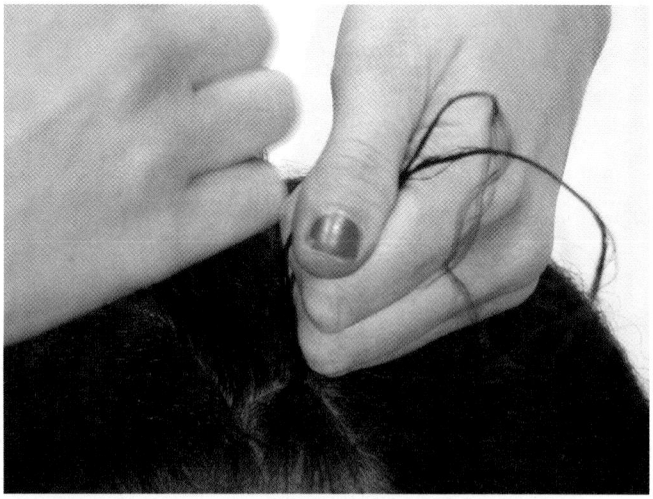

Figure 14.21 The channel of hair is subdivided into three. The section at the front is held in the left hand between the middle and third finger. The next section is held between the thumb and index finger. The last section is held in the right hand between the middle and third finger. Ensure that all the sections are the same width so that you get an even look.

Figure 14.22 The middle section held in the left hand is taken under the section held in the right hand using the index finger. The new middle section is now passed under the section on the outer of the left hand.

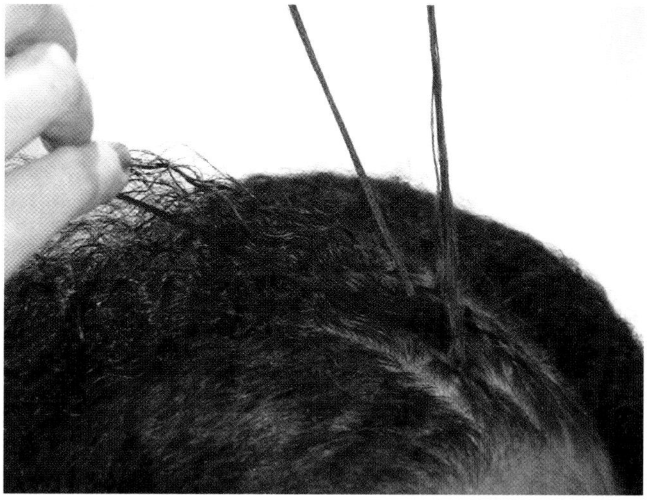

Figure 14.23 Some hair in the channel is taken with the fourth finger and included in the outer third section. The last two steps are repeated as far as the area where the plait hangs from the scalp.

Figure 14.24 The rest of the section is then plaited. The ends are secured with a band, beads or coloured thread.

Figure 14.25 Cornrows created throughout the top of the head.

Figure 14.26 Apply hairspray to the finished style.

Figure 14.27 The finished cornrows.

Twists

This technique is carried out by twisting the hair using either fingers or a comb. As with cornrows, different linear patterns can be created depending on the client's wishes. Twists in the hair can last up to 4 weeks. After this time they will look messy. A product application will help to hold the twist in place e.g. styling gel. The following will be shown:

- flat twist (on-scalp)
- two strand twists (off-scalp).

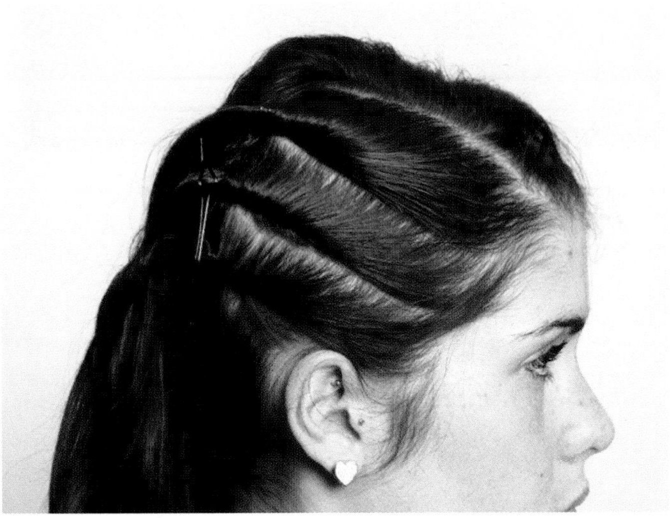

Figure 14.28 Flat twists

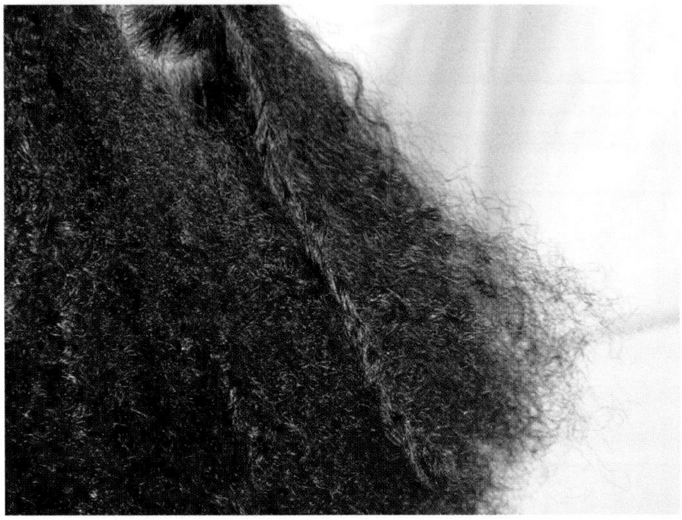

Figure 14.29 Two strand twists

Key information

They are described as on-scalp twists as they are tight to the scalp and not loose.

Flat twists

Flat twists look similar to cornrows but they are not weaved together. Less time is needed to create flat twists. They are described as on-scalp twists as they are tight to scalp and not loose.

After the hair has been shampooed, conditioned and dried roughly into shape, it is brushed to untangle. Using a tailcomb the hair is divided at the front.

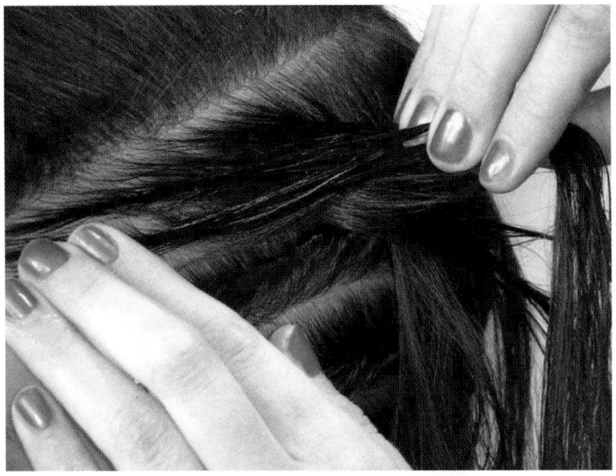

Figure 14.30 Styling gel is then applied to the section taken.

Figure 14.31 The hair is then twisted, close to the scalp but with the correct tension, towards the back of the head.

Figure 14.32 As the hair strand is twisted, another strand is picked up and twisted with this. This is continued towards the back of the head until the desired point is reached.

Figure 14.33 The strands should be of an equal width to keep the style looking even.

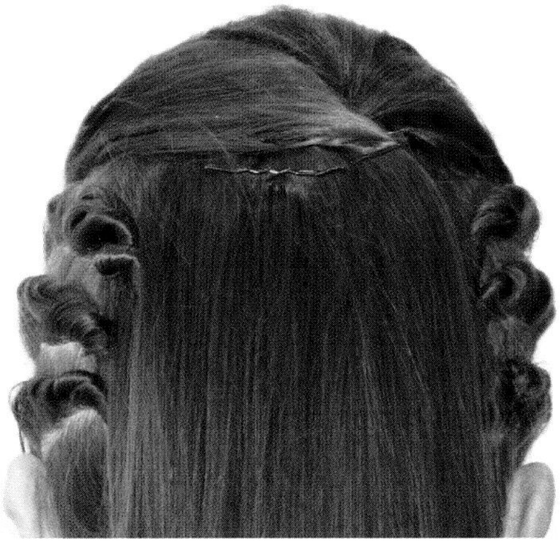

Figure 14.34 When each twist is finished, the hair is secured using bands or grips. This technique is continued on the rest of the hair to achieve the desired look.

Online activity 14.5 WWW

Drag into correct order

Two strand twists

This type of twist can be applied to the whole head or can be added to certain areas of a hairstyle e.g. a ponytail. Two sections of hair are taken and twisted over each other using your fingers in a clockwise direction. This is carried on as far as the ends of the hair. Curly hair does not need to be secured at the ends but straight hair may need to be.

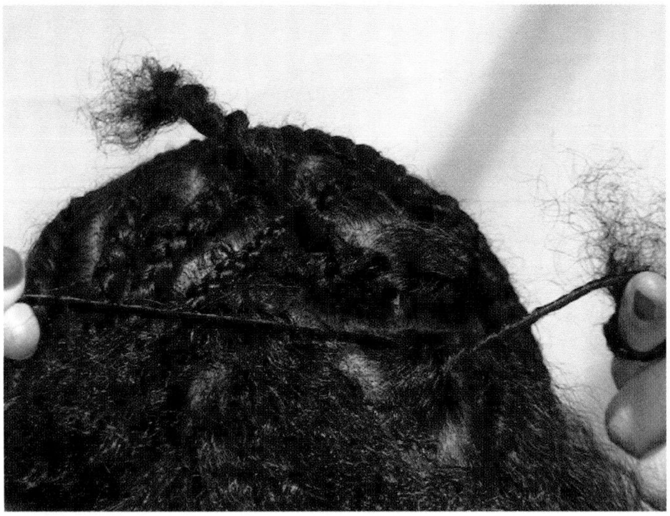

Figure 14.35 Two sections are taken.

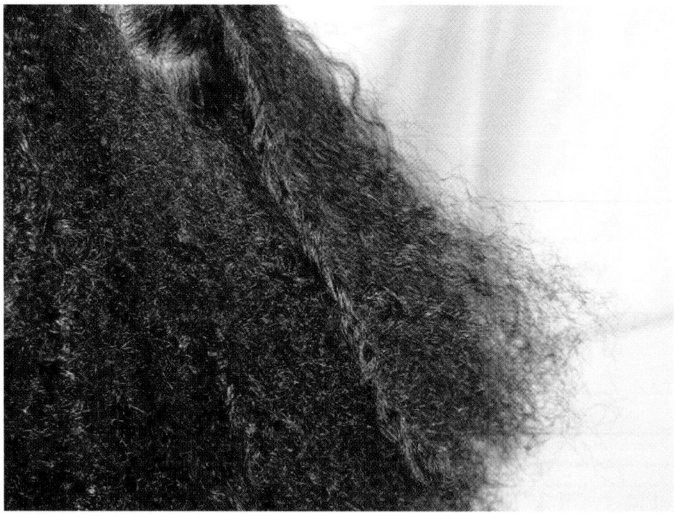

Figure 14.36 Curly hair does not need to be secured, unlike straight hair.

Key information

Use a back mirror from behind, angling the position so both the hairdresser and the client can see the finished result from the back.

Checking balance of completed style

Check the balance of the hairstyle, using the front mirror to ensure that the profile shape of the hairstyle and the finish are appealing to the client, and reinforce this by confirming with the client. Use a back mirror from behind, angling the position so both the hairdresser and the client can see the finished result from the back.

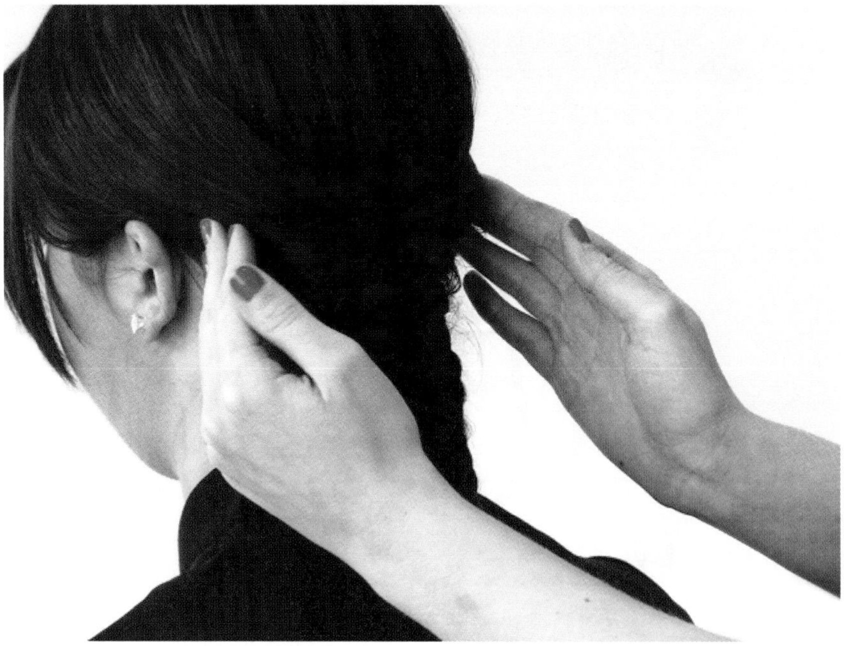

Figure 14.37 Checking balance of style

Key information

Throughout the service you must explain to the client what you are doing. Do this fully and accurately, repeating yourself if needed.

14.3 Provide aftercare advice

An important part of this service is to give the client aftercare advice. The client's lifestyle must be taken into consideration when creating a style that the client can maintain. Throughout the service you must explain to the client what you are doing. Do this fully and accurately, repeating yourself if needed.

Online activity 14.6 WWW

Round the board

Products

Advise the client on which products can be used at home. This should be based on the factors that influence the service. Refer to Chapter 6 for more information.

Removal of hairstyle

Explain to the client the way in which the hairstyle is taken down. Pins and grips must be removed carefully before brushing the hair.

Figure 14.38 Advise the clients on which products to use at home

Figure 14.39 Explain how a hairstyle is taken down

WORKSHEETS

14.4 Worksheets

You can carry out the worksheets during your study of a chapter or unit, or at the end. An example is presented here and there are more online. If your college or company is registered with ATT Training, lots more are available. Write your answers directly in the book, but only if you own it of course – if it is a library or college book, use a separate piece of paper!

14.4.1 The effects of plaiting and twisting on the hair

You should take care to use the correct tension when plaiting and twisting hair.

Answer the following questions:

1 Too much pulling will damage which area of the hair?

____

____

2 Describe the condition traction alopecia.

____

____

3 Suggest which plaits or twists would be most likely to cause traction alopecia.

____

____

4 What are the main causes of traction alopecia?

____

____

14.5 Assessment

Well done! If you have studied all the content of this unit you may be ready to test your knowledge.

Check out the 'Preparing for assessments' section in Chapter 1 if you have not already done so, and always remember:

- You can only do your best if you have. . .
  - studied hard
  - completed the activities
  - completed the worksheets
  - practised, practised, practised
  - and then revised!

Now carry out the online multiple-choice quiz

. . . and good luck in the final exam, which will be arranged by your tutor/assessor.

CHAPTER 15

Dry and finish men's hair

This chapter covers the NVQ/SVQ unit GB5, Dry and finish men's hair.

After every service the client will have their hair styled and finished. This unit covers the techniques of both blow-drying and finger-drying to create a variety of looks for men.

In this chapter you will learn about:

- maintaining effective and safe methods when drying hair
- drying and finishing hair
- providing aftercare advice.

Website www

www.atthairdressing.com

CHAPTER 15 DRY AND FINISH MEN'S HAIR: CONTENTS, SCREENS AND ACTIVITIES

Key:
Sections from the book are set in this colour
Screens available online are set in this colour
Online activity screens are set in this colour

Working safely

Introduction
Maintain effective and safe methods of working when drying hair
Hair is hygroscopic
Products used during styling and finishing
Correct selection
Creams
Gels
Heat protectors
Hairsprays
Wax
COSHH
Styling tools and equipment
Brushes
Drag correct picture
Hand dryers
Attachments
Electricity at work regulations
Consultation
Influencing factors
Preparing client for drying
Comfort during styling
Suggested time for service

Dry and finish hair

Introduction
Blow-drying hair
Blow-drying straight hair into shape 1
Blow-drying straight hair into shape 2
Blow-drying straight hair into shape 3
Drag into correct order
Finger-drying
Finger-drying curly hair
Checking balance of completed style

Provide aftercare advice

Provide aftercare advice
Round the board
Equipment and products
Worksheet – Control of Substances Hazardous to Health Regulations
Worksheet – Brushes
Online Multiple Choice Quiz

15.1 Working safely

When drying and finishing men's hair, the products, tools and equipment used will be less than is used during the hairdressing service. This is due to men's hair generally being shorter and so the time taken to style it will be reduced.

Chapter 2 covers health and safety working methods in more detail. Refer to this unit if needed.

Figure 15.1 Using tools for finishing and drying

Hair is hygroscopic

This means that it has the ability to absorb moisture.

Wet hair can be stretched to nearly double its normal length. This is called elasticity. Wet hair in its stretched state is called the 'beta keratin'. When it is in the natural state (unstretched), the hair is called the 'alpha keratin'. The reason why hair stretches is because the hydrogen bonds are broken down by water. It is these properties that allow us to alter the shape of hair. When heat is applied the hydrogen bonds can be re-formed into a new shape. The humidity in the air will affect the structure of the hair by making the hair feel damp. This will take the hair back to its natural state.

Definitions

Alpha keratin: Hair in its natural unstretched state.

Beta keratin: The stretched (wet) state of hair.

WWW

View the online video to learn more about the hair in its various states

Products used during styling and finishing

These include:

- creams
- gels
- heat protectors
- sprays
- wax.

To prevent wastage of products, use only the amount needed as according to manufacturers' instructions.

Figure 15.2 Selections of products used when drying and finishing men's hair

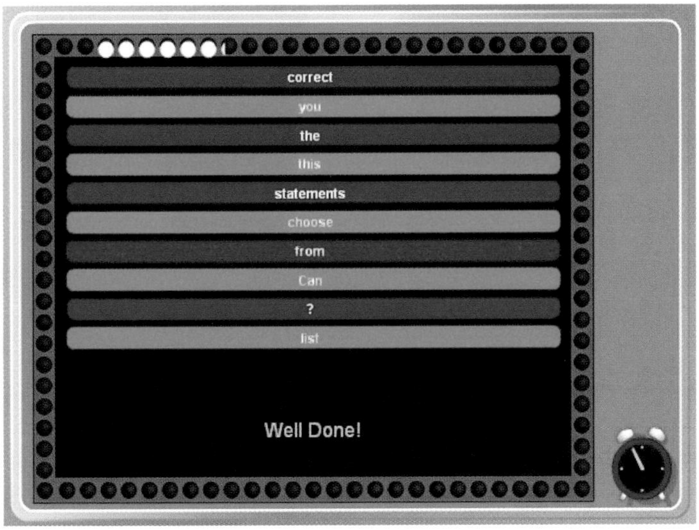

Figure 15.3 Online activity screen

WWW **Online activity 15.1**

Correct selection

Creams

Creams can be used on wet or dry hair and should be used sparingly.

Figure 15.4 Creams that can be used on men's hair

Gels

Gels can be used on wet or dry hair. They complement and give definition to the style.

Figure 15.5 Gels that can be used on men's hair

Heat protectors

These products protect the hair from damage caused by using heated styling equipment. When heated styling equipment is used frequently, the hair structure can become damaged as the cuticles swell and rise. When heat applicators are applied, they form a shield around the hair which acts as a barrier and absorbs the heat.

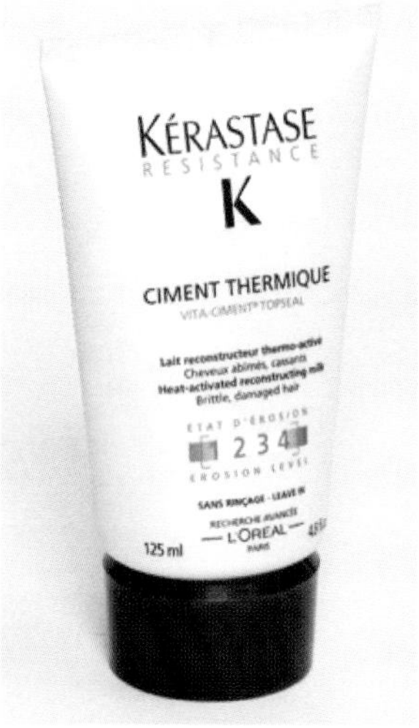

Figure 15.6 Heat protector

Hairsprays

Hairspray holds the hair in place and protects the hair from the weather and humidity. It comes in different strengths and it is easily removed from the hair by brushing or wetting as most hairsprays are water soluble. Application of hairspray should be made so that the direction of the spray is pointed away from the client's face. This can be achieved by standing in front of your client when you are applying the product. It should be held at approximately 10 – 12 inches from the head.

Figure 15.7 A type of hairspray used on men's hair

Wax

Wax is used on pre-dried hair to give definition. It is applied sparingly using the fingertips.

Figure 15.8 Wax and clay

Control of Substances Hazardous to Health Regulations 2002 (COSHH)

Safety first

A substance is considered to be hazardous if it can cause harm to the body.

These are commonly called the COSHH regulations and they lay down the essential requirements for controlling exposure to hazardous substances and for protecting people who may be affected by them.

It only poses a risk if it is:

- inhaled (breathed in)
- ingested (swallowed)
- in contact with the skin
- absorbed through the skin
- injected into the body
- introduced into the body via cuts etc.

For more information about the COSHH regulations refer to Chapter 2.

www

The associated learning screen for this part is interactive

Styling tools and equipment

Tools and equipment used for styling men's hair include:

- brushes
- hand dryers
- attachments.

Keep all tools and equipment clean and sterilised at all times to minimise products from building up and causing sticky areas. As the tools and equipment are used, the hair may become attached to these areas and get damaged. Ensure that all the equipment that you are to use is pre-selected and ready to use.

Figure 15.9 Blow-drying tools and equipment

Brushes

It is essential to have different types of brush so that you can produce the correct effects according to the client's wishes. The classic styling brush is used for all-purpose brushing creating a smooth effect on any length of hair. Vent brushes are used for all-purpose brushing creating a smooth effect on short or mid-length hair. Circular brushes are used to give volume to the hair or a curled effect on any length. The choice of brush will depend on the size of the curl and also the length of the hair. Tighter curls will need a smaller circular brush. Flat brushes are used for all-purpose brushing and for producing a smooth effect.

Figure 15.10 Styling brush

Figure 15.11 Vent brush

Figure 15.12 Circular brush

Figure 15.13 Flat brush

Online activity 15.2 WWW

Drag pictures

Hand dryers

There are many different types of hand dryer. You should be able to change the temperature and speed. It will be used for long periods of time and so should be durable. The hand dryer should also be easy to use and lightweight.

Figure 15.14 Hand dryer

Figure 15.15 Hand dryer

Attachments

Diffusers and nozzles can be attached to the hand dryer. The diffuser is attached to the end of the hand dryer. When switched on this disperses air evenly to the hair. It enables the hair to be dried gently and is suitable for creating movement in the hair. The nozzle enables air from the hand dryer to be distributed to one particular area. It is suitable for blow-drying the hair into shape.

Figure 15.16 Hand dryer with nozzle and diffuser

Electricity at Work Regulations 1989

These regulations state that you must:

- Always check electrical equipment before using. Look for loose wires and that the plug is not cracked or damaged in any way. Check that the cord is not frayed or cracked.
- Never use electrical equipment when your hands are wet.
- Electrical equipment should be maintained regularly and checked by a suitably qualified person. Once checked the equipment should have a certificate or label acknowledging it.
- Faulty electrical equipment in the workplace must be removed, labelled as faulty and reported to the relevant person.

Safety first

Faulty electrical equipment in the workplace must be removed, labelled as faulty and reported to the relevant person.

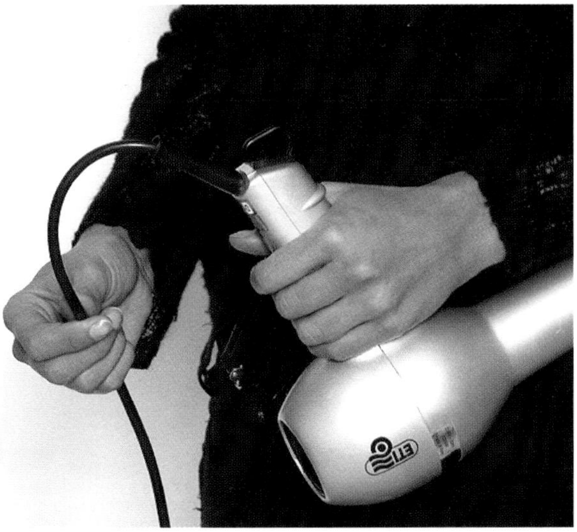

Figure 15.17 Check equipment

Consultation

Before any service begins the hairdresser must find out the client's expectations. The consultation is used to ensure the client's wishes are interpreted accurately and the desired look achieved. It is essential to be factual, honest, tactful, sincere, direct and clear. The consultation will give the opportunity to decide on products, the service that is carried out and the equipment that is used.

Figure 15.18 You can decide on the way the hair is dried during the consultation

Key information

The time the hair takes to dry will depend on how long and how much hair the client has.

Influencing factors

Check the client's current haircut as this will influence the way that you style it. Taking a look at how the client wears his hair will help if he would like to wear it in the same way. Also, look to assess the texture of the hair. There are three types of hair; fine, medium and coarse. The time the hair takes to dry will depend on how long and how much hair the client has.

Refer to Chapter 16 for other influencing factors to look out for during the consultation including growth patterns and head and face shapes.

Prepare client for drying

Drying and finishing the hair always follow another service, even if this is just a shampoo. Therefore the hair will be wet and so should be combed through before drying. Ensure that the client is gowned in the appropriate manner before drying and styling the hair.

Figure 15.19 Comb the hair

Comfort during styling

Whilst drying and finishing the client's hair, it is important for you to move around the client's head. However, the client's comfort should be considered at all times. Their back should be positioned right to the back of the chair and as flat as possible. They should have both feet on the footrest or the floor. Not only will this be a more comfortable position for the client but it also enables you to create a balanced hairstyle. Your own comfort during styling and finishing should be considered as well. Check your posture is correct, ensuring that your client's seat is at the correct height for you to work. Ensure that your work area is tidy and free from clutter.

Safety first

Ensure that your work area is tidy and free from clutter.

Definition

Posture: Working position of the body.

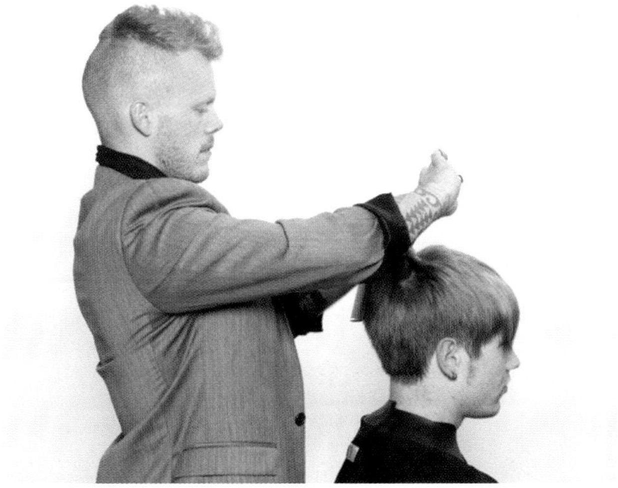

Figure 15.20 Correct posture during the hairdressing service

Suggested time for service

A commercially viable time for cutting, blow-drying/drying and finishing men's hair is 30 minutes.

15.2 Dry and finish hair

The consultation will allow you to agree a style with the client. Check the client is happy with the style you are creating before and during the service. Ensure that the hair does not dry out naturally, as this will stop you from achieving the desired look that is created through drying.

Blow-drying hair

When using any brush, it is important to be gentle otherwise the hair could become tangled or damaged. This is also uncomfortable for the client. An even tension should be kept at all times to avoid overstretching the hair and to ensure that you get an even finish. When drying, the angle of the brush determines how much root movement (lift or bounce) is achieved. Long hair will not allow much root lift because of the length and weight of the hair.

Figure 15.21 The angle of the brush determines how much root movement is achieved

Definition

Root lift: Creating volume at the root.

Blow-drying straight hair into shape

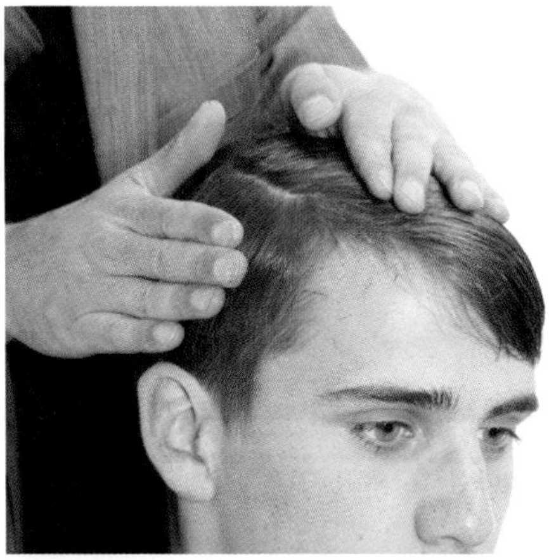

Figure 15.22 Apply products suitable for the client's hair type.

Figure 15.23 To achieve a smooth look, a flat brush is used.

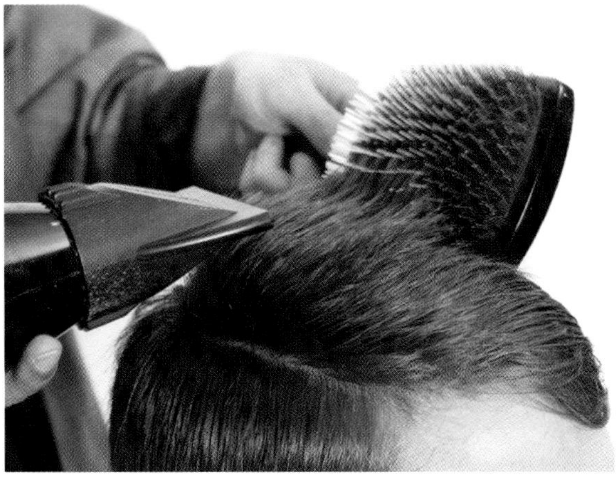

Figure 15.24 The direction of the air flow from the hand dryer must be directed along the hair shaft from roots to ends and in the same direction as the brush strokes. This will ensure an even and smoother finish. Continue this technique until the hair is dry.

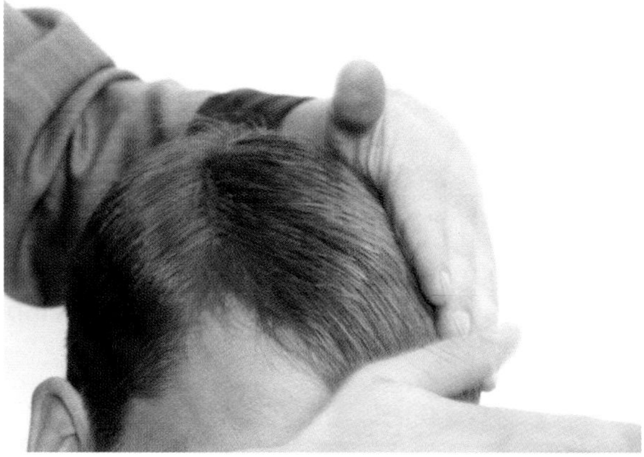

Figure 15.25 Apply suitable products to finish the hair.

Figure 15.26 Finished look.

Online activity 15.3 WWW

Drag into correct order

Finger-drying

This technique involves using manual dexterity to dry the hair into the required style. The fingers direct the hair, creating movement and volume for the desired look.

Definition

Dexterity: Having the skills to perform tasks with the hands.

Figure 15.27 Finger-drying hair

Finger-drying curly hair

Figure 15.28 Apply products appropriate to the client's hair. Distribute this evenly throughout.

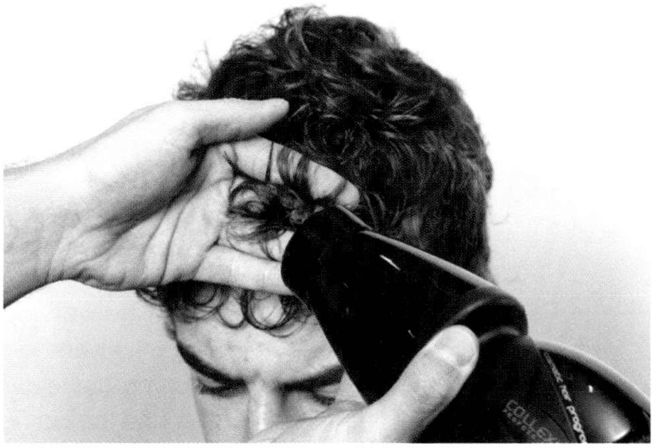

Figure 15.29 Using the fingers to direct the curls, dry the hair.

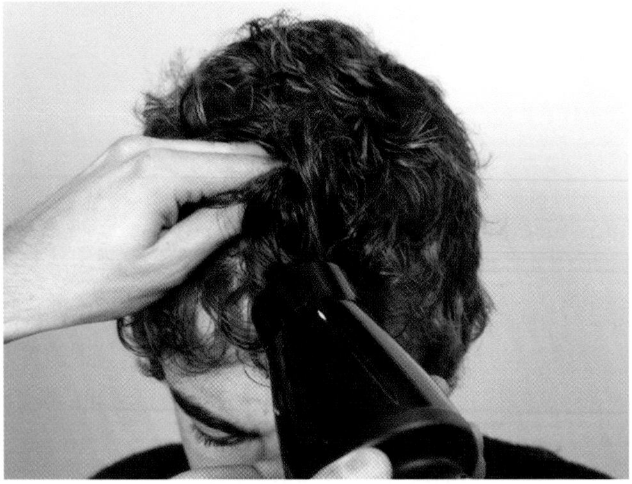

Figure 15.30 Small areas of the hair should be worked on.

Figure 15.31 Finished look.

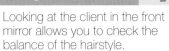

Key information

Looking at the client in the front mirror allows you to check the balance of the hairstyle.

Checking balance of completed style

Check the balance of the hairstyle, using the front mirror to ensure that the profile shape of the hairstyle and the finish are appealing to the client and reinforce this by confirming with the client. Use a back mirror from behind, angling the position so both the hairdresser and the client can see the finished result from the back.

15.3 Provide aftercare advice

Figure 15.32 Explain what you are doing throughout the service

An important part of this service is to give the client aftercare advice. The client should be able to recreate the look that you have given them. Ensure the client is aware that if the hair becomes damp through weather conditions, it is likely to drop or revert back to its natural state.

The client's lifestyle must be taken into consideration when creating a style that the client can maintain. For example an important factor for some would be a style that can be managed with minimum effort due to career and sports activities. Throughout the service you must explain to the client what you are doing. Do this fully and accurately, repeating yourself if needed.

WWW Online activity 15.4

Round the board

Equipment and products

As you are working, always explain to the client how best to use the equipment. They may want to recreate the style themselves at home. Advise the client on which products can be used at home. This should be based on the factors that influence the service. Refer to Chapter 6 for more information.

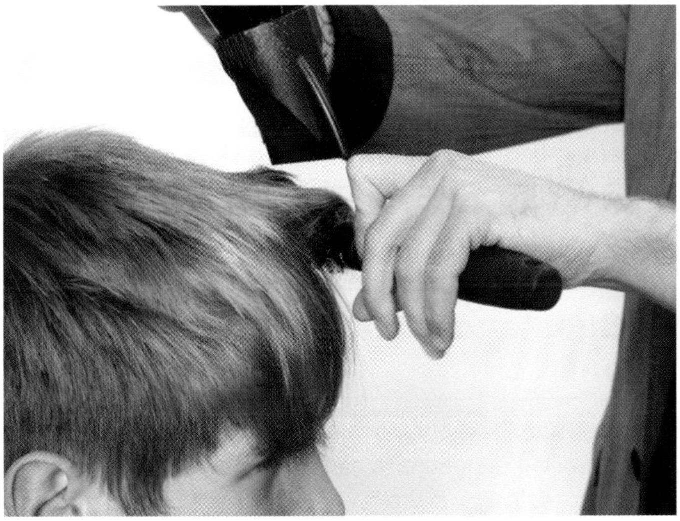

Figure 15.33 Talk to the client about the equipment you are using to create the style

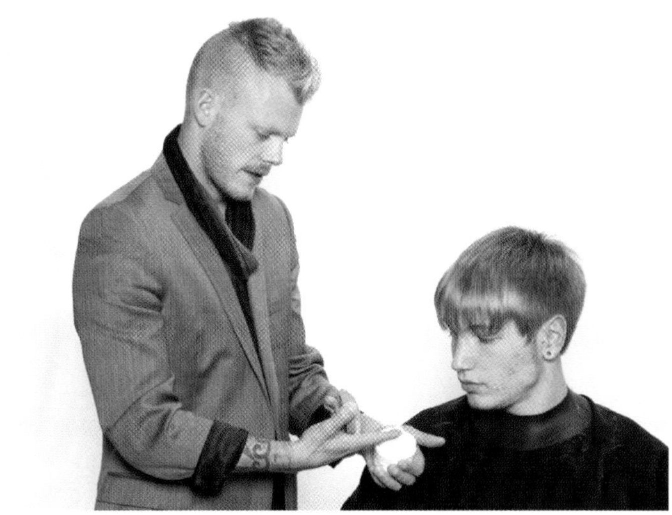

Figure 15.34 Explain to client which products can be used at home

WORKSHEETS

15.4 Worksheets

You can carry out the worksheets during your study of a chapter or unit, or at the end. An example is presented here and there are more online. If your college or company is registered with ATT Training, lots more are available. Write your answers directly in the book, but only if you own it of course – if it is a library or college book, use a separate piece of paper!

15.4.1 Control of Substances Hazardous to Health (COSHH) Regulations

These are commonly called the COSHH regulations and they lay down the essential requirements for controlling exposure to hazardous substances and for protecting people who may be affected by them.

A substance is considered to be hazardous if it can cause harm to the body. It only poses a risk if it is:

- inhaled (breathed in)
- ingested (swallowed)
- in contact with the skin
- absorbed though the body
- injected into the body
- induced into the body via cuts etc.

Here is a picture of Mr COSHH. Label him and write about situations that may occur in your salon that could cause you to be at risk from a hazardous substance. Also make a note of actions you can take to avoid this from happening.

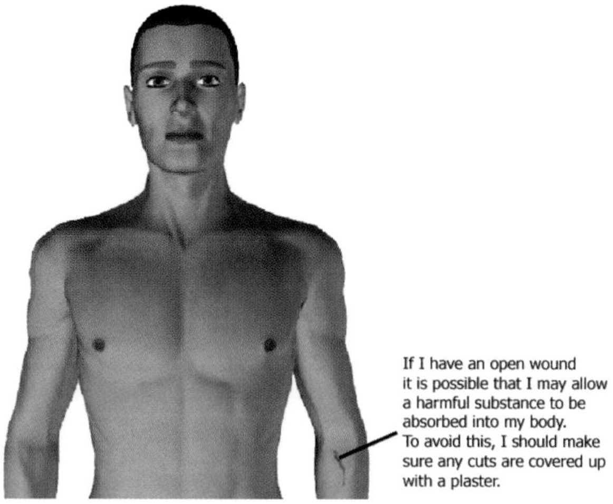
If I have an open wound
it is possible that I may allow
a harmful substance to be
absorbed into my body.
To avoid this, I should make
sure any cuts are covered up
with a plaster.

Figure 15.35 Mr COSHH

Make notes under each point to suggest action that could/should be taken.

15.5 Assessment

Well done! If you have studied all the content of this unit you may be ready to test your knowledge.

Check out the 'Preparing for assessments' section in Chapter 1 if you have not already done so, and always remember:

- You can only do your best if you have. . .
  - studied hard
  - completed the activities
  - completed the worksheets
  - practised, practised, practised
  - and then revised!

Now carry out the online multiple-choice quiz

. . . and good luck in the final exam, which will be arranged by your tutor/assessor.

CHAPTER 16

Cut men's hair

This chapter covers the NVQ/SVQ unit GB3, Cut hair using basic barbering techniques and the VRQ unit 210, Cut men's hair.

Many cutting techniques performed during barbering cross over with hairdressing as men and women have the same hair types and textures. Hairstyles have also become similar as many men are wearing hair in longer styles and women in shorter styles. The basic techniques of barbering include club cutting, scissor over comb, clipper over comb, freehand and thinning.

In this chapter you will learn about:

- maintaining effective and safe methods of working when cutting
- cutting hair to achieve a variety of looks
- providing aftercare advice.

Website
www.atthairdressing.com

CHAPTER 16 CUT MEN'S HAIR: CONTENTS, SCREENS AND ACTIVITIES

Key:
Sections from the book are set in this colour
Screens available online are set in this colour
Online activity screens are set in this colour

16.1 Working safely

Safety is the key issue when cutting hair. The tools that you use must allow you to perform the haircut that the client wishes to have. Be careful not to damage your tools as you work. Ensure that all of the equipment that you will be using is pre-selected and ready to use. Chapter 2 covers health and safety working methods in more detail. Refer to this unit if needed.

> **Safety first**
>
> Safety is the key issue when cutting hair.

Scissors

These come in a variety of materials such as stainless steel, with metal or plastic handles. They also come in a variety of designs, weights and prices. Picking scissors up and holding them is the best way to see if they are suitable. It is important that they feel comfortable. Scissors should always be clean and sharp. Before sterilising remember to remove all loose hairs.

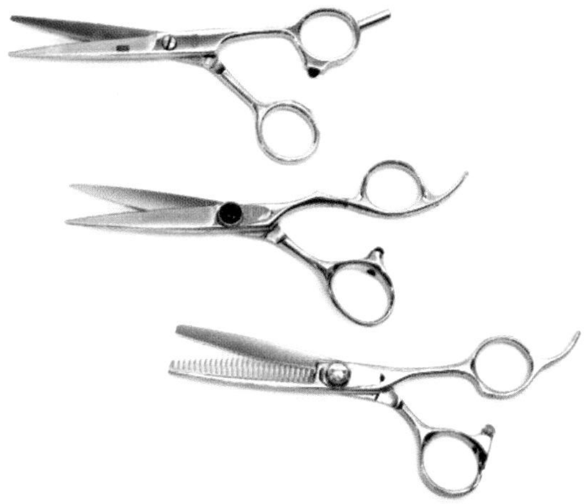

Figure 16.1 Different types of scissors

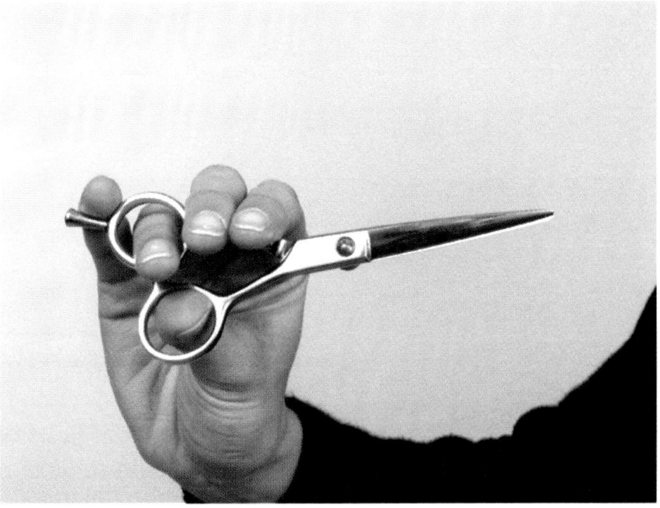

Figure 16.2 Pick scissors up to see if they are comfortable to hold

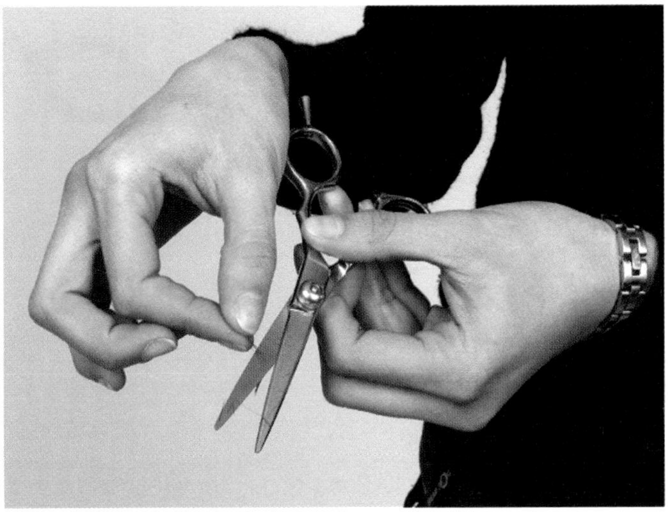

Figure 16.3 Pick off any loose hairs

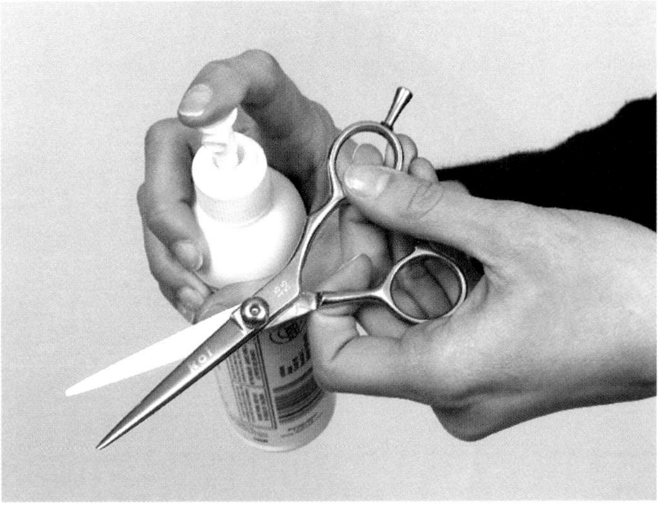

Figure 16.4 Sterilising scissors

Thinning scissors

These are scissors specifically designed for thinning the hair. They have one or possibly two blades that look like the teeth on a comb. The teeth of the blades are sharp and cut the hair. The gaps between the teeth just allow the hair to pass through without removing any hair at all. The size of the gap determines how much hair is removed.

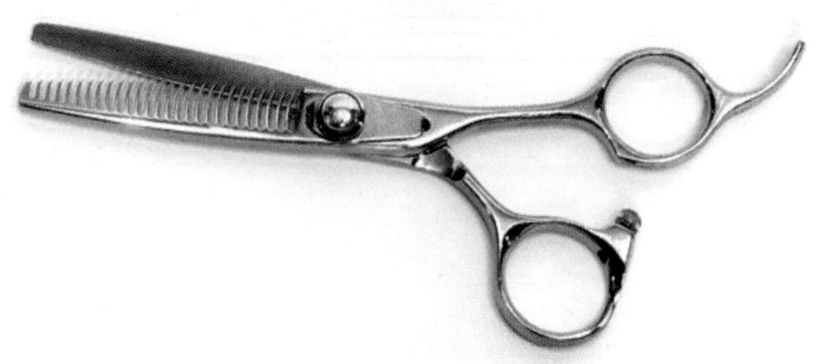

Figure 16.5 Thinning scissors with one blade serrated

Figure 16.6 And with two blades serrated

Razors

Definition

Disposable: Intended for use once and then thrown away.

The main types of razors used are cut-throat razors, safety razors and shapers. Cut-throat or open razors have a blade that folds into the handle. Safety razors have a disposable blade and so these can be changed between clients. This makes the service more hygienic. Shapers also have disposable blades and are used for cutting hair. They are not used for shaving.

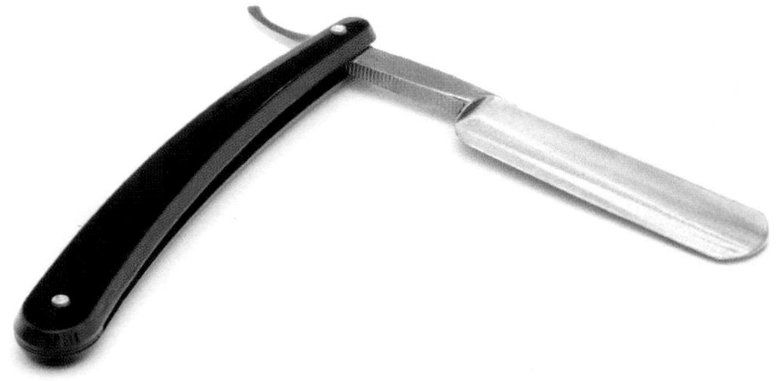

Figure 16.7 Cut-throat razor

Figure 16.8 Safety razor

Razors can only be used on wet hair. When used on dry hair they tear and shred the cuticles leaving the cortex frayed and exposed. It is also uncomfortable for the client. Salons using razor blades must dispose of them in a container such as a sharps box.

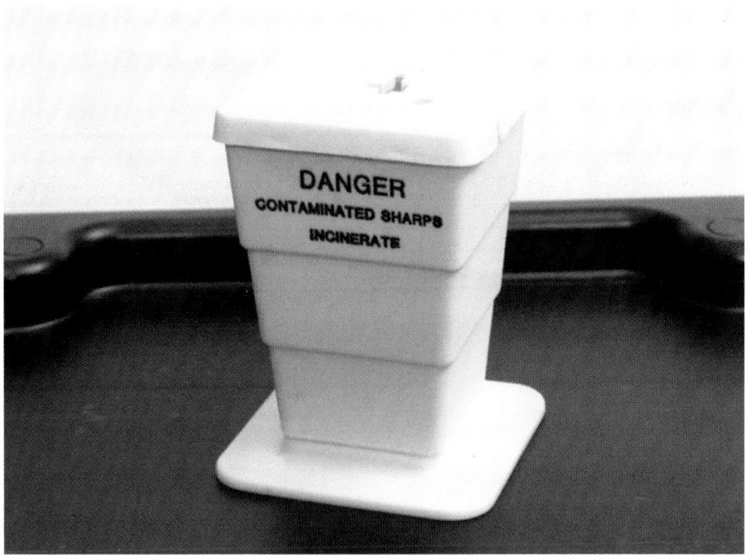

Figure 16.9 Dispose of razors in a box like this

Safety first

You must dispose of razor blades in a container such as a sharps box.

Online activity 16.1

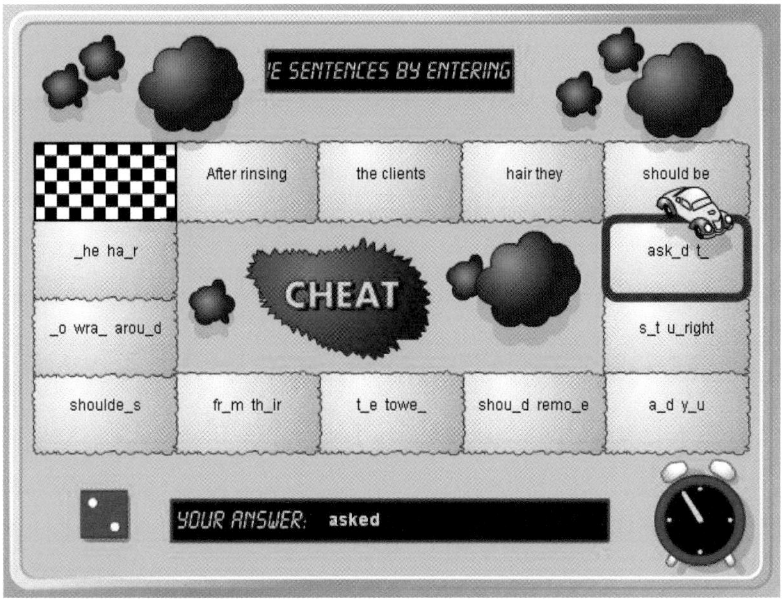

Round the board

Clippers

Always follow the manufacturer's instructions when using clippers so that you use them safely. When in use the bottom blade remains still whilst the top blade moves across it very quickly to cut the hair. Ensure that you check the alignment of the clipper blades before use. Small adjustments can be made by loosening the small screws that are positioned underneath. Remember to oil clippers using clipper oil after every use to keep them lubricated and clean. This also prolongs the life of the blades. After use, clean away hairs from the clippers. Sometimes the blades must be removed to clean away hair. If this is not done, the clippers may not work properly, causing discomfort to the client. All repairs to electric clippers should be carried out by a qualified electrician.

Safety first

Always follow the manufacturer's instructions when using clippers so that you use them safely.

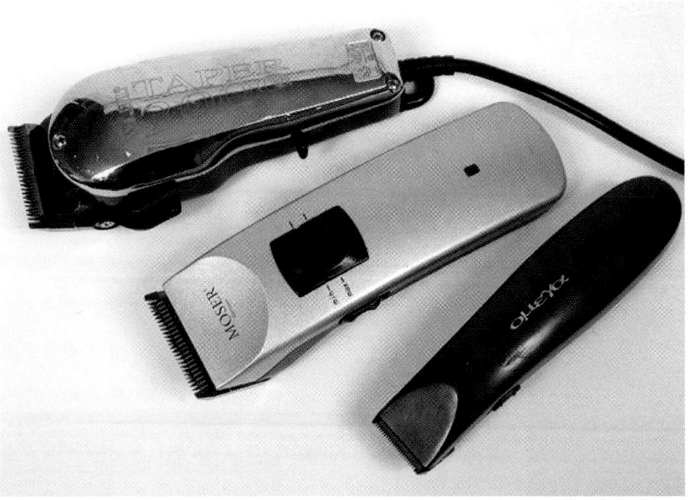

Figure 16.10 Electric clippers

Figure 16.11 Clippers with attachments

Clipper attachments

Clipper attachment sizes start at grade 1 and go up to grade 8 for cutting hair. This table shows the amount of hair that is left for each clipper grade.

Table 16.1 Grades of clipper attachment

Clipper grade	Length of hair left
1	3 mm / $^1/_8$ inch
2	6 mm / $^1/_4$ inch
3	10 mm / $^3/_8$ inch
4	13 mm / $^1/_2$ inch
5	16 mm / $^5/_8$ inch
6	19 mm / $^3/_4$ inch
7	22 mm / $^7/_8$ inch
8	25 mm /1 inch

Towels and gowns

All towels and gowns should be clean and sterile for each client to prevent cross infection of parasitic, viral, fungal and bacterial diseases.

These include:

- pediculosis capitis
- herpes simplex
- tinea capitis
- impetigo.

Figure 16.12 Towels and gowns must be clean and sterile

Consultation

Before any service begins the hairdresser must find out what the client wants or needs. The consultation is used to ensure the client's wishes are interpreted accurately and the desired look achieved. It is essential to be factual, honest, tactful, sincere, direct and clear.

Figure 16.13 Find out what the client would like

Analyse hair and scalp

Prior to all barbering tasks it is necessary to analyse the hair and scalp. This includes a visual and physical examination. The hair should be combed through to check for factors that will influence the client's choice of style. The following factors may influence the client's choice of style:

- male pattern baldness
- hair growth patterns
- head and face shapes

Safety first

See Chapter 4 for information on hair and scalp disorders or contraindications to the hairdressing service (including infections and infestations).

- hair density
- hair texture
- hair elasticity
- piercings.

Figure 16.14 Always analyse the client's hair and scalp

WWW Online activity 16.2

Correct selection

Male pattern baldness

Definitions

Alopecia totalis: Baldness all over the head.

Alopecia areata: Baldness starting as a small round patch and spreading outwards.

Before cutting men's hair, it is essential to look for any signs of male pattern balding (MPB). The cause of this condition is believed to be heredity and due to an excess level of the hormone testosterone.

Alopecia totalis is a total baldness of the head. When the baldness starts as a small round patch that spreads outwards, this is known as alopecia areata. The hair grows back from the middle of the balding patch and there may be a more than one patch at any time.

Your advice will depend on the stage of baldness. If there is a slow loss of hair, then reassurance should be given and the different styling options explained. If there is a great deal of hair loss, there will be a limited number of styles that you can create.

If your client has a toupee, the hairstyle you create must allow for this. It must be a balanced style, blending the client's real hair into the added hair. If your client has a full hairpiece then it is likely the client will wish to have their hair short underneath.

Figure 16.15 Patterns in male baldness

Growth patterns

The natural hair-fall and the hair growth patterns are particularly important for you to be aware of before starting any haircut. Some growth patterns may prevent you from cutting the hair in a particular style.

Key information

Hair growth patterns include:
widow's peak
crowns
cowlick
nape whorls.

Widow's peak

A widow's peak is a very strong centre forward growth on the front hairline. It is best to avoid light fringes as they will lift and separate.

Crown

A crown is a circular movement of the hair (whorl) positioned towards the back, on the top of the head. It is important to identify the crown area because it can be a very strong movement. In some cases a double crown or two crowns are present, moving in different directions. Keeping length in the crown may help styling.

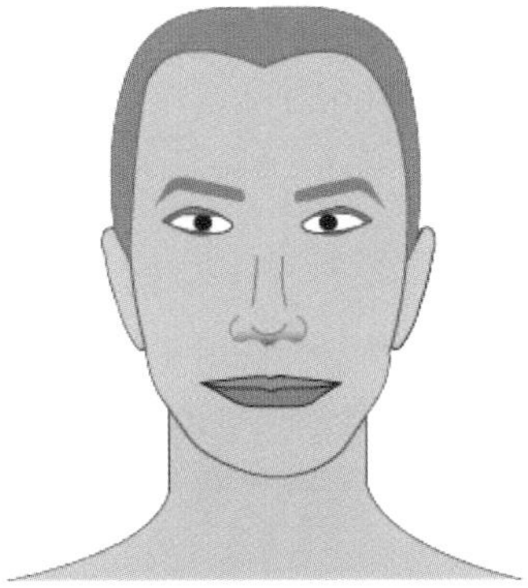

Figure 16.16 Widow's peak

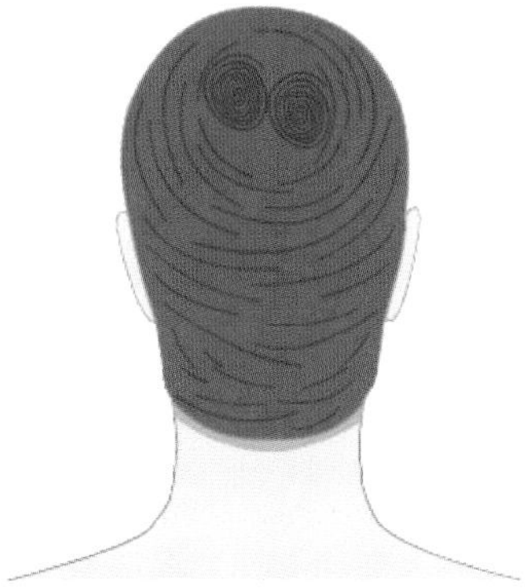

Figure 16.17 Double crown

Cowlick

A cowlick is usually found on the front hairline across the forehead. The roots of the hair grow backwards and the mid-lengths and ends of the hair are forward, causing the hair to spring up. Cutting a straight fringe may be difficult as the hair tends to separate naturally. Moving the parting may help this.

Nape whorl

Nape whorl describes the movement of the hair in the nape area which is below the occipital bone. They can be at one side or both sides. Styles are best kept very short or long.

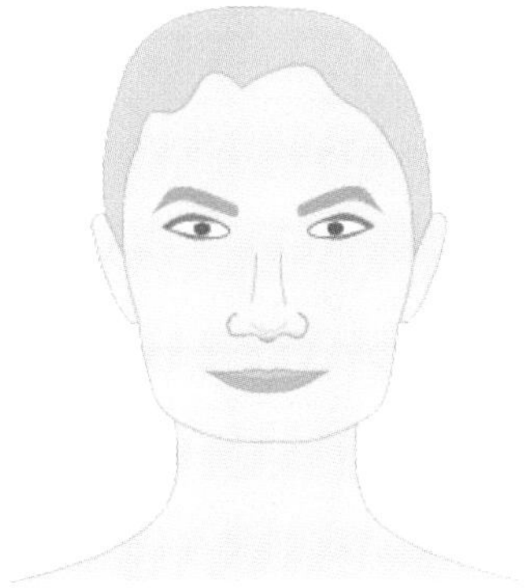

Figure 16.18 Cowlick

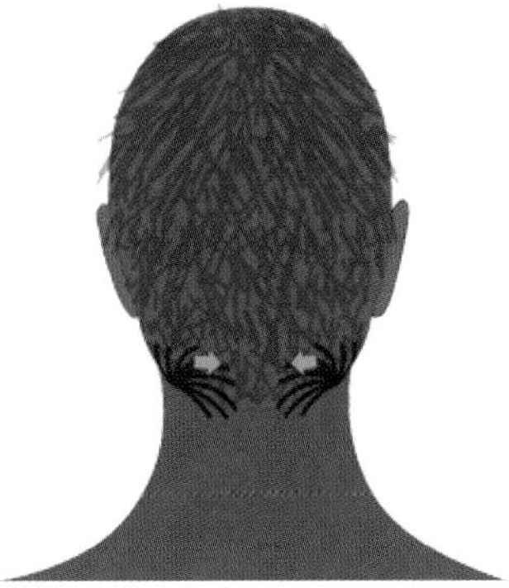

Figure 16.19 Nape whorls

Online activity 16.3

Scrambled words

Head and face shapes

The client may have the following head or face shape:

- oval
- square
- oblong
- round.

The oval shaped face is considered to be the perfect shape that suits any style. However, many people have differing features and it is important to choose the hairstyle to suit each client's face shape and features.

Men with a square facial shape tend to appear masculine looking, with a strong angular jawline and square hairline. This type of face shape enables a hairstyle that gives a classic traditional look for short hair.

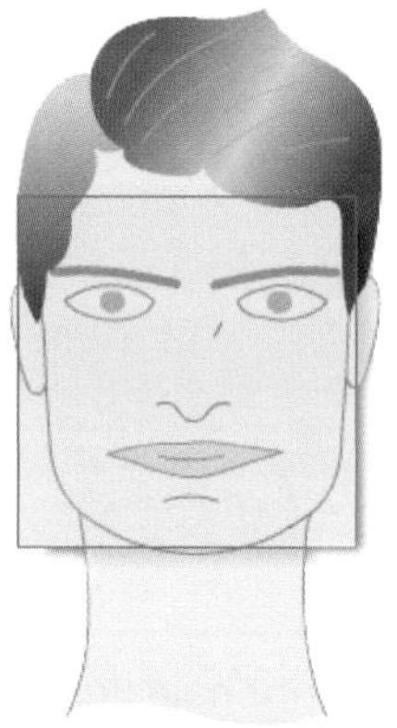

Figure 16.20 Square shaped face

Most hairstyles work well with an oblong shaped face as it is similar to an oval shape.

Figure 16.21 Oblong shaped face

If your client has a round face, a hairstyle that is flat at the sides with volume on top will flatter them. Long hair will also give the illusion of length.

Figure 16.22 Round face

Large ears that protrude need to be covered for a flattering effect.

Figure 16.23 Possible haircut for client with large ears

If the client has a big nose or broken nose a centre parting will exaggerate this. Choose an asymmetric style. This will be more flattering.

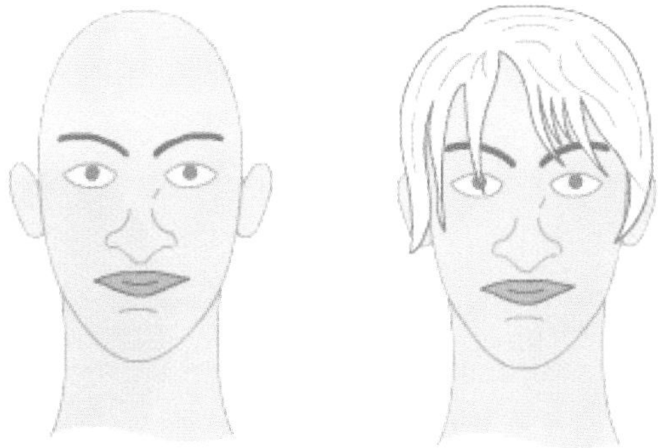

Figure 16.24 An asymmetric style would work for a client with a big/broken nose

A fringe will achieve the best effect for a client with a high forehead or receding hairline.

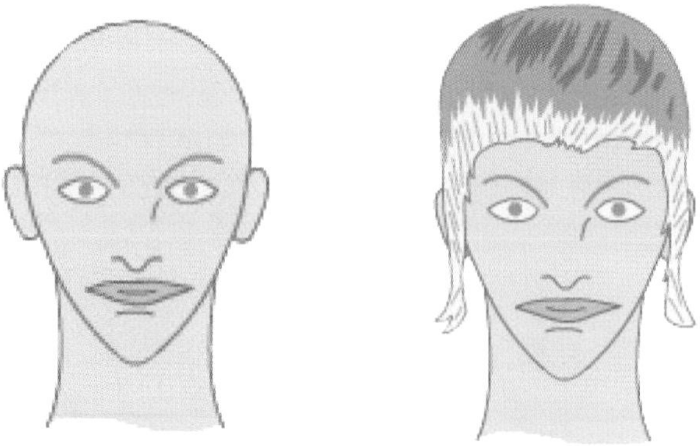

Figure 16.25 A fringe can be helpful for a client with a large forehead

A short, stocky neck requires a softer hairstyle which is more flattering to the client.

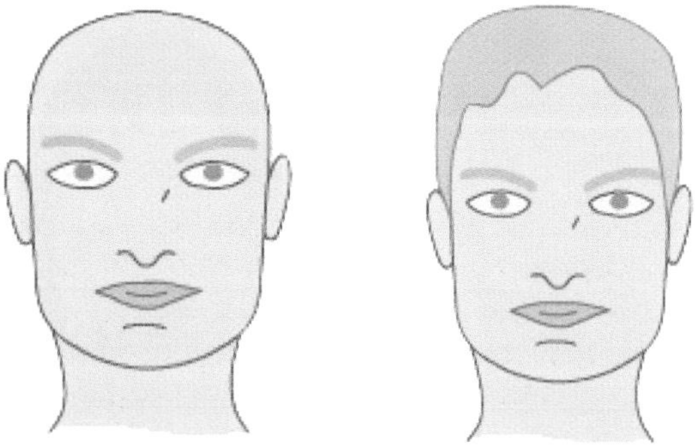

Figure 16.26 A softer hairstyle would suit a client with a stocky neck

Hair density

This refers to the amount of hair that the client has on his or her head. If a client has dense hair this means that you will not be able to see the client's scalp. If you can see the client's scalp then they have a low density of hair on their head.

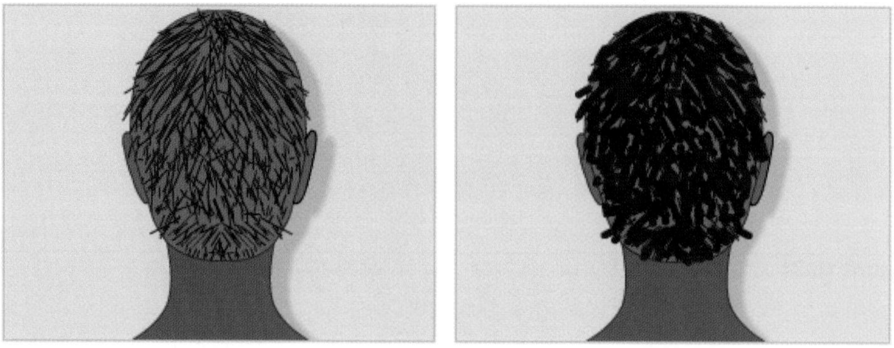

Figure 16.27 Low density hair and dense hair

Hair texture

There are three types of hair. These will need different strengths of products:

- Fine textured hair requires firm hold.
- Medium and coarse textured hair will need normal strength hold.

Figure 16.28 Assess texture of hair

Definition

Coarse: Rough in texture. Coarse hair has a thick shaft.

Elasticity

This test assesses the extent of damage to the cortex of the hair. It measures the ability of the hair to be stretched. Hold a single strand of hair firmly at each end with finger and thumb. Pull back gently and see how much the hair stretches and springs back. A hair in good condition can stretch up to a third of its length and return to its original length. If the hair snaps it indicates that the hair has a weak cortex.

Online activity 16.4 WWW

Round the board

Piercings

If you notice that the client has piercings around the ears and mouth, take care when cutting the hair near these areas. If the piercings cause a high risk, you can ask the client to remove them, or cover them with a plaster.

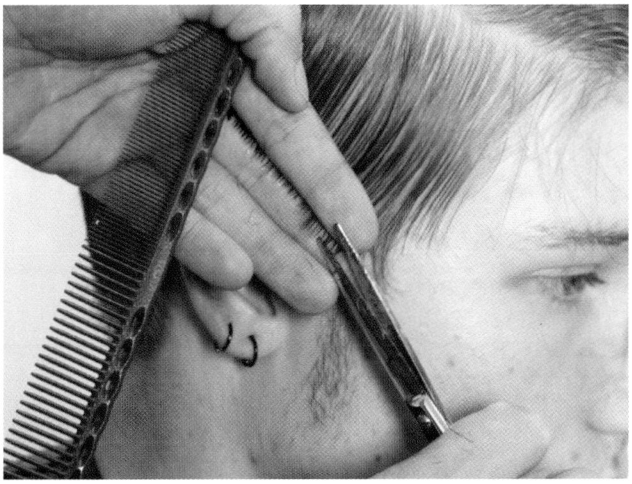

Figure 16.29 Take care when working near piercings

Safety first

If the piercings cause a high risk, you can ask the client to remove them or cover them with a plaster.

Preparing the client for a haircut

It is important to gown the client effectively prior to cutting the hair. This is to protect the client's clothes and to ensure that the client is comfortable. Hair cuttings are extremely prickly when they go down the back of the neck and can penetrate the skin causing an infection. Cuttings are also very difficult to remove from clothes. Do not have too much bulk from clothes and towels around the neck; this restricts the accuracy when cutting and in some cases the mobility of the client's neck.

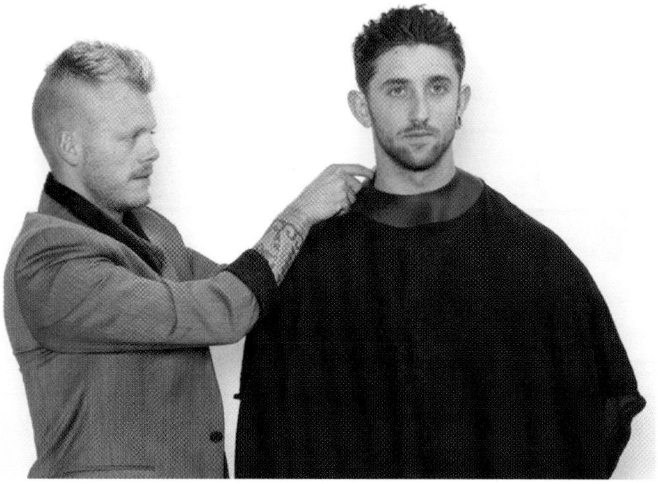

Figure 16.30 Gown the client

Comfort during cutting

Whilst cutting the client's hair, it is important for you to move around the client's head. However, the client's comfort should be considered at all times. Their back should be positioned right to the back of the chair and as flat as possible. They should have both feet on the footrest or the floor. Not only will this be a more comfortable position for the client but it also enables you to create a balanced hairstyle. Your own comfort during cutting should be considered as well. Check your posture is correct, ensuring that your client's seat is at the correct height for you to work. Ensure that your work area is tidy and free from clutter.

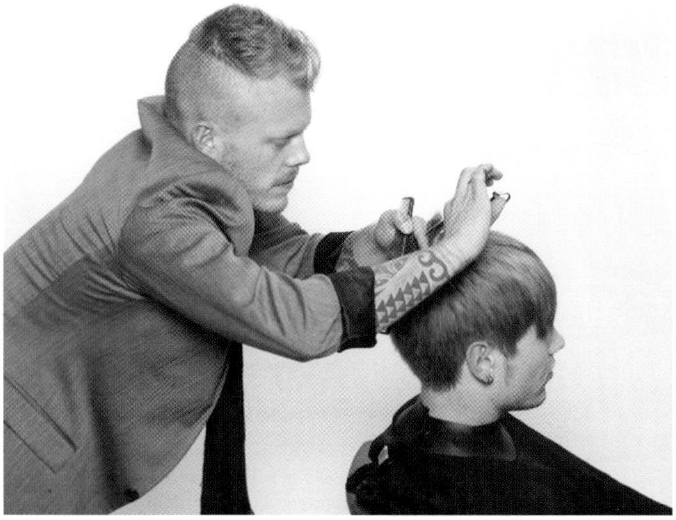

Figure 16.31 Incorrect posture

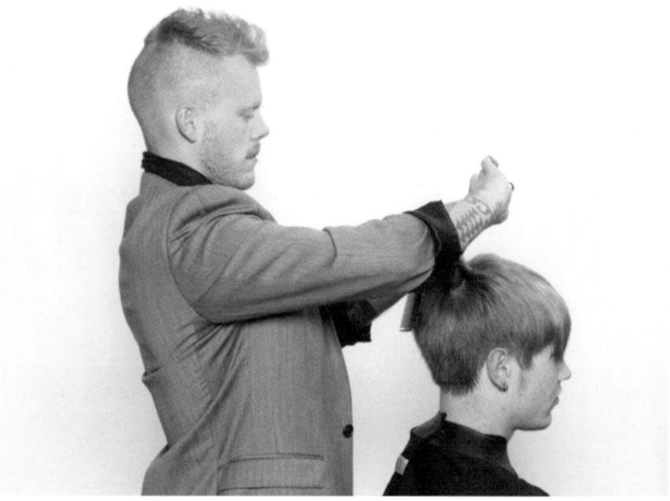

Figure 16.32 Correct posture

After cutting always remember to sweep up the hair cuttings off the floor and dispose of them in the appropriate place.

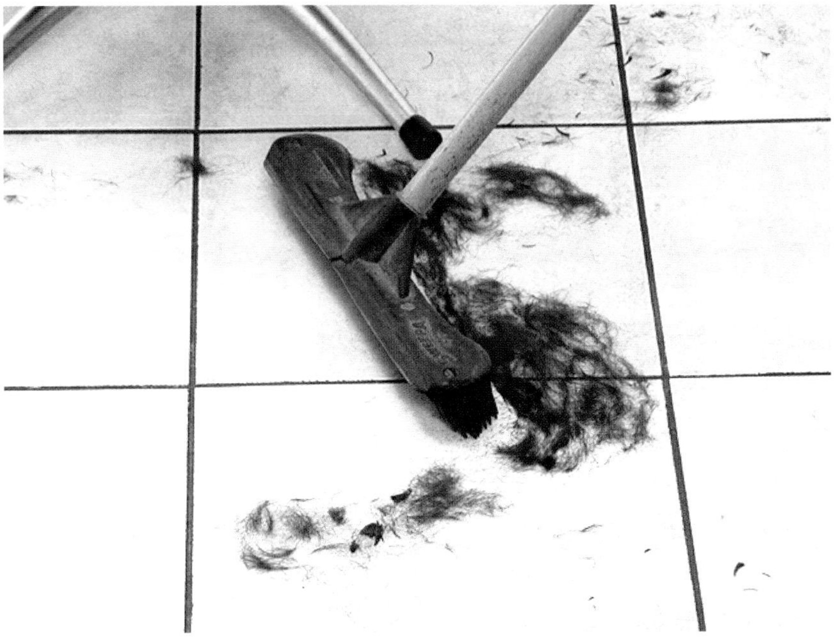

Figure 16.33 Sweep the floor after cutting

Suggested time for cutting

A commercially viable time for cutting, blow-drying/drying and finishing men's hair is 30 minutes.

16.2 Cut hair to achieve a variety of looks

In this section you will learn how to perform several haircuts using basic cutting techniques whilst keeping in mind any important factors, for example head and face shapes.

Wet and dry cutting

The benefits of cutting hair when it is dry include:

- any growth patterns and movement to the hair can be seen clearly
- a quicker haircut can be carried out
- the client's desired length is easily achieved.

The benefits of cutting hair when it is wet include:

- combing and managing the hair will be easier
- sections will be clearer
- more accurate and controlled cut
- any curl to the hair will be visible.

Wet hair will have more elasticity so needs to be held with less tension or you may cut the hair too short.

Figure 16.34 Cutting dry hair

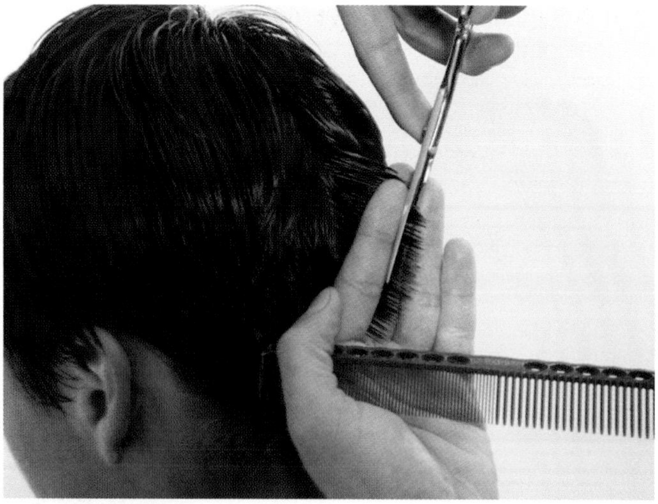

Figure 16.35 Cutting wet hair

Key information

Styling products must be washed out of hair otherwise it may be sticky and it will be hard to cut accurately.

WWW Online activity 16.5

Correct selection

Preparing the client's hair before cutting

If the client has products on his hair, e.g. styling gel, it must be washed to remove it. If not the hair will be sticky and it will be hard to cut accurately. It is always best to wash the hair, even if carrying out a dry cut, for this reason. It will also help you to see the natural fall of the hair. Before any haircut, the hair must be combed through to detangle. This is very important as you need to be able to see any growth patterns and natural partings.

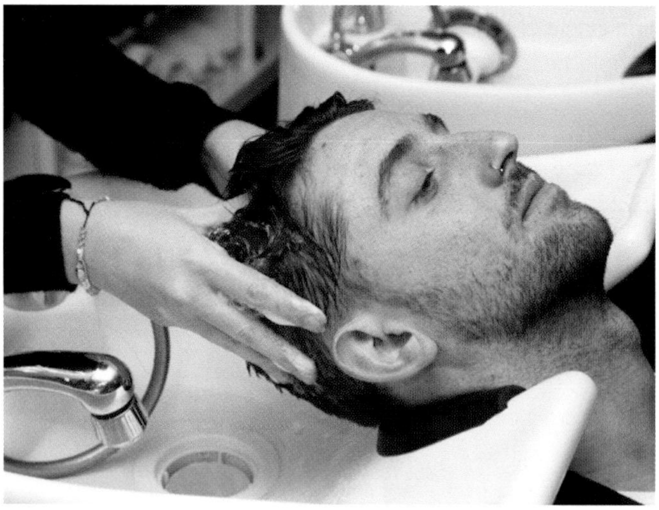

Figure 16.36 Washing the client's hair

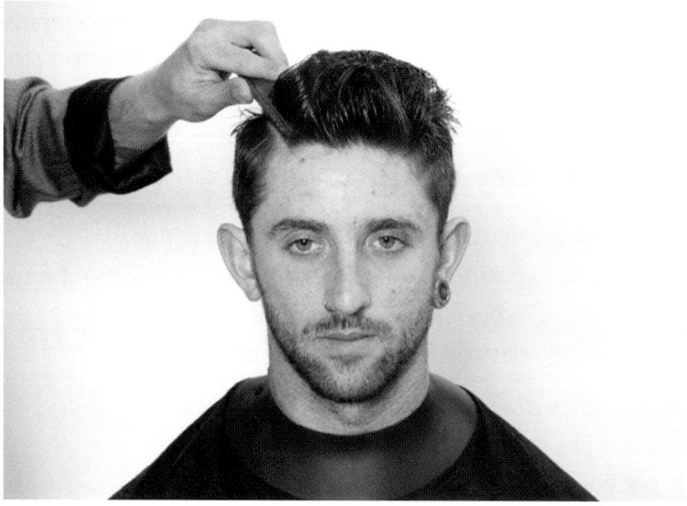

Figure 16.37 Comb the hair through before a cut

Cutting angles and guidelines

You should be aware of the cutting angles you are using throughout the haircut. The holding and cutting angle will affect the balance and amount of graduation it has. A guideline is the first section of hair that is cut and the next section/s are subsequently cut to. The number of guidelines will depend on how simple or complex the haircut is.

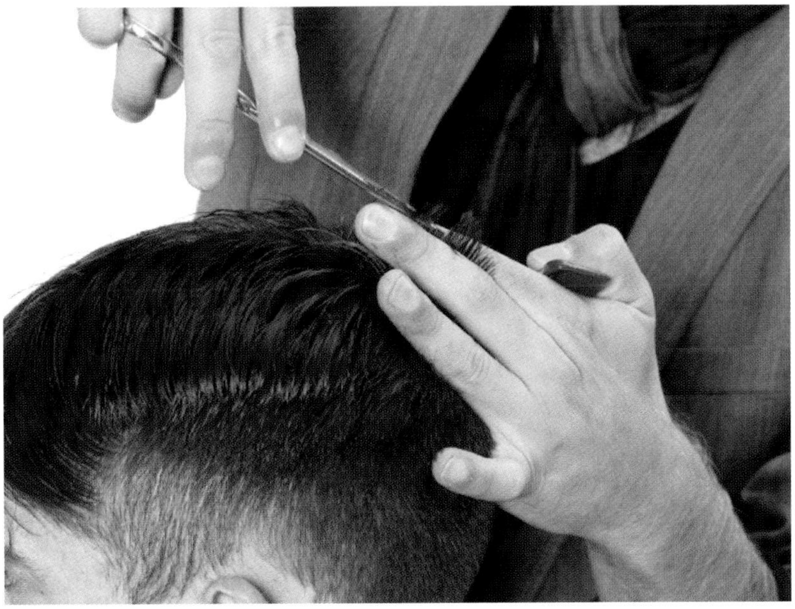

Figure 16.38 Holding the hair at a 90 degree angle

Key information

A guideline is the first section of hair that is cut and the next section/s are subsequently cut to.

Natural fall

As mentioned previously, when preparing the client's hair, it is important to look for their hair's natural fall. This applies during the haircut as well, as you must always work with the client's natural fall, e.g. partings, nape whorls etc. This will make the style easier to manage for the client.

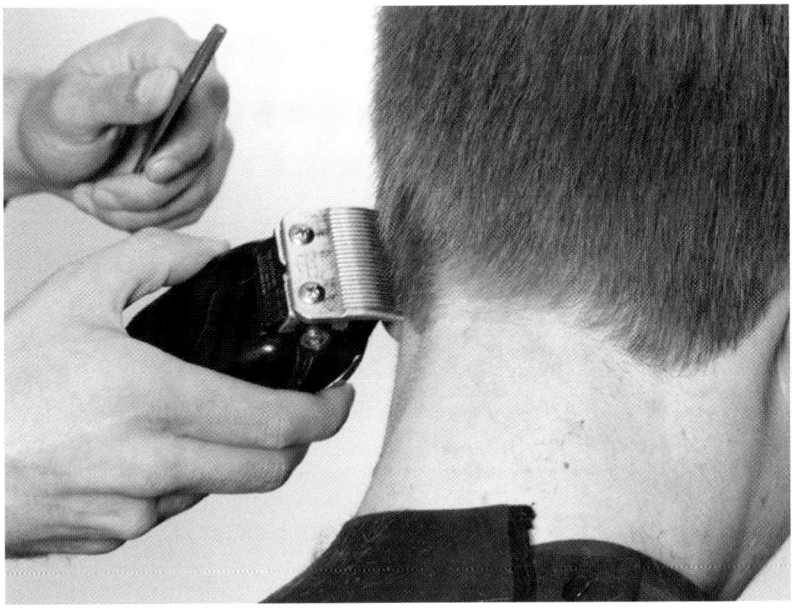

Figure 16.39 Work with the client's natural fall

Key information

When cross checking you should hold sections of hair out at right angles to the original sections.

Cross checking

At the end of a haircut and possibly during, it is important to check the cut you have created. You do this by holding sections of hair out at right angles to the original sections. This enables you to see how accurate the cut is. If you find any areas that are not even, you can cut the hair accordingly.

Outline and neckline shapes

When creating a haircut, you should try to use the natural hairline as the perimeter. Doing this will enable the style to look balanced. If the perimeter is above the natural hairline, then once the hair grows back, it will look untidy. If this is not possible, e.g. the client has a very short style with an even growth around hairline, then it should be defined. The look will be less harsh if the nape line looks natural.

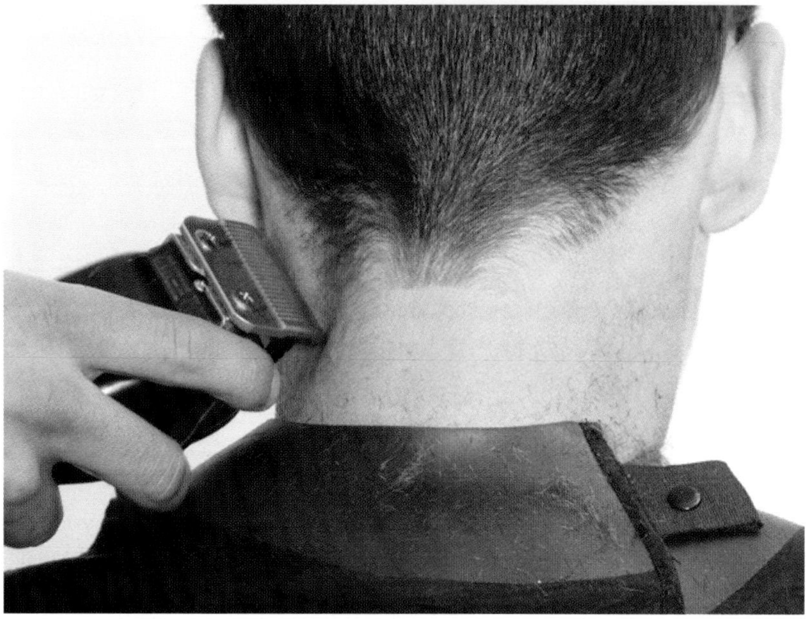

Figure 16.40 Work with the client's natural hairline to ensure tidiness

The neckline could be shaped in the following ways:

- rounded
- squared
- tapered.

A rounded neckline takes the square corners off and it has the benefit of adding balance to a wide neck.

A square neckline has the appearance of a hard line against the neck. It should be shaved to follow the natural hairline as closely as possible. This kind of neckline will add width to a slim neck. The disadvantage is that when the hair grows back it can appear untidy.

A tapered hairline follows the natural hairline. A wide neck will appear slim with this neckline and as the hair grows back it will not look untidy.

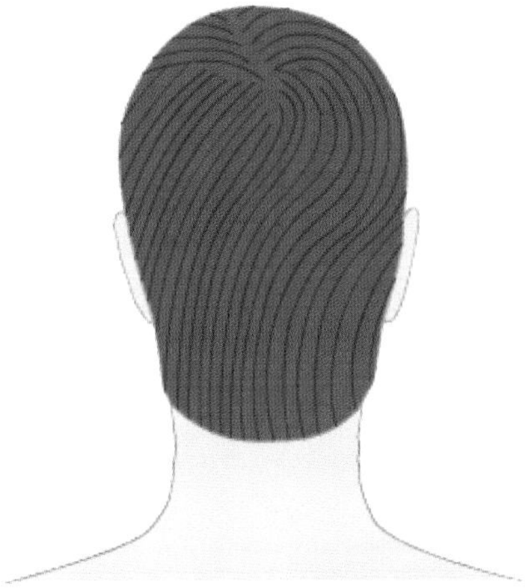

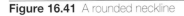

Figure 16.41 A rounded neckline

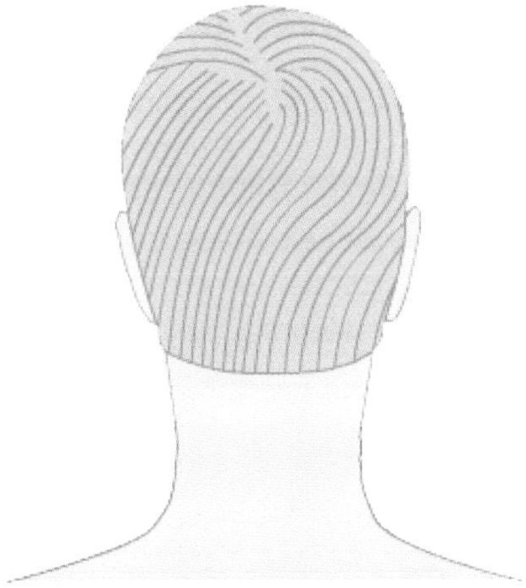

Figure 16.42 A square neckline

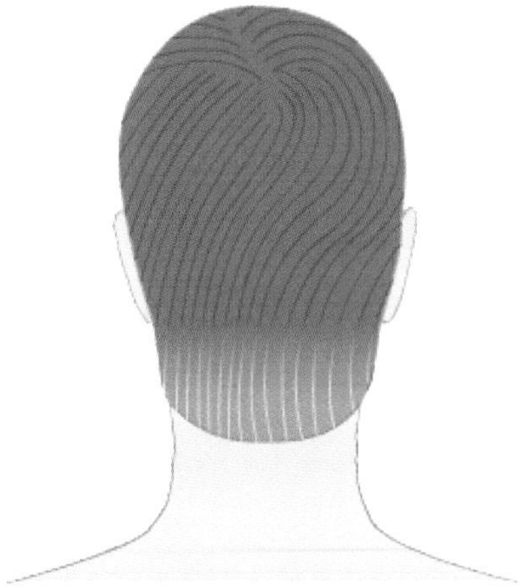

Figure 16.43 A tapered neckline

Cutting techniques

These include:

- club cutting
- scissor over comb
- clipper over comb
- freehand
- thinning
- fading.

Online activity 16.6 WWW

Select correct box

Club cutting

Each section of hair is cut straight across bluntly, usually with scissors, but can also be achieved with clippers. The hair mesh is cut straight across to produce level ends.

Figure 16.44 Club cutting technique

Scissors over comb

Used when the hair is required to be very short and finely graduated. When using this cutting method a smooth flowing movement is required to avoid 'steps' in the hair. Keep the head up in a sitting position. Use the points of the scissors to lift a section of hair. Place a comb under the section of hair. Glide the comb in an upward direction. Follow the comb with the scissors and carefully cut the hair to the required length. Open and close the scissors rapidly clipping away at the length.

Figure 16.45 Scissors over comb technique

Clipper over comb

This eliminates the hard work from the scissor over comb technique. Place the comb and hold at the appropriate angle under a section of hair. Glide the clippers across the comb. Repeat this until the required length is achieved.

Figure 16.46 Clipper over comb technique

Freehand cutting

This is the way of cutting the hair without holding it with the fingers. It is mainly used when cutting fringes, around the perimeter edges near the ears and for trimming hair around growth patterns. Comb the hair into place and then cut freehand without using tension on the hair. By not using tension on the hair when dry, it gives a better indication of where the hair will sit.

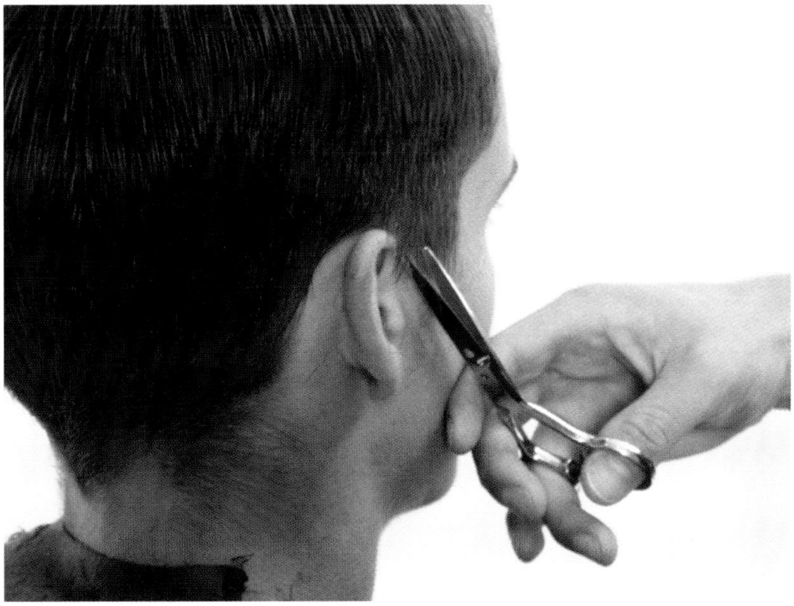

Figure 16.47 Freehand cutting

Thinning

This removes bulk from the hair. Many cutting techniques can be used for thinning the hair, not only the use of thinning scissors. It can be carried out on wet or dry hair.

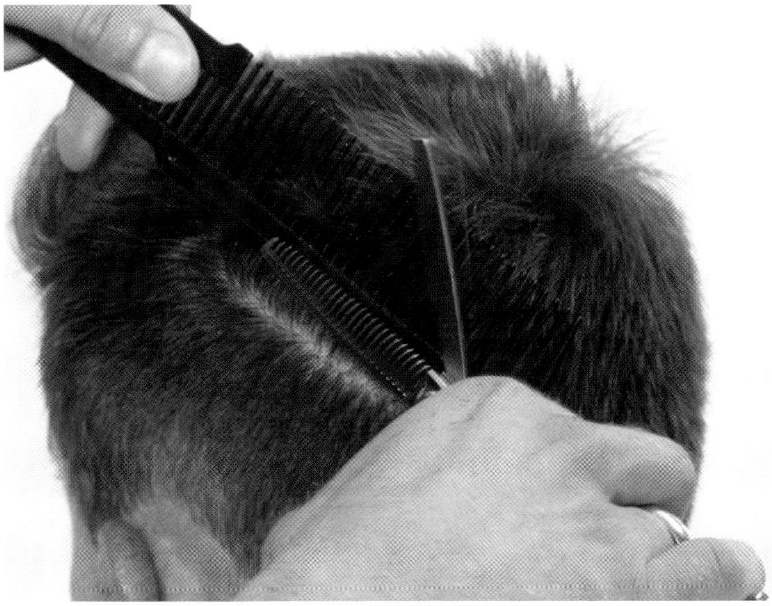

Figure 16.48 Thinning the hair

Fading

This technique is carried out using clippers. Very short hair at the bottom is blended into longer hair at the top of the head. This produces a haircut where the length of the hair increases or decreases gradually without any lines.

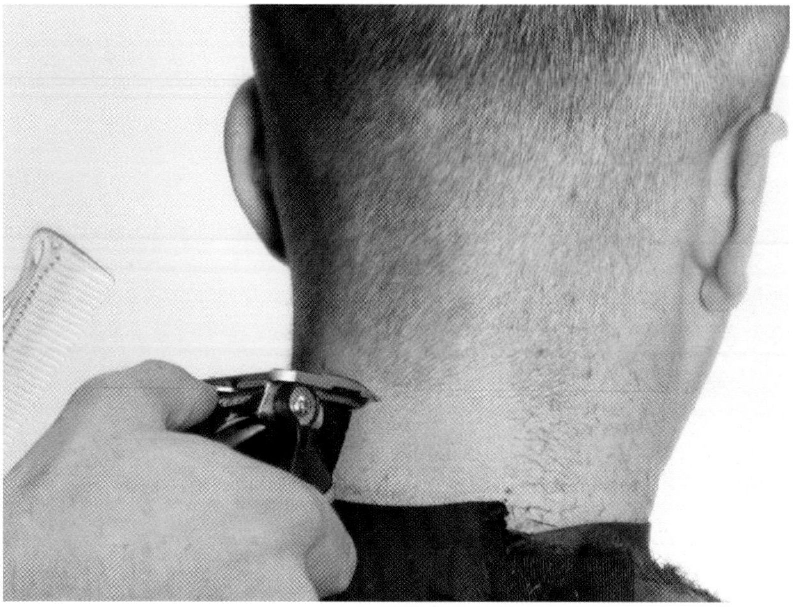

Figure 16.49 Fading the hair

WWW Online activity 16.7

Five in a row

Website WWW

www.atthairdressing.com

Clipper graduation haircut on straight hair

A graduation haircut tapers in at the neck and sides with the angle of the hair being held out from the head.

Figure 16.50 After gowning in the appropriate manner and combing the hair through, section both sides of the hair.

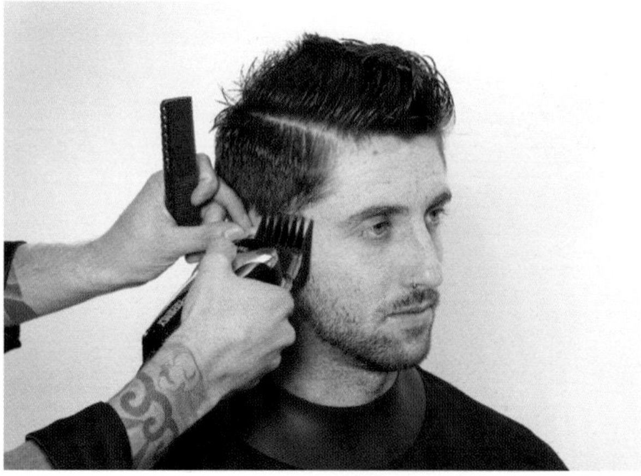

Figure 16.51 Using clippers with longest grade attachment, move in an upwards direction at the sides. Continue to the back of the head.

Figure 16.52 Hold the clippers in parallel with the outline of the lower part of the back of the head. Repeat on the other side.

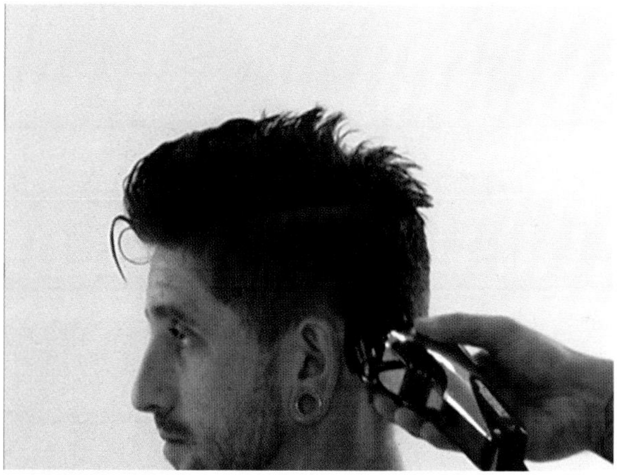

Figure 16.53 Use a smaller grade attachment to fade the haircut out and form a graduation (online video).

Figure 16.54 Change the angle of the clippers as you go to ensure that all hair that should be, is cut. Remember to hold the client's ears away from the clippers. Cross-check to make sure that all hair is cut.

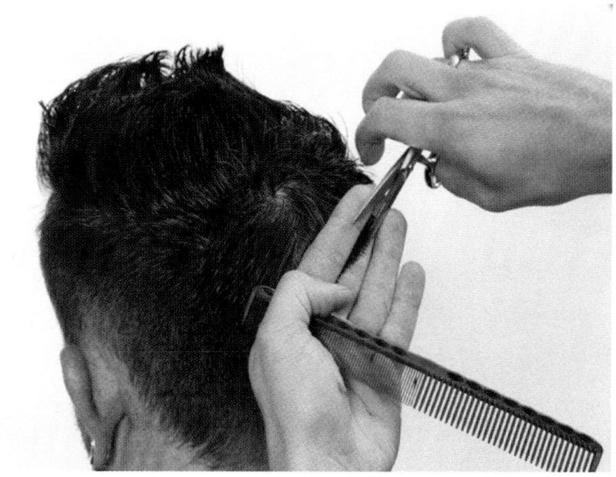

Figure 16.55 Blend the edge of the already cut hair into the back of the haircut by holding the hair at a 45 degree angle and cutting.

Figure 16.56 Move around the head to blend in the sides.

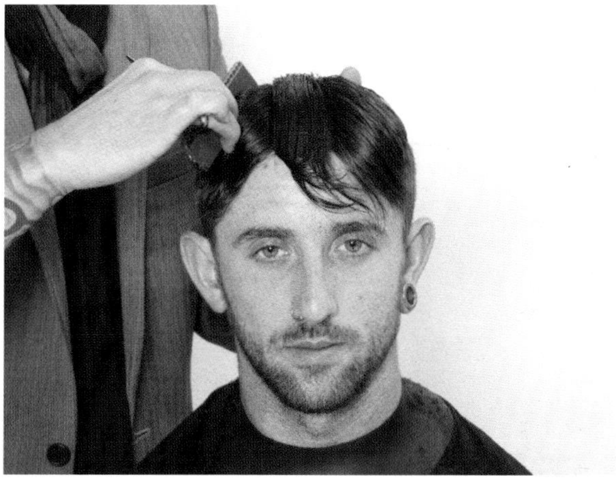

Figure 16.57 Create a central profile parting and join the back to the top.

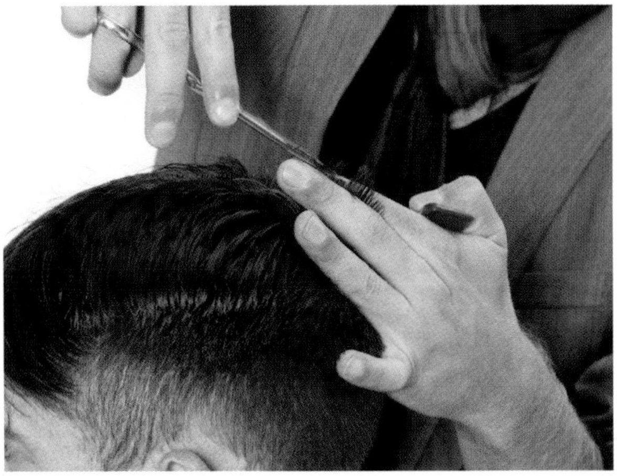

Figure 16.58 Hold the hair at 90 degrees to cut.

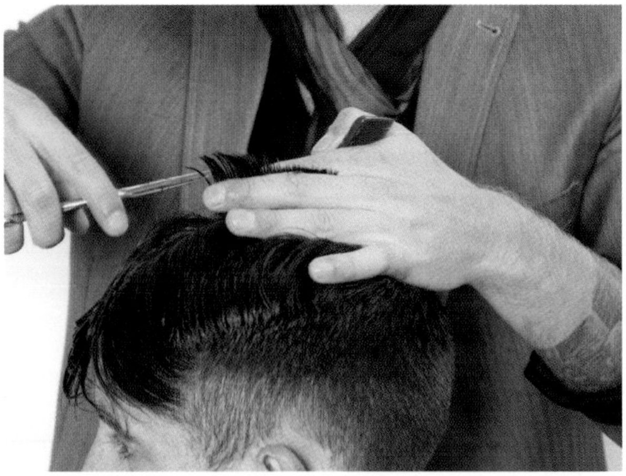

Figure 16.59 Carry this on over the top of the head, following the guideline.

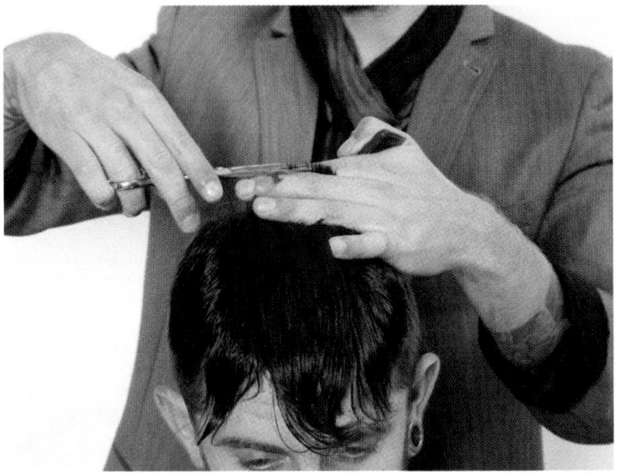

Figure 16.60 Move to the back of the head and take sections across the central profile parting. Club cut the hair to the guideline in the middle.

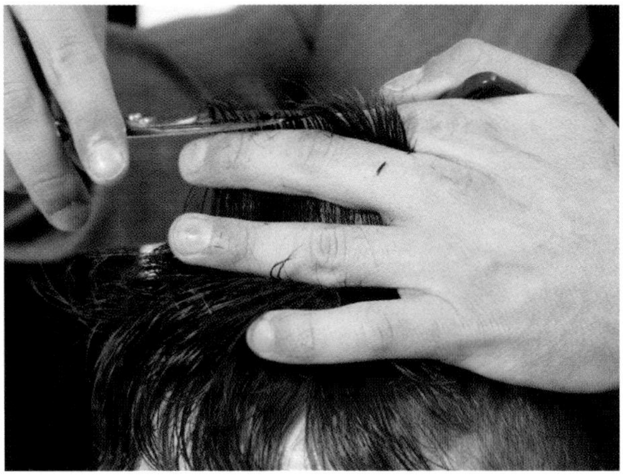

Figure 16.61 Move towards the front of the head, taking sections of the parting.

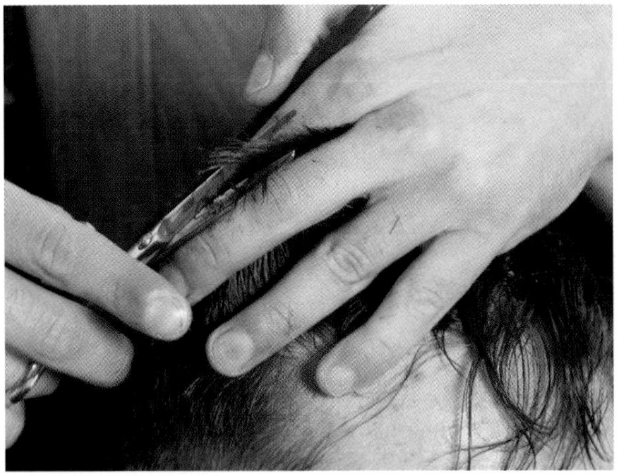

Figure 16.62 The left and right sections next to the central profile parting are then blended in.

Figure 16.63 After the hair is dried, a scissor over comb effect is used to blend the edge of the clipper area into the area the scissors have cut. The angle of the comb is held in line with the graduation angle.

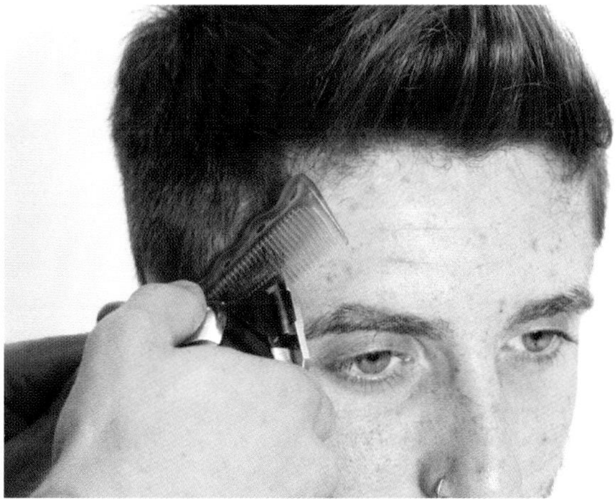

Figure 16.64 The hair is tapered close to the head using a clipper over comb technique.

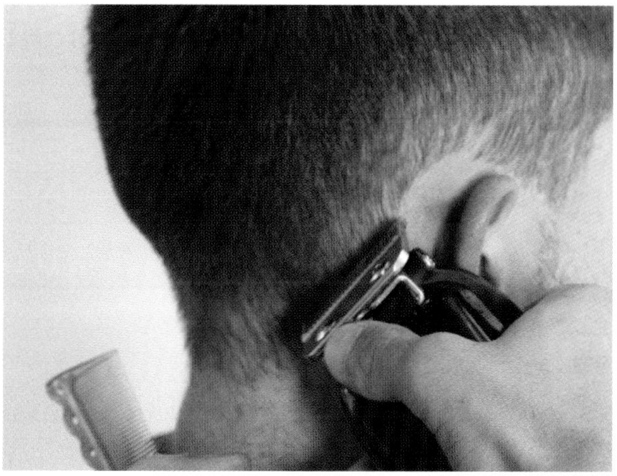

Figure 16.65 The outline shape is tidied using the clippers in an upturned position.

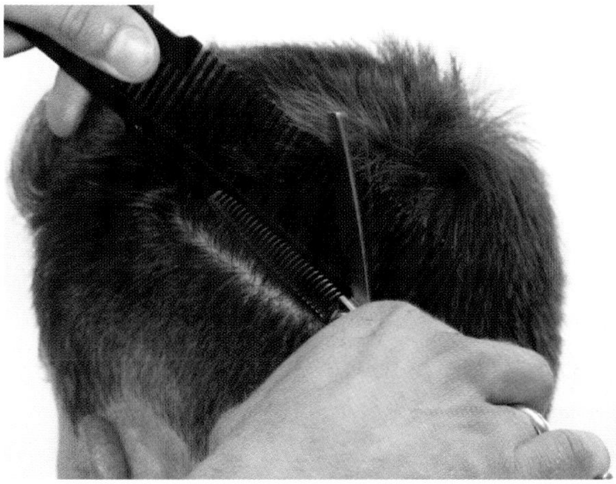

Figure 16.66 Finally the hair is thinned/texturised using the thinning scissors and finishing products applied.

Figure 16.67 Finished look.

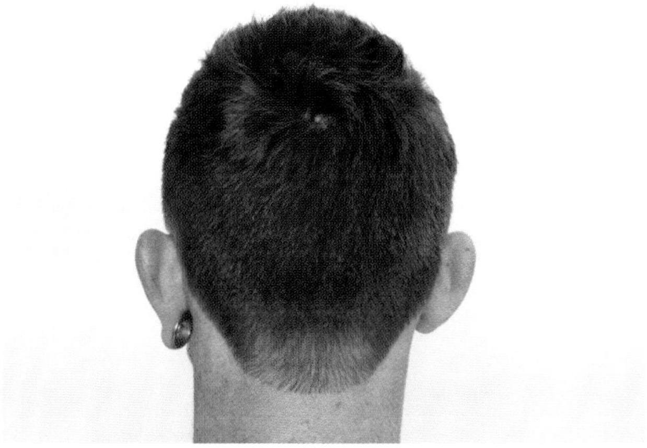

Figure 16.68 Finished look.

Scissor graduation haircut with parting on straight hair

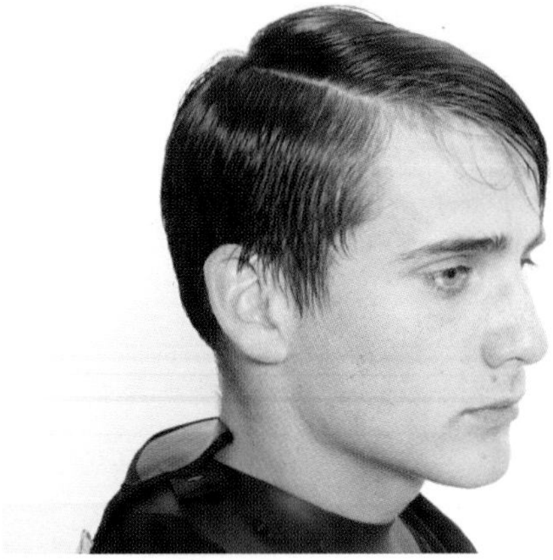

Figure 16.69 After the client is gowned in the appropriate manner, the hair is combed through and sectioned in line with the client's natural parting.

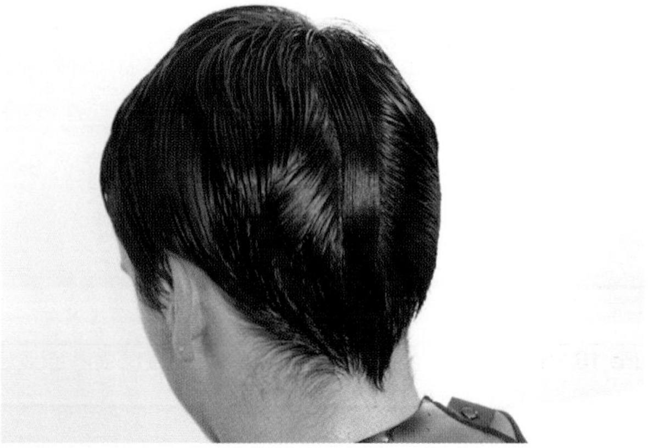

Figure 16.70 At the back of the head a parting is created approximately 3 cm wide.

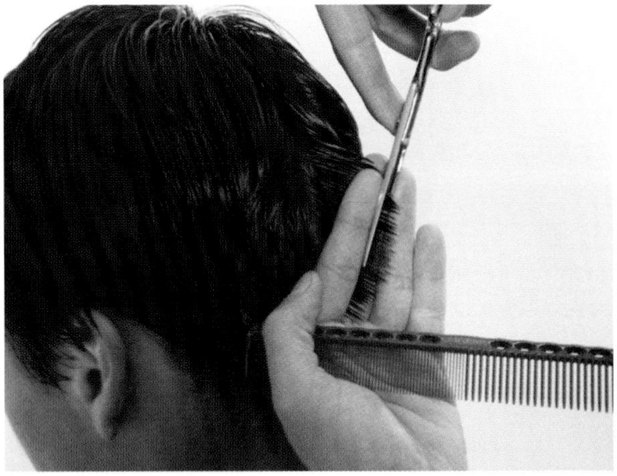

Figure 16.71 Starting at a top section from the occipital bone going down to the nape, hold the hair at a 45 degree angle and cut. This creates the guideline.

Figure 16.72 Follow the guideline down to the nape.

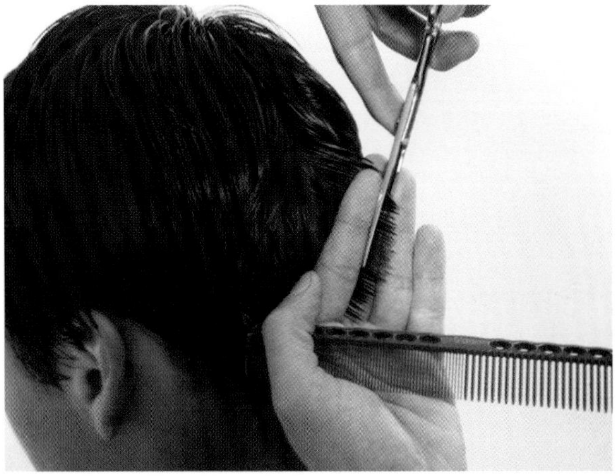

Figure 16.73 Follow this guideline to the sections to the left and right of the central parting at the back of the head.

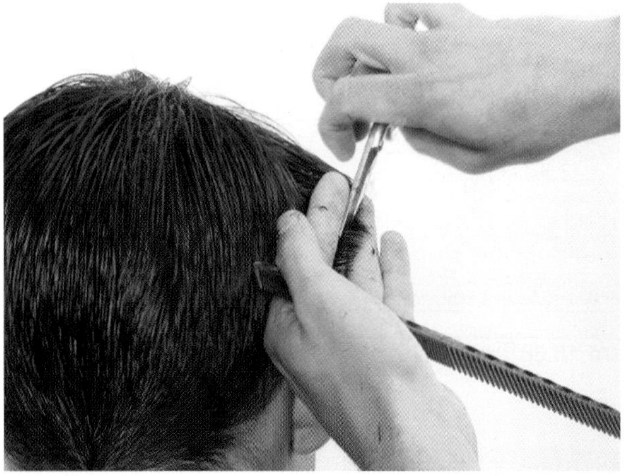

Figure 16.74 Move to the sides and graduate, following the guideline.

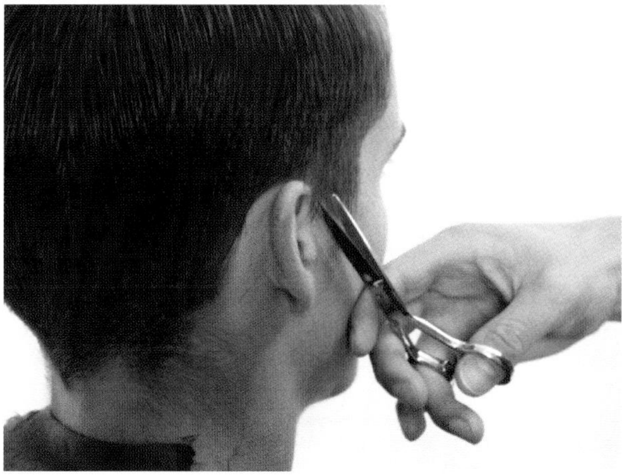

Figure 16.75 Freehand cut the profile shape around the ears.

Figure 16.76 Carry this out on the other side of the head.

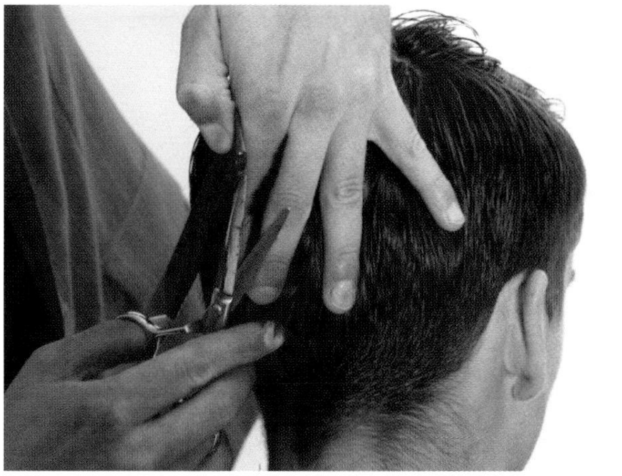

Figure 16.77 At the back of the head, the hair is held at a 90 degree angle, to join the back to the top.

Figure 16.78 Wide sections of hair are taken next to the parting and club cut following the guideline.

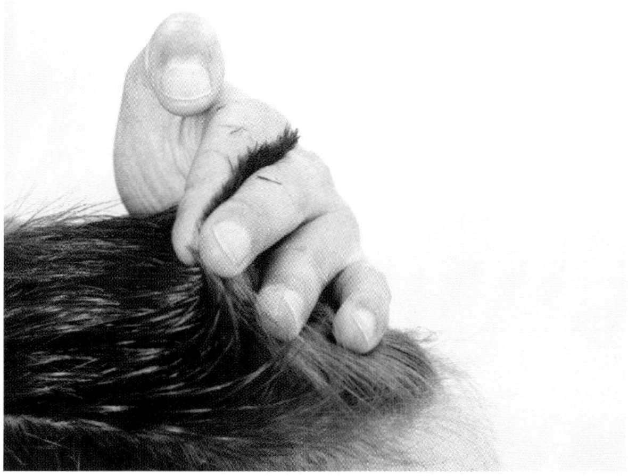

Figure 16.79 The fringe is pulled back when cutting to maintain length.

Figure 16.80 Cross check the haircut.

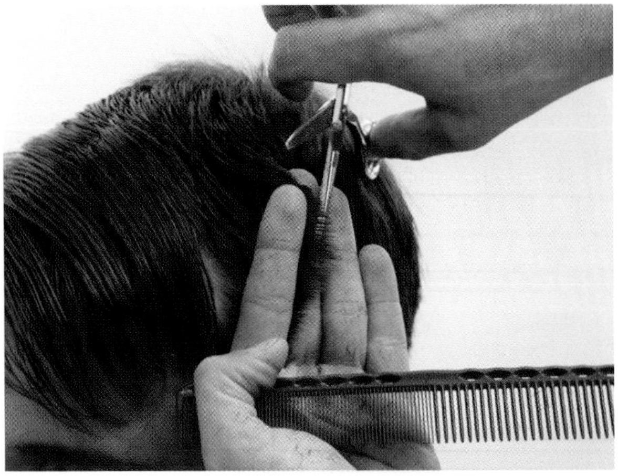

Figure 16.81 Blend in the sides of the hair. Dry the hair.

Figure 16.82 Create a tapered neckline using the clipper over comb technique.

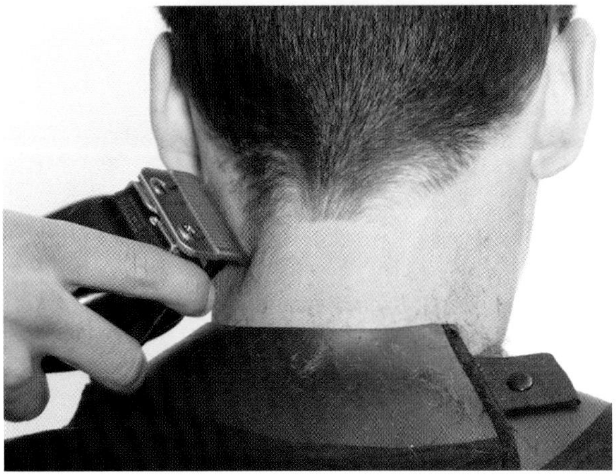

Figure 16.83 Tidy up the neckline using the clippers in the inverted position.

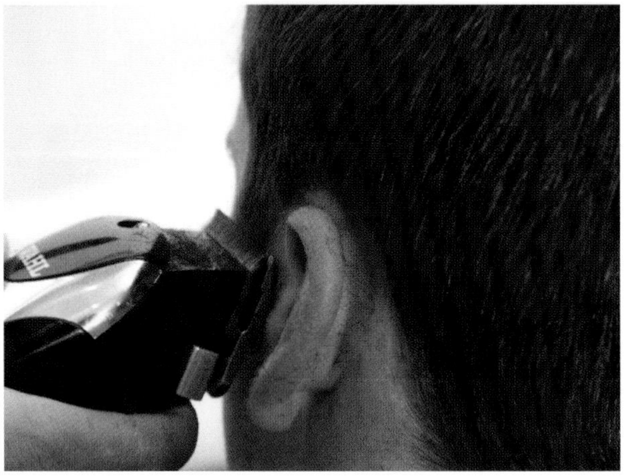

Figure 16.84 Cut the profile shape around the ears. When cutting sideburns, the clippers should be flat to the head.

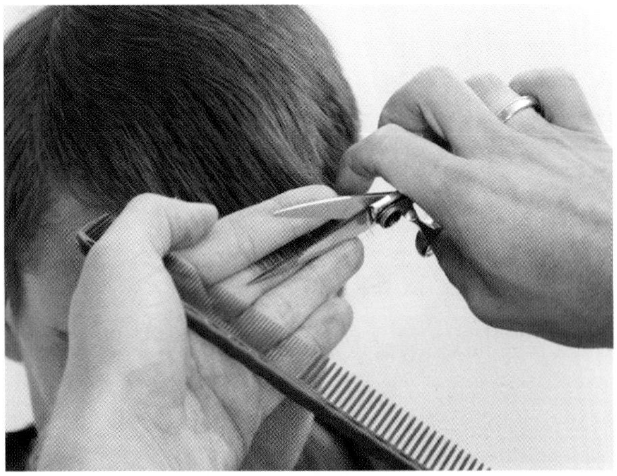

Figure 16.85 To cut the fringe, hold the hair in the direction it falls and club cut.

Figure 16.86 It is then slice cut to texturise.

Figure 16.87 Products are applied to finish the look.

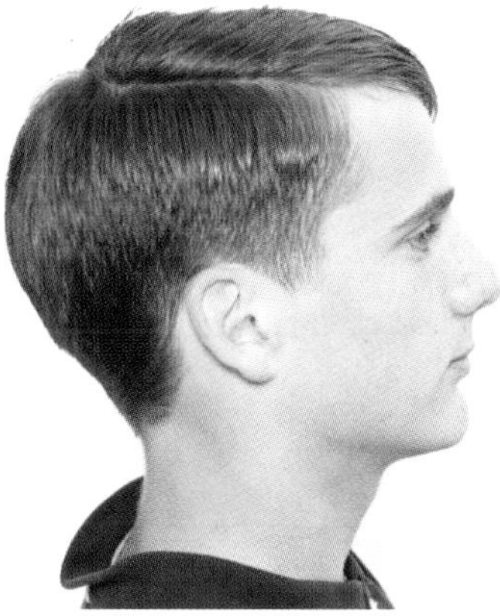

Figure 16.88 Finished look.

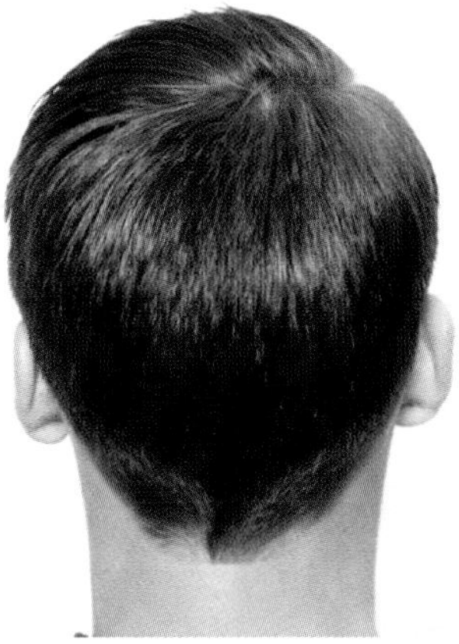

Figure 16.89 Finished look.

Uniform cut

Uniform layers produce a style where the inside length is the same length as the perimeter hair length.

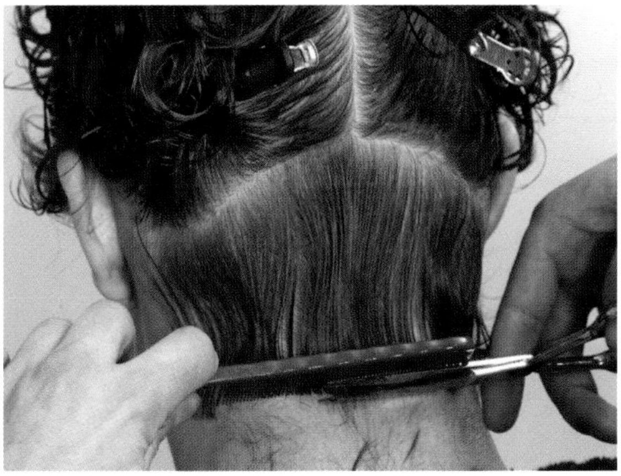

Figure 16.90 After the hair is combed to detangle it the hair is sectioned at the back. Using the centre parting as a guide, comb approximately 1.5 cm of hair from both sides of the centre section.

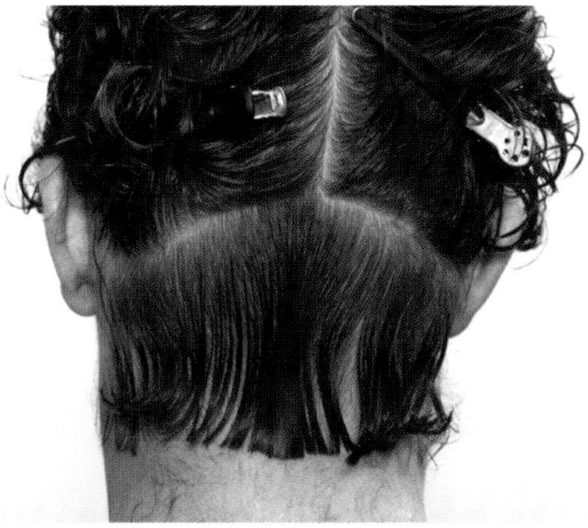

Figure 16.91 Cut the baseline to the required length.

Figure 16.92 Working in vertical sections from the centre of the nape, hold the hair out from the scalp at 90 degrees. Cut hair to this guideline. Do not cut into the baseline, cut to it or from it. Continue around the lower nape cutting at the same length.

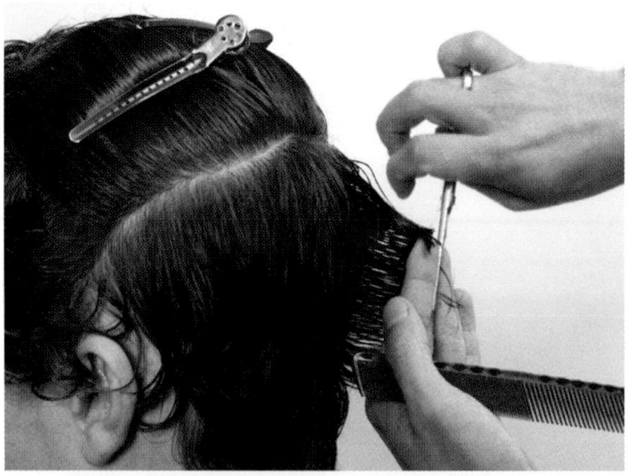

Figure 16.93 Comb down the second section. Working in vertical sections from the centre of head, again hold the hair out at 90 degrees and cut to the guideline. Continue working around the head.

Figure 16.94 The sides of the hair are joined in by working in vertical sections from the back of the ear to the front of the hairline.

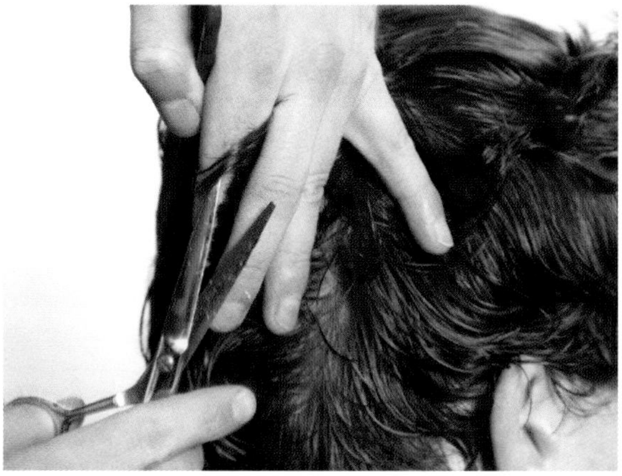

Figure 16.95 Continue following the guideline over the back of the head towards the crown.

Figure 16.96 Club cut the hair working towards the front of the head.

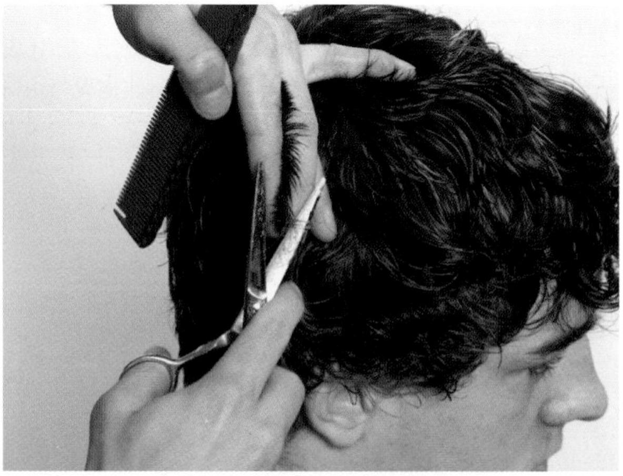

Figure 16.97 Join the top into the hair that has been previously cut at the sides.

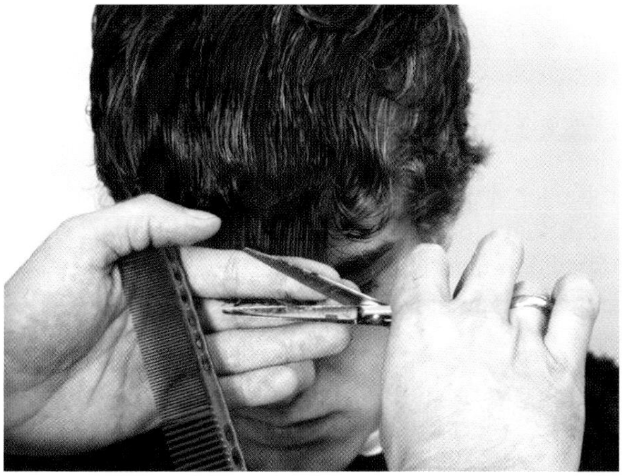

Figure 16.98 Club cut the fringe, holding the hair at the correct tension for curly hair.

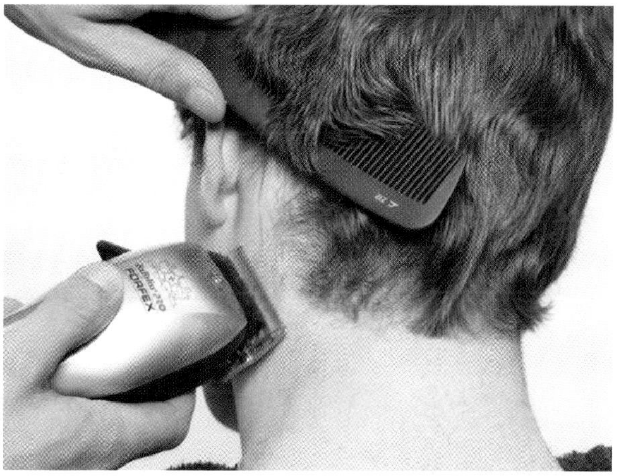

Figure 16.99 Dry or finish hair as required. Unwanted hair is removed from the neckline.

Figure 16.100 Finished look.

Client care

After cutting, remove any loose clippings of hair from the client's face, neck and shoulders. Make sure that you are happy with the cut you have created and check the balance of the style. Check with the client that they are happy with the finished look. Hold a back mirror up to help the client see the back profile.

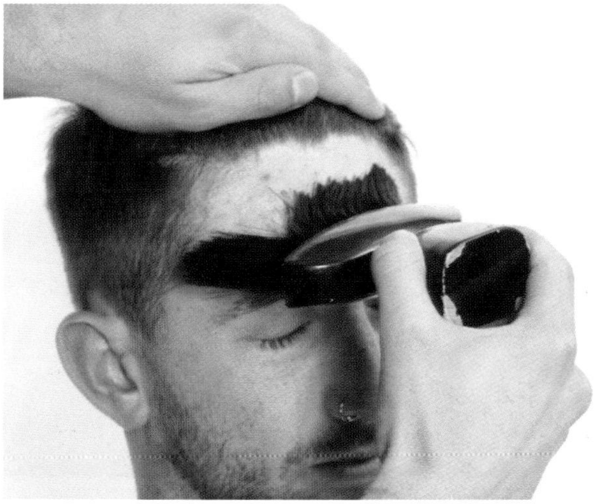

Figure 16.101 Remove loose clippings.

Safety first

Loose clippings should always be removed from the client's face, neck and shoulders after cutting.

16.3 Provide aftercare advice

An important part of this service is to give the client aftercare advice. You should explain to the client how often they should return to the salon to maintain their haircut. This will depend on the length of the client's hair. Clients with shorter styles will need to return to the salon for a trim more often than clients with longer styles. The client's lifestyle must be taken into consideration when creating a style that the client can maintain.

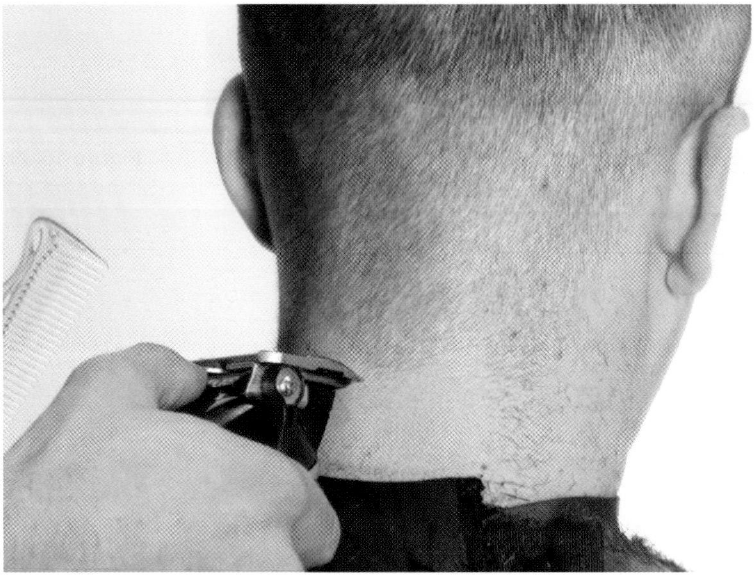

Figure 16.102 This type of style will need regular maintenance.

Equipment and products

As you are working, always explain to the client how best to use the equipment. They may want to recreate the style themselves at home. Advise the client which products can be used at home. This should be based on the factors that influence the service. Refer to Chapter 6 for more information.

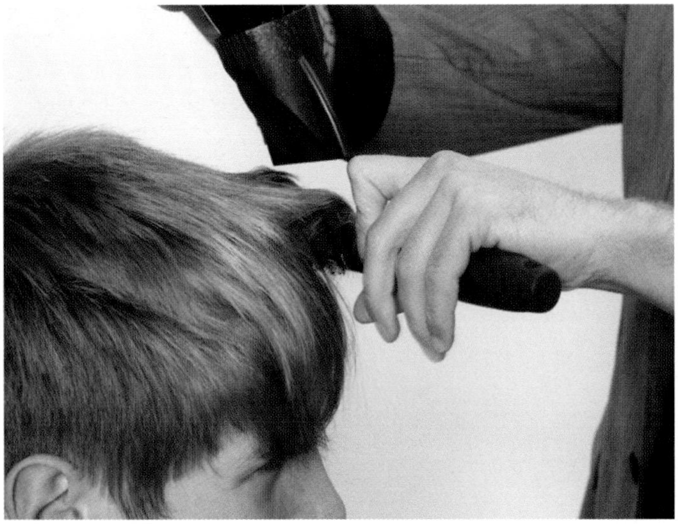

Figure 16.103 Talk to the client about the equipment you are using to create the style

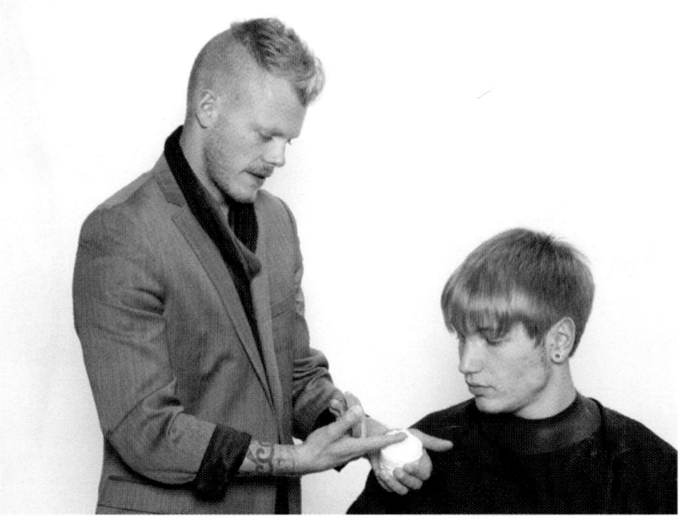

Figure 16.104 Explain to client which products can be used at home

16.4 Worksheets

WORKSHEETS

You can carry out the worksheets during your study of a chapter or unit, or at the end. An example is presented here and there are more online. If your college or company is registered with ATT Training, lots more are available. Write your answers directly in the book, but only if you own it of course – if it is a library or college book, use a separate piece of paper!

16.4.1 Cutting techniques

Label each of these photos to say which cutting technique is shown and suggest when this would be used.

Figure 16.109

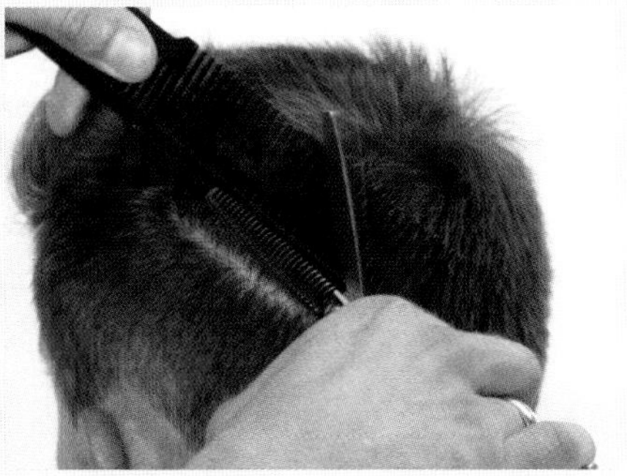

Figure 16.110

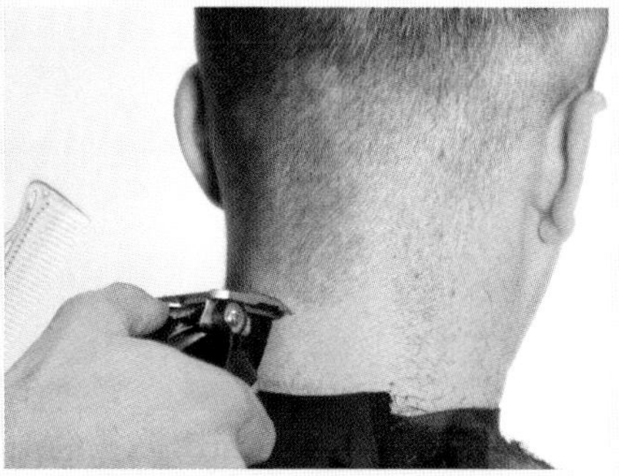

Figure 16.111

Figure 16.112

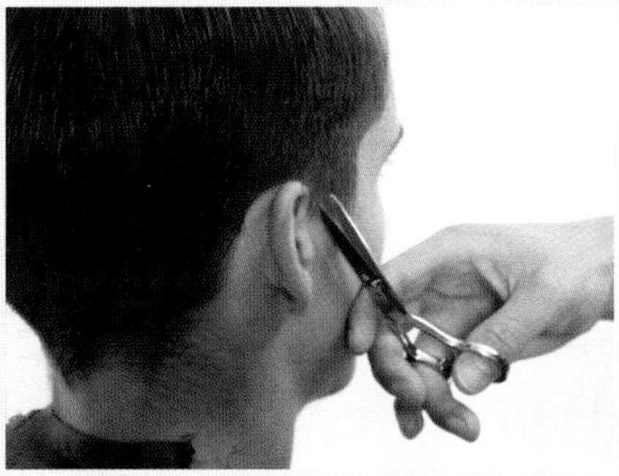

Figure 16.113

Figure 16.114

16.5 Assessment

Well done! If you have studied all the content of this unit you may be ready to test your knowledge.

Check out the 'Preparing for assessments' section in Chapter 1 if you have not already done so, and always remember:

- You can only do your best if you have. . .
  - studied hard
  - completed the activities
  - completed the worksheets
  - practised, practised, practised
  - and then revised!

Now carry out the online multiple-choice quiz

. . . and good luck in the final exam, which will be arranged by your tutor/assessor.

CHAPTER 17

Cut facial hair to shape

This chapter covers the NVQ/SVQ unit GB4, Cut facial hair to shape using basic techniques and the VRQ unit 211, Cut facial hair.

Men's barbering services have always included beard and moustache shaping and this chapter will cover the skills required to do this. As in hairdressing, when carrying out the cutting techniques, certain factors must always be taken into account, e.g. hair growth patterns, clients' features and face shapes.

In this chapter you will learn about:

- maintaining effective and safe methods of working when cutting facial hair
- cutting beards and moustaches to maintain their shape
- providing aftercare advice.

Website WWW
www.atthairdressing.com

CHAPTER 17 CUT FACIAL HAIR TO SHAPE: CONTENTS, SCREENS AND ACTIVITIES

Key:
Sections from the book are set in this colour
Screens available online are set in this colour
Online activity screens are set in this colour

17.1 Working safely

Safety is the key issue when cutting facial hair. The tools that you use must allow you to perform the barbering service that the client wishes to have. Be careful not to damage your tools as you work. Ensure that all the equipment that you are to use is pre-selected and in easy reach.

Safety first

Chapter 2 covers health and safety working methods in more detail. Refer to this unit if needed.

Scissors

These come in a variety of materials such as stainless steel, with metal or plastic handles. They also come in a variety of designs, weights and prices. Picking scissors up and holding them is the best way to see if they are suitable. It is important that they feel comfortable. Scissors should always be clean and sharp. Before sterilising remember to remove all loose hairs. The blades should be sprayed with sterilising spray or wiped carefully with sterile wipes before being placed in the ultraviolet cabinet for the correct length of time according to the manufacturer's instructions.

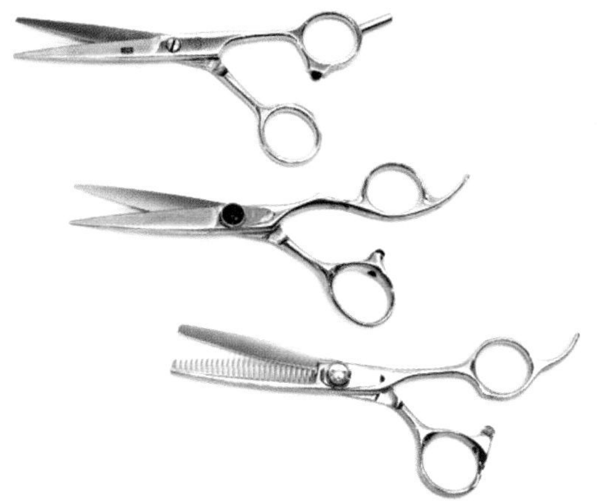

Figure 17.1 Different types of scissors

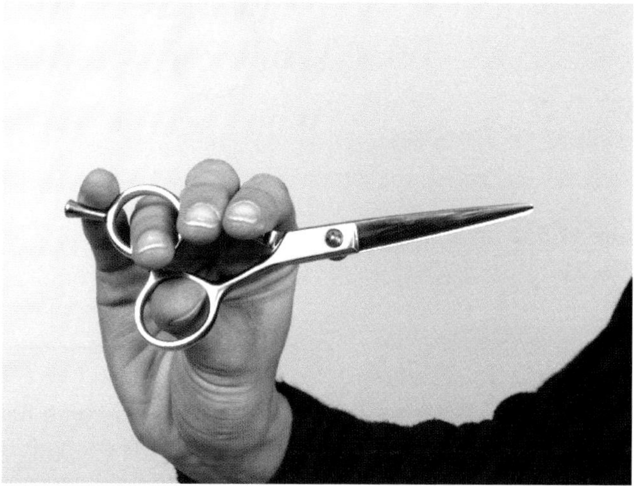

Figure 17.2 Pick scissors up to see if they are comfortable to hold

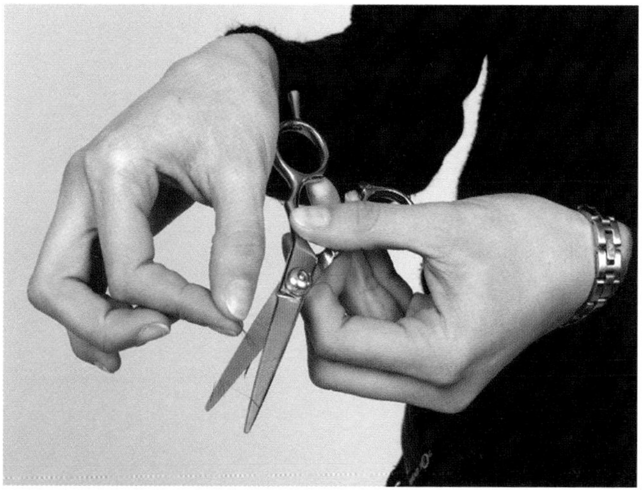

Figure 17.3 Pick off any loose hairs

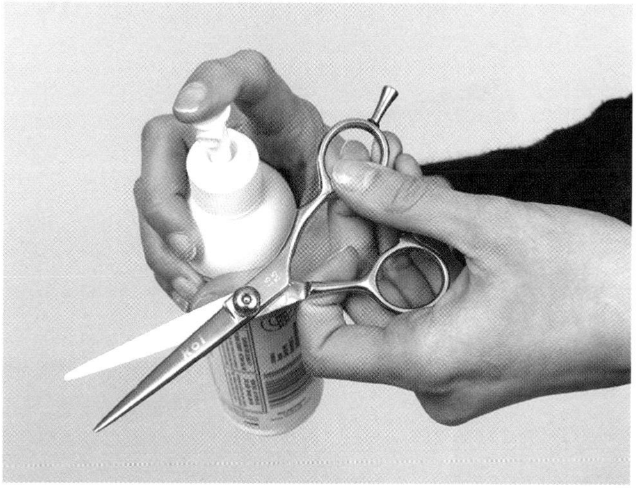

Figure 17.4 Sterilising scissors

Online activity 17.1

Round the board

Thinning scissors

Definition

Serrated: Having a jagged edge.

There are scissors specifically designed for thinning the hair. They have one or possibly two blades that look like the teeth on a comb. The teeth of the blades are sharp and cut the hair.

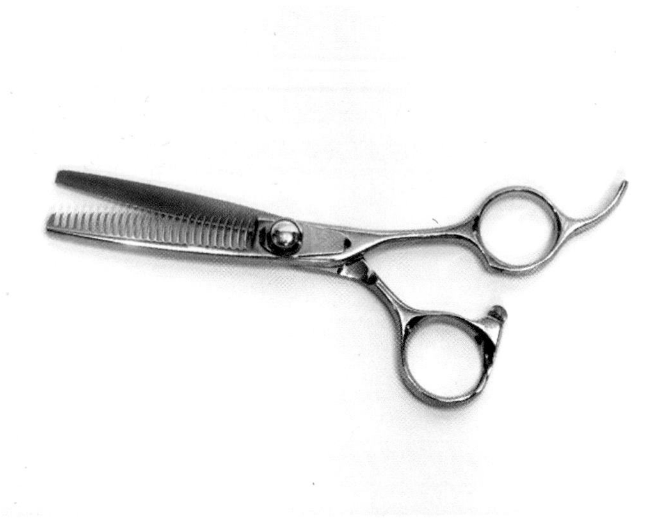

Figure 17.5 Thinning scissors with one blade serrated

Figure 17.6 And with two blades serrated

Combs

Key information

The barbering comb has a tapered edge and is more flexible than the hairdressing comb.

Combs used for barbering are different to those used in hairdressing. The barbering comb has a tapered edge and is more flexible than the hairdressing comb. The length of the comb should be based on how comfortable it is for you to hold and work with. To clean, combs should be washed in water with detergent and then placed in sterilising solution for the correct length of time according to the manufacturer's instructions.

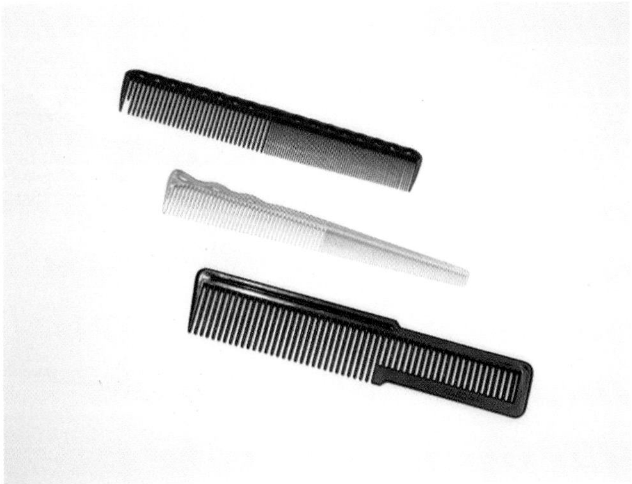

Figure 17.7 Combs used in barbering

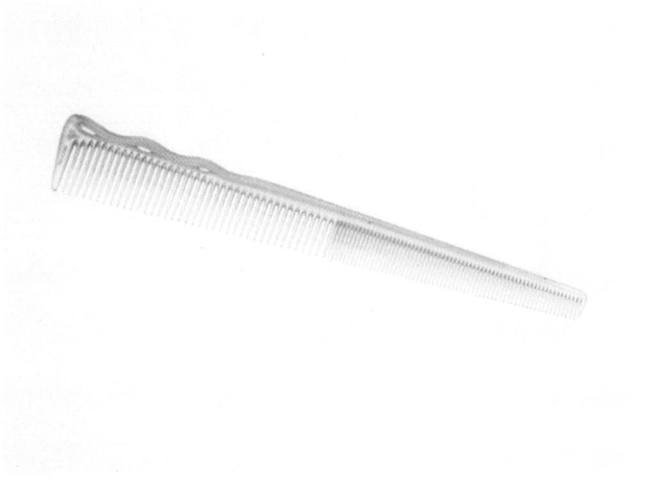

Figure 17.8 Barbering comb

Clippers

Always follow the manufacturer's instructions when using clippers so that you use them safely. When in use the bottom blade remains still whilst the top blade moves across it very quickly to cut the hair. Ensure that you check the alignment of the clipper blades before use. Small adjustments can be made by loosening the small screws that are positioned underneath.

Remember to oil clippers using clipper oil after every use to keep them lubricated and clean. This also prolongs the life of the blades. After use, clean away hairs from the clippers. Sometimes the blades must be removed to clean away hair. If this is not done, the clippers may not work properly, causing discomfort to the client.

Safety first

All repairs to electric clippers should be carried out by a qualified electrician.

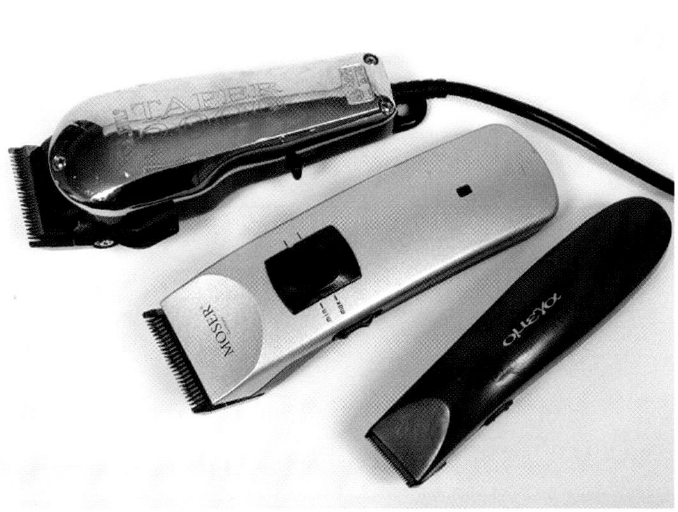

Figure 17.9 Electric clippers

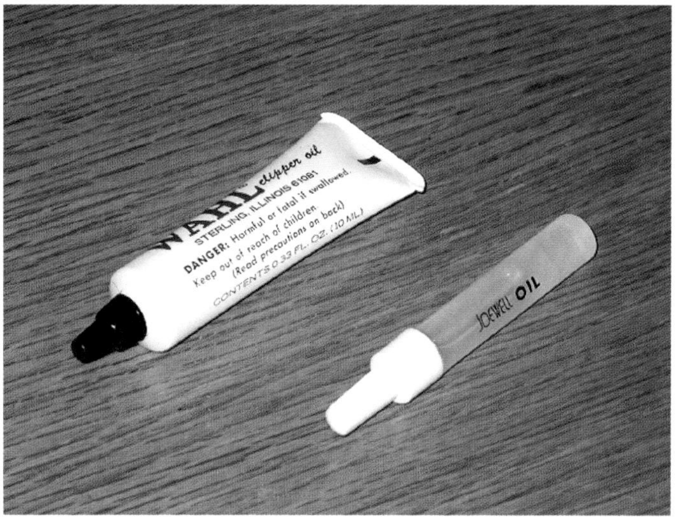

Figure 17.10 Clipper oil

Clipper attachments

Figure 17.11 Clippers with attachments

Clipper attachment sizes start at grade 1 and go up to grade 8 for cutting hair. This table shows the amount of hair that is left for each clipper grade.

Table 17.1 Grades of clipper attachment

Clipper grade	Length of hair left
1	3 mm / $^1/_8$ inch
2	6 mm / $^1/_4$ inch
3	10 mm / $^3/_8$ inch
4	13 mm / $^1/_2$ inch
5	16 mm / $^5/_8$ inch
6	19 mm / $^3/_4$ inch
7	22 mm / $^7/_8$ inch
8	25 mm /1 inch

Towels and gowns

All towels and gowns should be clean and sterile for each client to prevent cross infection of parasitic, viral, fungal and bacterial diseases. These include:

- pediculosis capitis
- herpes simplex
- tinea capitis
- impetigo.

Definitions

Pediculosis capitis: Also known as head lice. Tiny insects that are spread by head-to-head contact.

Herpes simplex: A viral infection affecting the skin and nervous system.

Tinea capitis: Fungal infection that is contagious.

Impetigo: Contagious bacterial skin disease.

Figure 17.12 Towels and gowns should be clean and sterile

Consultation

Before any service begins the barber must find out what the client wants or needs. The consultation is used to ensure the client's wishes are interpreted accurately and the desired look achieved. It is essential to be factual, honest, tactful, sincere, direct and clear.

Figure 17.13 Find out what the client needs

Factors influencing the service

You should identify any factors that may influence the client's choice of facial style.

These include:

- facial features
- head and face shapes
- hairstyle
- hair density
- hair growth patterns
- skin elasticity.

Safety first

See Chapter 4 for information on adverse skin conditions including infections or infestations that may prevent you from performing this service.

Online activity 17.2 WWW

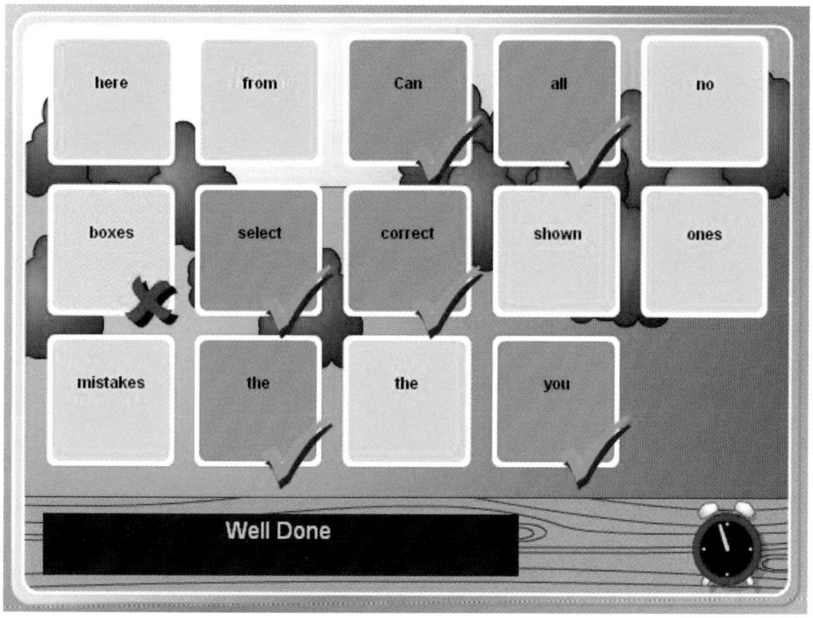

Correct selection

Facial features

Generally the larger the client's facial features, the thicker the beard or moustache can be (Figures 17.14, 17.15). If the client has finer features they should have a smaller design. This is shown in Figures 17.16 and 17.17, with the client having a small mouth so a moustache that is short and narrow would best suit him.

Figure 17.14 Large facial features. . .

Figure 17.15 . . . allow for a thicker beard

Figure 17.16 A small mouth. . .

Figure 17.17 . . . suits a short and narrow moustache

If the client has a large prominent nose, a thicker moustache would suit him. Any facial scarring can be hidden with beards or moustaches.

Figure 17.18 A large prominent nose. . .

Figure 17.19 . . . suits a thicker moustache

Figure 17.20 Facial scarring can be hidden. . .

Figure 17.21 . . . with a beard

If the client has any facial piercings, then either ask the client to remove them or take extra care when combing and cutting around these areas.

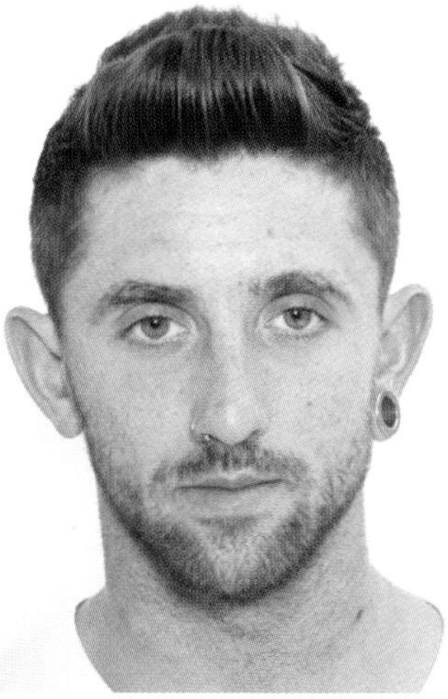

Figure 17.22 Take extra care if a client has piercings

WWW **Website**

www.atthairdressing.com

Head and face shapes

Men with square faces can soften their look by having beards or moustaches that are rounded.

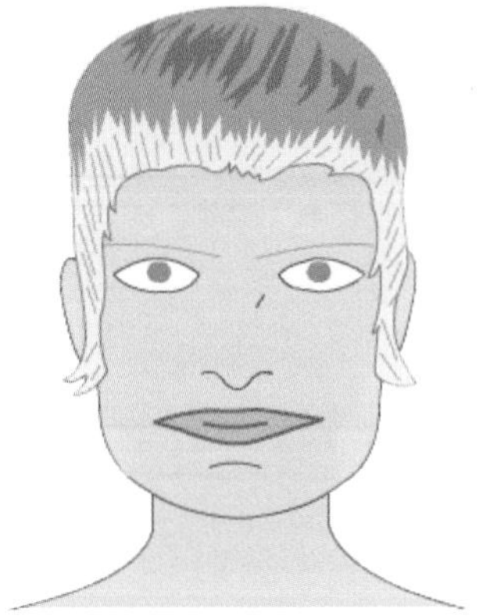

Figure 17.23 Square shaped face

Figure 17.24 Rounded beard

Round faces can be lengthened by choosing beard designs that have angles and lines instead of curves.

Figure 17.25 Round shaped face

Figure 17.26 Beard design with angles and lines

Oval shaped faces tend to suit any facial style. A beard or moustache should be chosen that enhances the client's features.

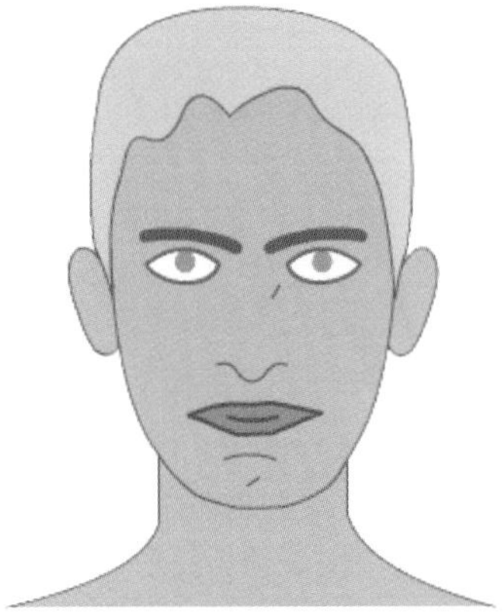

Figure 17.27 Oval shaped face

Figure 17.28 A beard that enhances the client's features

Small faces should keep small facial hair designs that are cut close and are the same in length.

Figure 17.29 A small face

Figure 17.30 A beard that is cut close

If the client has a wide head, a beard that is full and long will flatter him. It should be cut close at the side and lengthened at the chin.

Figure 17.31 A wide head

Figure 17.32 A long beard cut close at the sides

Hairstyle

The beard or moustache the client wishes to have should complement his hairstyle. A client with little or no hair should choose a beard or moustache that is small and close cut whereas thick long hair would suit a client with a larger beard. Work together with the client to find a style that suits him and he is happy with.

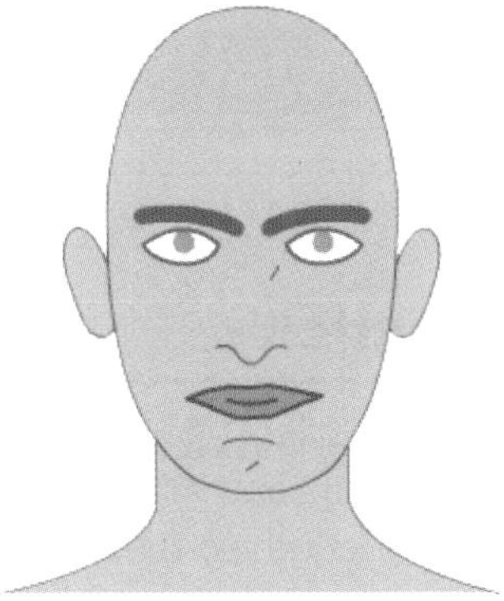

Figure 17.33 A client with no hair. . .

Figure 17.34 . . . should choose a beard or moustache that is small and cut close

Figure 17.35 A client with thick, long hair. . .

Figure 17.36 . . . should choose a larger beard

Hair density

The client's choice of style will be influenced by the density of facial hair. If a client has thick facial hair, they may not be able to have a narrow, fine moustache. The density will also affect the tools and techniques that are used, e.g. clippers may need to be used instead of scissors for a thick beard.

Figure 17.37 The density of the client's facial hair will affect his style

Definition

Density: The thickness.

Hair growth patterns and skin elasticity

Check to see if there are any hair growth patterns in the client's facial hair. This might affect the way it is cut. For example, if the client has any whorls, the hair may need to be cut close to the skin or left at a longer length so that they are unnoticed. This is also the case if there are any thinning or missing areas. As the skin ages, it will lose its elasticity; therefore it will be less taut. To avoid cutting the skin, it must be pulled slightly to create tension.

Key information

As the skin ages, it will lose its elasticity; therefore it will be less taut.

Figure 17.38 Checking for hair growth patterns

Preparing the client for facial cutting

It is important to gown the client effectively prior to cutting facial hair. This is to protect the client's clothes and to ensure that the client is comfortable. Hair cuttings are extremely prickly when they go down the back of the neck, and can penetrate the skin causing an infection. Cuttings are also very difficult to remove from clothes.

Safety first

Hair cuttings are extremely prickly when they go down the back of the neck, and can penetrate the skin causing an infection.

Protective equipment varies from salon to salon but your salon may use the following:

- gown covering all clothing ensuring there are no gaps
- towel fastened at the client's back
- cotton wool strip or neck wool placed around client's neck.

Figure 17.39 The client is gowned

After the client has been gowned, the eyes should be covered with dampened eye pads to ensure that no clippings enter the eyes. Do not have too much bulk from clothes and towels around the neck; this restricts the accuracy when cutting and in some cases the mobility of the client's neck.

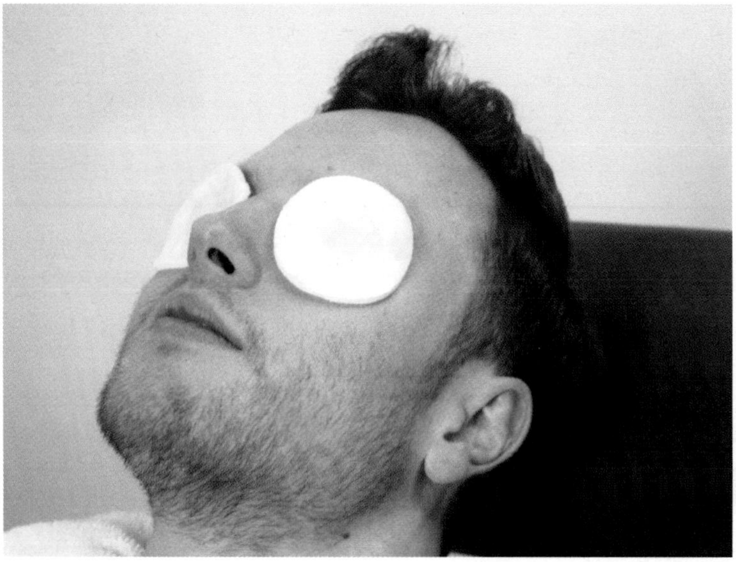

Figure 17.40 The eyes are covered with dampened eye pads

WWW **Online activity 17.3**

Round the board

Comfort during cutting facial hair

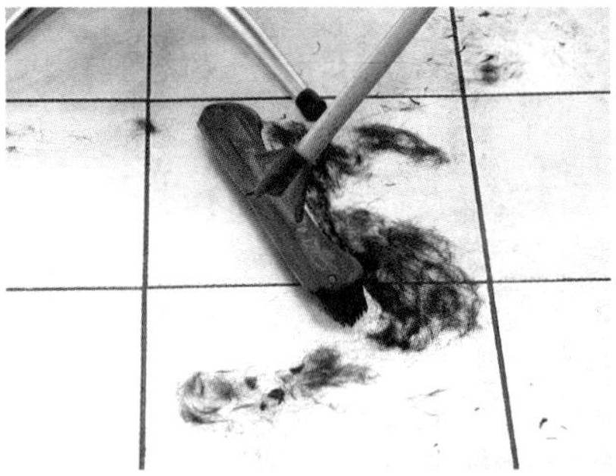

Figure 17.41 Keep the salon clean

When cutting men's facial hair, the client must have their head tilted back in order for you to work safely and accurately. The barbering chair has a reclining facility and headrest allowing the client to be comfortable in this position. The client should have both feet squarely on the footrest which will help both the client to be comfortable and you to work safely. Your own comfort during cutting should be considered as well. Check your posture is correct, ensuring that your client's seat is at the correct height for you to work. Ensure that your work area is tidy and free from clutter.

After cutting always remember to sweep up the hair cuttings off the floor and dispose of them in the appropriate place.

Suggested time for cutting facial hair

The table shows the suggested times for cutting facial hair.

Table 17.2 Suggested time for cutting facial hair

Facial cut	Time
Full beard	15 minutes
Moustache	5 minutes

17.2 Cut beards and moustaches to maintain their shape

In this section you will learn the basic cutting techniques for maintaining facial hair shape whilst keeping in mind any important factors. Your consultation will have established the service that you will be providing but ensure that throughout the cutting process your client is happy with what you are doing. This may mean uncovering their eyes to check they are comfortable with the design you are creating.

Figure 17.42 The consultation will establish which service is to take place

Preparing the client's facial hair before cutting

You should untangle the facial hair before cutting. Then the hair should be cleansed as this will make the cut easier. If the client is having another service which involves shampooing, this can be done at the same time. If there is no other service, the client can wash his face and beard at the front wash basin. Alternatively cleansers or cleansing wipes can be used.

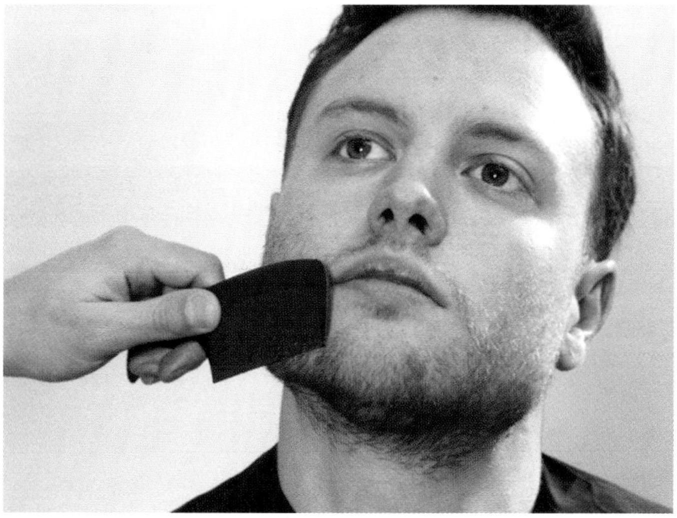

Figure 17.43 Combing the client's beard

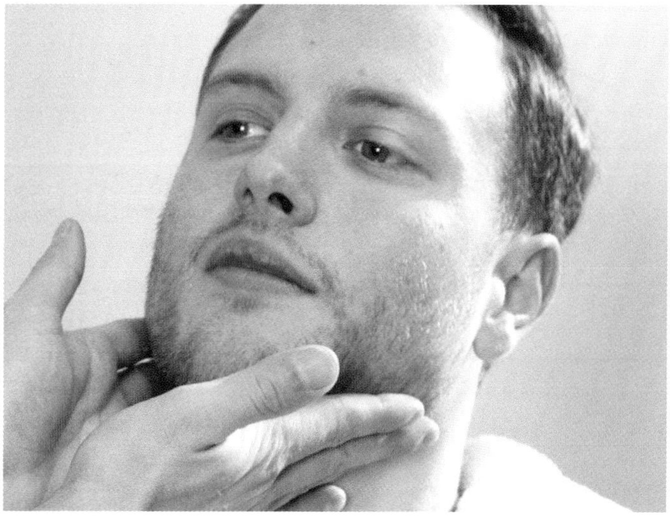

Figure 17.44 Cleansing the beard

Definition

Systematic: To complete in a set order/follow a set system.

Key information

Moustaches are usually trimmed with the scissors for better control and to stop the clippers vibrating and tickling the client.

Definition

Inverted: Turned upside down or in the opposite direction.

Methods of cutting beards/moustaches

When cutting beards and moustaches, it will be easier if you work in a systematic manner. That way the pattern you are following will be clear. Working from either side or the middle, it is helpful to cut channels of hair which follow the guidelines you are creating. Remember to try to follow the client's natural hairline on the face. If you don't do this the style will look out of balance and uneven. It will also be difficult for the client to maintain.

It is important to check the balance of the shaping throughout to ensure that you are creating an even finish. Moustaches are usually trimmed with the scissors for better control and to stop the clippers vibrating and tickling the client. This may make them pull away.

Removing unwanted hair from the outside of the perimeter line

To finish the look, make sure that any hair that is not wanted from the outside of the perimeter line is removed. This is done once the client is happy with the shape you have created. The clippers are inverted and the edge used to mark a clear line. Once this is done they are turned back around and the unwanted hair is removed. If needed, gently pull the skin so that it is taut to get a closer cut.

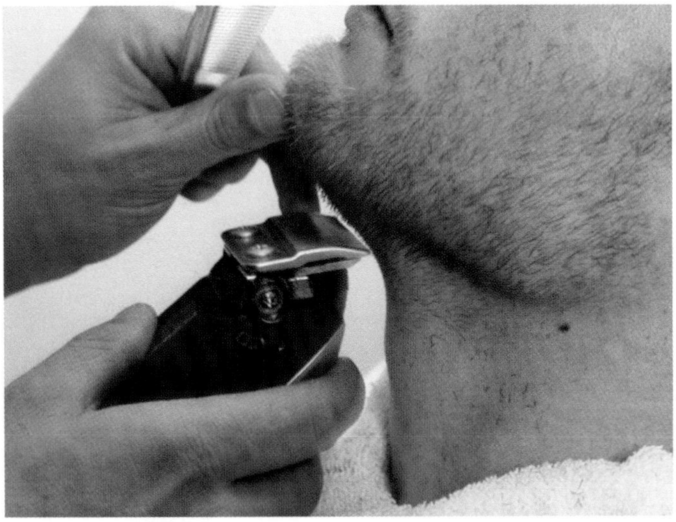

Figure 17.45 Making out the edge of the perimeter line

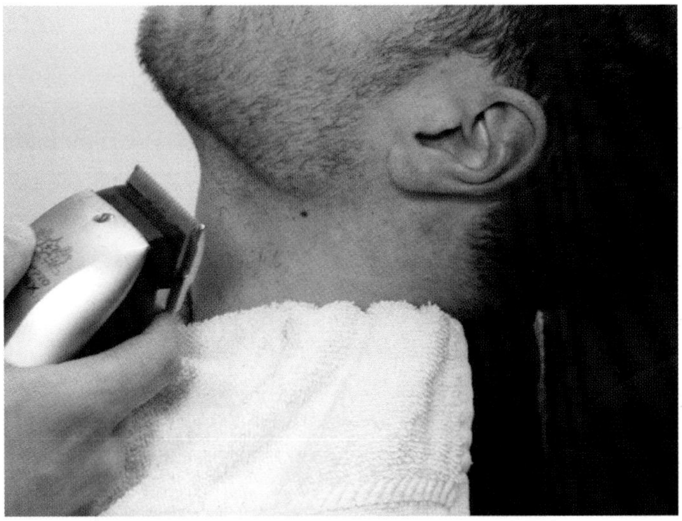

Figure 17.46 Remove unwanted hair outside the edge

Online activity 17.4

Five in a row

Cutting techniques

Techniques used during facial hair trimming include:

- scissors over comb
- clipper over comb
- clippers with attachment
- freehand.

Scissors over comb

Used when the hair is required to be very short and finely graduated. When using this cutting method a smooth flowing movement is required to avoid 'steps' in the hair. The comb is placed against the skin and the hair cut as the comb is moved away from the face.

Clipper over comb

This eliminates the hard work from the scissor over comb technique. Clipper over comb is used for removing bulk and shaping beards and moustaches. Place the comb and hold at the appropriate angle under a section of hair. Glide the clippers across the comb. Repeat this until the required length is achieved.

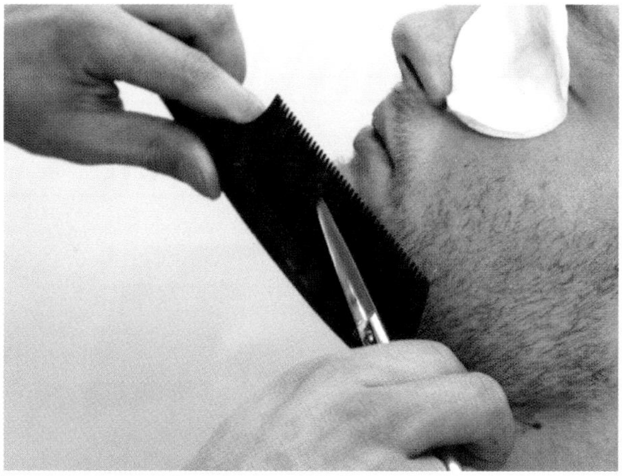

Figure 17.47 Scissor over comb technique

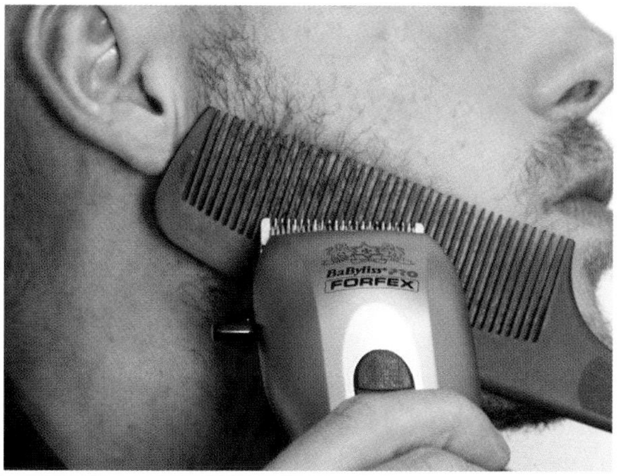

Figure 17.48 Clipper over comb technique

Clippers with attachments

The correct grade must be chosen when performing this technique. See previous section for more information on attachments. Place the clippers directly onto the skin when using as this will create an even length.

Freehand cutting

When you cut the beard or moustache without holding with the fingers, this is known as freehand cutting. It is usually carried out to tidy the beard or moustache once the main bulk has been removed.

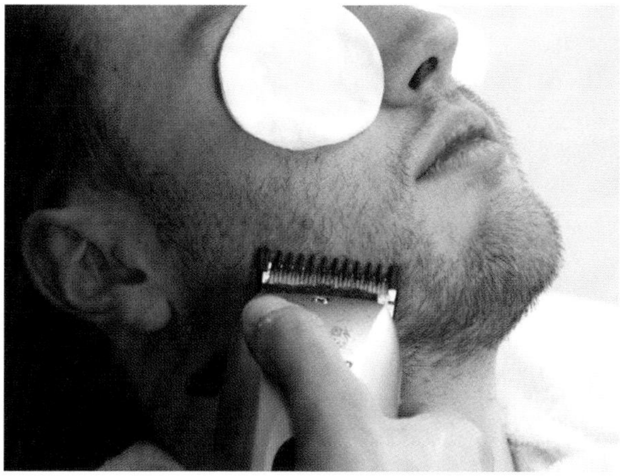

Figure 17.49 Clippers with attachment

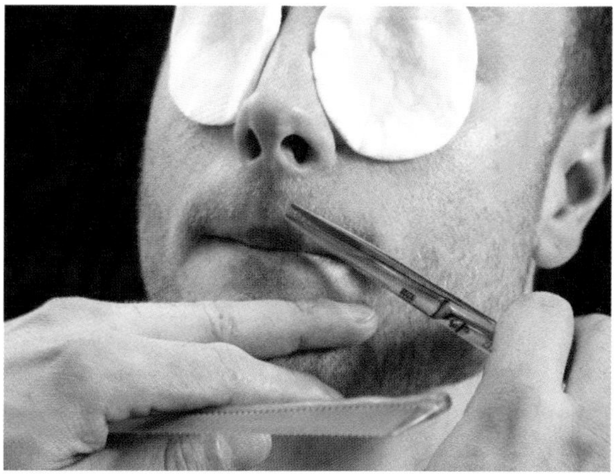

Figure 17.50 Freehand cutting

Moustache and beard shapes

There are many moustache and beard shapes. The following are some that the client may wish for you to cut and shape.

Figure 17.51 Examples of moustache and beard shapes

Cutting beard and moustache to shape

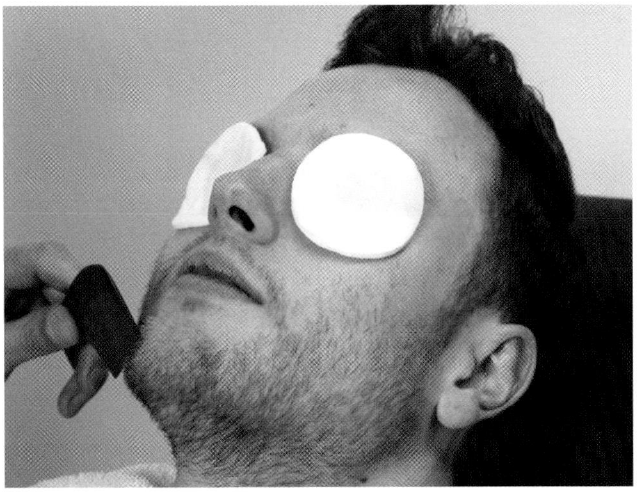

Figure 17.52 After the client is protected and seated correctly in a comfortable position, the beard is combed through to detangle.

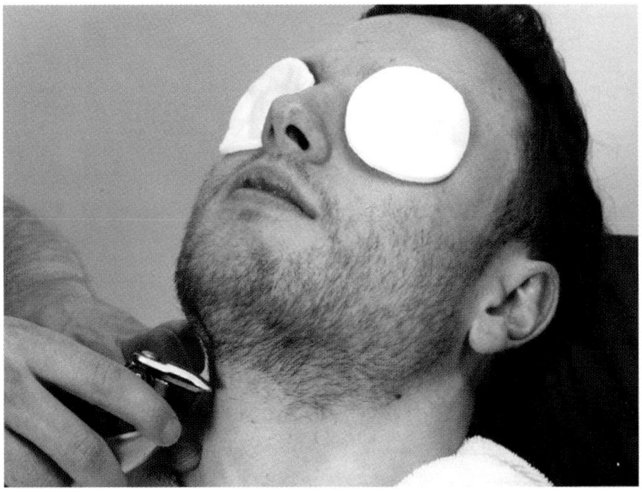

Figure 17.53 The clippers are then inverted and an edge is created. This is the outline shape.

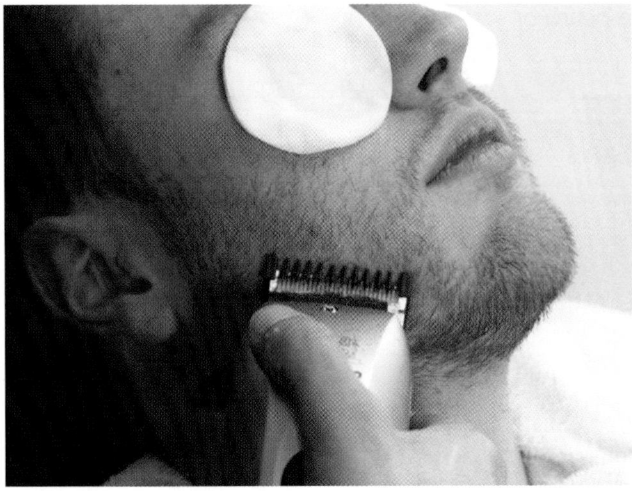

Figure 17.54 Using the clippers with attachment, shorten the beard according to client's wishes.

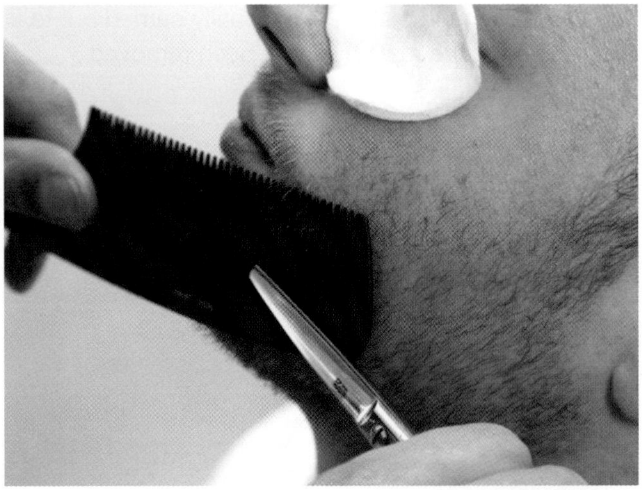

Figure 17.55 Use the scissors over comb technique to cut closer to the skin.

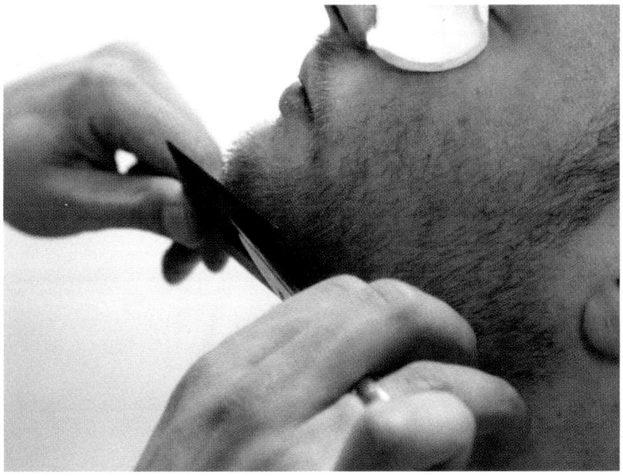

Figure 17.56 The hair is held at 90 degrees from the head whilst performing this technique. The guideline is followed throughout.

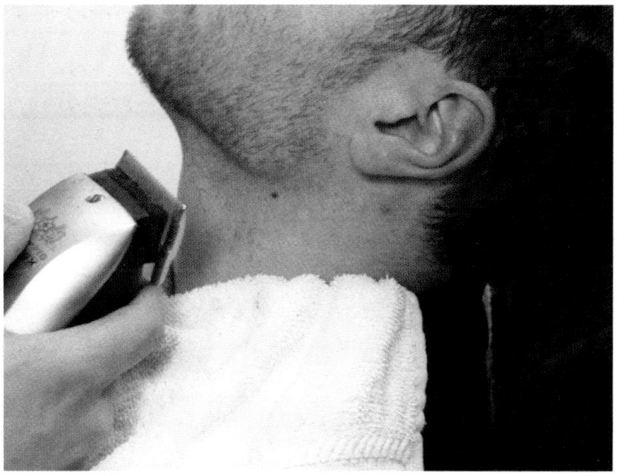

Figure 17.57 Using the clippers, unwanted hair outside the beard area is removed.

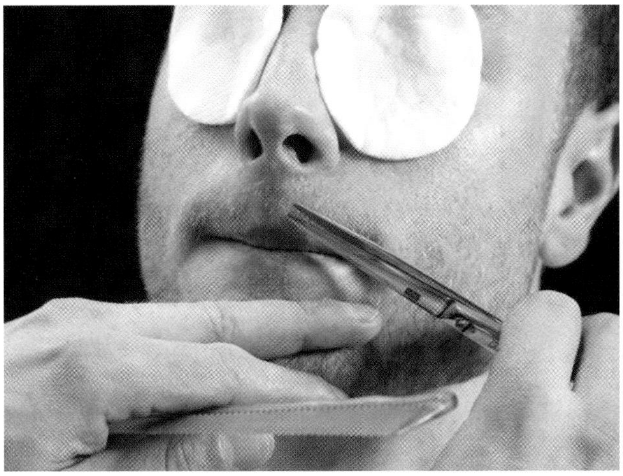

Figure 17.58 Trim the moustache using the scissors and a free-hand technique.

Figure 17.59 Finished look.

Figure 17.60 Finished look.

Online activity 17.5 WWW

Drag into correct order

Shaping eyebrows

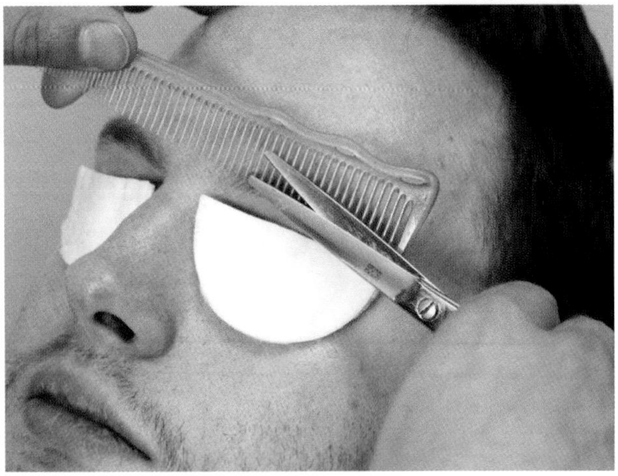

Figure 17.61 Use the scissors over comb technique to shape eyebrows.

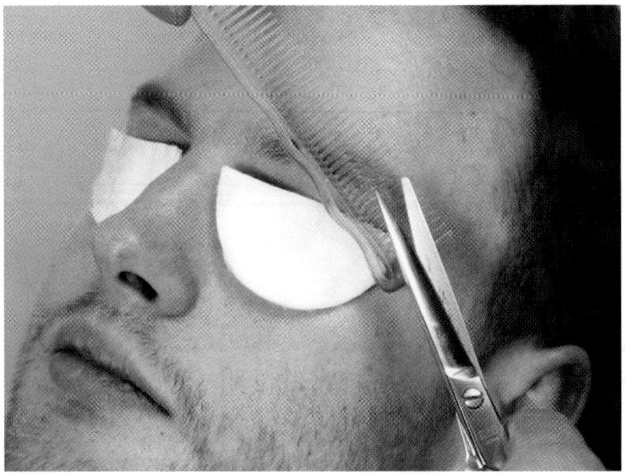

Figure 17.62 Follow the contours of the eyebrow and cut any loose hairs off.

Client care

After cutting, remove any loose clippings of hair from the face. This can be carried out with a cloth. Check with the client that they are happy with the finished look.

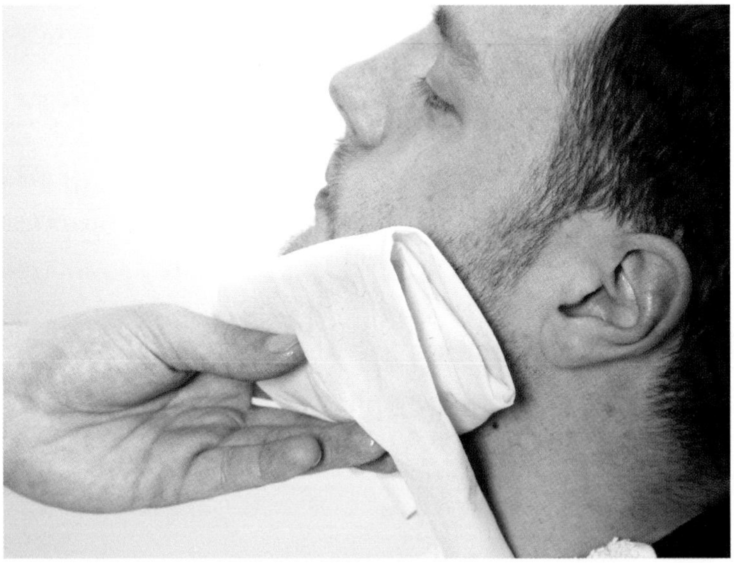

Figure 17.63 Remove loose clippings with a cloth.

17.3 Provide aftercare advice

Key information

The average rate of growth of hair is 1.25 cm every month.

An important part of this service is to give the client aftercare advice. You should explain to the client how often they should return to the salon to maintain their beard and/or moustache. This will depend on the length; the average rate of growth of facial hair is 1.25 cm every month so it is likely between 3 and 5 weeks. Clients with shorter styles will need to return to the salon more often than clients with longer styles.

The client should be given advice on tidying up the perimeter of his beard or moustache as he may wish to do this himself. This will usually be carried out using nail scissors or electric razors. The client's lifestyle must be taken into consideration when creating a style that the client can maintain.

Online activity 17.6 WWW

Round the board

Products

Advise the client on which products can be used at home. This should be based on the factors that influence the service.

Figure 17.64 Advise the client on which products can be used at home

WORKSHEETS

17.4 Worksheets

You can carry out the worksheets during your study of a chapter or unit, or at the end. An example is presented here and there are more online. If your college or company is registered with ATT Training, lots more are available. Write your answers directly in the book, but only if you own it of course – if it is a library or college book, use a separate piece of paper!

17.4.1 Facial features

The facial features of your client must be considered when cutting facial hair.

Each of these images shows a type of facial feature. Draw the style of beard or moustache onto each one that you think will suit them best. Explain your reasons alongside each image.

Figure 17.65 A small face

Figure 17.66 Scarring on face

Figure 17.67 Large facial features

Figure 17.68 A prominent nose

17.5 Assessment

Well done! If you have studied all the content of this unit you may be ready to test your knowledge.

Check out the 'Preparing for assessments' section in Chapter 1 if you have not already done so, and always remember:

- You can only do your best if you have. . .
  - studied hard
  - completed the activities
  - completed the worksheets
  - practised, practised, practised
  - and then revised!

Now carry out the online multiple-choice quiz

. . . and good luck in the final exam, which will be arranged by your tutor/assessor.

Top tips

The most important attribute to have when working as a hairdresser is excellent communication and customer service skills. You may be an amazing hairdresser, but if you do not make your clients feel valued and comfortable, they will not come back to you.
Lindsay Bellis, Lecturer in Hairdressing and Bridal Hair at Yale College

Health and safety

Following health and safety legislation shows your clients and employer that you take your job seriously.
Samantha Raybould, Yale College, Wrexham

Create a positive impression

Think like a client; would you rather walk through the door of a salon where everyone looks miserable or happy?
Carly Embling-Loxton, Helen Ward and Linda Powell, Swindon College

When you greet a client for the first time, don't be afraid to shake their hand when you introduce yourself. It's professional and shows confidence, which all clients look for in a hair stylist.
Samantha Raybould, Yale College, Wrexham

Advise and consult

Sit next to the client, at eye level, when carrying out a consultation. This will stop the client feeling intimidated by you standing over them and will also help you talk to them face to face rather than through the mirror, as although this is normal to hairdressers, clients may feel uncomfortable.
Mandy Durkin, Saks Education

As well as asking your client what they *would* like, also ask them what they *do not* like.
Carly Embling-Loxton, Helen Ward and Linda Powell, Swindon College

Reception duties

Reception is your salon's 'first impression'. It must be clean, warm and welcoming and so must the people that are behind it!
Carly Embling-Loxton, Helen Ward and Linda Powell, Swindon College

Promote additional services or products

Never assume that your client wants 'the usual'. Always tell them about new products, services and techniques available in your salon. Even if they are not wanted they will be happy that you have offered.
Carly Embling-Loxton, Helen Ward and Linda Powell, Swindon College

Effectiveness at work

Being able to recognise your salon's unique selling point is vital for success within the hair and beauty industry.
Karen Wright, Head of School Hair and Beauty Therapy, Runshaw College

When creating your own 'look book', give your signature services names to highlight your individuality as a hairdresser. For example, 'hidden lights' is a lowlighting technique used to complement the client's natural depth and tone.
Andrea Larter, Hairdressing Lecturer at Redbridge College

Shampoo, condition and treat the hair and scalp

A scalp massage whilst conditioning is normally the part of the service that the client enjoys the most, so make sure your technique keeps them coming back for more!
Carly Embling-Loxton, Helen Ward and Linda Powell, Swindon College

Style and finish hair

When styling long hair that is thick and heavy, secure it up to the crown area using small bands, then design your curls around this. Hair will stay in place for longer and it will stop the hair sagging.
Sue Sweeny, A. P. & Section Leader for hairdressing, Chichester College

Only apply serum to the mid lengths and ends of thick/dense hair. Doing this will avoid oily roots.
Sarah Flecknor, Hairdressing Tutor, Graduate Salon, Grimsby Institute and University Centre

Give every client a 'commentary' of the way you are blow-drying their hair and the products/tools you are using. This way they are much more likely to be able to recreate the look at home.
Mandy Durkin, Saks Education

Always show your client the back of their hair before you apply hairspray. If they aren't happy with the finish it will be harder to change once the hairspray is on.
Carly Embling-Loxton, Helen Ward and Linda Powell, Swindon College

Use a few Velcro rollers around the crown when the hair is still warm from blow-drying. This will give added lift, and can then be secured in place with a little hairspray.
Vanda Dean, Graduate Salon, Grimsby Institute and University Centre

Straightening irons are not only for styling hair poker straight. Think of them as styling irons, experiment with different styles creating waves, curls and root lift on styles. You can even use them for pin curling.
Lindsay Bellis, Lecturer in Hairdressing and Bridal Hair at Yale College

Set and dress hair

With any setting technique, always allow the hair to cool prior to removing the rollers. This will ensure a nice firm result with a shiny finish and it will help to avoid static.
David Rabjohns, East Surrey College

Be sure not to leave any gaps amongst your rollers as it will leave gaps in the hair once dry.
Carly Embling-Loxton, Helen Ward and Linda Powell, Swindon College

Never open grips and pins in your mouth; this is unhygienic and could cause cross infection.
Natalie Stephens, Hairdressing Level 2 and Level 3 Curriculum Leader, Creative Academies, Gloucestershire College

When you have spent hours putting someone's hair up for an occasion, advise them that if they are having a bath in the evening, to run the cold water first before adding warm water, as this neutralises steam and stops their hair dropping (the hydrogen bonds will not break).
Carly Embling-Loxton, Helen Ward and Linda Powell, Swindon College

When dry setting the hair with Velcro rollers, spritz the ends with a light volume spray. This will make the ends easier to wrap around the roller, smooth the ends and will make the set last longer.
Lindsay Bellis, Lecturer in Hairdressing and Bridal Hair at Yale College

Cutting hair

Right-handed people tend to cut base lines that slope longer towards the left. This is due to the fact that the direction we cut in is from right to left (and vice versa for left-handed people). Knowing this makes it easier to self-correct the cutting angle and create even and balanced base lines.
David Rabjohns, East Surrey College

When performing a one length cut **always** ensure the client's head is looking down towards the floor. This will prevent graduation on the perimeter line.
Paula Shaw, Lecturer – Hairdressing, Knowsley Community College

When cutting hair, always make sure your client's legs are uncrossed to prevent the cut becoming unbalanced.
Abby Crowhurst, Divisional Lead Manager Hair & Beauty, The Manchester College

Remember the fringe is the part of the haircut the client will see the most, so pay particular attention to this area when cutting. It will define your cut.
Mandy Durkin, Saks Education

When cutting a one length style, try to keep the cutting line at eye level. On very long hair this may require asking your client to stand.
Virginia Collins, Graduate Salon, Grimsby Institute and University Centre

When cutting, don't be scared to turn your client around in their chair so they are sideways to the mirror; that way you can check whether you are elevating your sections enough or not.
Nicki Chaplin, Graduate Salon, Grimsby Institute and University Centre

When carrying out a cut, ensure that you always have a water bottle to hand before you start. The hair should be wet at all times; this creates even tension and makes the hair easier to work with.
Lindsay Bellis, Lecturer in Hairdressing and Bridal Hair at Yale College

When cutting hair, make the most use of your tools and equipment. Use your mirror to continuously check your client's and your own posture and how you are angling, sectioning and cutting the hair. You should also think of your comb as a ruler, using it to help you achieve your required angles.
Lindsay Bellis, Lecturer in Hairdressing and Bridal Hair at Yale College

Colour hair

Never wash your tint bowl up until the service is over. Tint removes tint from the client's skin and can also be used if any touch-ups are needed rather than mix up more products!
Zoe Grimes, Assessor, Redbridge College

When you have finished weaving a full head of bleach foils application, take small strips of cotton wool and put one between each foil at the root area. This will prevent any seepage from touching the scalp when the bleach expands during development.
Susie Phillips, Lead Personal Learning Advisor, Redbridge College

When choosing a colour for a client always check their eye colour and skin tone as these will tell you whether your client would suit a cool or warm tone colour.
Sue Sweeny, A. P. & Section Leader for hairdressing, Chichester College

When describing colours to clients always use terms that a client can relate to such as 'honey highlights' or 'chocolate'.
Suzanne Szepeta, Vision West Notts

As well as using antioxy between colour processes, condition the hair. This will keep it in optimum condition and will give an improved colour result.
Janice Yardley, Graduate Salon, Grimsby Institute and University Centre

When diluting peroxide, always do so at eye level and on a flat surface, using eye protection.
Nicki Chaplin, Graduate Salon, Grimsby Institute and University Centre

Perm and neutralise hair

After applying your perm lotion, change your cotton wool after five minutes. If you do not change the cotton wool, most of the excess will have dripped through and will be lying against the client's skin.
Carly Embling-Loxton, Helen Ward and Linda Powell, Swindon College

Plait and twist hair

If hair is too clean and slippery to work with, lightly spray some hairspray through it to give it some grip.
Carly Embling-Loxton, Helen Ward and Linda Powell, Swindon College

Cut facial hair to shape

Moustaches can be worn as part of the beard, or as a separate entity. Likewise, sideburns can also be integrated or separate from a beard.
Dawn Buttle, Academy Manager, Salon Services, Hairdressing, South Essex College of Further and Higher Education

Glossary

This glossary is also available online at www.atthairdressing.com where you can search for important words and phrases and even translate them into other languages.

We have added a guide to the pronunciation of unusual words in this format: (proh-nun-see-ay-shun), at the front of the book.

Abrasion *An area of the skin which has worn away.*

Absorbed *Taken in through the surface of an object.*

Accessories *Jewellery or other items worn in the hair.*

Accident *A mishap that can often lead to injury.*

Account *A record of financial transactions.*

Accuracy *How close the data given is to the true value.*

Accurate *Exact.*

Acetic acid *Used in acid rinses (vinegar rinse).*

Acid balanced *Lotion with the same pH as the skin (4.5-5.5).*

Acid *A solution with a pH of less than 7.*

Action plan *A method of outlining steps and actions in order to achieve a particular goal.*

Adapt *To suit another purpose.*

Added hair *Extensions and hairpieces.*

Additional media *Materials other than ornamentation used for creating a look, e.g. accessories, make-up and clothes.*

Additive *Substance added to improve a product.*

Adequate *Sufficient.*

Adhere *To stick to.*

Adhesions *Scar tissue.*

Advertising *Promoting product or services.*

Advice *Guidance offered by someone.*

Afro *Type of hair.*

Afro comb *Comb to detangle afro or curly hair.*

Aftercare *Continuing service given to the client.*

Agitation *To keep a substance or object moving.*

Alcohol *Solvent used in setting lotions.*

Alcoholics Anonymous *A worldwide group of men and women who meet in order to help one another stop drinking alcohol and remain sober.*

Alkaline *Solution with a pH above 7.*

Allergic reaction *Abnormal reaction to a substance.*

Allergy *Abnormal reaction to a substance.*

Almond oil *Vegetable oil used for hot oil scalp treatments. Ingredient of control creams.*

Alopecia *A general term meaning baldness.*

Alopecia areata *Balding condition made up of small round patches which often follow the line of a nerve.*

Alpha keratin *Hair in its natural unstretched state.*

Alphabetical *In the order of the letters of the alphabet.*
Alter *To change.*
Alternative *A choice.*
Amino-acid *The component units of protein.*
Ammonia *Colourless fluid used as a solvent.*
Anagen *During the period of active growth the hair is said to be in anagen.*
Analyse *Examine in detail, e.g. the condition of the hair.*
Androgenic alopecia *Hereditary male pattern baldness.*
Annual income *Amount of money you earn each year.*
Annual *Yearly.*
Anonymous *To be unknown.*
Antiseptic *A substance which prevents the multiplication of germs but does not necessarily kill them. Examples are cetrimide and chloroxylenol.*
Antivirus software *A software package that prevents computer viruses from damaging or destroying the system.*
Appeal *To ask urgently.*
Appearance *The way that somebody looks.*
Application *Another name for a computer program such as Microsoft Word.*
Appointment *A specified time for a meeting.*
Appraisal *A system of reviewing an employee's job performance carried out by the employee and employer.*
Area *Length x width.*
Artificial *To be man-made.*
Assemble *To gather together.*
Assess *To judge the condition (of hair).*
Assessor *The candidate's teacher or tutor who assesses the portfolio of evidence.*
Assistance *Help.*
Asymmetric *Unbalanced profile.*
Attract *To draw an object or substance closer.*
Authorisation *Agreed by the supervisor.*
Autoclave *Apparatus used for sterilising tools. It works on the same principle as a pressure cooker.*
Avant-garde *A term used to describe artwork that breaks away from tradition.*
Average *The sum divided by the number of items.*
Awarding body *There are several awarding bodies, for example City and Guilds, AQA, Edexcel and OCR.*
Back brushing *Achieves a soft effect and will 'fluff' the hair with more bounce.*
Back combing *Achieves a stiff style.*
Backup *A second copy of work in case the original is damaged or destroyed. Should be stored away from the computer.*
Backwash *Flow of water directed backwards.*
Bacteria *Disease causing micro-organisms.*
Balance *Equal distribution.*
Bands of colour *Areas of the hair that appear lighter or darker than the rest of the hair.*
Barbicide *Chemical used to sterilise tools.*
Barrel curl *Used on very short hair to achieve the same result as rollers.*
Barrier *Something that blocks things from going past it.*

Barrier cream *A cream used to protect skin from contact with products.*

Base colour *The client's natural hair colour.*

Baseline *Lowest point and foundation of haircut.*

Basic skills *Reading, writing, speaking in English (or Welsh) and using numbers sufficiently well to be able to function in society and at work. Key skills and basic skills overlap at levels 1 and 2.*

Basin *A sink. Used to wash clients' hair.*

Beta keratin *The stretched (wet) state of hair.*

Biased *Favouring one thing over another.*

Bicarbonate *Mineral of hard water.*

Binds *Ties to.*

Bleach *Chemical used to lighten (whiten) hair colour by oxidisation.*

Blending *Combining two sections.*

Block colouring technique *Colouring the hair in a large area.*

Blow-drying *The method of drying the hair using a hand dryer.*

Bluetooth *Wireless technology. A chip is responsible for the transmission of data between a wide range of devices (mobile phone and hands-free system) through short range digital two-way radio.*

Bob *A one length haircut.*

Body language *Refers to facial expressions, gestures or a particular way a person is standing. Non-verbal communication.*

Brick cutting *A technique of texturising by cutting small parts of hair in a 'brick' fashion.*

Brickwork *Term used for positioning rollers correctly.*

Brittle *Hair that can be easily broken.*

Buckled *To be out of shape.*

Budget *A list of incomings and outgoings used in financial planning.*

Burdock root oil *Used in shampoos for dry scalp.*

Calcium *Mineral affecting the hardness of water.*

Canities *Pigmentation cells not functioning; hair turns white.*

Capability *The ability to complete a task.*

Cape *Waterproof gown used to protect a client's clothes.*

Capillary *Very thin blood vessel.*

Career prospect *The direction in which your career could move.*

Cash *Money, banknotes and coins.*

Catagen *Stage of hair growth: hair falls out, follicle shrinks.*

CD-ROM *Compact Disc Read Only Memory. Stores up to 800Mb of data. The data is "read only" which means that you cannot change or overwrite it.*

Ceramic *An object that is made into a shape and then hardened using heat.*

Cetrimide *Antiseptic chemical used for pityriasis capitis.*

Characteristic *A feature or quality of a person, place or thing.*

Checking *Hair has a balanced front; sides, sections match.*

Cheque guarantee card *Guarantee by bank for payment of the order.*

Cheque *Written order to bank for payment.*

Chip and PIN *Customers key in a PIN at point of sale instead of signing a receipt.*

Chlorinated water *Water with added chlorine; can damage the hair.*

Cicatrical alopecia *Baldness caused by physical/chemical damage to skin.*

Circular brush *Used to loosen out the set or achieve a softer look.*

Circumference *The boundary line of a circle.*
Clarify *To make clear.*
Clarifying *To make clear.*
Classic *A look that will not age.*
Client suggestion box *A box used by clients to post written feedback.*
Climazone *Equipment to dry hair and speed chemical processes.*
Clipboard *A temporary area used to store copied information.*
Clipper over comb *Technique for cutting hair. Clippers are used to cut hair following the movement over a comb.*
Clock spring curls *Tight curls or wave movements.*
Clockwise *To move in the same direction as the hands on a clock.*
Closed question *A question with a definite answer, e.g. yes/no.*
Club cutting *Hair cut straight across.*
Coal tar *Chemical with antiseptic qualities.*
Coarse hair *Hair with thick shaft.*
Coconut *Used in shampoos for dry scalps.*
Colleagues *The people who you work with.*
Collodion *A syrupy, clean solution of pyroxylin, alcohol and ether.*
Colour correction *The way in which hair colour or bleach problems are corrected.*
Colour reducer *A product used to remove permanent hair colour.*
Colour reduction *A product used to remove permanent colour from the hair.*
Colour star *Colour chart to achieve desired colour.*
Colour test *Test used to monitor colour development.*
Colour tone *Warm/cool shades of colour tints.*
Commitment *To bind yourself to a certain action.*
Communicate *To exchange information.*
Communication *An exchange of thoughts and information.*
Complementary skills *Skills other than hairdressing but nonetheless essential.*
Comprehensive *To cover a wide area.*
Compression ratio *The volume above the piston when it is at BDC compared to the volume above the piston when it is at TDC.*
Compulsory *Must be completed.*
Computer application *Programs such as Word, Excel and PowerPoint.*
Computer crash *An event that causes the computer to become inactive. This can often result in the loss of unsaved work.*
Computerised *Performed by using a computer.*
Concave *To curve inwards.*
Concentrated *A liquid that has had its dilution reduced.*
Concise *Expressing a lot but in few words.*
Condition *Reference to the state of the hair's health.*
Conditioner *Product used to enhance hair condition.*
Confidence *A feeling of trust.*
Confidential information *Information that is private and should be protected.*
Confidentiality *To keep secret.*
Confirm *To make more firm by repeating.*
Constricted *Made smaller than normal.*
Constructive *To improve.*

Consultation *Discuss individual needs with the client.*
Contagious *Infection can be transferred by contact.*
Contamination *Spread of disease by contact of non-sterile objects.*
Contradictory *To oppose in disagreement.*
Contraindication *A condition preventing a treatment.*
Contribution *To give.*
Conventional *Ordinary.*
Conversion factor *Used to make it easier when converting from one form of 'measurement' to another.*
Conversions *To change one expression to another. For example, expressing miles in kilometres.*
Convex *To curve outwards.*
Cool shade *Colours such as blue.*
Co-operative *To join in and help others in your team.*
Cornrows *Braids that are plaited close to the scalp.*
Cortex *Middle layer of the hair shaft.*
Courteous *To be polite.*
Cowlick *Growth pattern of the hair.*
Creative *To be artistic.*
Credit *System of allowing customers to pay later for services.*
Creeping oxidation *Active product left on the hair separating the cuticle plates.*
Crimping iron *Tool used for crimping the hair.*
Crocodile clamps *Used to hold hair while sectioning.*
Cross check *Checking haircut.*
Cross infection *The spreading of infection between individuals and objects.*
Cross-section *The area exposed if a cut were to be made through the centre of an object.*
Crown *The top of the head.*
Crucial *Very important.*
Curl rearranger *The product used in the first step of a two-step perm.*
Curling *To form curls in the hair.*
Curling tongs *Used for curling the hair.*
Currency *A unit of exchange used as a form of money.*
Current *A look that is fashionable.*
Cuticles *Outer layer of the hair shaft.*
Cut-throat razor *Used for tapering wet hair and shaving.*
Cysteine *An amino acid joined by sulphur bonds.*
Cystine *An amino acid joined by sulphur bonds.*
Damaged cuticle *Cuticle scale open; absorbs moisture.*
Data Protection Act *An Act that provides rights for individuals regarding the obtaining, use, holding and disclosure of information about themselves.*
Debit *Cash deducted from a customer's account.*
Debit card *A card guarantee that a debit will be honoured by the bank.*
Decimal *A number system that uses a base of 10.*
Decimal place *The position of numbers after (to the right of) the decimal point.*
Decomposition *The breakdown of a material.*
Defamatory *Untrue and harmful information.*
Denman brush *A type of brush used for achieving a thorough brush.*
Dense *Thick.*
Depth *The natural lightness/darkness of the hair.*

Dermal papilla *Situated at the hair follicle base, supplying all the materials needed for growth.*

Dermatitis *Abnormal skin condition.*

Dermis *Lower layer of the skin.*

Design *The arrangement of elements.*

Design plan *A document used for planning a project outlining objectives, budget, roles and responsibilities, resources, health and safety issues etc.*

Designated *To have been selected for a task or duty.*

Detergent *Cleaning substance used in shampoos.*

Determine *To decide.*

Dexterity *To perform tasks with the hands, using skill.*

Diagnose *Identify the problem, need or want.*

Diameter *The line that goes through the centre of the circle.*

Dictionary *A book containing a list of words in alphabetical order. Each word has information given about it (i.e. the definition).*

Diet *Nutrient content and food calorific value.*

Diffuse alopecia *Condition in which the hair thins gradually.*

Diffuser *Attachment to a dryer for special effect.*

Digit *A number.*

Dilute *Weaken the concentration (strength) of a solution.*

Disconnected *A type of haircut featuring different lengths without being blended together.*

Discriminatory *Unfair or unequal treatment of a person due to their age, sex, disability, race, religion etc.*

Disk drives *The primary data storage device used by computers. It stores and retrieves data.*

Dispense *To give out.*

Disposable *Designed to be thrown away after use.*

Dissatisfied *Not happy.*

Distribute *Spread out.*

Distributed *Spread out.*

Di-sulphide bond *Sulphur link of two cystine amino acids.*

Dizziness *A spinning sensation.*

Double base-line *Working (cutting) on an extra line over a shorter one.*

Double booking *Two treatments scheduled at the same time.*

Double crown *A growth pattern where the crowns jump and swirl in opposite directions.*

Dressing hair *The way in which hair is finished using different techniques, e.g. smoothing or curling.*

Dressing out brush *Brush that has a rubber base for more gentle brushing.*

Dressing out *Styling hair.*

Droop *To sag, or hang loosely.*

Dry setting *Hair is altered temporarily using heated rollers.*

Dryer *Equipment for drying hair; can be hand held or floor standing.*

Duty *Something that you are obliged to do.*

Effect *The consequence of.*

Effective *To work well.*

Efficient *To get the job done with little waste of time or energy.*

Effleurage *Smooth stroking massage movement, using palm of the hand.*

EFTPOS *Electronic Point of Sale.*

Elasticity test *Test used to assess damage to cortex of hair.*

Eliminate	*To remove.*
Email	*Electronic mail. Messages sent from one person to another electronically via a computer.*
Emergency services	*Fire, ambulance, police.*
Emerging	*A look that is nearly in fashion.*
Emoticons	*A way of expressing emotions in online communication, e.g.:-).*
Emotion	*State of feeling, associated with stress, which can affect the condition of the hair.*
Empathise	*To understand someone else's feelings.*
Emulsify	*To blend two liquids that wouldn't naturally combine together.*
Emulsifying agent	*To blend two liquids that wouldn't naturally combine together.*
Emulsion	*A mixture of two or more liquids that do not blend together.*
Emulsion bleach	*Type of bleach used for full head treatment.*
Enhance	*To make the best of.*
Enquiry	*A question.*
Ensure	*To make certain.*
Epidermis	*Outer layer of the skin.*
Equal opportunities	*Everyone to be given equal rights.*
Equipment	*An instrument.*
Establish	*To find out.*
Estimate	*To guess, but based on experience!*
Ethical	*Morally correct.*
Eumelanin	*Black and brown pigments.*
Evacuate	*To remove.*
Evaluate	*To assess.*
Evidence	*This is what a candidate needs to produce to prove they have the skills required.*
Exaggerate	*To emphasise.*
Exerting	*To use or apply.*
Exhibition	*An event at which products and services are advertised and sold.*
Expire	*To finish.*
Expression	*A way to communicate.*
Extension	*An additional set of numbers that connects to the same telephone line.*
External assessment	*A test set externally to check portfolio evidence.*
Extinguish	*To put out.*
Fatigue	*Tiredness: can be caused by poor working posture.*
Faulty	*Does not work.*
Feasible	*To be capable of being achieved.*
Feathering	*Technique used to remove volume or length of hair.*
Feature	*A characteristic of a person's face.*
Feedback	*The opinions of others or yourself concerned with a product or service.*
Filing system	*Method of keeping records of client treatments.*
Financial	*Monetary.*
Fine hair	*Term used to describe thin or delicate hair strands.*
Fine pins	*Equipment used to secure pin curls or dress hair up.*
Finger-drying	*To dry hair using a hairdryer and your hands.*
Finger-waving	*Technique where hair is moulded into an 'S' shape using fingers and comb. Also known as water waving.*
Finishing spray	*A product that holds hair in place and protects against weather and humidity.*

Fire extinguisher *A device for putting out small fires.*
Fixing *Alternative name for neutralising hair.*
Flamboyant *To be excessively ornamented.*
Flammable *Can catch fire.*
Flat brush *A brush used for smoothing the hair. Also known as spiral brush.*
Flexible *Being able to accept change.*
Floppy disk *A portable disk that stores 1.44Mb of information.*
Focused *To the point.*
Foils *Thin sheets of metal generally used for highlighting/lowlighting hair.*
Follicle *Sac containing the hair shaft in the epidermis.*
Folliculitis *Bacterial infection of the follicle.*
Forgery *A copy that is illegal.*
Fractions *A number of parts out of another number of parts.*
Fragilitas crinium *Hair splits at the ends and along the shaft.*
Fraud *The act of deceiving to obtain money.*
Freehand cutting *Cutting without tension.*
Friction massage *Used during shampooing to work from the front of the scalp to the nape using the pads of the fingers in a vigorous movement.*
Fungi *Parasitic organisms that do not contain chlorophyll. Includes mushrooms and yeast.*
Gel *Lotion used to make hair spiky or stand-up.*
General practitioner *A doctor.*
Gesture *A hand or body motion.*
Glare *Reflection from the sun or a light onto the computer screen making it difficult to see properly.*
Gloss *Lotion used to make hair look shiny.*
Goals *Objectives relating to a particular time. Can be short-term or long-term.*
Google *Popular search engine.*
Gown *Protective garment used to cover a client's clothes.*
Gradient *The degree of incline.*
Graduation *The shape of a style created by cutting hair to achieve a look where the inner length is longer than the outer length.*
Grammar *Forming well written, easy to read sentences, paragraphs and documents with the use of punctuation (full stops, commas etc.).*
Grievance *To have felt grief after a wrongdoing has occurred. A formal complaint.*
Growth pattern *The direction of the hair growth.*
Guideline *Mesh of hair used to measure other sections.*
Hair balance *Profile shape of the hairstyle.*
Hair extensions *Additional pieces of hair attached to current hair.*
Hair shaft *The part of the hair that is above the skin.*
Hair straighteners *Heated styling equipment designed to straighten the hair. Can also be used for other styling techniques.*
Hair structure *The microscopic make-up of hair.*
Hairline *Natural hairline around the neck and face.*
Hairspray *A product that holds hair in place and protects against weather and humidity.*
Hard disk *A storage device that holds large amounts of data.*
Hardware *The physical components of a computer system.*

Hard water *Water with increased levels of calcium; requires more soap and detergent; forms scum.*

Hazard *A source of danger.*

Hazardous *Involving risk or danger.*

Heart shape *Face shape for which suitable hairstyles include a fringe and hair between ear and jaw.*

Heat protectors *Products applied to prevent the hair becoming damaged from heated styling equipment.*

Heated rollers *Creates volume root lift, curl and hair direction.*

Heated tongs *An electrical device used to curl hair.*

Henna *Permanent vegetable tint.*

Hereditary *Passed on from parents (genetic).*

Herpes simplex *A viral infection affecting the skin and nervous system.*

Hexachlorophene *Chemical used with antiseptic properties used on dry scalp.*

Hierarchy *A group of people ranked in order of job position.*

Highlights *Lightening strands of hair.*

Hinder *To prevent something.*

Hologram *A 3-D image.*

Hood dryer *Floor mounted dryer; creates an overall even drying effect quickly.*

Hormone *Chemical produced by the body controlling chemical reactions in the body.*

Hospitality *The way in which a client is welcomed and received into the salon.*

Hostility *Unfriendly.*

Humidity *The dampness in the hair.*

Hydrogen *Flammable gas occurring in water and ammonia.*

Hydrogen bond *A chemical bonding linking oxygen to hydrogen to form water.*

Hydrogen peroxide *An agent used for oxidising when colouring and perming.*

Hydrophilic *Will mix with water.*

Hydrophobic *Will not mix with water (repelled).*

Hygiene *Principles and practice of sanitation to ensure good health.*

Hygroscopic *Absorbs moisture.*

ICT *Information and Communication Technology.*

Identify *To consider.*

Image *A perception of (hair salon's image).*

Immiscible *Liquids that are incapable of mixing together.*

Imperial Measurement *Defined by three measures: the gallon, the yard and the pound.*

Impetigo *Contagious bacterial skin disease.*

Impression *Outward appearance.*

Incapacitated *A person with a mental, emotional or physical impairment.*

Incoming telephone call *To receive a telephone call.*

Incompatibility test *Method of detecting products used in previous treatments that may contra-react.*

Incompatible *Cannot be used with (other chemicals).*

Incorporating *To include.*

Infection *A disease caused by micro-organisms.*

Infectious *The spreading of disease.*

Infestation *A group of parasites.*

Infirm *A person lacking in strength.*

Inflation *The general increase in the price of goods and services.*

Ingest *Take into the body by the mouth.*
Ingredient *Part of.*
Inhalation *Take into the body through the airways.*
Initial and diagnostic assessment *This is carried out to find a candidate's strengths and weaknesses, current levels of attainment and potential.*
Initiative *To take the first step.*
Innovative *To be forward thinking in terms of ideas and themes.*
Input device *A device that allows you to put information into the computer, e.g. keyboard, mouse.*
Interactive *Two-way communication.*
Internal *Inside.*
Internal shape *Internal shape of the haircut.*
Internal verification *The process whereby a centre ensures it operates consistently and to national standards in interpreting and assessing the key skills.*
Internet *A worldwide network of computers that allows us to view the World Wide Web.*
Interpersonal skills *The ability to deal well with several different people.*
Interpret *To understand and be able to explain something.*
Interpreted *To make sense of.*
Inter-quartile mean *The average of the values in the inter-quartile range.*
Inter-quartile range *The range of numbers with the upper and lower quartiles removed.*
Intertwining *To twist together.*
Intimidating *To make somebody feel uncomfortable, timid or even fearful.*
Inversion *Create a concave shape in the hair.*
Inward nape *Nape hair grows strongly to the centre.*
Irritant *A chemical that can cause irritation or inflammation to the skin.*
Irritate *To annoy or cause discomfort.*
IT *Information Technology.*
Itemise *To list individually.*
Job description *A set of responsibilities given by an employer for a particular job.*
Journal *Day by day diary or similar.*
Keloid *Irregular fibrous tissue which is formed at the place of a scar or injury.*
Keratin *Protein that makes up hair. Contains large amounts of sulphur.*
Key data *Important, relevant information.*
Keyboard *The typewriter-like keys used to input data into a computer. An input device.*
Knowledge *To know something.*
Lanolin *Product used in shampoos used for a dry scalp.*
Lanugo *Foetal body hair.*
Latent heat *Body heat from the scalp.*
Layering *Hair cut at various angles.*
Legislation *A law.*
Libellous *Untrue and harmful information.*
Library *Collection of materials, e.g. books or CDs.*
Lice *Fleas, insects that infest the hair.*
Lift pic *Root lift achieved by setting rollers on the section.*
Lift *Lightening the hair colour.*
Lightening *To remove colour from the hair.*
Lime scale *Deposit of bicarbonates caused by boiling water.*

Long shape *Face shape suited by fuller sides hairstyle and flatter on top.*

Lotion *Product that has the consistency of a light cream.*

Lower quartile *Data is split into 4 equal quarters. The lowest quarter is referred to as the lower quartile. For example the lower quartile of 100 is the lowest 25 of the number.*

Lowlights *Sections of hair that have been toned darker than the full head of hair.*

Magnesium *Mineral affecting the hardness of the water.*

Maintain *To keep something at a specific level.*

Maintenance *To care for.*

Manoeuvre *To move.*

Manual *Not computerised.*

Mapping *Used to identify opportunities for developing and assessing key skills within the curriculum.*

Marcel iron *Equipment used for setting hair.*

Marketing *The method of advertising, promoting and selling to customers.*

Massage *Manipulative movement using the fingers and palms of the hand.*

MasterCard *Type of credit card.*

MB *Megabyte. Used to measure computer memory. 1 Mb = 1,000,000 bytes or 1024 Kb (kilobytes).*

Mean *The average value (the sum divided by the number of items).*

Median *The middle number of a series when the data is arranged in ascending order.*

Medicated *Contains healing or medical additives.*

Medium hair *Hair shaft is middle-range in size.*

Medulla *The central part of the hair shaft.*

Melanin *Colouring pigment of the hair.*

Melanocytes *A cell that contains the pigment melanin.*

Memory chip *A chip that stores data.*

Merchandise *Goods that are to be sold.*

Merely *No more than.*

Meshes *Smaller sections of main sections.*

Method *The way in which a task is carried out.*

Methodically *To work through something in the correct order.*

Metric measurement *A system designed to regulate measurement. Each quantity has a single unit. These include metre, kilogram, ampere.*

Micro-organisms *Tiny forms of life, only seen through a microscope.*

Microphone *A device that converts sound waves to audio signals.*

Microsoft Office *A package of programs including Word Processor (Word), Spreadsheet (Excel), Presentation (PowerPoint), Email and Organisation (Outlook).*

Misconception *To have a thought that is incorrect.*

Mobility *Movement.*

Mode *The most common number in a series.*

Modifications *Changes made.*

Moisturise *Add or restore moisture to the hair.*

Molecule *Chemical unit of two or more atoms.*

Monilethrix *Uneven production of cells in dermal papilla causing brittle hair.*

Monitor *The screen that displays information produced on a computer. An output device.*

Moulding *To sculpture the hair.*

Mouse *An input device that allows the user to move the pointer around the screen and click on different items to operate computer applications.*

Mousse foam *Lotion used for setting hair.*

Multiple choice *A selection of answers.*

Nape *Lowest point of hair growth at the back of the head.*

Natural base *Natural colour of the hair.*

Natural parting *A natural parting where the hair falls making a dividing line.*

Navigation *The way in which you get around a program or website.*

Negative communication *A comment or statement expressing lack of approval.*

Negative ions *Electrically charged atoms.*

Network card *A piece of hardware that allows computers to be connected to a network.*

Network *Interlinked group of computers so that resources can be shared.*

Neutralise *Fixing the structure of the hair after permanent waving or relaxing.*

Nitro-dyes *Semi-permanent colouring dyes.*

Non-contagious *Infection that cannot be transferred by contact.*

Non-verbal *Any form of communication that does not use words, e.g. traffic lights, shaking somebody's hand and smiling.*

Normalising *Alternative word for neutralising.*

Nozzle *Attachment for dryer to achieve a special effect.*

Objective information *Information that is unbiased and open minded.*

Objectives *The goals to be achieved.*

Obligatory *Compulsory.*

Obscene *Offensive, foul, disgusting.*

Obstacles *Objects that are in the way.*

Occipital bone *Convex protruding bone at the back of the skull.*

Occupation *The job that you do. For example, training to be a motor mechanic is training for an occupation.*

Odour *Smell or fragrance.*

Offensive *To attack somebody/something by words or physically.*

Office applications *A package of programs including Word Processor (Word), Spreadsheet (Excel), Presentation (PowerPoint), Email and Organisation (Outlook).*

One length cut *Hair cut in a 'bob'.*

Open centred pin curls *Loose, soft pin curls.*

Open question *A question used to allow respondent to expand on their answer.*

Opinion *A personal belief.*

Organisms *A life form made of a complex system of cells and tissues.*

Ornamentation *Decoration to be added to hair once it has been styled.*

Outgoing telephone call *To make a telephone call to somebody.*

Output device *A device that allows information from the computer to be displayed, e.g. monitor, printer.*

Outside shape *Shape of the hair cut on the base line.*

Oval shape *The perfect shaped face to suit any hair style.*

Overlap *Time of a treatment going into the time scheduled for another.*

Oxidation *The addition of oxygen in a chemical reaction.*

Oxymelanin *Melanin reduced by bleach.*

Packet *An item used to colour hair in sections.*

Paddle brush *Used for smoothing hair.*

Parasite *An organism that feeds from and lives on another organism.*

Participate *To take part in.*

Particle *A tiny part of an object.*

Pear shape *Face shape for which suitable hairstyles should have lots of volume around the temples but flat around the jaw line.*

Pediculosis capitis *To be infected with lice on the scalp.*

Penetrate *To enter.*

Penetrating conditioner *Work by penetrating the cortex and help to repair damage by adding protein. They are known as substantive products.*

Per cent *The proportion of one part of something to the whole. Per means 'out of' and 'cent' means 'hundred'.*

Percentage change *Changed amounts divided by the original value, then multiplied by 100.*

Performance criteria *The standards from which you (the student) will be evaluated.*

Perimeter *The sum of all the outside edges of a shape.*

Perm rod *Rod around which hair is re-shaped.*

Permanent colour *Colour containing molecules that penetrate the cuticle and are absorbed into the cortex. The tint remains until it is cut out.*

Perming *The method of curling hair by altering the structure using chemicals.*

Petrissage *A deep kneading massage movement.*

pH *Level of acidity/alkalinity.*

Pharmacist *Somebody who carries out the service of preparing and distributing medicine.*

Pheomelanin *Natural pigment of hair causing a red/yellow hair colour.*

Phrase *A group of words in sequence.*

Pi *3.141592 (3.142).*

Pigment *Colour matter of the hair.*

Pin curling *Open centre pin curl used to achieve loose flat look.*

Pine *Product used in shampoos for dry scalp.*

Pityriasis capitis *Continuous flaking of the epidermis (dandruff).*

Plagiarise *Taking another person's work as your own.*

Plaiting *Used to achieve a secure finish after dressing hair out.*

Planning *The act of forming and following a programme to achieve a specific goal.*

Pleating *Folds of hair secured with pins and grips.*

Pli *Hair set in rollers or pin curls.*

Point to root *Winding the hair from the ends of the hair to the root.*

Pointing *Technique used to break up the points of the hair.*

Policy *A plan of action.*

Polite *To show regard to others. To use good manners.*

Polythene *Lightweight plastic.*

Ponytail *A hairstyle where the hair is drawn to the back of the head and secured with a band.*

Population of UK *Number of people that live in the UK (about 60 Million in 2010).*

Porosity *Ability to absorb moisture.*

Portfolio *This is usually a folder that contains the evidence chosen to illustrate competence to satisfy individual key skills requirements.*

Positive communication *A comment or statement expressing approval.*

Positive ions *Electrically charged atoms.*

Posture *Working position of the body.*

Potential *Possibility that something may happen.*

Powder bleach *Type of bleach used for highlights. Not usually recommended for full head.*

PPE *Personal Protective Equipment. Equipment that is worn to protect people at work from risks to their health and safety.*

Precaution *A method of reducing risk.*

Precise *To be exact and accurate.*

Pre-colouring *Applying a treatment to the hair before colouring to improve the condition.*

Pre-perm shampoo *Soapless detergent shampoo with no additives.*

Pre-perm test *Detection of extent of curl from previous perm.*

Pre-pigmentation *The method of adding a warm shade to the hair to replace missing pigments before re-colouring bleached hair.*

Presentation *The way in which something is displayed.*

Pre-softening *The application of a treatment to lift the cuticle from the hair allowing the colour to penetrate the cortex.*

Prevalent *To be widespread.*

Pre-wrap lotion *Method used to even out the porosity of hair.*

Pricing scanner *A device that converts a visual form into a price.*

Prickly *Sensation of cut hair next to client's skin.*

Primary colours *Yellow, blue and red.*

Printer *An output device that allows data from the computer to be displayed on paper.*

Probationary *A trial period.*

Procedure *A course of action.*

Processing time *The length of time it takes for colour to develop.*

Processor *The central processing unit oversees all of the other components of the system. Can be thought of as the brain of the computer.*

Product *Items sold as part of the hair care process.*

Professional *Term given to use of effective and efficient working methods.*

Profile *Shape of the hairstyle.*

Profitable *To obtain positive income from a transaction.*

Progress *Positive development.*

Promotional *To advertise or publicise.*

Promptly *Straight away.*

Proportion *The size of different parts in relation to each other.*

Props *Items used for events.*

Protective gloves *Rubber gloves used to protect hands from chemicals.*

Protective treatment *Products used to stop damage to hair that has previously been treated. Applied before treatment.*

Protein *Hair structure, made from amino acids.*

Protrude *To stick out.*

Provenance *The origins of information.*

PSI *Pounds per square inch.*

Psoriasis *Red patches on scalp covered by silver white scales.*

Pubic *Type of terminal hair.*

Publicity *To get attention for a product/service by advertising etc.*

Punctuation *The use of marks and signs to form words, sentences, paragraphs etc.*

Qualified *To have the necessary skills and abilities to perform a job.*

Quantify *To put something into figures.*

Quartile *Any three points that divide an ordered distribution into four parts. Each of these parts contains a quarter of the score.*

Quasi-permanent *Non-permanent method of colouring hair. Fades over a period that is longer than semi-permanent.*

Questionnaire *A set of questions used for collecting feedback.*

Racist *Intolerance of race. A person with prejudiced belief that one race is superior to (better than) another.*

Radius *A line running from the centre of the circle to the circumference.*

Rake comb *Large toothed comb for wet/tangled hair.*

Range *The difference between the highest and lowest numbers.*

Rapport *An agreement of trust between hairdresser and client.*

Rash *Contraindication response by the body to a chemical.*

Rate of lift *Lightening of hair colour.*

Ratio *The comparison of two numbers.*

React *To respond.*

Reaction *When chemicals cause a substance to change.*

Rebonding *Re-fixing amino acids in the neutralising process to re-form cystine.*

Receding *Moving from the front to the back gradually.*

Reception *Greeting.*

Recession areas *Growth pattern – bald areas around the hairline.*

Recognition *To identify a thing or person.*

Record *History of client's treatments.*

Record card *Method of recording client's treatments.*

Rectify *To set right.*

Referral *To suggest or recommend.*

Regenerate *To renew or replace.*

Regime *A method or plan.*

Regulate *Adjust (the temperature of the water).*

Regulations *Rules.*

Reinforce *To make information sink in. To confirm.*

Relaxing *The method of reducing a natural curl by altering the structure either temporarily or permanently using chemicals.*

Relevant information *The suitability of information based upon your needs.*

Repel *To reject.*

Represent *Acting on behalf of someone.*

Reputable *To have a good reputation.*

Research *To study something thoroughly.*

Resistant *To not be affected by.*

Resolution *The number of pixels per square inch shown on the computer screen. The greater the resolution the better the picture.*

Resolve *To correct.*

Resources *Sources of information, expertise and knowledge.*

Respect *To think of highly.*

Respond *To answer to.*

Retail *To be sold.*

Revenue *Income.*

Review *To look over and study information again.*

Revision *To review information in order to remind yourself of its content.*

Ringworm *A fungal skin infection.*

Rinse *Process of cleaning, usually with water.*

RIRO *Rubbish In Rubbish Out. In relation to the Internet.*

Risk *The likelihood of an accident occurring from a hazard.*

Risk assessment *The process of calculating the risk associated with a hazard and the actions taken to avoid it.*

Role *A set of activities or actions attached to a job.*

Roll *A hairstyle created by folding the hair and securing with pins.*

Roller *A cylindrical styling tool used to create waves or curls.*

Root lift *Creating volume at the root.*

Root movement *Amount of lift achieved at the hair root.*

Root to point *Winding the hair from the roots to the ends of the hair.*

Rotary massage *Second massage movement in shampooing using the pads of the fingers in quick, circular movements.*

Round shape *Face shape suited by flat sides, full on top hair style.*

Rounding off *Express as a round number (e.g. 4.7 rounded off becomes 5).*

Routine *A course of action that is followed every day.*

RSI *Repetitive strain injury. This type of injury occurs from repeated physical movements. It can be caused by bad typing technique, bad posture and lack of adequate rest and breaks. RSI is common in the wrists.*

Sale *To sell.*

Satisfied *To be happy with something.*

Scabies *Raised red lines on the skin caused by itch mite.*

Scalding *Burning of the skin by (water) that is too hot.*

Scales *Outer part of the cuticle.*

Scalp protector *Product applied to hairline and scalp to protect against chemicals in products.*

Scalp *Skin of the top of the head.*

Scanning *To skim/scan text in order to get a general idea about it.*

Schedule *To plan a time and place.*

Scissors over comb *A cutting technique. Scissors are used to cut hair rapidly following the movement over a comb.*

Scrunch drying *A technique of drying the hair using a diffuser to enhance curls or waves.*

Scum *Calcium stearate formed from soap and mineral salts in hard water.*

Sea *Salted water causes damage to hair.*

Search engine *A program that enables you to locate information on the World Wide Web using keyword searches.*

Sebaceous cyst *Lump on scalp caused by blocked sebaceous gland.*

Sebaceous gland *Produces sebum.*

Seborrhoea *Condition in which excess sebum is produced from the sebaceous gland.*

Sebum *Oily secretion from the sebaceous gland.*

Secondary colours *Colours made from mixing primary shades together: orange, green and violet.*

Section clips *Used for sectioning hair.*

Section *Main divisions when dividing the hair for a particular hairdressing service.*

Seminar *A conference or meeting to discuss a certain subject.*

Semi-permanent *Type of colour group (nitro-dyes).*

Semi-permanent colour *Colour molecules deposited in the hair cuticle or under the open cuticle. They will lighten each time the hair is shampooed.*

Sequence *One thing that follows on to the next.*

Serum *Product applied during styling to give the hair shine.*
Services *Alternative name for hair treatment.*
Sesame *Product used in shampoos for dry scalp.*
Setting comb *A comb used for finger waving or dressing hair.*
Setting hair *Setting hair into range of styles and effects.*
Setting mousse *A product that is applied to wet hair in order to keep style in place.*
Setting pins *Used for securing rollers in place.*
Shade chart *Method of identifying the target shade.*
Shadowing *Following a more experienced member of staff for training purposes.*
Shampoo *Detergent to wash or clean hair.*
Shine *Spray lotion applied to hair to achieve a shiny finish.*
Significant figures *The number of digits expressed in a measurement. Sig. fig. can appear before and/or after the decimal point.*
Signposting guidance *Within the specifications for the new AS levels A levels and GNVQs, opportunities for developing or producing evidence for assessment of key skills.*
Simulations *Activities that simulate or model reality.*
Sincere *To be genuine.*
Skim-reading *To skim/scan text in order to get a general idea about it.*
Skin test *Application of the product to the skin to assess the reaction.*
Slice colouring technique *Colouring small sections of hair.*
Slide cutting *Scissors are slipped through the hair to achieve tapering (feathering) effect.*
Sodium hydroxide *Lye contained in relaxers.*
Soft water *Reduced level of mineral content. Water suds easily.*
Software *A computer program.*
Sparingly *To use a small amount.*
Sparse *Not dense. Thin.*
Speakers *Device that converts audio signals to sounds that humans can hear.*
Specialise *To devote yourself to a particular area of work.*
Spell checker *Most computer applications (e.g. Microsoft Word, Excel etc.) will enable you to check documents for incorrect spelling.*
Spelling *To form a word with a series of letters.*
Spider diagrams *A series of lines and boxes containing relevant information. A form of note taking.*
Spiral *Type of setting technique. Also a type of brush, also known as circular brush.*
Spot colouring *Applying colour to certain parts of the hair that need it.*
Spreadsheet *A computer program often used to create financial forecasting documents.*
Square metre *The area enclosed by a square with sides of 1 metre long.*
Square shape *Shape of face suited by softer hairstyle and jaw-line partially covered.*
Stainless steel *A very durable metal.*
Stance *The way you stand.*
Standard form *Used so that very large or very small numbers can be written in a more convenient way.*
Standards moderation *The means by which awarding bodies ensure consistency across centres and ensure that national standards are being maintained and applied.*
State *To express.*
Stationery *Paper and office materials.*
Statistics *Numerical data.*
Sterile *Free from disease causing micro-organisms.*

Sterling *Currency of the UK.*
Stimulate *To provoke or cause feeling.*
Stock *Products held in the salon for sale or treatment.*
Stopcock *A valve that opens and closes a gas or water supply pipe.*
Straight pins *Strong pins used for long hairstyles and holding rollers.*
Straighteners *Electrical devices used to straighten hair.*
Straightening *Method used to make curly hair straight.*
Straightening irons *Electrical devices used to straighten hair.*
Strand *Term used for small group of hairs.*
Strand test *Test used to monitor colour development.*
Strength *Something that is done well.*
Stretch *Test used to measure the tensile strength of hair.*
Structure *A build-up of parts.*
Sturdy *Strong.*
Subdivided *To divide something that has already been divided.*
Substantive *A thing or idea.*
Sulphur *Main chemical of the amino acid cystine.*
Sunlight *Natural light rays that can damage hair.*
Supervisor *The person in charge.*
Surface conditioner *Work on the surface layer of the hair, coating the hair shaft and filling any gaps in the cuticle layer that have been caused by previous treatments.*
Surfactant *Detergent that can damage the hair.*
Survey *A method of collecting measured information.*
Symmetric *To have equal distribution.*
Sympathetically *To be sympathetic. To understand how someone may feel.*
Tactful *To show skills in sensing the correct way to deal with others.*
Tail comb *Used to help sectioning hair while setting.*
Tangled *In a mess.*
Tapering *Alternative term for 'feathering'.*
Target *Objective set down for staff to reach.*
Target colour *The hair colour chosen by the client.*
Team working *A group of people working together.*
Technician *A person who is trained in the technicalities (small details) of a subject.*
Technique *A specific method of working.*
Telogen *Stage of hair growth when follicles and papilla are in a stage of rest.*
Temperature *The heat level.*
Temporary *Type of colour group (azo dyes).*
Tensile (strength) *Ability of hair to be stretched.*
Tension *Stretched.*
Terminal *Hair of face, arms, pubic regions.*
Test curl *Test to determine if full head can be permed.*
Test cut *Test sample of hairs to assess the effect of colouring.*
Texture *The coarseness or fineness of hair.*
Theme *A subject matter.*
Thinning *Reduce the volume of hair.*
Timeliness *Reference to the time that information was recorded.*

Tinea capitis *Fungal infection, contagious.*
Tinting *Colouring with highlights or lowlights.*
Tinting cap *Cap through which strands of hair are pulled to be tinted.*
Tolerance *The amount that somebody can resist.*
Tone *Warm or cool shade of colour tint.*
Toner *Colour used to neutralise unwanted tones in lightened hair.*
Tool *An implement used for working.*
Toxic *Poisonous and harmful.*
Tracking *The method by which learners' achievements are recorded across a range of activities.*
Traction alopecia *A condition in which the hair falls out due to excessive pulling.*
Trainee *A person who is training for a particular job role.*
Training *To learn skills.*
Transaction *The agreement between a seller and buyer for goods or services.*
Transfer *To move from one area to another.*
Translucent *Has no colour.*
Treatment *A service.*
Treatment conditioners *Work by penetrating the cortex and help to repair damage by adding protein. They are known as substantive products.*
Trichologist *A specialist in hair and scalp conditions.*
Trichorrhexis nodosa *Small white nodules along the hair shaft.*
Twist *A channel of hair that has been wound around itself.*
Twisting *The method of twisting a channel of hair around itself.*
Ultraviolet *Type of light ray; can be harmful.*
Unauthorised *Not allowed.*
Under cut *To remove hair under the base line.*
Uniform layer cut *Both sides of the hair cut evenly.*
Uniform *To be evenly spaced.*
Upper quartile *Data is split into 4 equal quarters. The highest quarter is referred to as the upper quartile. For example the upper quartile of 100 is the highest 25 of the numbers.*
Upward nape *Hair grows upward from the nape.*
UV *Ultraviolet. Type of light ray, can be harmful.*
VAT *Value Added Tax.*
Vellus *Fine body hair.*
Velocity *The speed or rate of motion that something is travelling at.*
Vent brush *Type of brush; creates a broken casual effect.*
Venue *A place where an event is held.*
Verbal *Any form of communication that uses words, e.g. speaking and writing in the form of letters, newspapers, emails etc.*
Vigorously *Active strength.*
Virgin hair *Hair that has not been chemically treated or bleached.*
Virus *A tiny organism that causes infectious disease.*
VISA *Credit card company.*
Vocabulary *Words and their meanings.*
Volume *Length x width x height.*
Warm shade *Colour such as red or orange.*
Warts *Caused by viral infection of epidermis: non-contagious if not damaged.*

Waste *To throw away.*

Water soluble *Dissolves in water.*

Water waving *Another name for finger waving.*

Watermark *A design that is visible when held up to the light.*

Wax *A product used during styling and setting, usually made from beeswax.*

Weakness *Tasks that need improvement in performance.*

Weave cutting *Scissors 'snip' at roots, create texture and strengthen root support.*

Weave foil *Method of tinting hair by placing sections on foil.*

Weaving *Interlacing hair.*

Web browser *A software package that allows you to view pages from the World Wide Web. Examples are Internet Explorer and Google Chrome.*

Web page *A document, usually written in HTML (Hypertext Mark-up Language), that can be accessed on the Internet.*

Web Site *A collection of electronic "pages".*

Website *A collection of electronic "pages".*

Weight *Distribution of hair length within a haircut.*

Wet shampoo *Shampoo that requires water.*

Whorl *A growth pattern that follows a circular shape.*

Widow's peak *Growth pattern: hairline points in middle of forehead.*

Winding *Technique to change the shape of hair.*

Word processor *A computer program used to create text based documents such as letters and memos, although graphics may also be added.*

World Wide Web *The www is a collection of electronic "pages" that can be accessed over the Internet. The World Wide Web is NOT the same as the Internet, it is only a part of it.*

Woven hair *Interlacing hair to other pieces of hair or other items.*

Wrapping lotion *The product used in the second step of a two-step perm.*

Zinc pyrithione *Chemical in shampoo that lifts off top layer dead skin cells.*

Index

Where the page numbers are in **bold** this means there is a whole chapter on that subject. Headings in *italics* refer to the sample worksheets at the end of chapters

D